BATMAN

THE

CHALICE

CHUCK DIXON
writer

JOHN VAN FLEET
artist

JACK MORELLI (*THE CHALICE*)
JOHN WORKMAN (*THE ANKH*)
letterers

JOHN VAN FLEET
collection and original series cover artist

BATMAN created by BOB KANE
with BILL FINGER

SUPERMAN created by
JERRY SIEGEL and JOE SHUSTER

By special arrangement
with the JERRY SIEGEL FAMILY

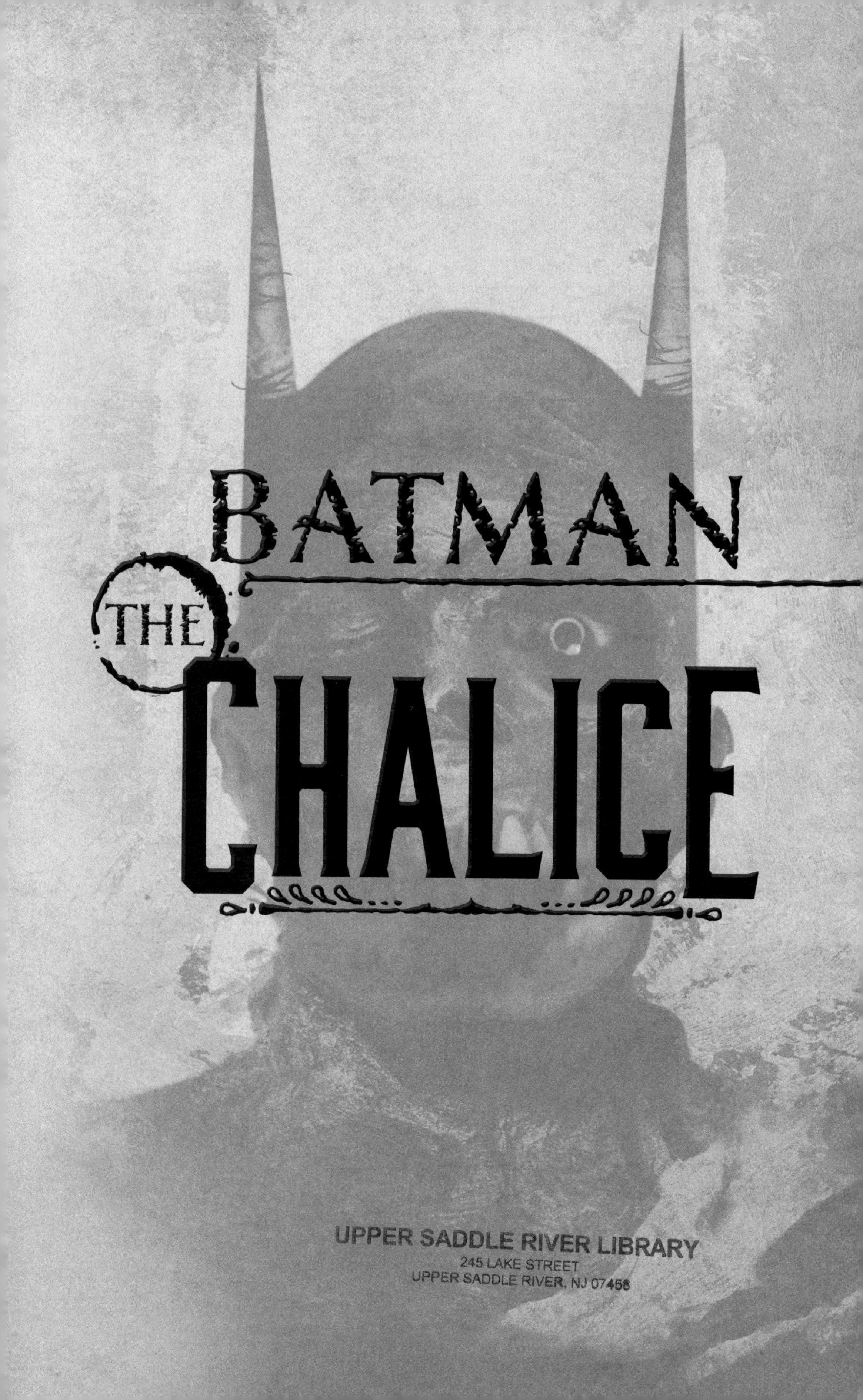

BATMAN THE CHALICE

DENNIS O'NEIL
MATT IDELSON   Editors – Original Series
DARREN VINCENZO   Associate Editor – Original Series
NACHIE CASTRO   Assistant Editor – Original Series
JEB WOODARD   Group Editor – Collected Editions
REZA LOKMAN   Editor – Collected Edition
STEVE COOK   Design Director – Books
AMIE BROCKWAY-METCALF   Publication Design
SUZANNAH ROWNTREE   Publication Production

BOB HARRAS   Senior VP – Editor-in-Chief, DC Comics

JIM LEE   Publisher & Chief Creative Officer
BOBBIE CHASE   VP – Global Publishing Initiatives & Digital Strategy
DON FALLETTI   VP – Manufacturing Operations & Workflow Management
LAWRENCE GANEM   VP – Talent Services
ALISON GILL   Senior VP – Manufacturing & Operations
HANK KANALZ   Senior VP – Publishing Strategy & Support Services
DAN MIRON   VP – Publishing Operations
NICK J. NAPOLITANO   VP – Manufacturing Administration & Design
NANCY SPEARS   VP – Sales
JONAH WEILAND   VP – Marketing & Creative Services
MICHELE R. WELLS   VP & Executive Editor, Young Reader

DC Comics, 2900 West Alameda Ave., Burbank, CA 91505
Printed by LSC Communications, Owensville, MO, USA.
12/4/20. First Printing.
ISBN: 978-1-77950-745-7

Library of Congress Cataloging-in-Publication Data is available.

PART I

THE CHALICE

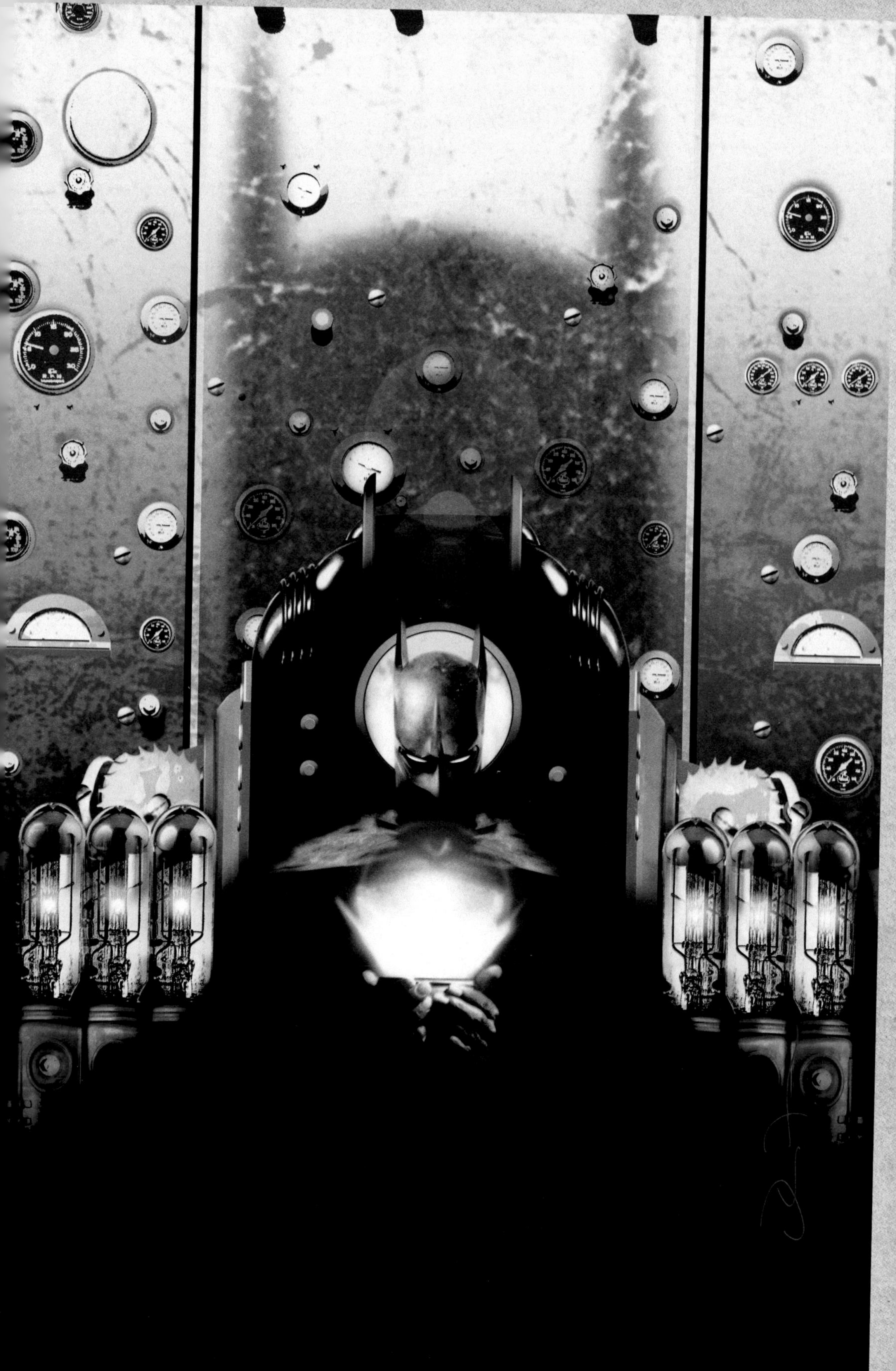

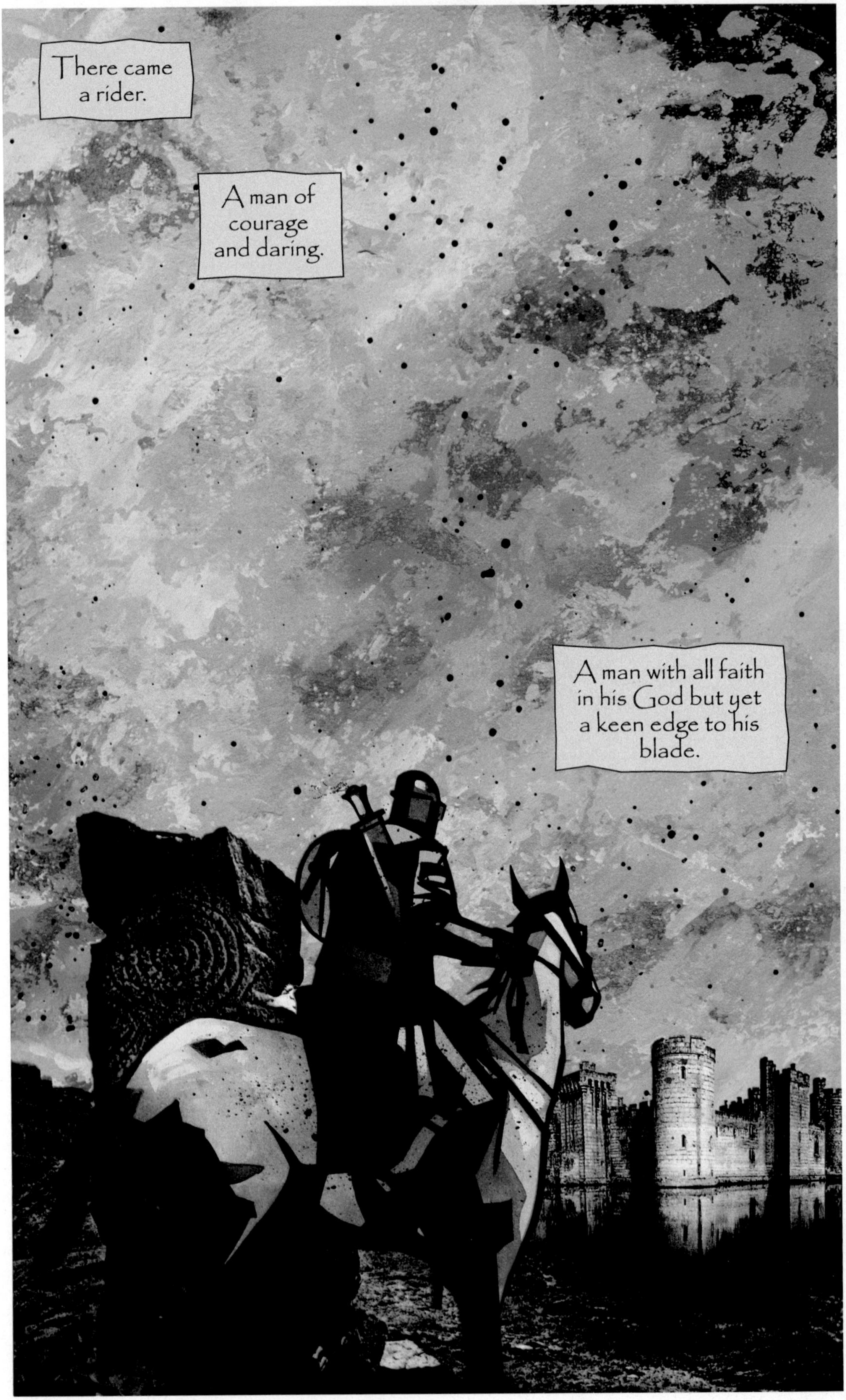
There came a rider.
A man of courage and daring.
A man with all faith in his God but yet a keen edge to his blade.

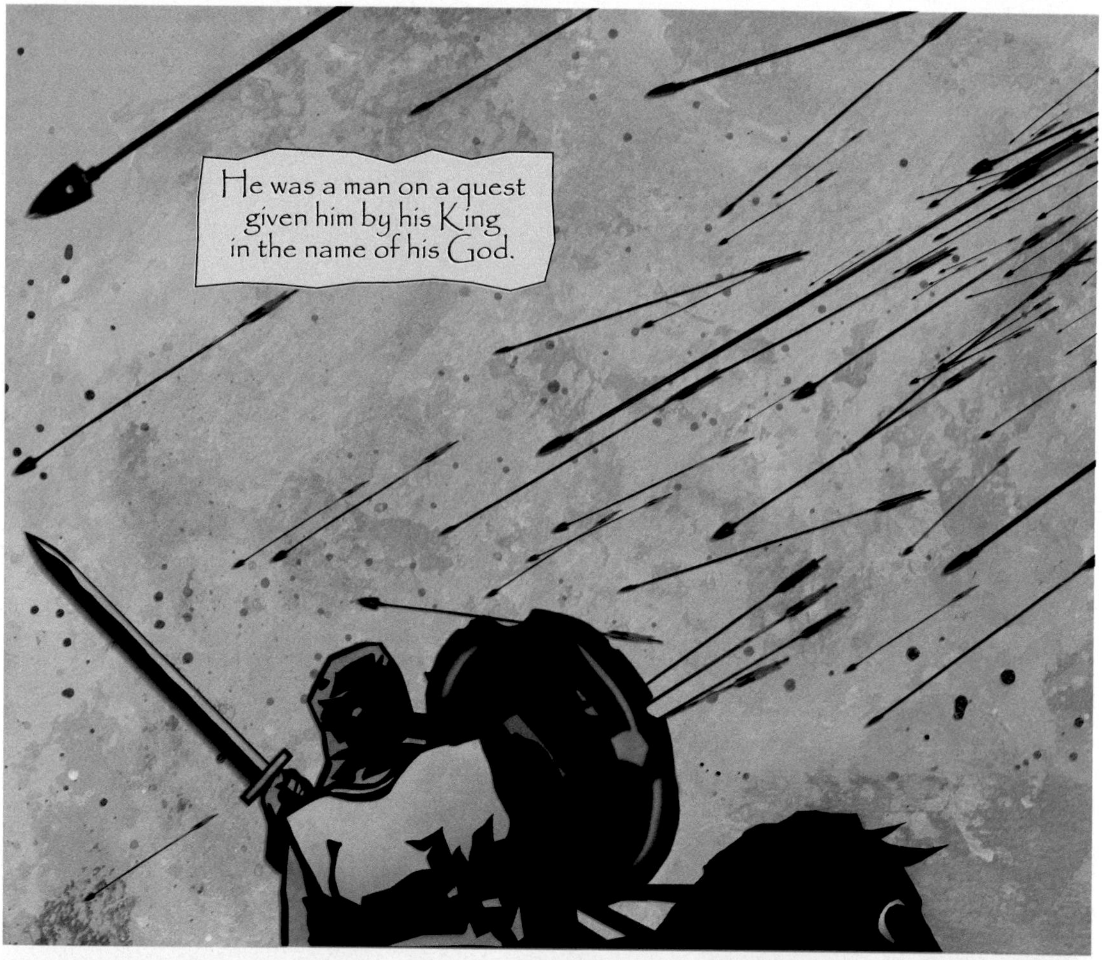
He was a man on a quest given him by his King in the name of his God.

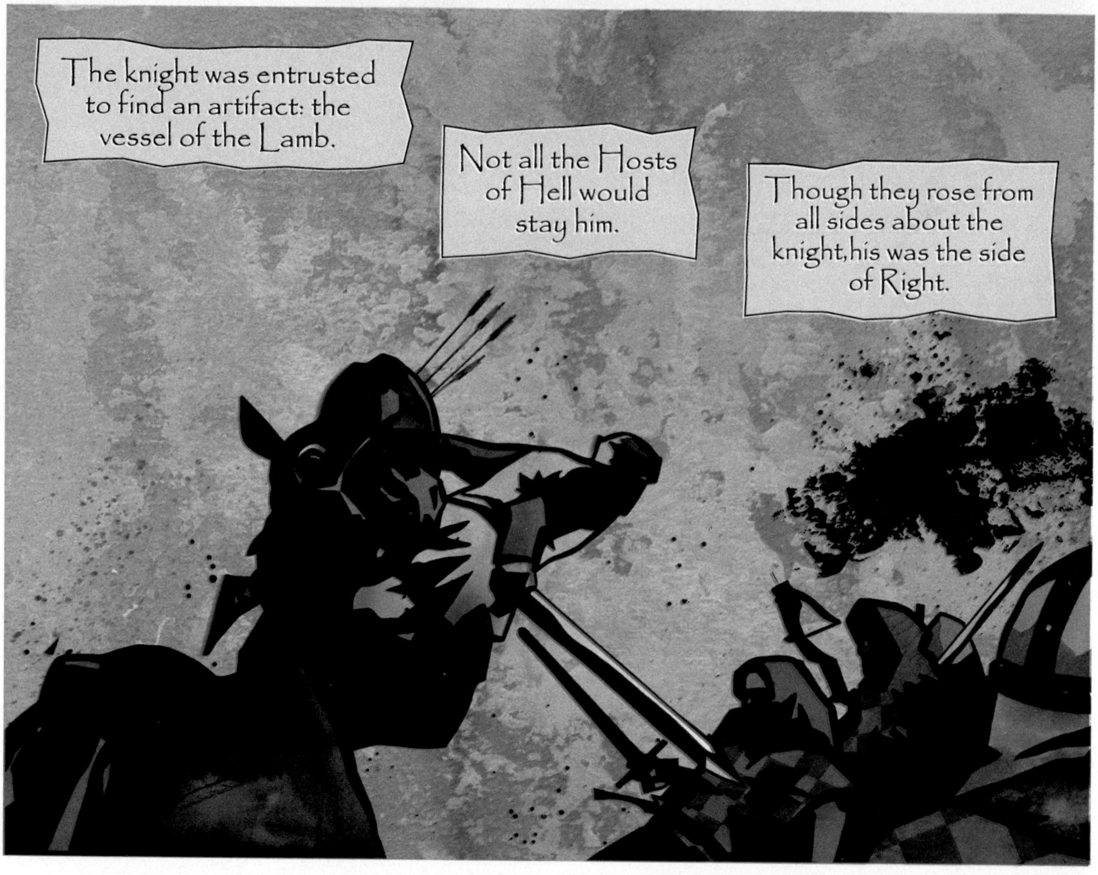
The knight was entrusted to find an artifact: the vessel of the Lamb.
Not all the Hosts of Hell would stay him.
Though they rose from all sides about the knight,his was the side of Right.

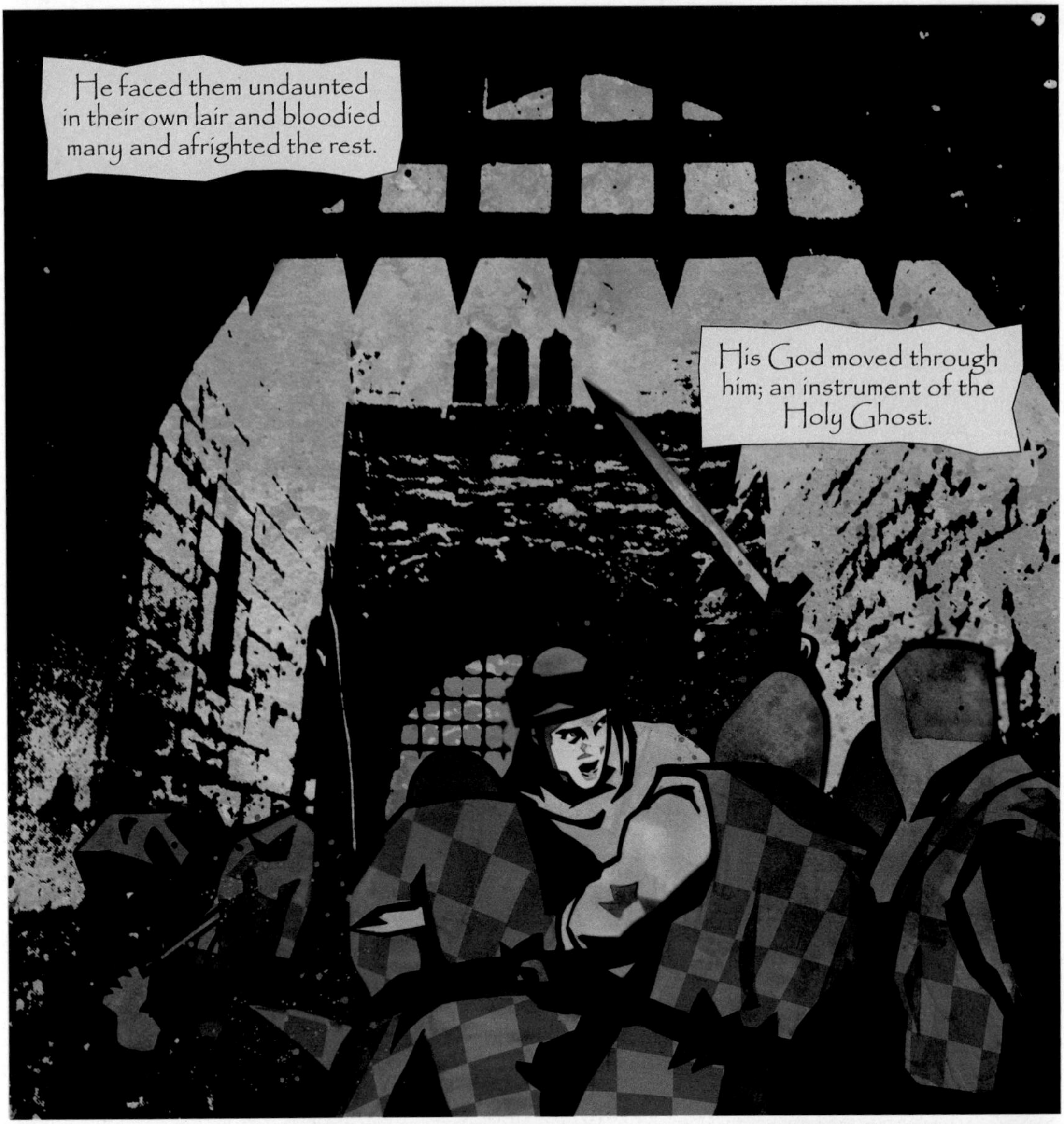
He faced them undaunted in their own lair and bloodied many and afrighted the rest.
His God moved through him; an instrument of the Holy Ghost.

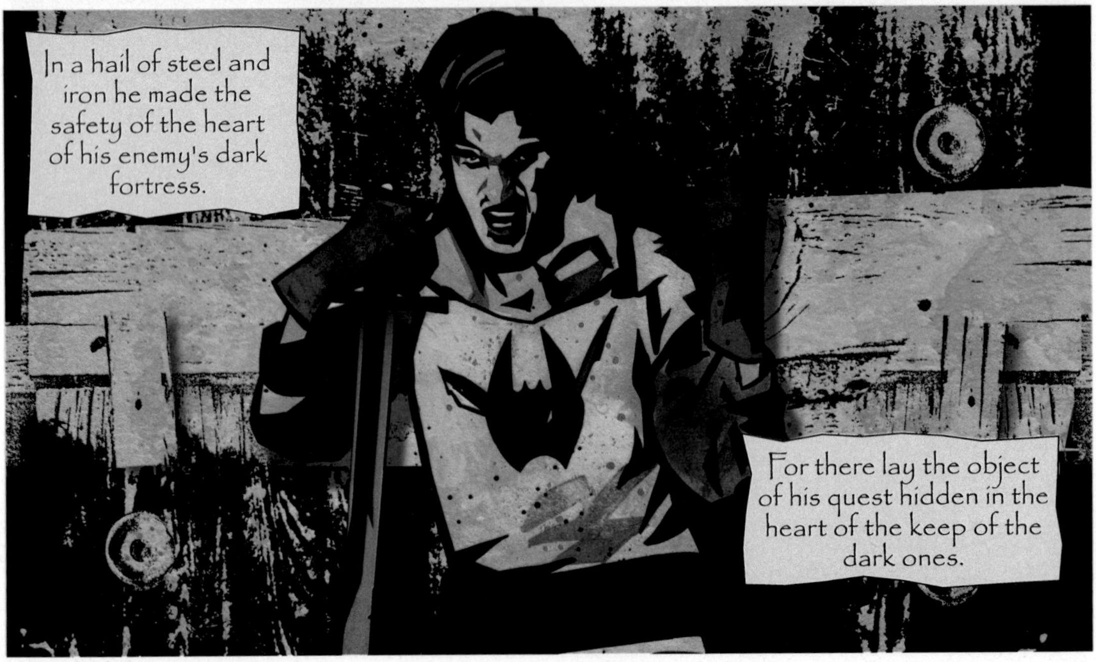
In a hail of steel and iron he made the safety of the heart of his enemy's dark fortress.
For there lay the object of his quest hidden in the heart of the keep of the dark ones.

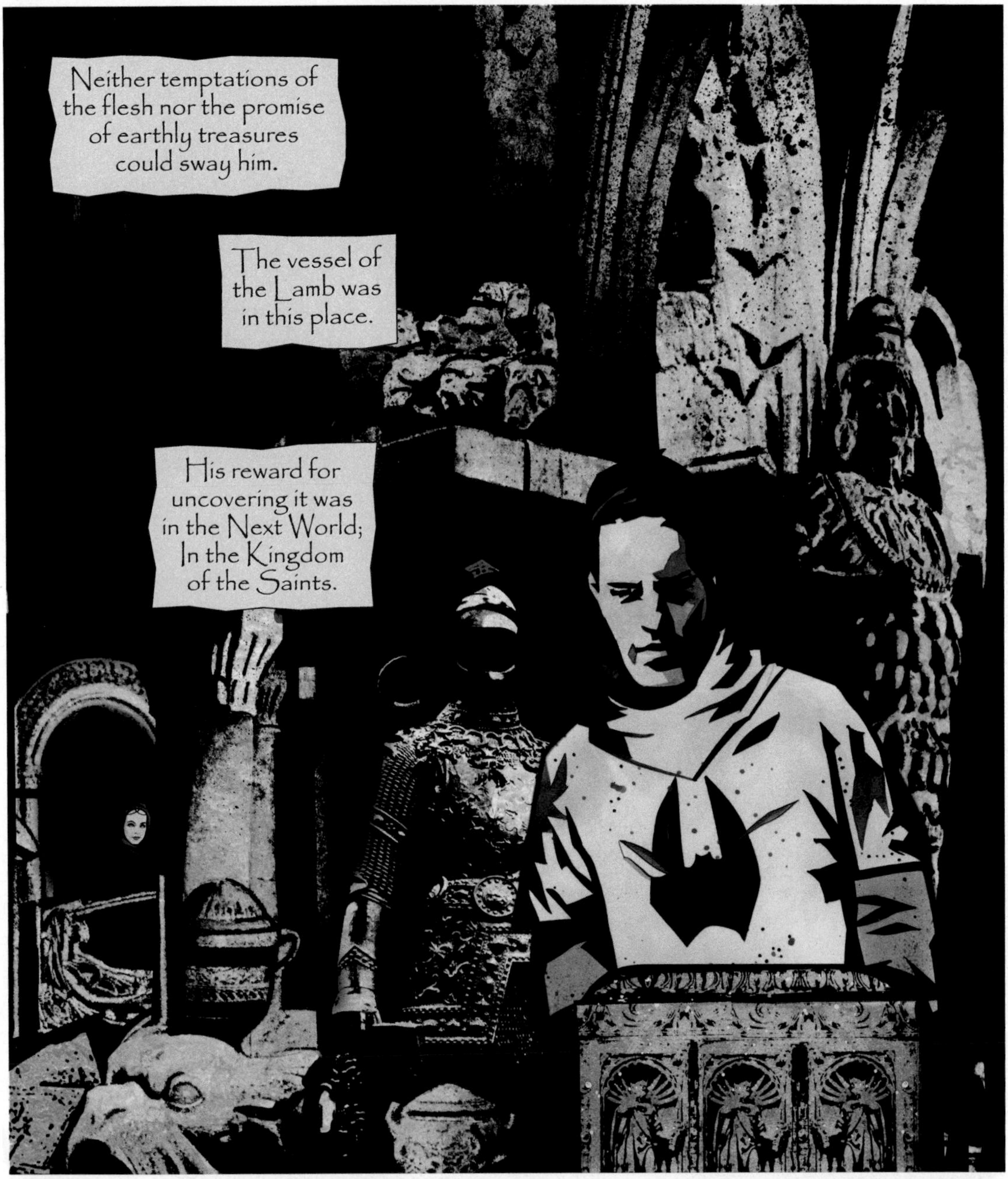
Neither temptations of the flesh nor the promise of earthly treasures could sway him.
The vessel of the Lamb was in this place.
His reward for uncovering it was in the Next World; In the Kingdom of the Saints.

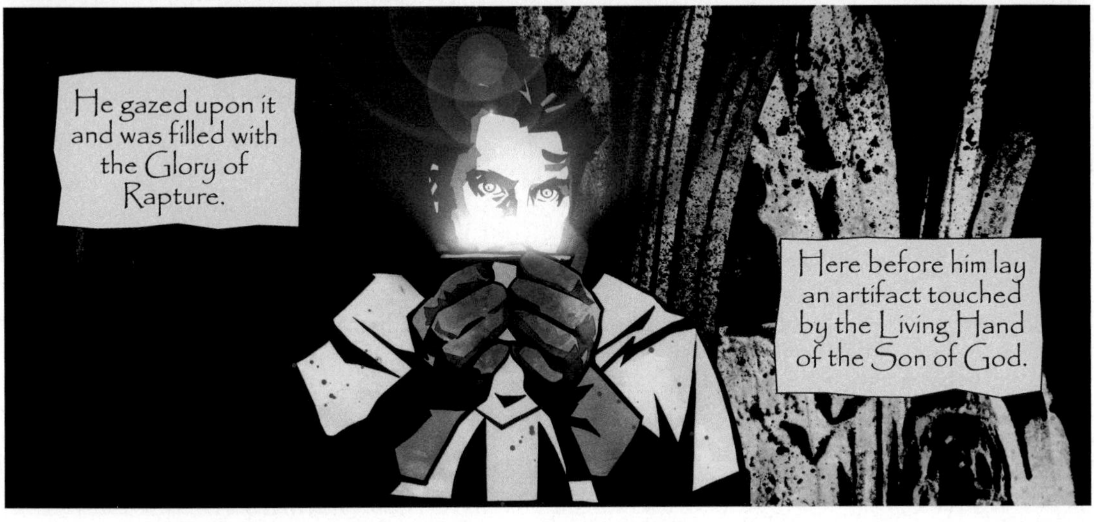
He gazed upon it and was filled with the Glory of Rapture.
Here before him lay an artifact touched by the Living Hand of the Son of God.

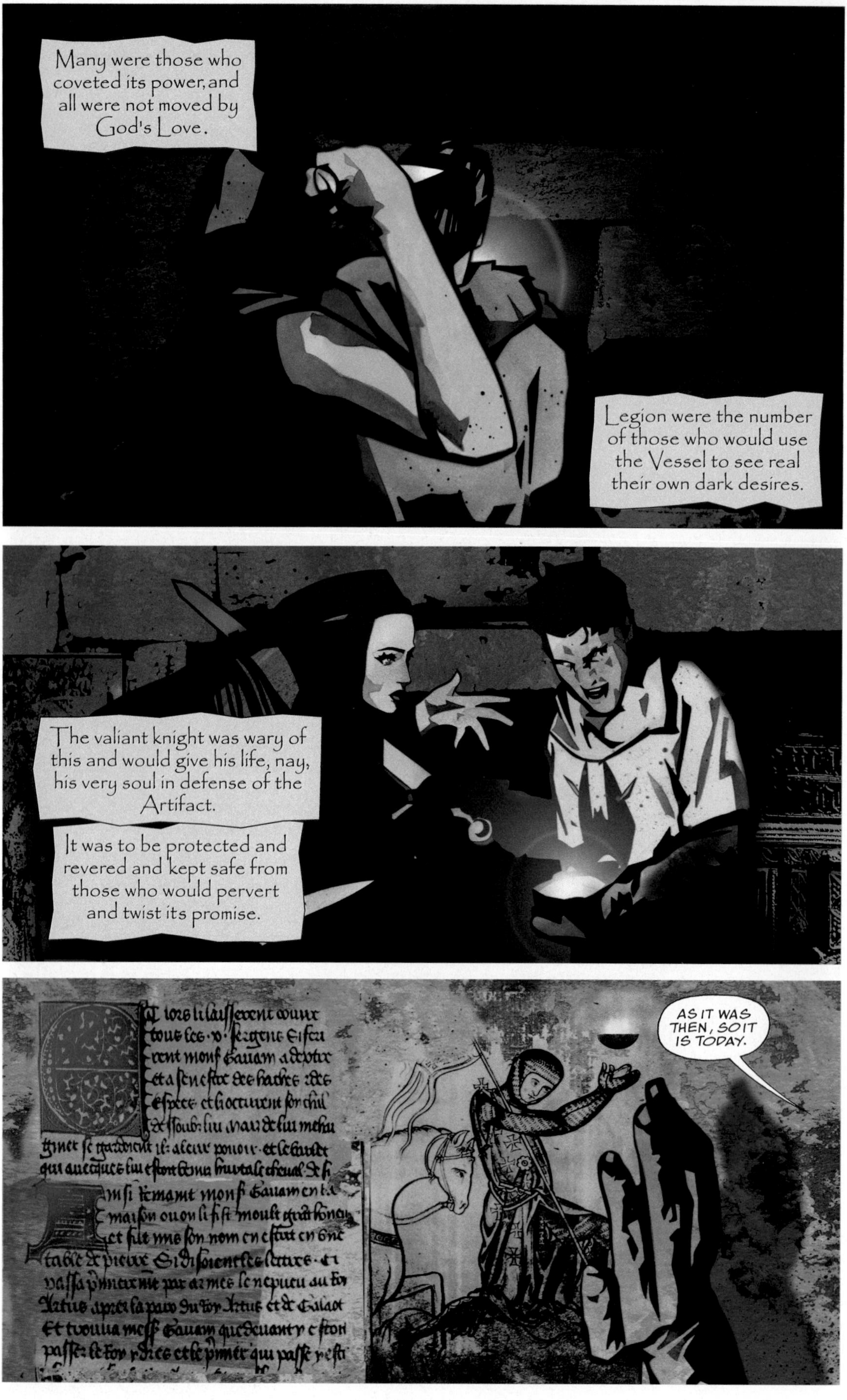
Many were those who coveted its power, and all were not moved by God's Love.
Legion were the number of those who would use the Vessel to see real their own dark desires.
The valiant knight was wary of this and would give his life, nay, his very soul in defense of the Artifact.
It was to be protected and revered and kept safe from those who would pervert and twist its promise.
AS IT WAS THEN, SO IT IS TODAY.

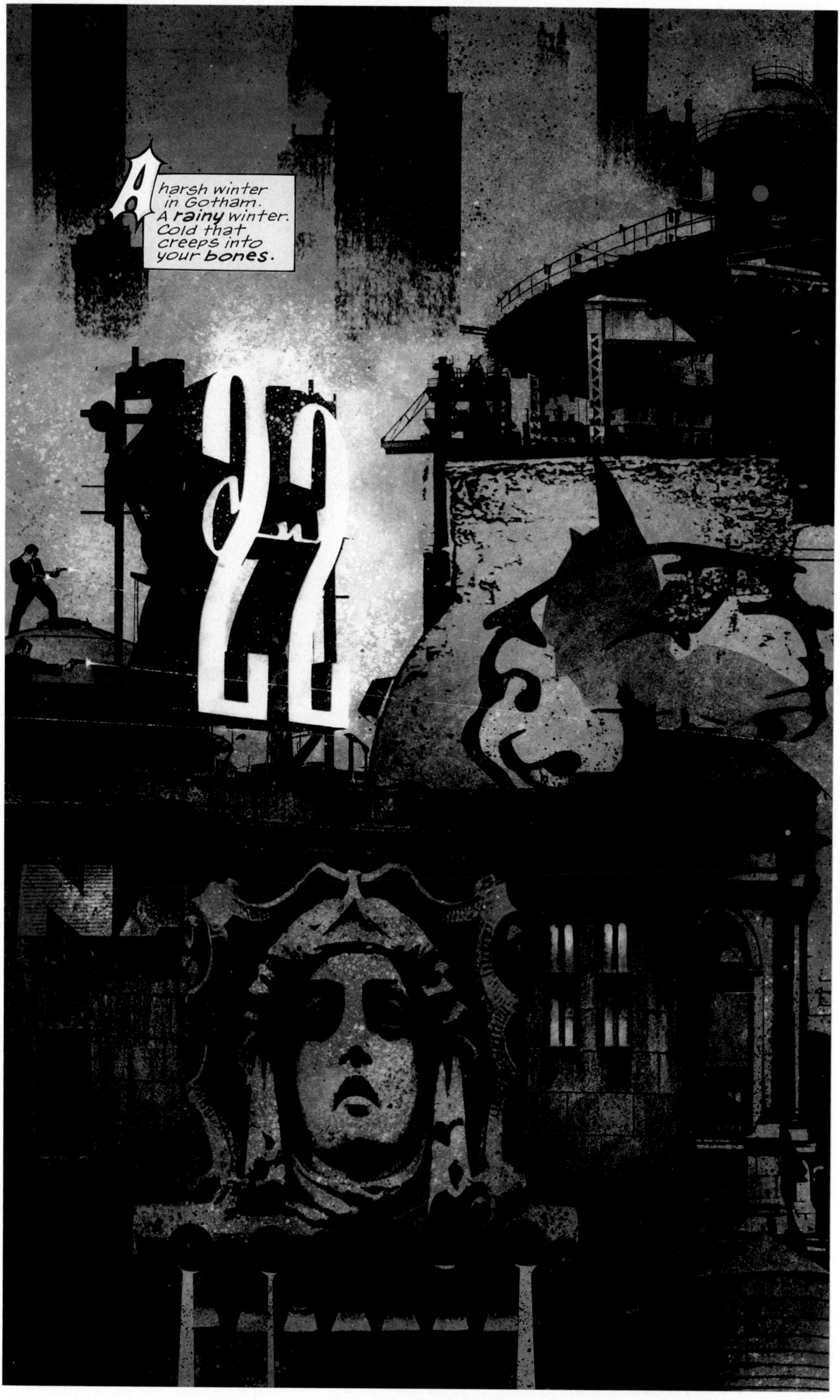
A harsh winter in Gotham. A rainy winter. Cold that creeps into your bones.
22

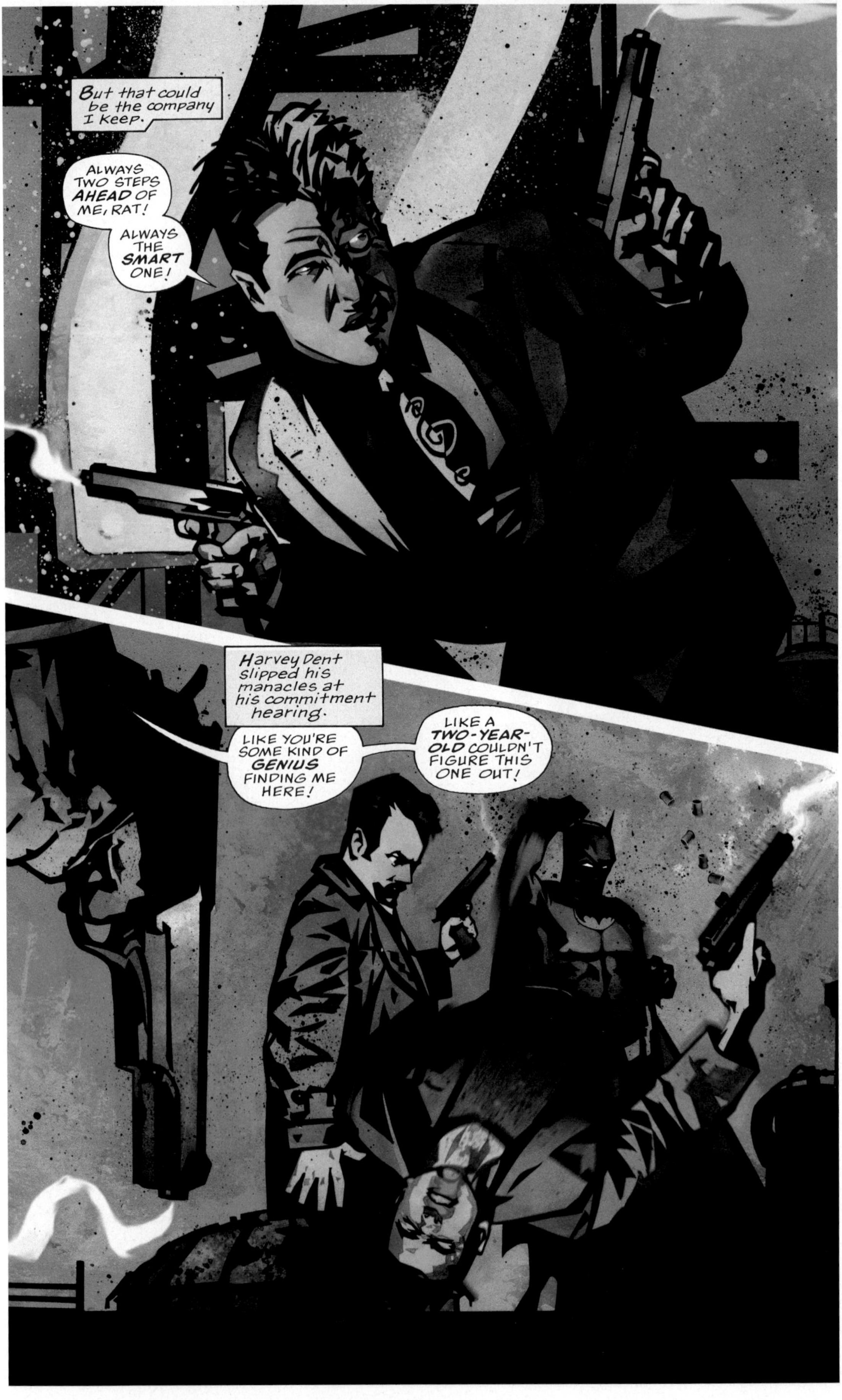

But that could be the company I keep.
ALWAYS TWO STEPS AHEAD OF ME, RAT!
ALWAYS THE SMART ONE!
Harvey Dent slipped his manacles at his commitment hearing.
LIKE YOU'RE SOME KIND OF GENIUS FINDING ME HERE!
LIKE A TWO-YEAR-OLD COULDN'T FIGURE THIS ONE OUT!

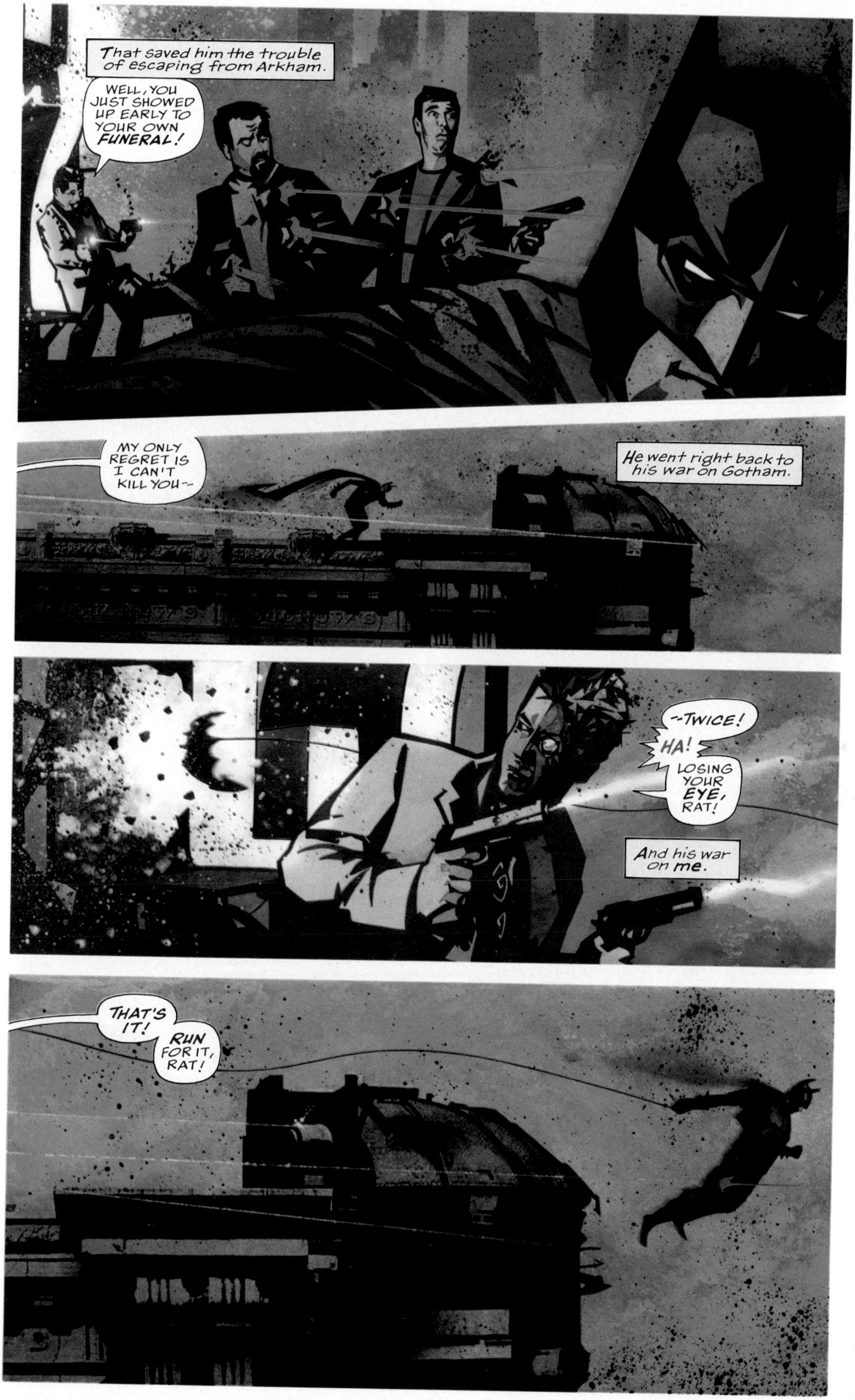
That saved him the trouble of escaping from Arkham.
WELL, YOU JUST SHOWED UP EARLY TO YOUR OWN FUNERAL!
MY ONLY REGRET IS I CAN'T KILL YOU--
He went right back to his war on Gotham.
--TWICE!
HA!
LOSING YOUR EYE, RAT!
And his war on me.
THAT'S IT!
RUN FOR IT, RAT!

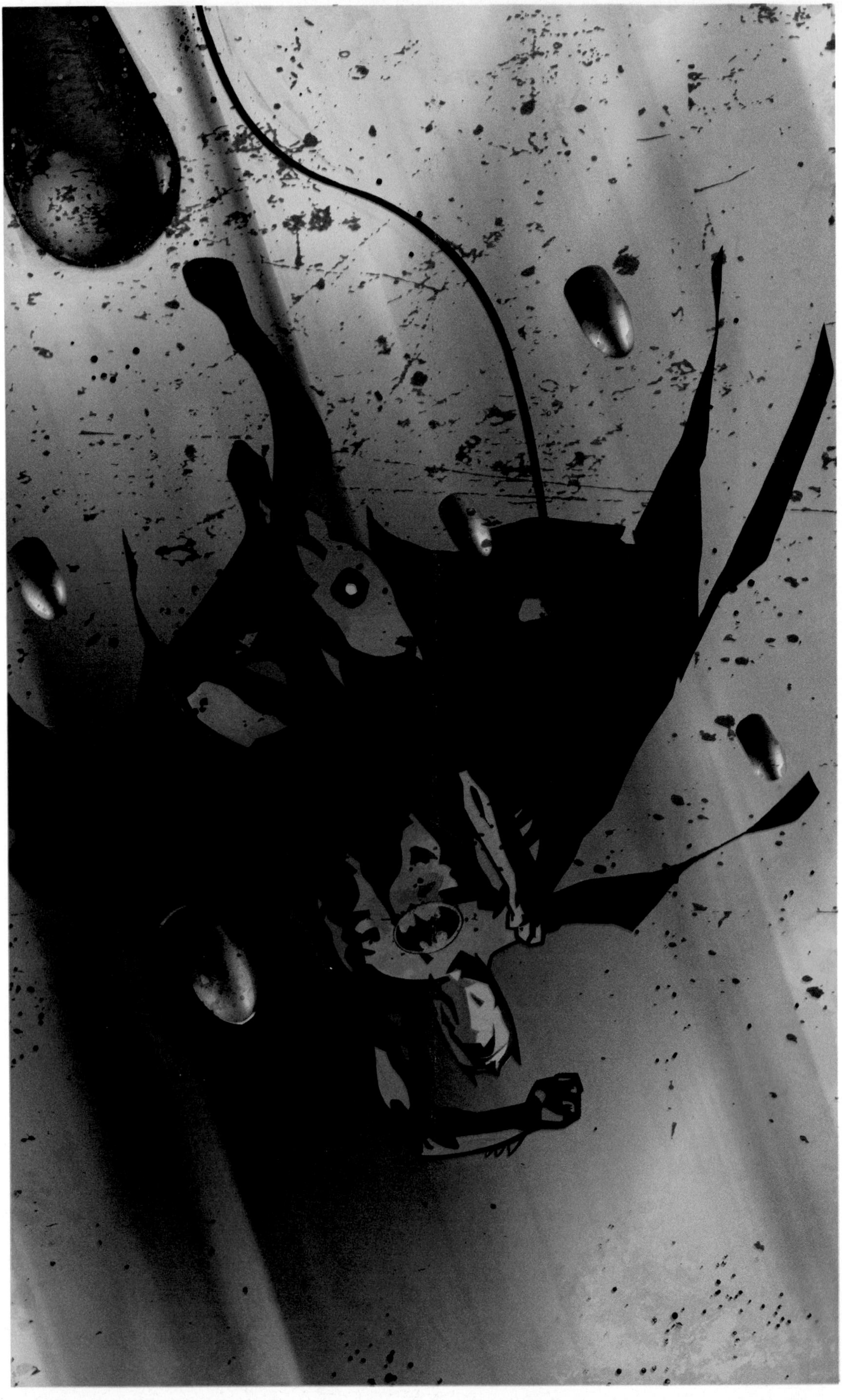

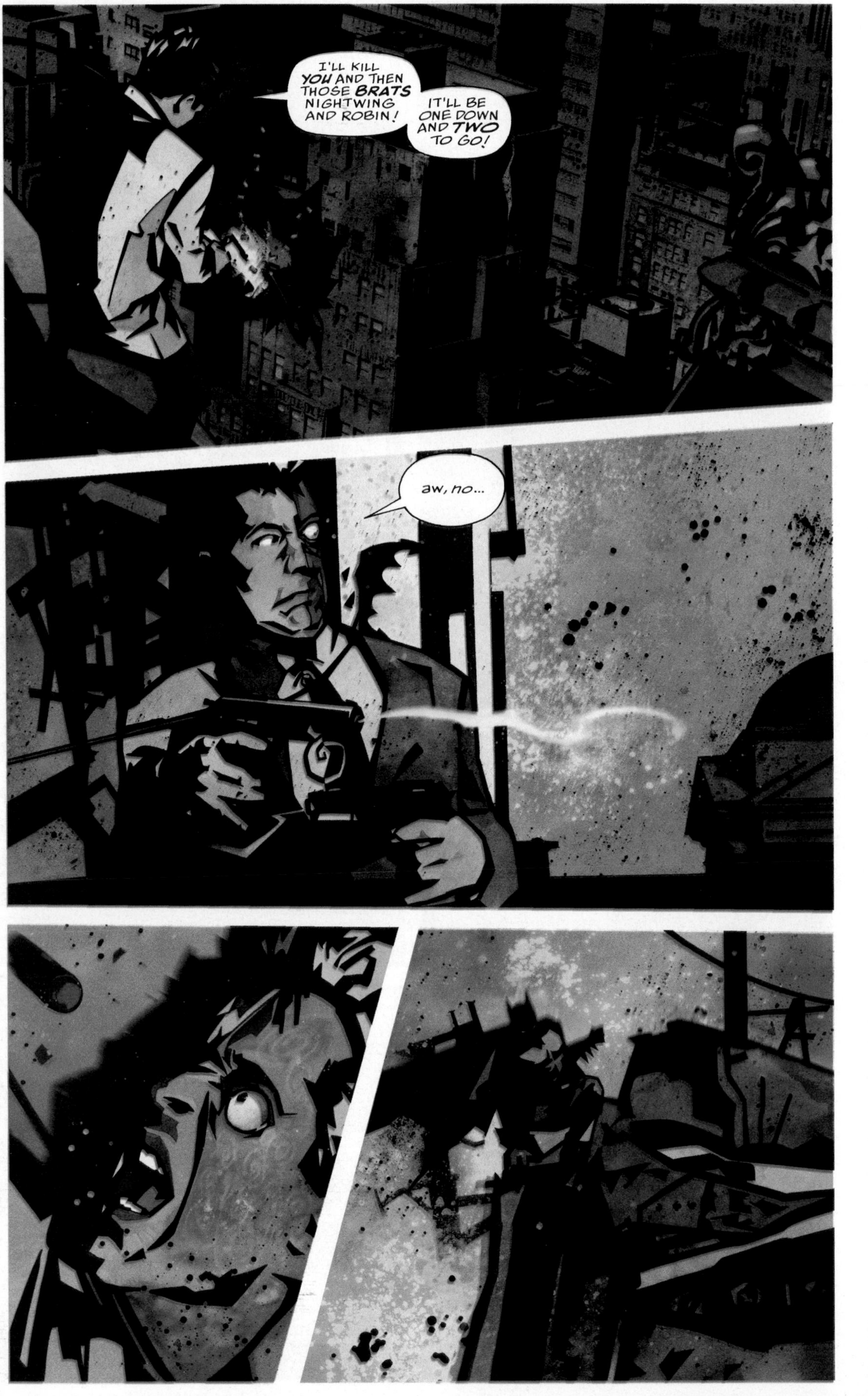
I'LL KILL YOU AND THEN THOSE BRATS NIGHTWING AND ROBIN!
IT'LL BE ONE DOWN AND TWO TO GO!
aw, no...

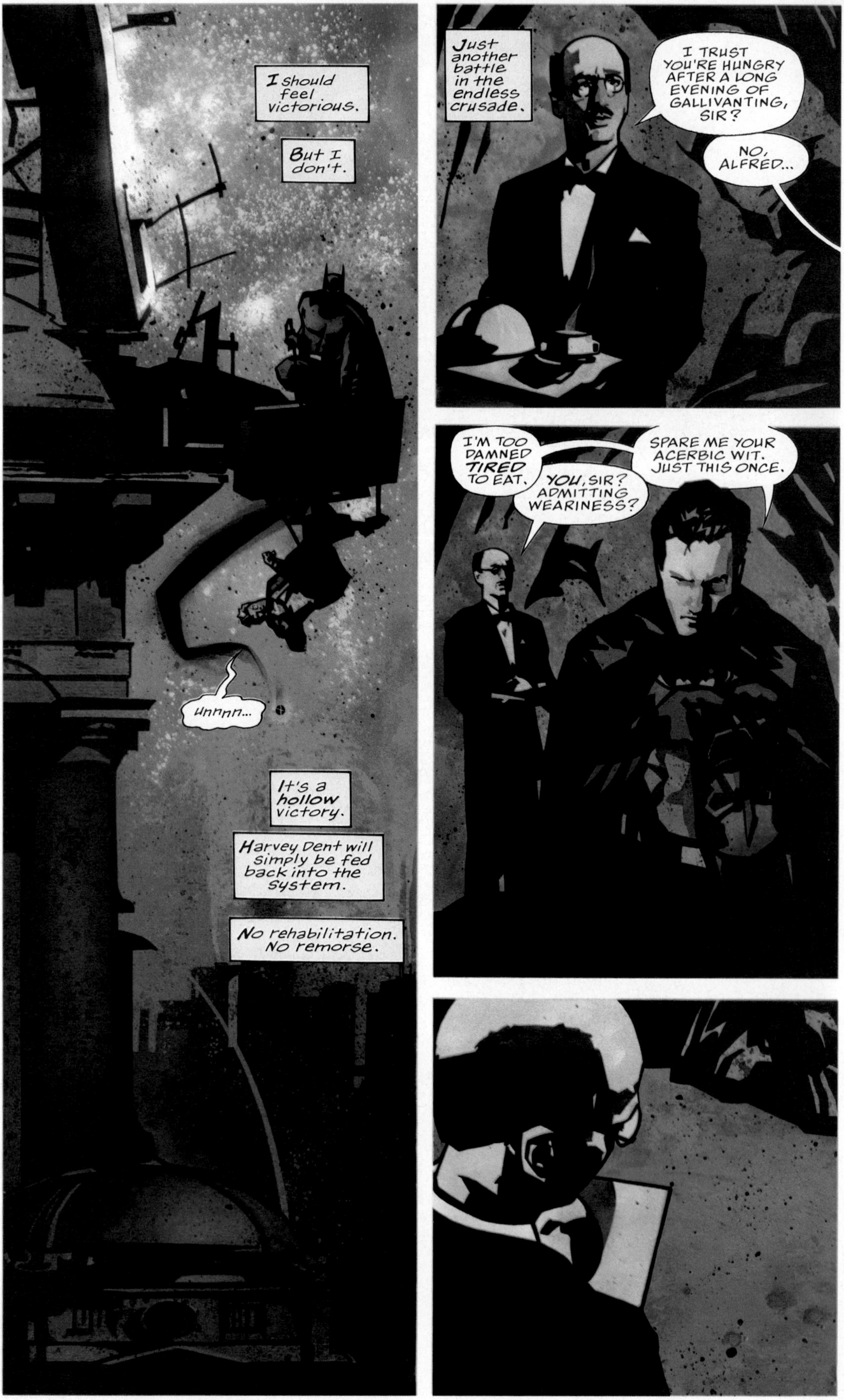
I should feel victorious.
But I don't.
unnnn...
It's a hollow victory.
Harvey Dent will simply be fed back into the system.
No rehabilitation. No remorse.
Just another battle in the endless crusade.
I TRUST YOU'RE HUNGRY AFTER A LONG EVENING OF GALLIVANTING, SIR?
NO, ALFRED...
I'M TOO DAMNED TIRED TO EAT.
YOU, SIR? ADMITTING WEARINESS?
SPARE ME YOUR ACERBIC WIT. JUST THIS ONCE.

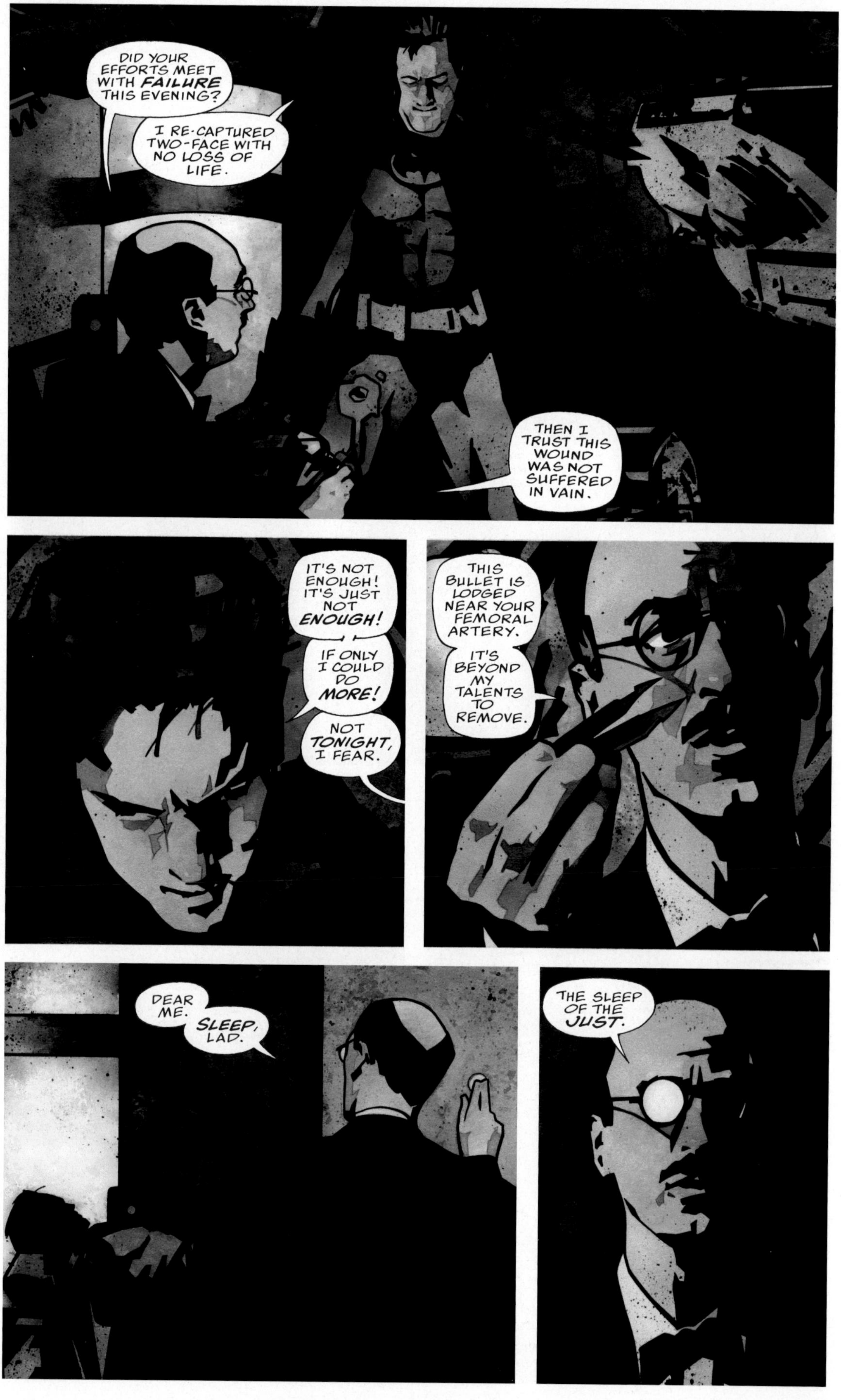
DID YOUR EFFORTS MEET WITH FAILURE THIS EVENING?
I RE-CAPTURED TWO-FACE WITH NO LOSS OF LIFE.
THEN I TRUST THIS WOUND WAS NOT SUFFERED IN VAIN.
IT'S NOT ENOUGH! IT'S JUST NOT ENOUGH!
IF ONLY I COULD DO MORE!
NOT TONIGHT, I FEAR.
THIS BULLET IS LODGED NEAR YOUR FEMORAL ARTERY.
IT'S BEYOND MY TALENTS TO REMOVE.
DEAR ME.
SLEEP, LAD.
THE SLEEP OF THE JUST.

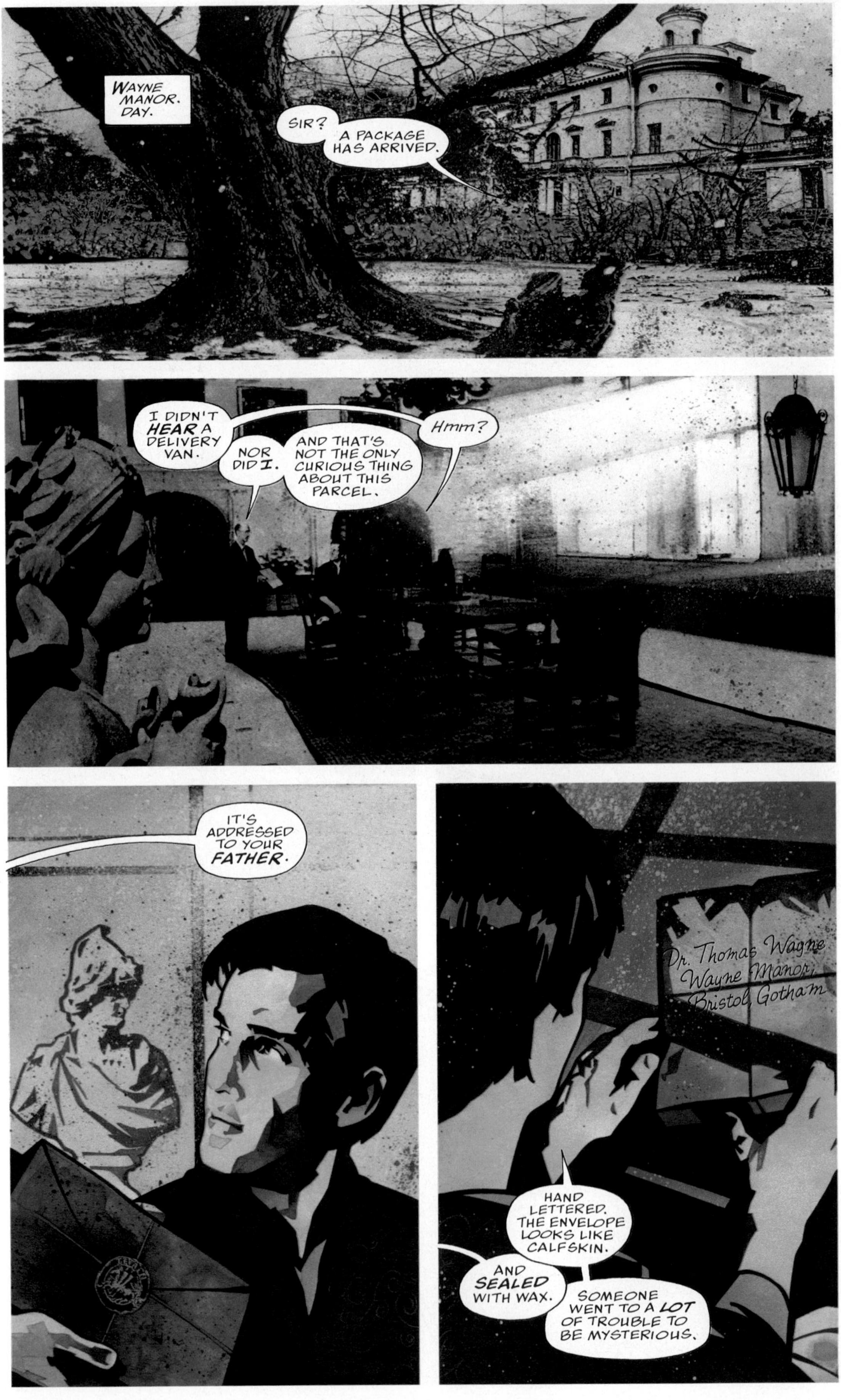
WAYNE MANOR. DAY.
SIR?
A PACKAGE HAS ARRIVED.
I DIDN'T HEAR A DELIVERY VAN.
NOR DID I.
AND THAT'S NOT THE ONLY CURIOUS THING ABOUT THIS PARCEL.
Hmm?
IT'S ADDRESSED TO YOUR FATHER.
Dr. Thomas Wayne
Wayne Manor,
Bristol, Gotham
HAND LETTERED. THE ENVELOPE LOOKS LIKE CALFSKIN.
AND SEALED WITH WAX.
SOMEONE WENT TO A LOT OF TROUBLE TO BE MYSTERIOUS.

IT'S OLD EARLY MIDDLE AGES. THE BINDING IS IRISH. THE PAPER IS ITALIAN LINEN.

SHALL WE OPEN IT?

I SUPPOSE.

SO CAUTIOUS? ARE YOU AFRAID THE BOOK WILL EXPLODE?

OR HAVE TOXINS IN THE FIBERS. A PAPER CUT WOULD BE DEADLY.

DEAR.

Josephus
Bron
Alainsohn

IT'S A LIST OF NAMES. THE EARLIEST PAGES ARE ALL IN THE SAME HAND.

SOMEONE OBVIOUSLY COPIED IT FROM AN EARLIER WORK. THE FIRST NEW HAND IS IN 1050 A.D.

THE FIRST NAME IS JOSEPHUS. THE NEXT IS BRONS AND THEN ALAINSOHN.

Oh, MY--

oh, MY.

IF THIS IS SOME KIND OF SICK JOKE...

Grambling Hall
Shadow Falls Road
Chapin, Gotham

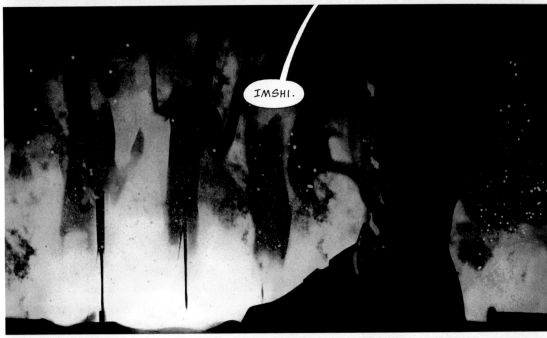

IMSHI.

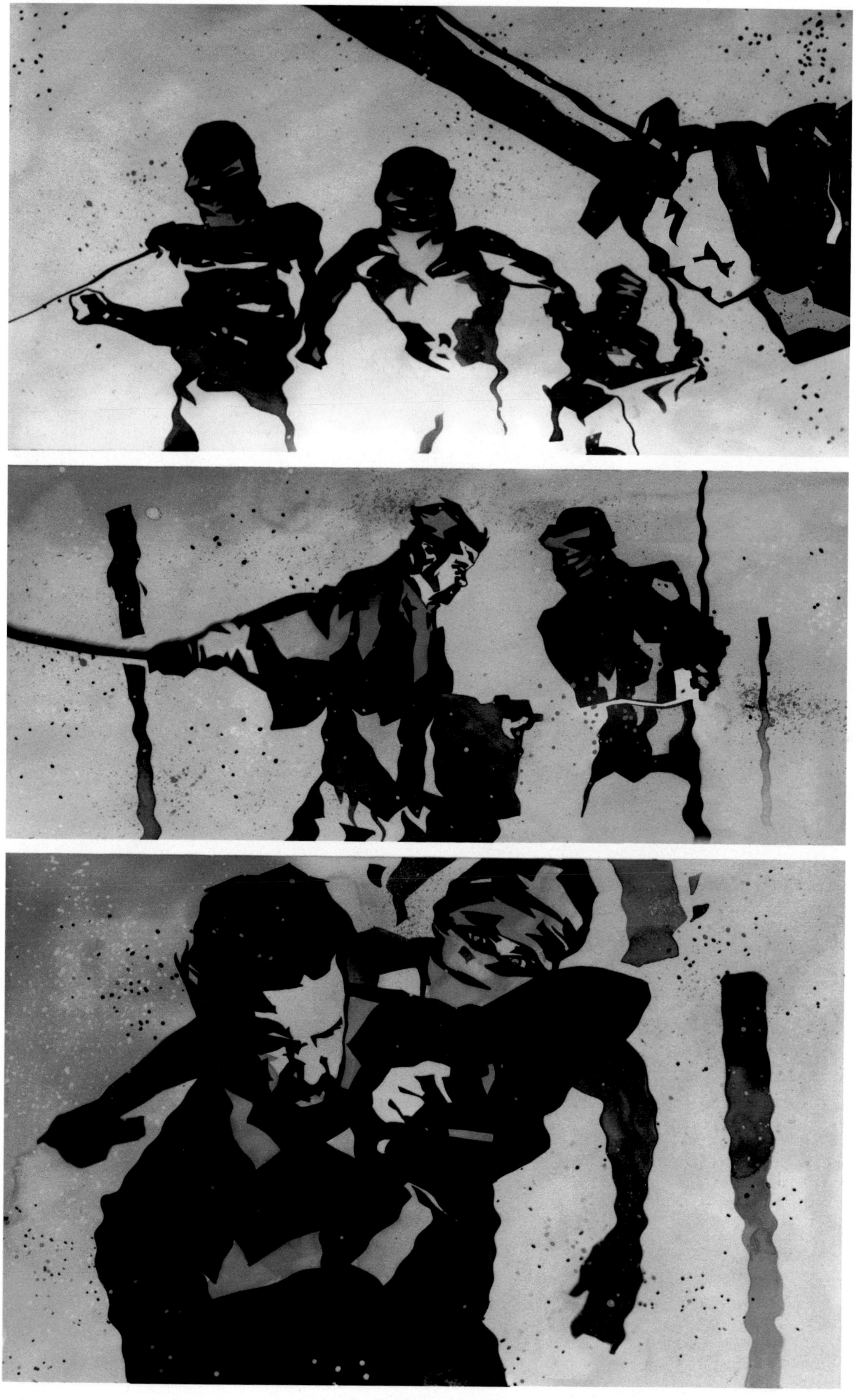

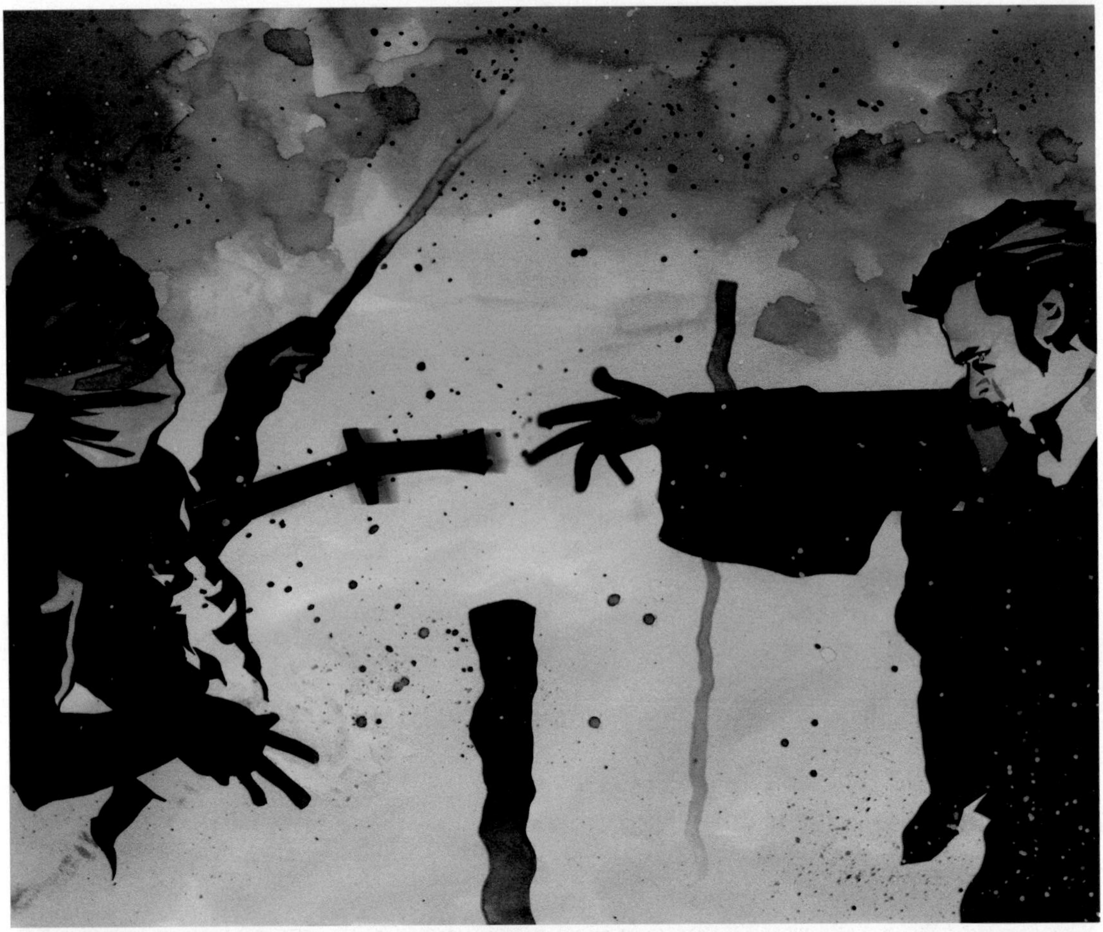

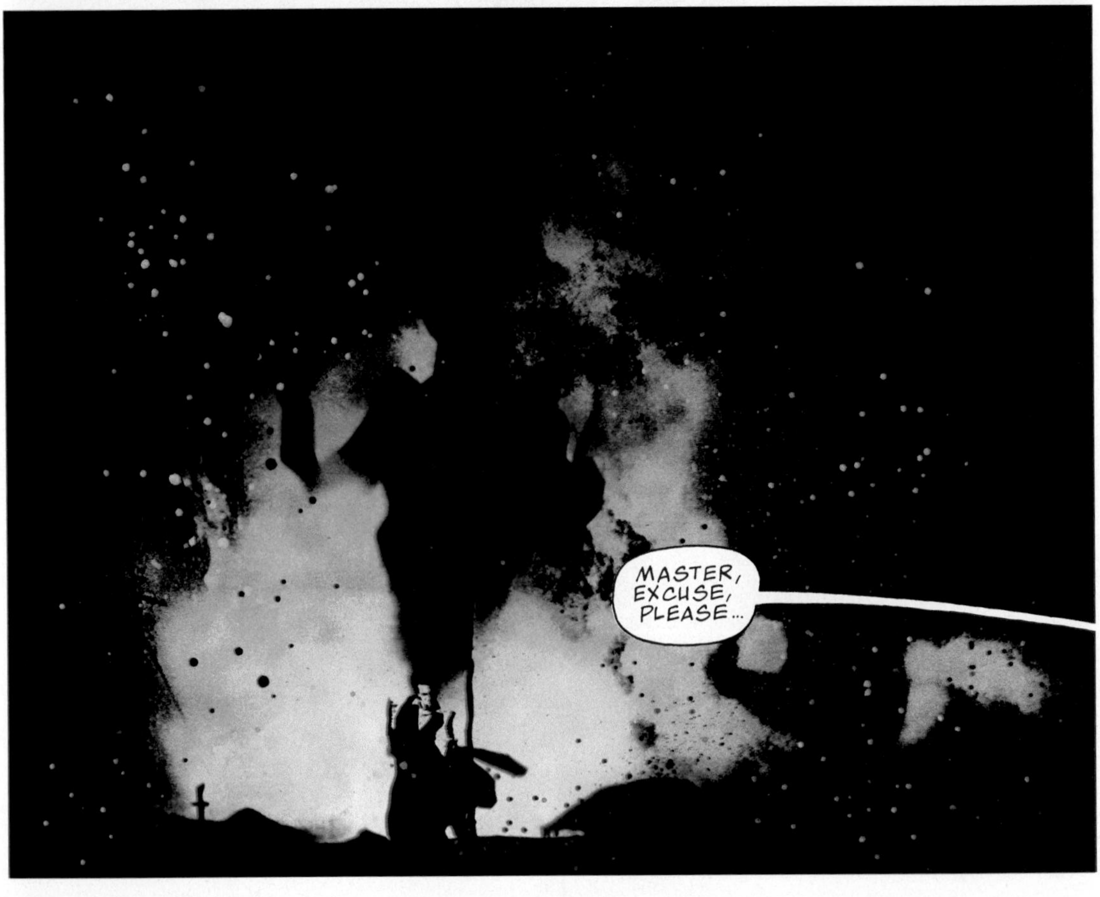
MASTER, EXCUSE, PLEASE...

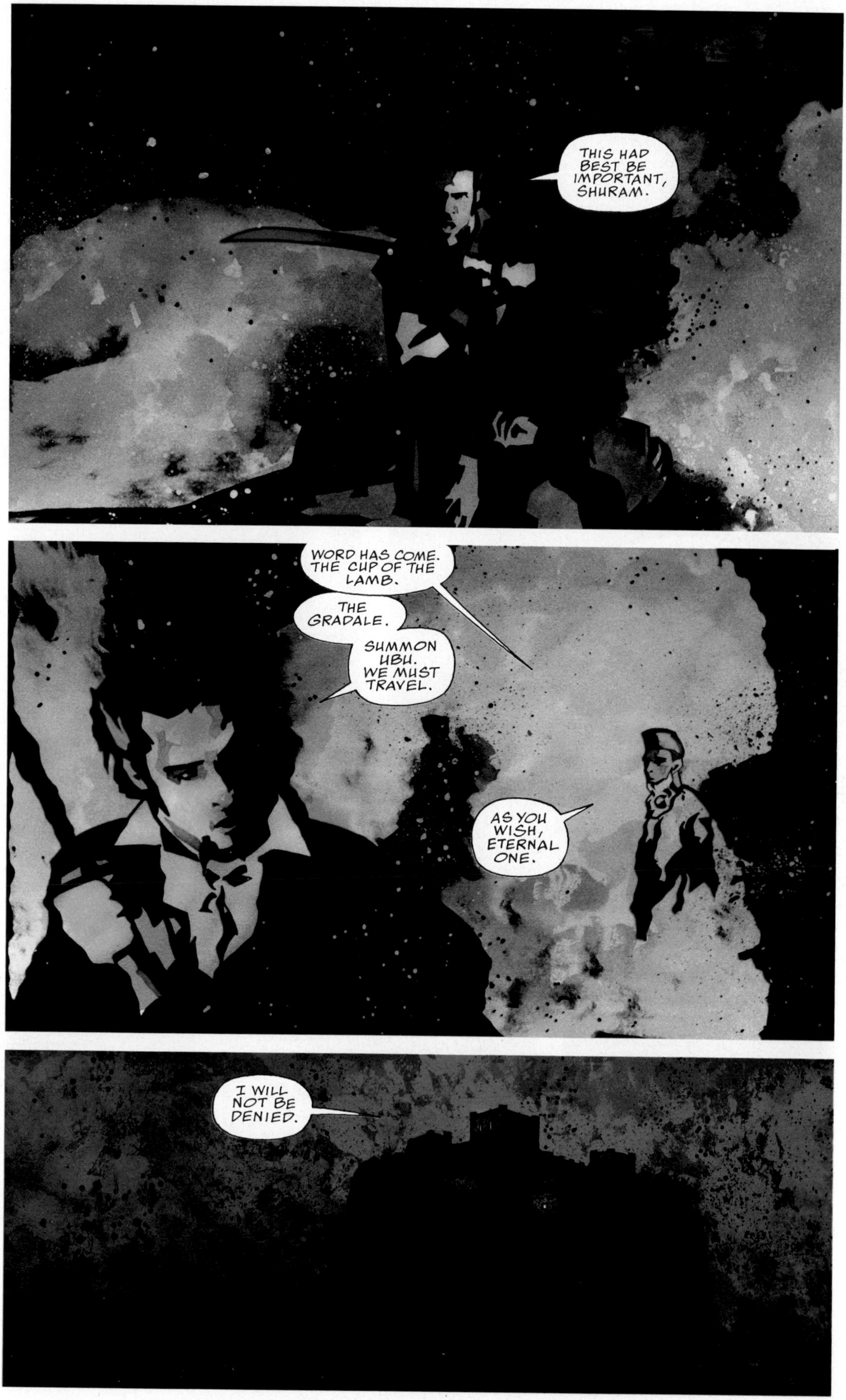
THIS HAD BEST BE IMPORTANT, SHURAM.
WORD HAS COME. THE CUP OF THE LAMB.
THE GRADALE.
SUMMON UBU. WE MUST TRAVEL.
AS YOU WISH, ETERNAL ONE.
I WILL NOT BE DENIED.

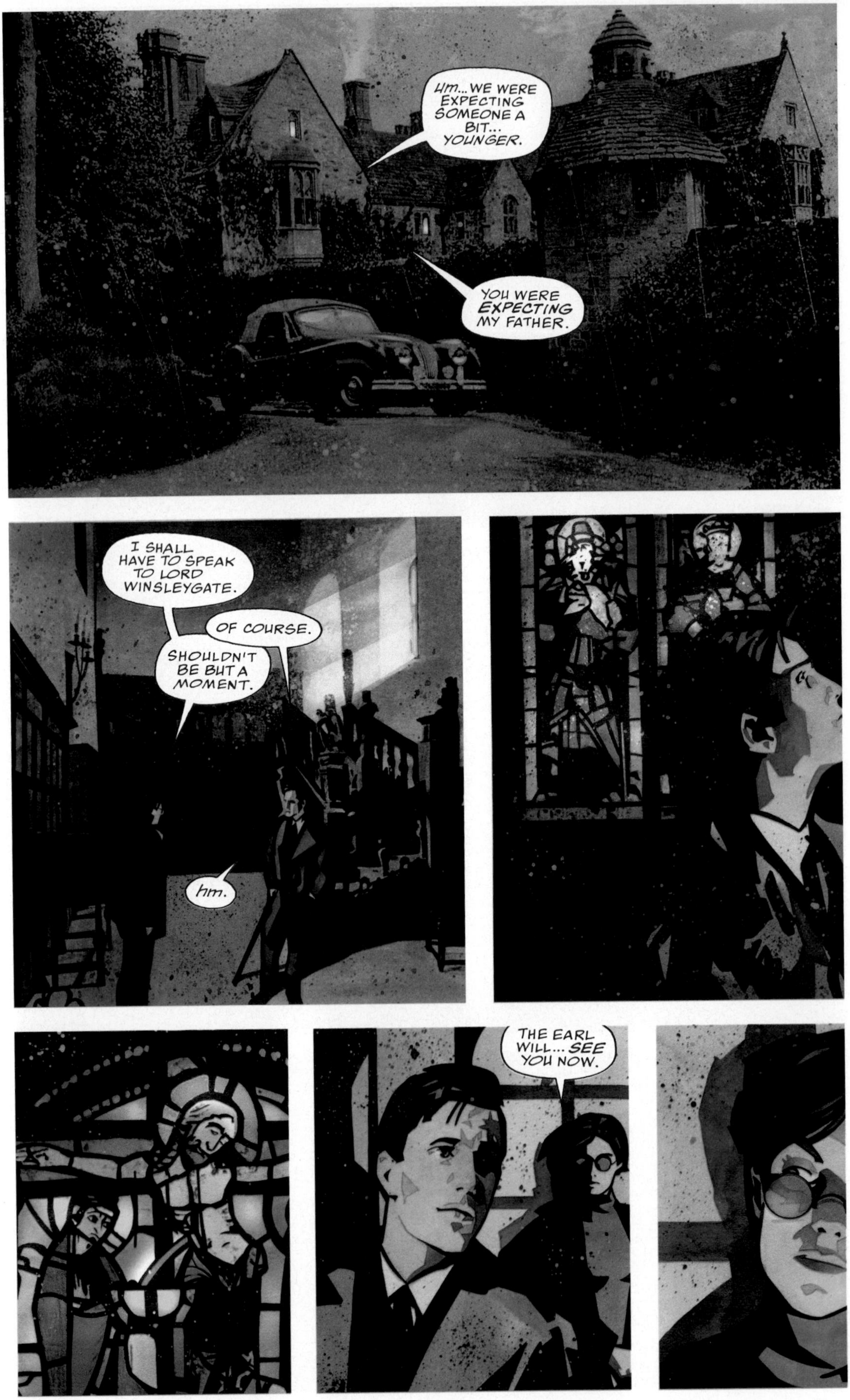
UM... WE WERE EXPECTING SOMEONE A BIT... YOUNGER.
YOU WERE EXPECTING MY FATHER.
I SHALL HAVE TO SPEAK TO LORD WINSLEYGATE.
OF COURSE.
SHOULDN'T BE BUT A MOMENT.
hm.
THE EARL WILL... SEE YOU NOW.

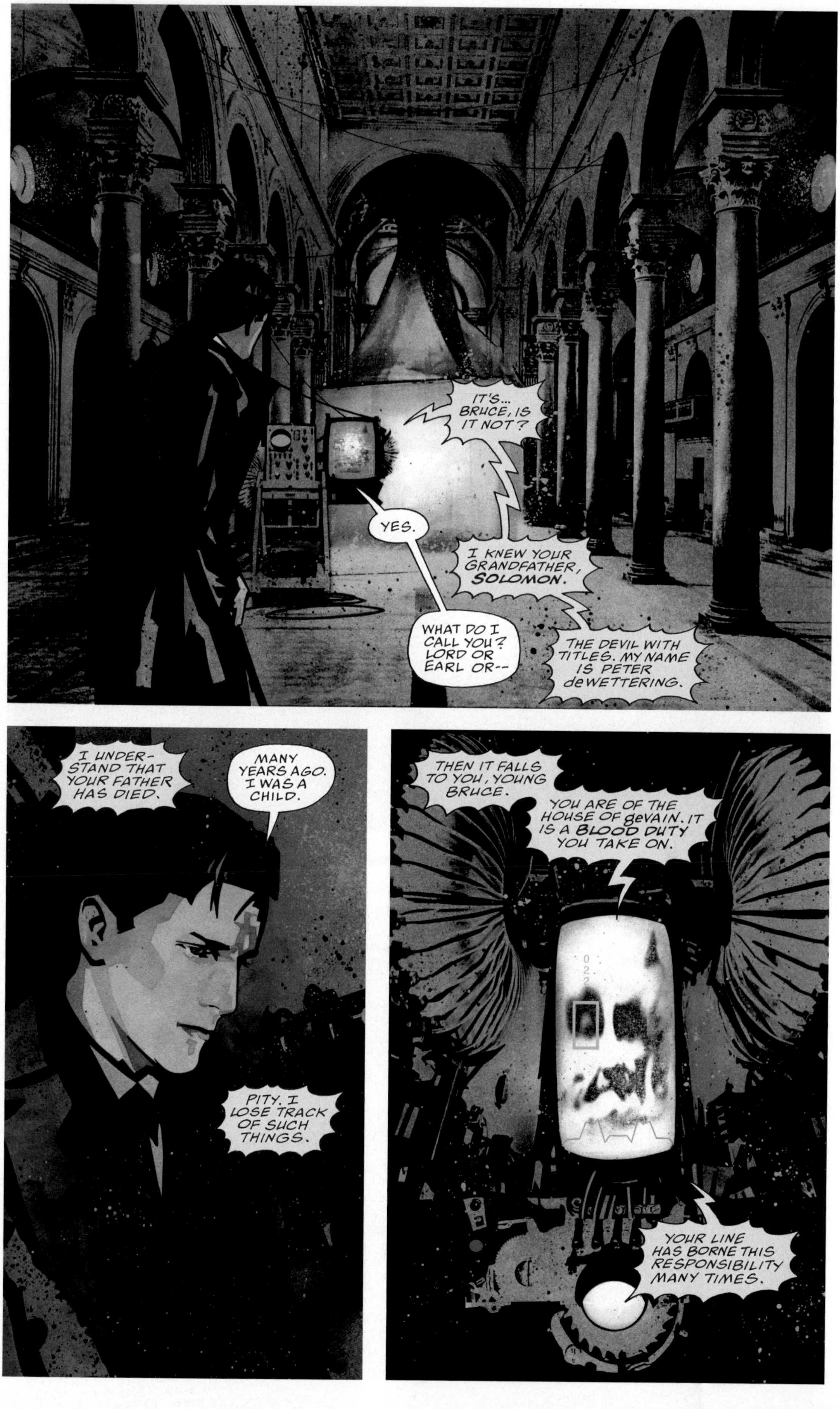

IT'S... BRUCE, IS IT NOT?
YES.
I KNEW YOUR GRANDFATHER, SOLOMON.
WHAT DO I CALL YOU? LORD OR EARL OR--
THE DEVIL WITH TITLES. MY NAME IS PETER deWETTERING.
I UNDER-STAND THAT YOUR FATHER HAS DIED.
MANY YEARS AGO. I WAS A CHILD.
PITY. I LOSE TRACK OF SUCH THINGS.
THEN IT FALLS TO YOU, YOUNG BRUCE.
YOU ARE OF THE HOUSE OF geVAIN. IT IS A BLOOD DUTY YOU TAKE ON.
YOUR LINE HAS BORNE THIS RESPONSIBILITY MANY TIMES.

"DUTY"?
MY NAME IS WAYNE, NOT GEVAIN.
IT WAS ONCE GEVAIN. MANY AGES AGO.
THIS IS THE OBJECT. MORE PRECIOUS THAN ANY LIFE, IT IS.
WHAT IS IT?
THE GREEL. THE CUP OF KINGS.
THE HOLY GRAIL, SON.
1.0269
THE BOWL OF THE CHRIST. THE CUP THAT HELD THE BLOOD OF THE MESSIAH.
WHAT AM I SUPPOSED TO--
beeeeeeeeeee
1.0000

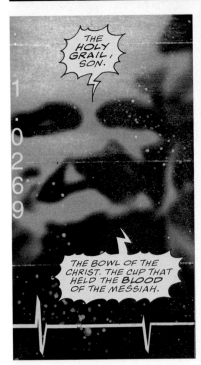

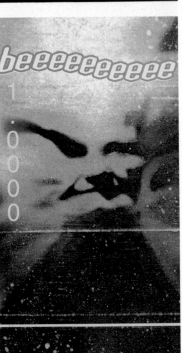

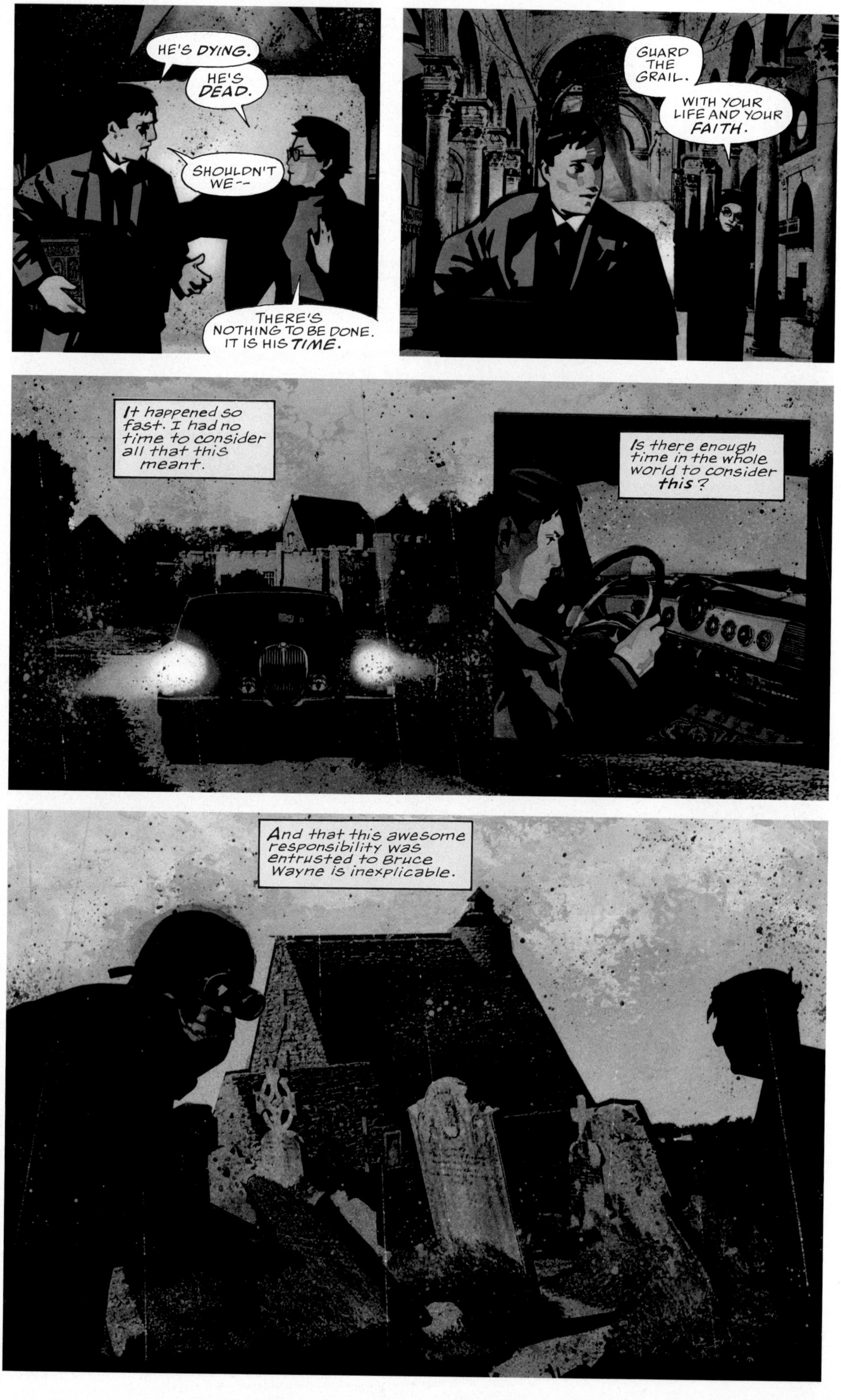
HE'S DYING.
HE'S DEAD.
SHOULDN'T WE--
THERE'S NOTHING TO BE DONE. IT IS HIS TIME.
GUARD THE GRAIL.
WITH YOUR LIFE AND YOUR FAITH.
It happened so fast. I had no time to consider all that this meant.
Is there enough time in the whole world to consider this?
And that this awesome responsibility was entrusted to Bruce Wayne is inexplicable.

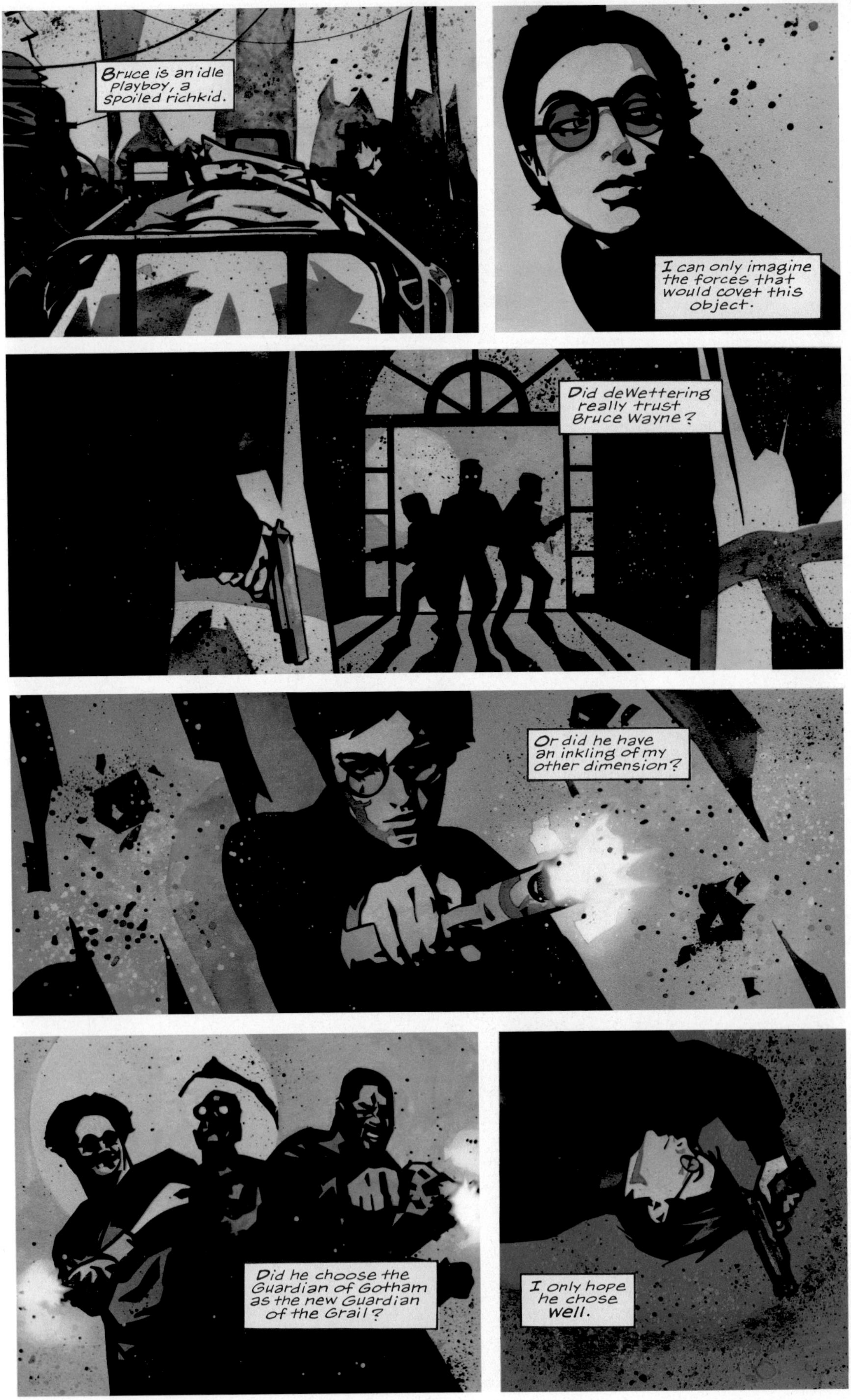
Bruce is an idle playboy, a spoiled richkid.
I can only imagine the forces that would covet this object.
Did deWettering really trust Bruce Wayne?
Or did he have an inkling of my other dimension?
Did he choose the Guardian of Gotham as the new Guardian of the Grail?
I only hope he chose well.

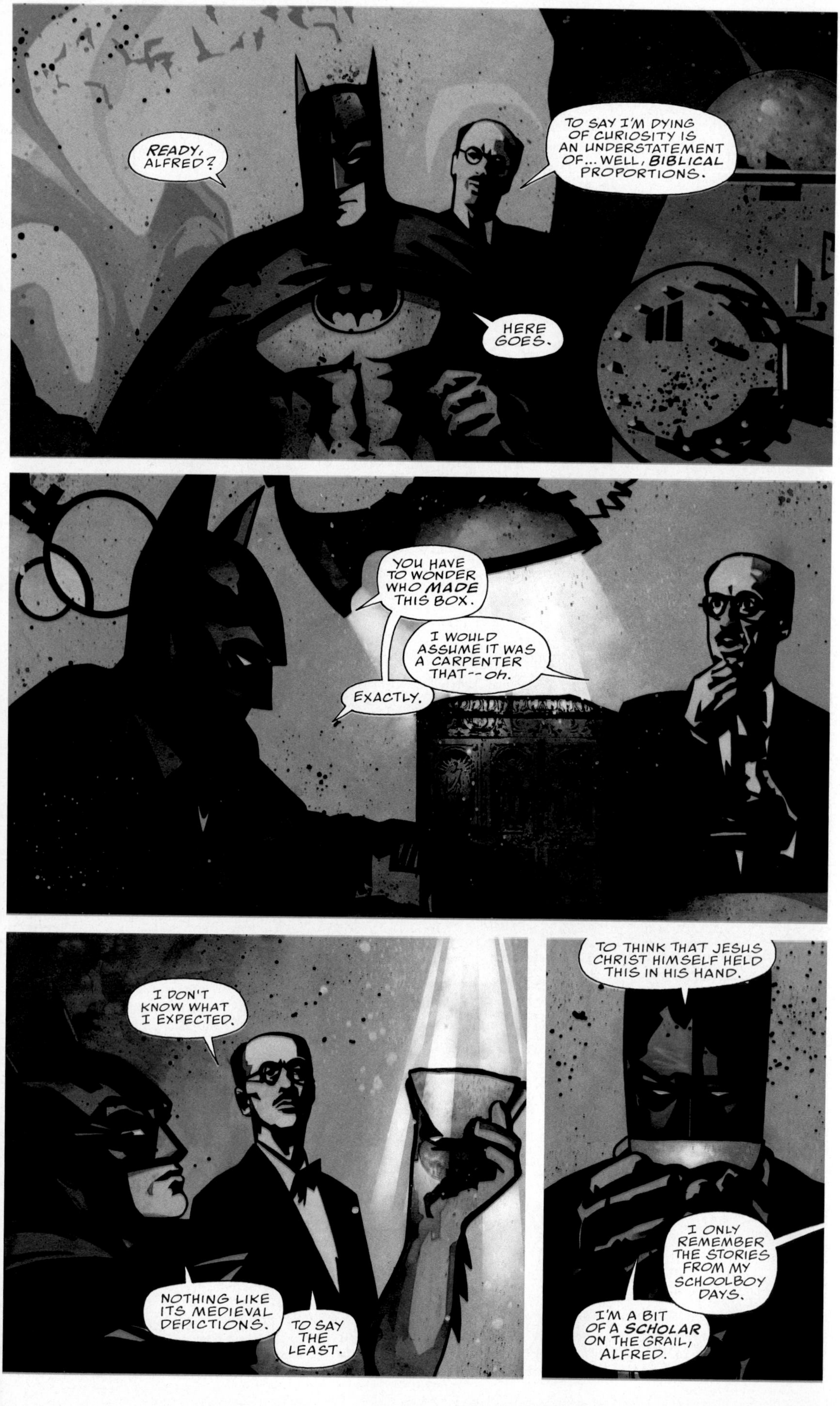
READY, ALFRED?
TO SAY I'M DYING OF CURIOSITY IS AN UNDERSTATEMENT OF... WELL, BIBLICAL PROPORTIONS.
HERE GOES.
YOU HAVE TO WONDER WHO MADE THIS BOX.
I WOULD ASSUME IT WAS A CARPENTER THAT--oh.
EXACTLY.
I DON'T KNOW WHAT I EXPECTED.
NOTHING LIKE ITS MEDIEVAL DEPICTIONS.
TO SAY THE LEAST.
TO THINK THAT JESUS CHRIST HIMSELF HELD THIS IN HIS HAND.
I ONLY REMEMBER THE STORIES FROM MY SCHOOLBOY DAYS.
I'M A BIT OF A SCHOLAR ON THE GRAIL, ALFRED.

IT'S SAID THAT THIS IS THE BOWL THAT JESUS ATE LAMB FROM AT THE LAST SUPPER.
IT WAS LATER USED BY JOSEPH OF ARIMATHEA TO CATCH CHRIST'S BLOOD WHEN HE HUNG FROM THE CROSS.
IT WAS SUPPOSEDLY LOST FOR CENTURIES AND SOUGHT ON QUESTS BY KNIGHTS FROM THE ROUND TABLE.
ONE OF THEM WAS AN *ANCESTOR* OF MINE ACCORDING TO THE GRAIL BOOK.

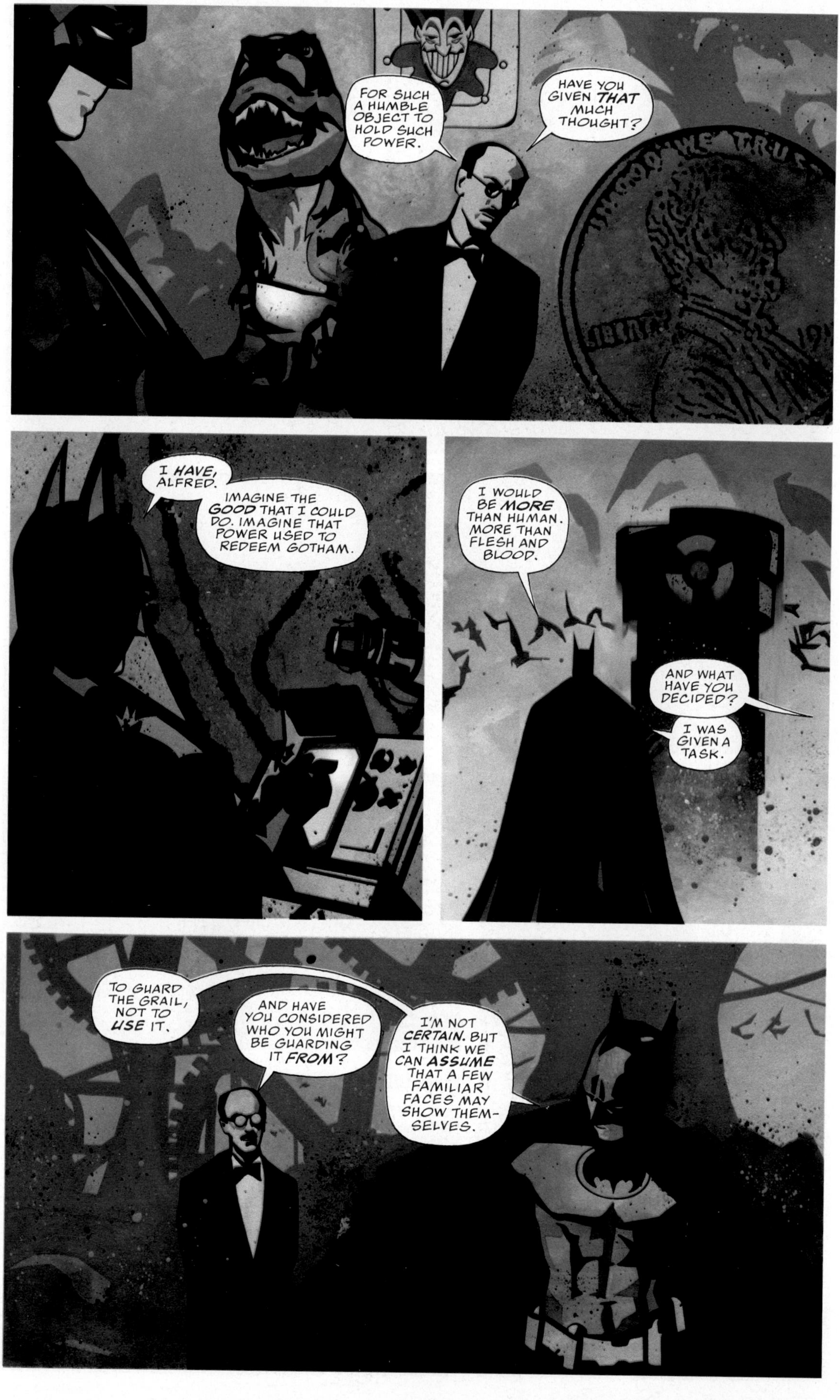
FOR SUCH A HUMBLE OBJECT TO HOLD SUCH POWER.
HAVE YOU GIVEN **THAT** MUCH THOUGHT?
I **HAVE,** ALFRED.
IMAGINE THE **GOOD** THAT I COULD DO. IMAGINE THAT POWER USED TO REDEEM GOTHAM.
I WOULD BE **MORE** THAN HUMAN. MORE THAN FLESH AND BLOOD.
AND WHAT HAVE YOU DECIDED?
I WAS GIVEN A TASK.
TO GUARD THE GRAIL, NOT TO **USE** IT.
AND HAVE YOU CONSIDERED WHO YOU MIGHT BE GUARDING IT **FROM**?
I'M NOT **CERTAIN.** BUT I THINK WE CAN **ASSUME** THAT A FEW FAMILIAR FACES MAY SHOW THEM-SELVES.

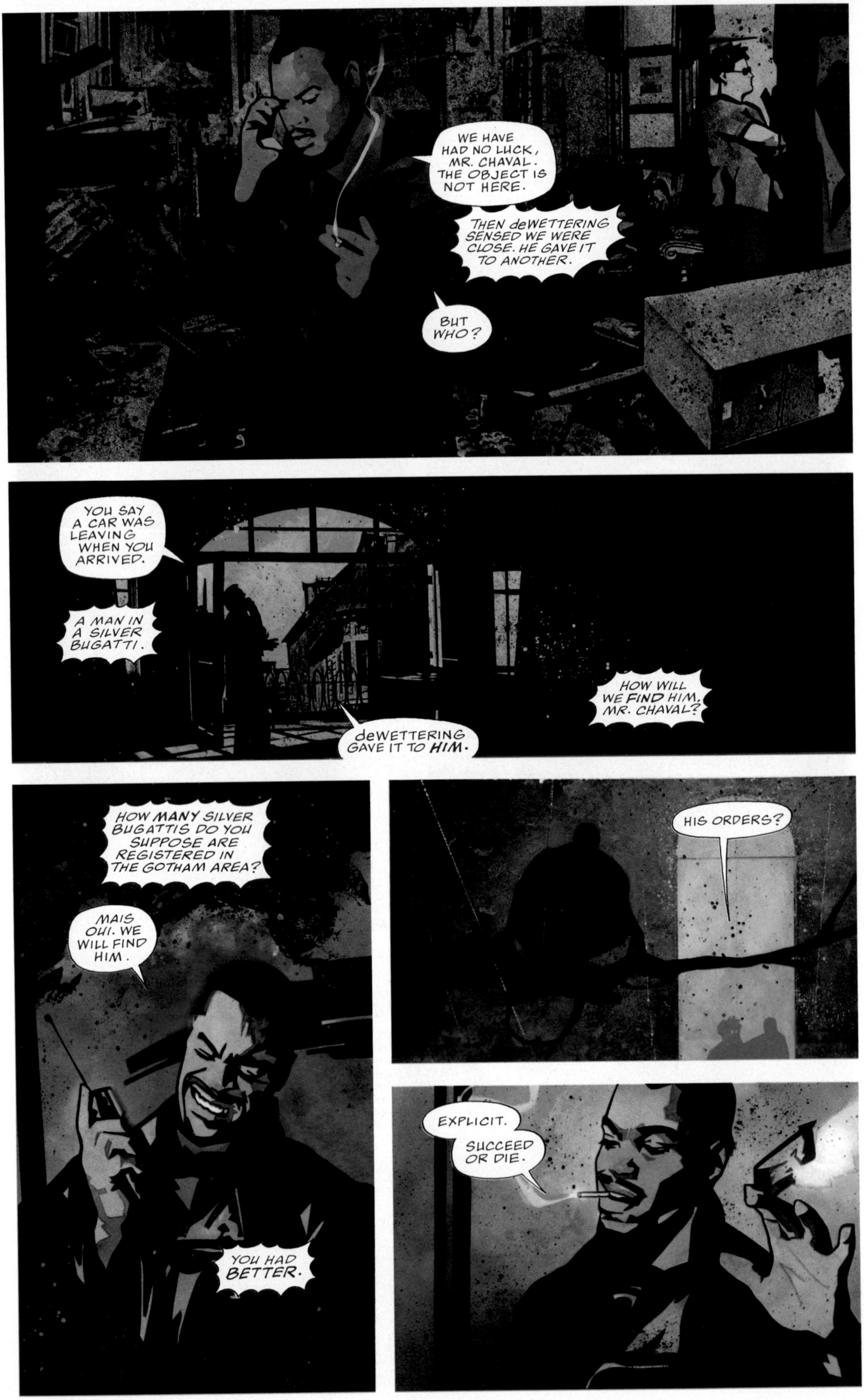
WE HAVE HAD NO LUCK, MR. CHAVAL. THE OBJECT IS NOT HERE.
THEN deWETTERING SENSED WE WERE CLOSE. HE GAVE IT TO ANOTHER.
BUT WHO?
YOU SAY A CAR WAS LEAVING WHEN YOU ARRIVED.
A MAN IN A SILVER BUGATTI.
deWETTERING GAVE IT TO HIM.
HOW WILL WE FIND HIM, MR. CHAVAL?
HOW MANY SILVER BUGATTIS DO YOU SUPPOSE ARE REGISTERED IN THE GOTHAM AREA?
MAIS OUI. WE WILL FIND HIM.
YOU HAD BETTER.
HIS ORDERS?
EXPLICIT.
SUCCEED OR DIE.

AS ALWAYS.

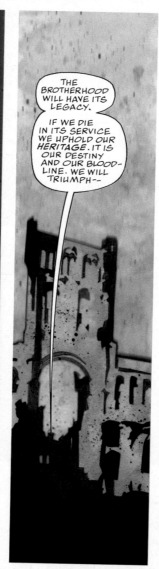

THE BROTHERHOOD WILL HAVE ITS LEGACY. IF WE DIE IN ITS SERVICE WE UPHOLD OUR *HERITAGE*. IT IS OUR DESTINY AND OUR BLOODLINE. WE WILL TRIUMPH--

--THOUGH ALL HELL'S *DEMONS* STAND BEFORE US.

A SOUND--

ONLY THE FLAMES. THAT IS A HOUSE OF THE DEAD BEHIND US.

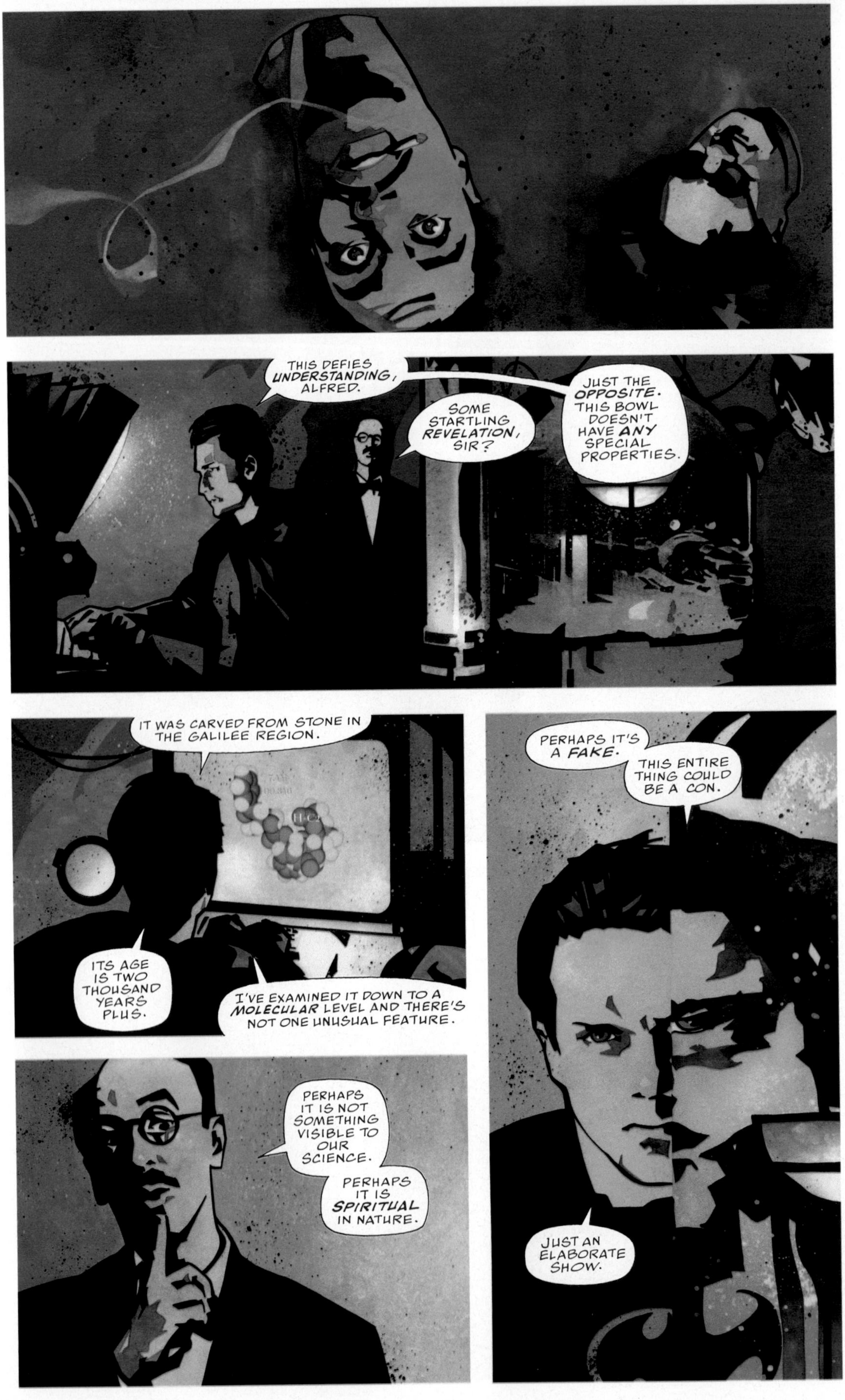

THIS DEFIES UNDERSTANDING, ALFRED.
SOME STARTLING REVELATION, SIR?
JUST THE OPPOSITE. THIS BOWL DOESN'T HAVE ANY SPECIAL PROPERTIES.
IT WAS CARVED FROM STONE IN THE GALILEE REGION.
ITS AGE IS TWO THOUSAND YEARS PLUS.
I'VE EXAMINED IT DOWN TO A MOLECULAR LEVEL AND THERE'S NOT ONE UNUSUAL FEATURE.
PERHAPS IT IS NOT SOMETHING VISIBLE TO OUR SCIENCE.
PERHAPS IT IS SPIRITUAL IN NATURE.
PERHAPS IT'S A FAKE.
THIS ENTIRE THING COULD BE A CON.
JUST AN ELABORATE SHOW.

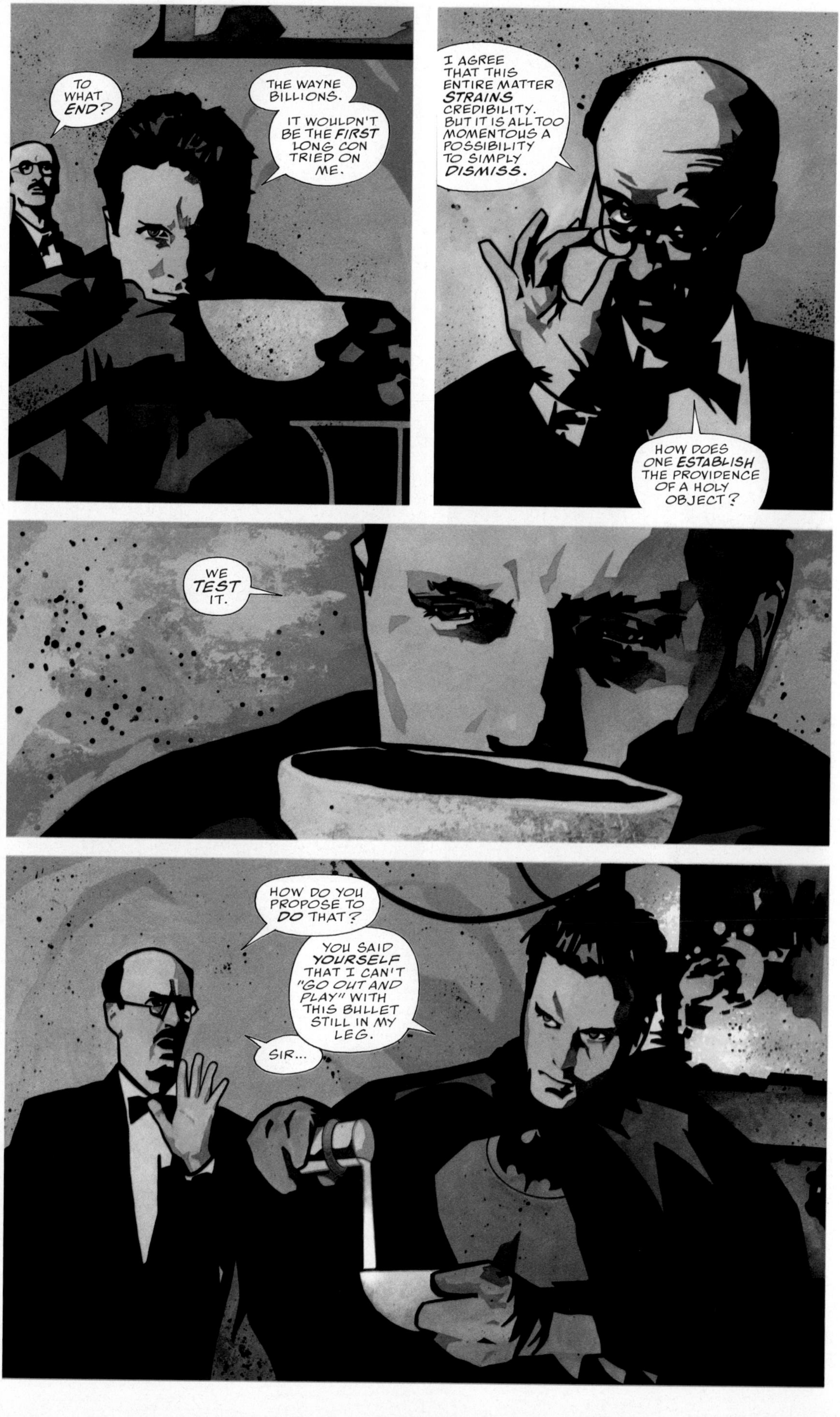
TO WHAT END?
THE WAYNE BILLIONS.
IT WOULDN'T BE THE FIRST LONG CON TRIED ON ME.
I AGREE THAT THIS ENTIRE MATTER STRAINS CREDIBILITY. BUT IT IS ALL TOO MOMENTOUS A POSSIBILITY TO SIMPLY DISMISS.
HOW DOES ONE ESTABLISH THE PROVIDENCE OF A HOLY OBJECT?
WE TEST IT.
HOW DO YOU PROPOSE TO DO THAT?
YOU SAID YOURSELF THAT I CAN'T "GO OUT AND PLAY" WITH THIS BULLET STILL IN MY LEG.
SIR...

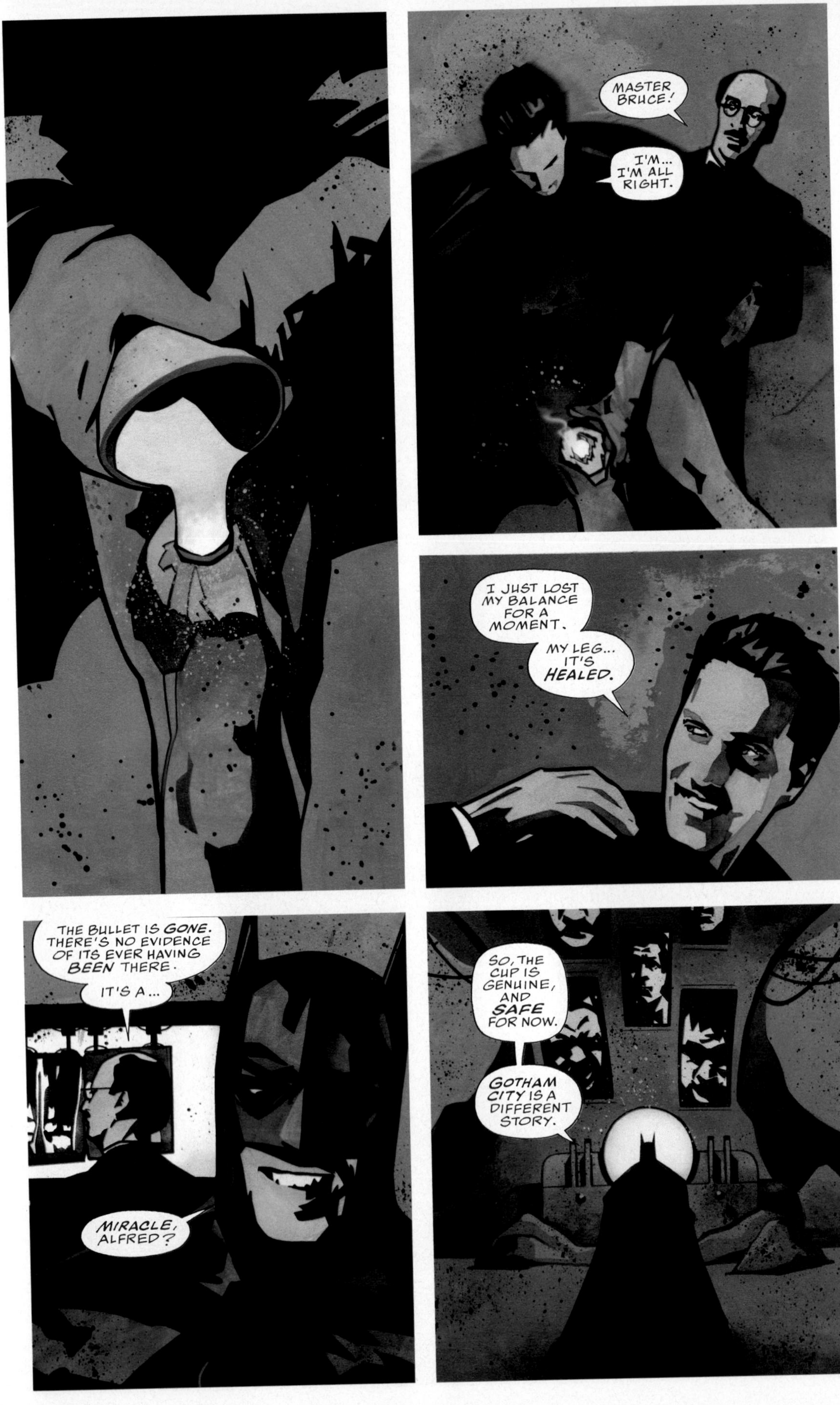
MASTER BRUCE!
I'M... I'M ALL RIGHT.
I JUST LOST MY BALANCE FOR A MOMENT.
MY LEG... IT'S HEALED.
THE BULLET IS GONE. THERE'S NO EVIDENCE OF ITS EVER HAVING BEEN THERE.
IT'S A...
MIRACLE, ALFRED?
SO, THE CUP IS GENUINE, AND SAFE FOR NOW.
GOTHAM CITY IS A DIFFERENT STORY.

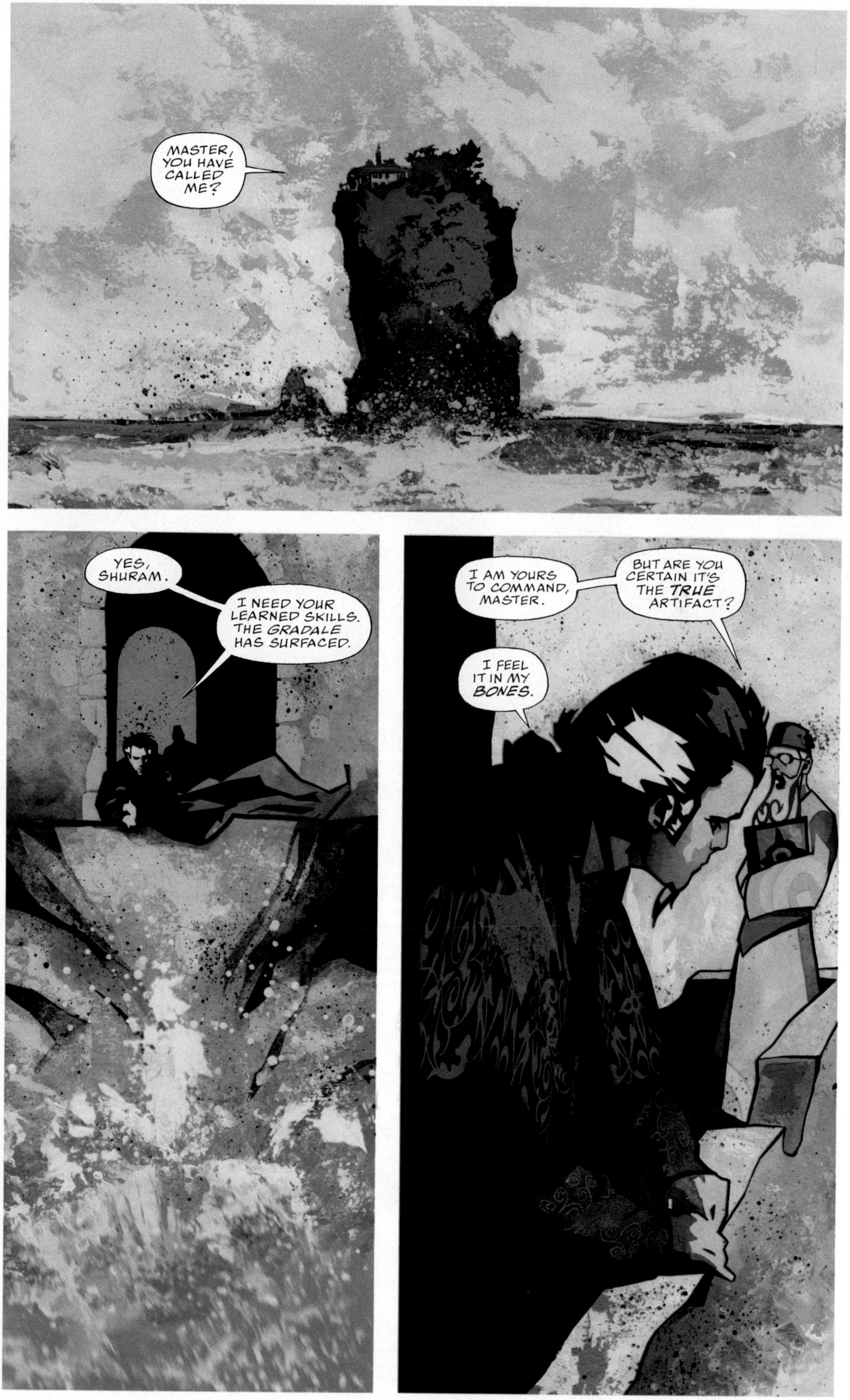
MASTER, YOU HAVE CALLED ME?
YES, SHURAM.
I NEED YOUR LEARNED SKILLS. THE GRADALE HAS SURFACED.
I AM YOURS TO COMMAND, MASTER.
BUT ARE YOU CERTAIN IT'S THE TRUE ARTIFACT?
I FEEL IT IN MY BONES.

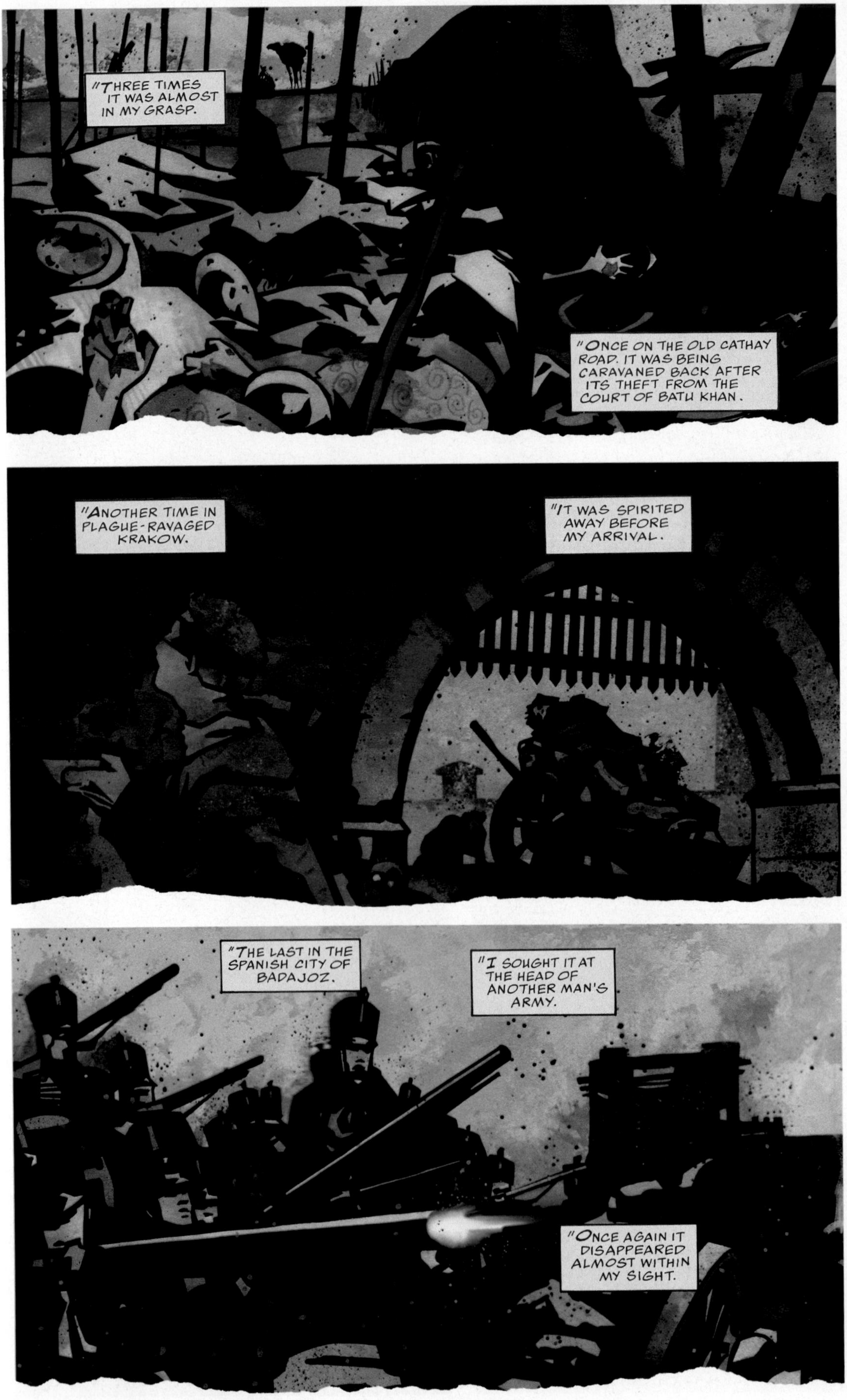
"THREE TIMES IT WAS ALMOST IN MY GRASP.
"ONCE ON THE OLD CATHAY ROAD. IT WAS BEING CARAVANED BACK AFTER ITS THEFT FROM THE COURT OF BATU KHAN.
"ANOTHER TIME IN PLAGUE-RAVAGED KRAKOW.
"IT WAS SPIRITED AWAY BEFORE MY ARRIVAL.
"THE LAST IN THE SPANISH CITY OF BADAJOZ.
"I SOUGHT IT AT THE HEAD OF ANOTHER MAN'S ARMY.
"ONCE AGAIN IT DISAPPEARED ALMOST WITHIN MY SIGHT.

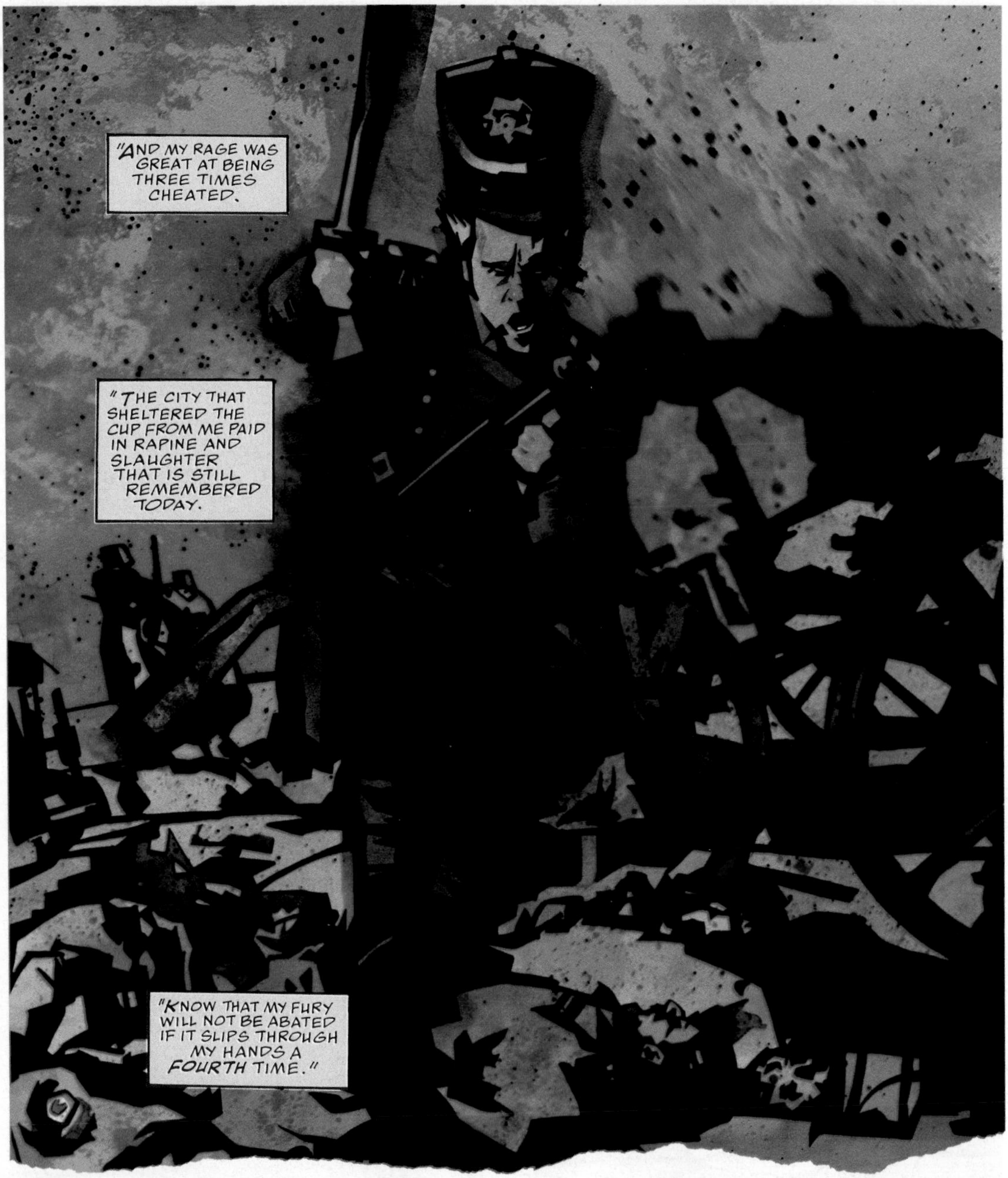
"AND MY RAGE WAS GREAT AT BEING THREE TIMES CHEATED.
"THE CITY THAT SHELTERED THE CUP FROM ME PAID IN RAPINE AND SLAUGHTER THAT IS STILL REMEMBERED TODAY.
"KNOW THAT MY FURY WILL NOT BE ABATED IF IT SLIPS THROUGH MY HANDS A FOURTH TIME."

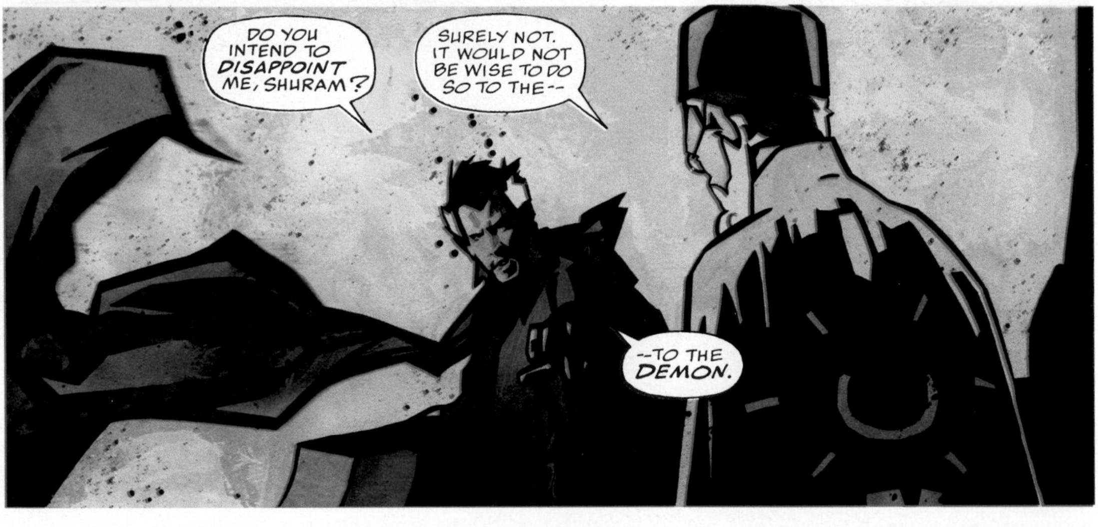
DO YOU INTEND TO DISAPPOINT ME, SHURAM?
SURELY NOT. IT WOULD NOT BE WISE TO DO SO TO THE--
--TO THE DEMON.

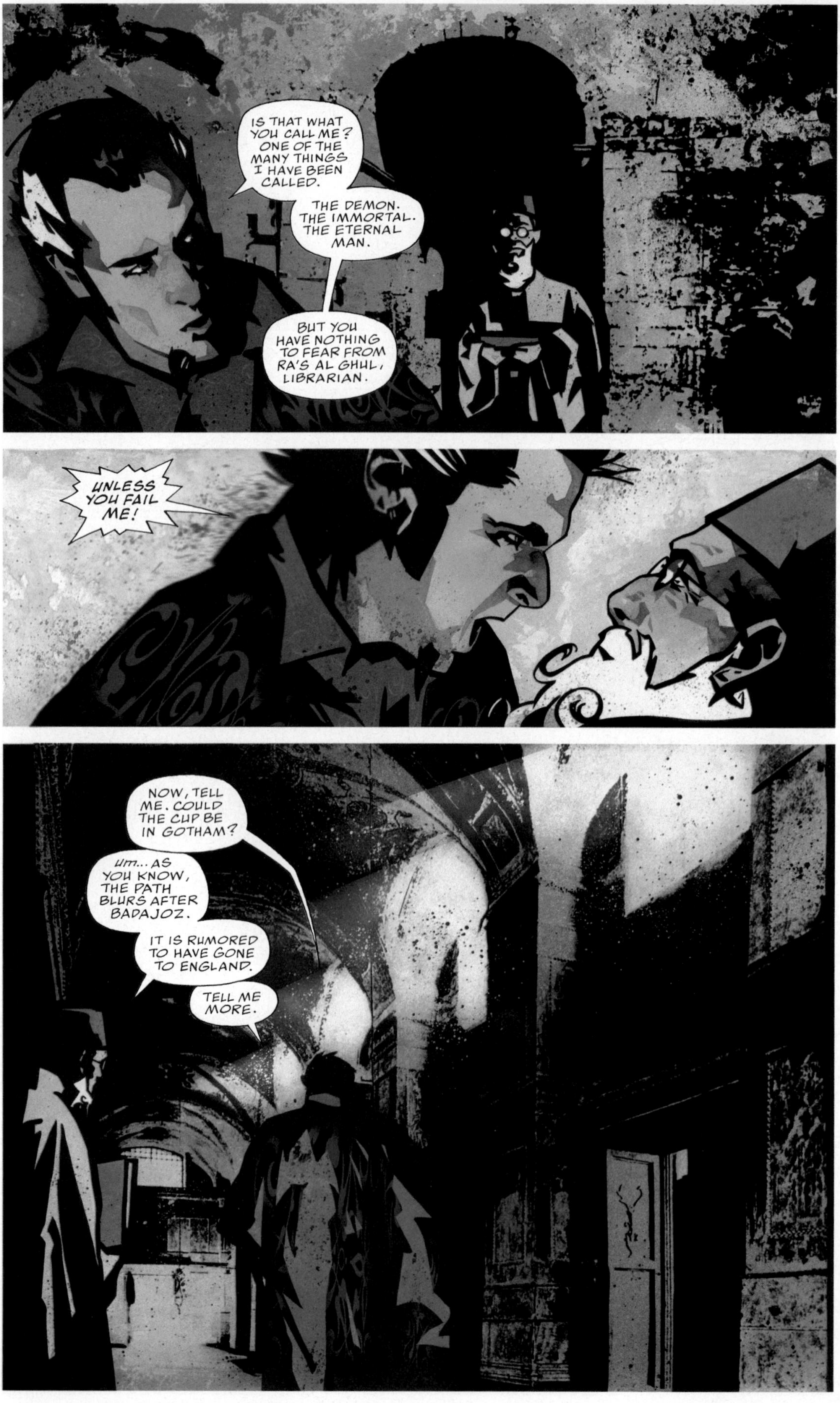
IS THAT WHAT YOU CALL ME? ONE OF THE MANY THINGS I HAVE BEEN CALLED.
THE DEMON. THE IMMORTAL. THE ETERNAL MAN.
BUT YOU HAVE NOTHING TO FEAR FROM RA'S AL GHUL, LIBRARIAN.
UNLESS YOU FAIL ME!
NOW, TELL ME. COULD THE CUP BE IN GOTHAM?
UM... AS YOU KNOW, THE PATH BLURS AFTER BADAJOZ.
IT IS RUMORED TO HAVE GONE TO ENGLAND.
TELL ME MORE.

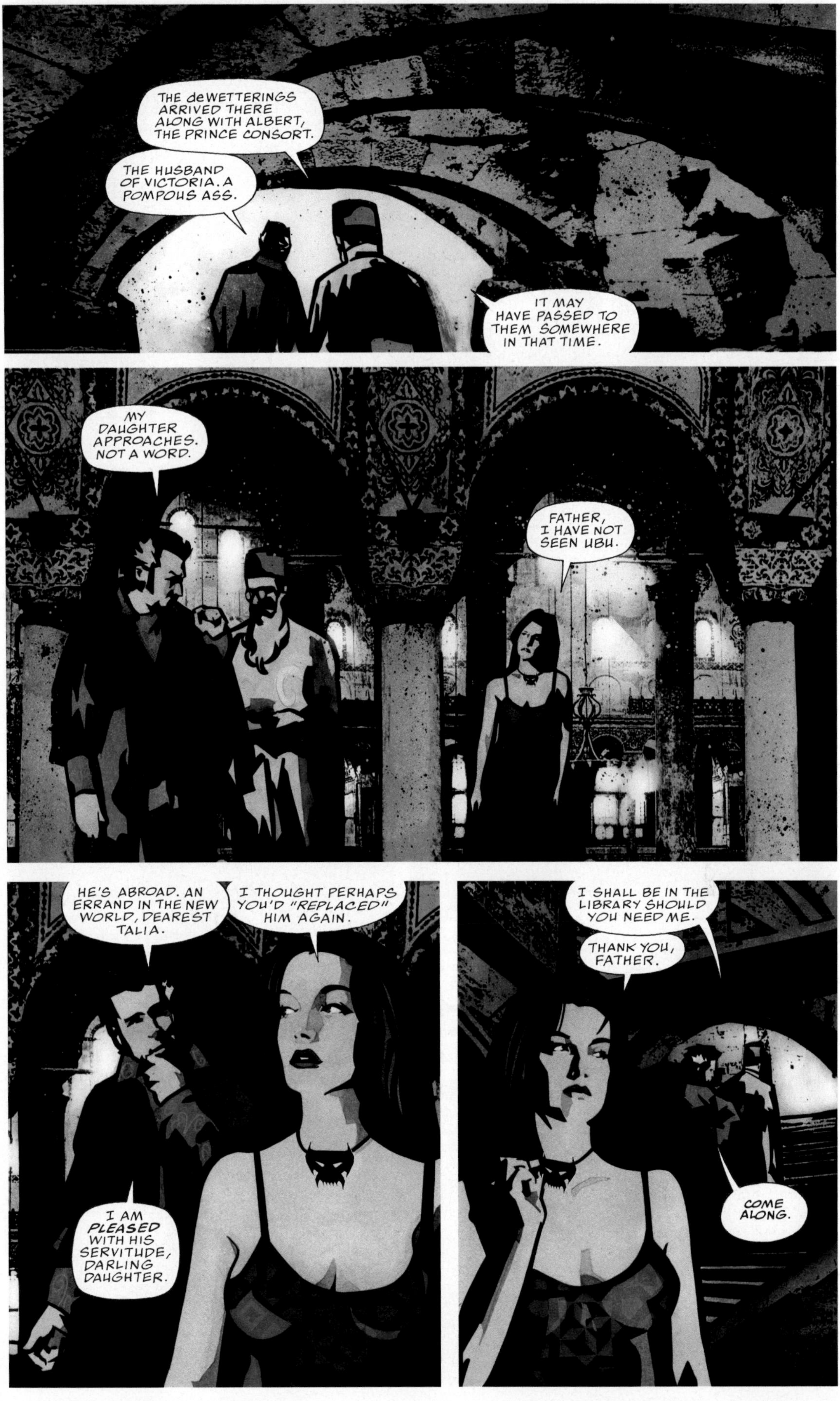
THE deWETTERINGS ARRIVED THERE ALONG WITH ALBERT, THE PRINCE CONSORT.
THE HUSBAND OF VICTORIA. A POMPOUS ASS.
IT MAY HAVE PASSED TO THEM SOMEWHERE IN THAT TIME.
MY DAUGHTER APPROACHES. NOT A WORD.
FATHER, I HAVE NOT SEEN UBU.
HE'S ABROAD. AN ERRAND IN THE NEW WORLD, DEAREST TALIA.
I THOUGHT PERHAPS YOU'D "REPLACED" HIM AGAIN.
I AM PLEASED WITH HIS SERVITUDE, DARLING DAUGHTER.
I SHALL BE IN THE LIBRARY SHOULD YOU NEED ME.
THANK YOU, FATHER.
COME ALONG.

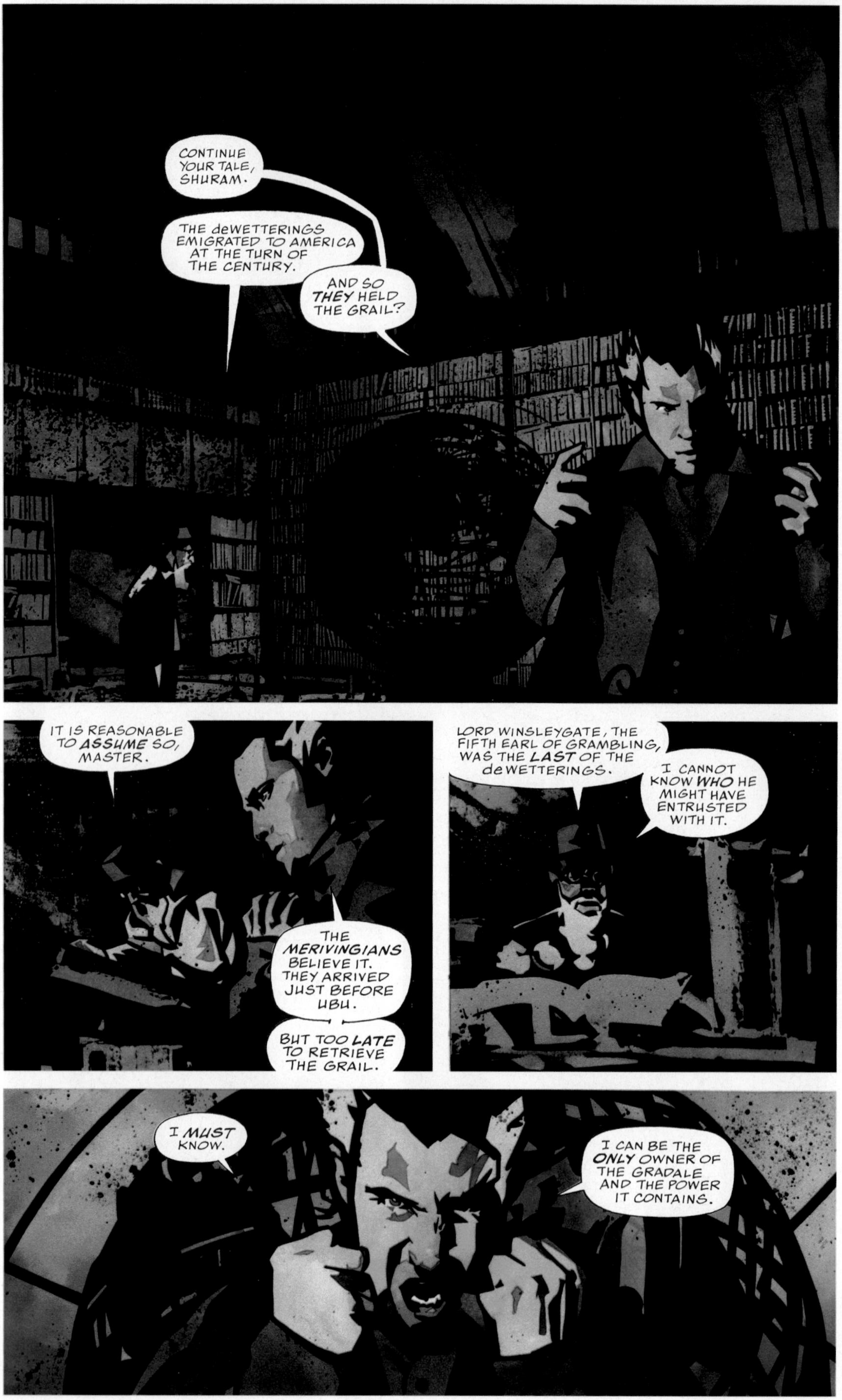
CONTINUE YOUR TALE, SHURAM.
THE deWETTERINGS EMIGRATED TO AMERICA AT THE TURN OF THE CENTURY.
AND SO THEY HELD THE GRAIL?
IT IS REASONABLE TO ASSUME SO, MASTER.
THE MERIVINGIANS BELIEVE IT. THEY ARRIVED JUST BEFORE UBU.
BUT TOO LATE TO RETRIEVE THE GRAIL.
LORD WINSLEYGATE, THE FIFTH EARL OF GRAMBLING, WAS THE LAST OF THE deWETTERINGS.
I CANNOT KNOW WHO HE MIGHT HAVE ENTRUSTED WITH IT.
I MUST KNOW.
I CAN BE THE ONLY OWNER OF THE GRADALE AND THE POWER IT CONTAINS.

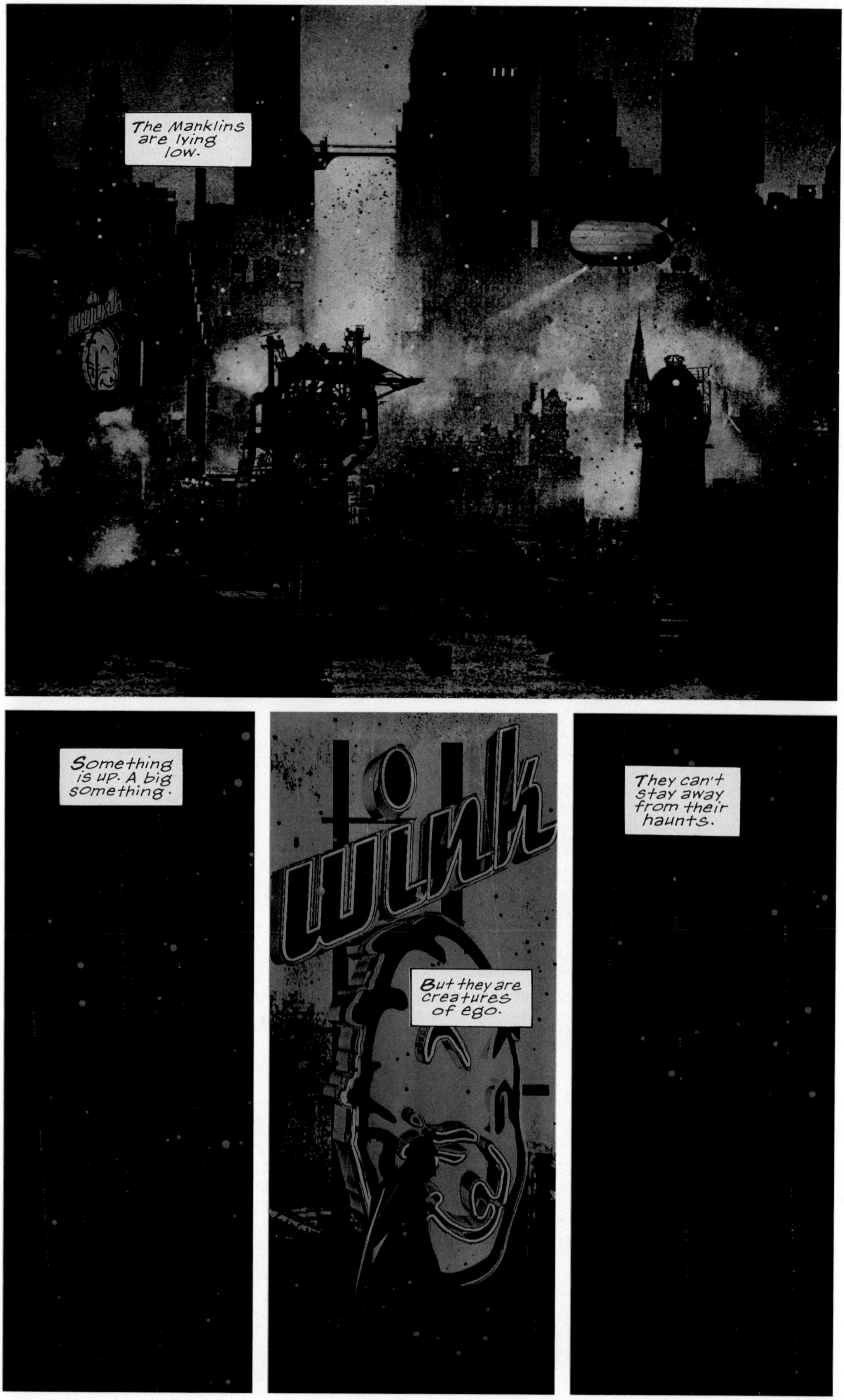
The Manklins are lying low.
Something is up. A big something.
wink
But they are creatures of ego.
They can't stay away from their haunts.

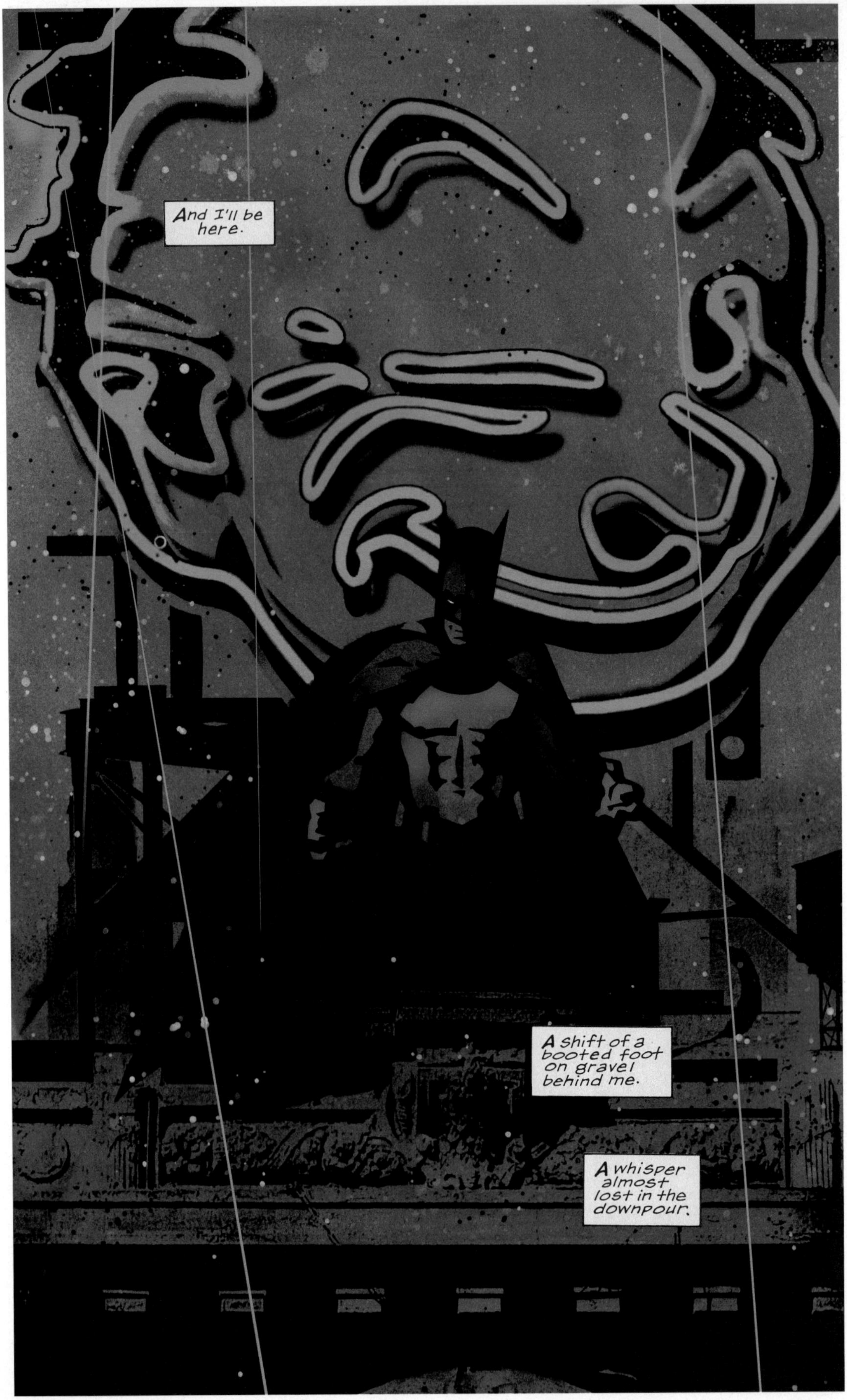
And I'll be here.
A shift of a booted foot on gravel behind me.
A whisper almost lost in the downpour.

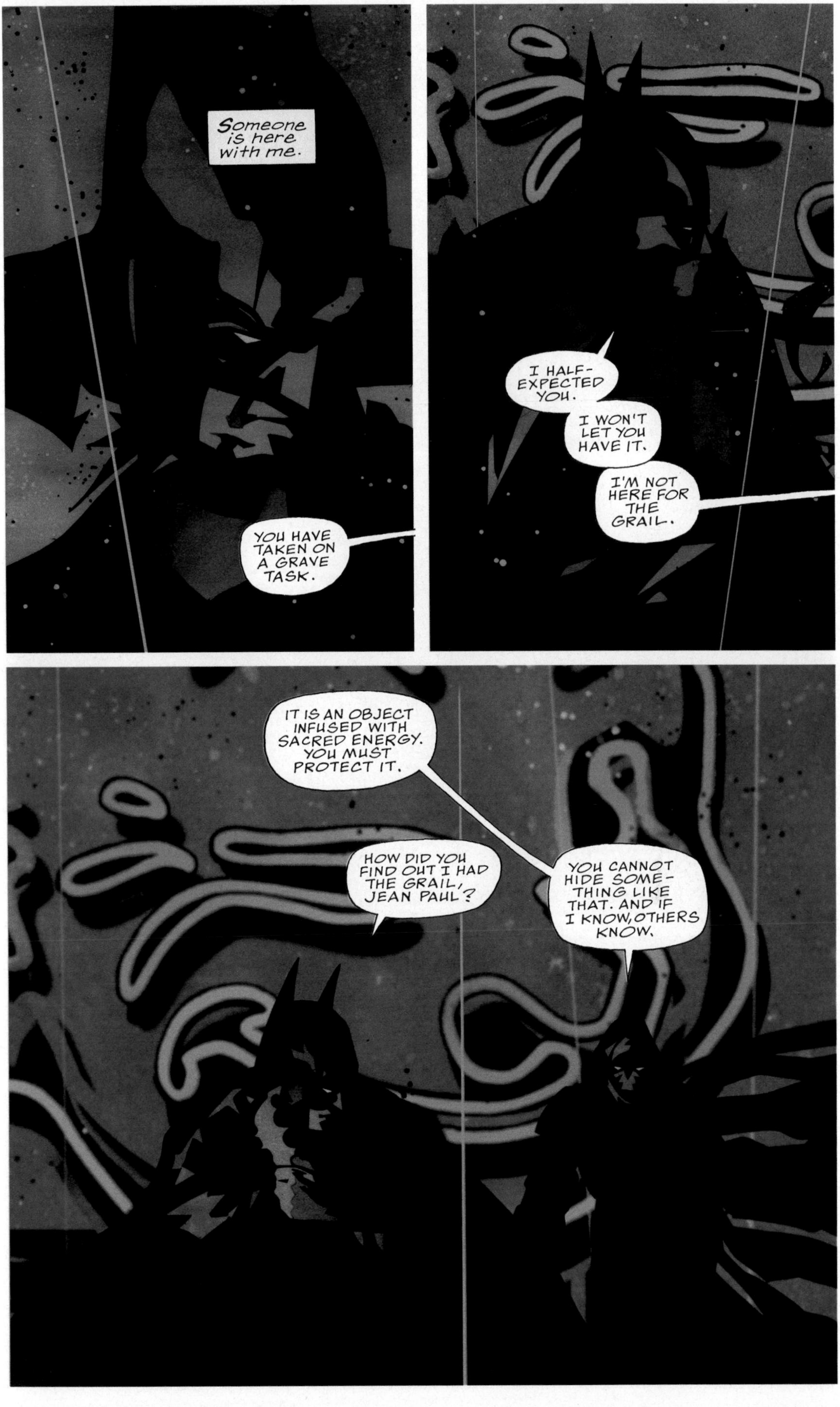
Someone is here with me.
YOU HAVE TAKEN ON A GRAVE TASK.
I HALF-EXPECTED YOU.
I WON'T LET YOU HAVE IT.
I'M NOT HERE FOR THE GRAIL.
IT IS AN OBJECT INFUSED WITH SACRED ENERGY. YOU MUST PROTECT IT.
HOW DID YOU FIND OUT I HAD THE GRAIL, JEAN PAUL?
YOU CANNOT HIDE SOME-THING LIKE THAT. AND IF I KNOW, OTHERS KNOW.

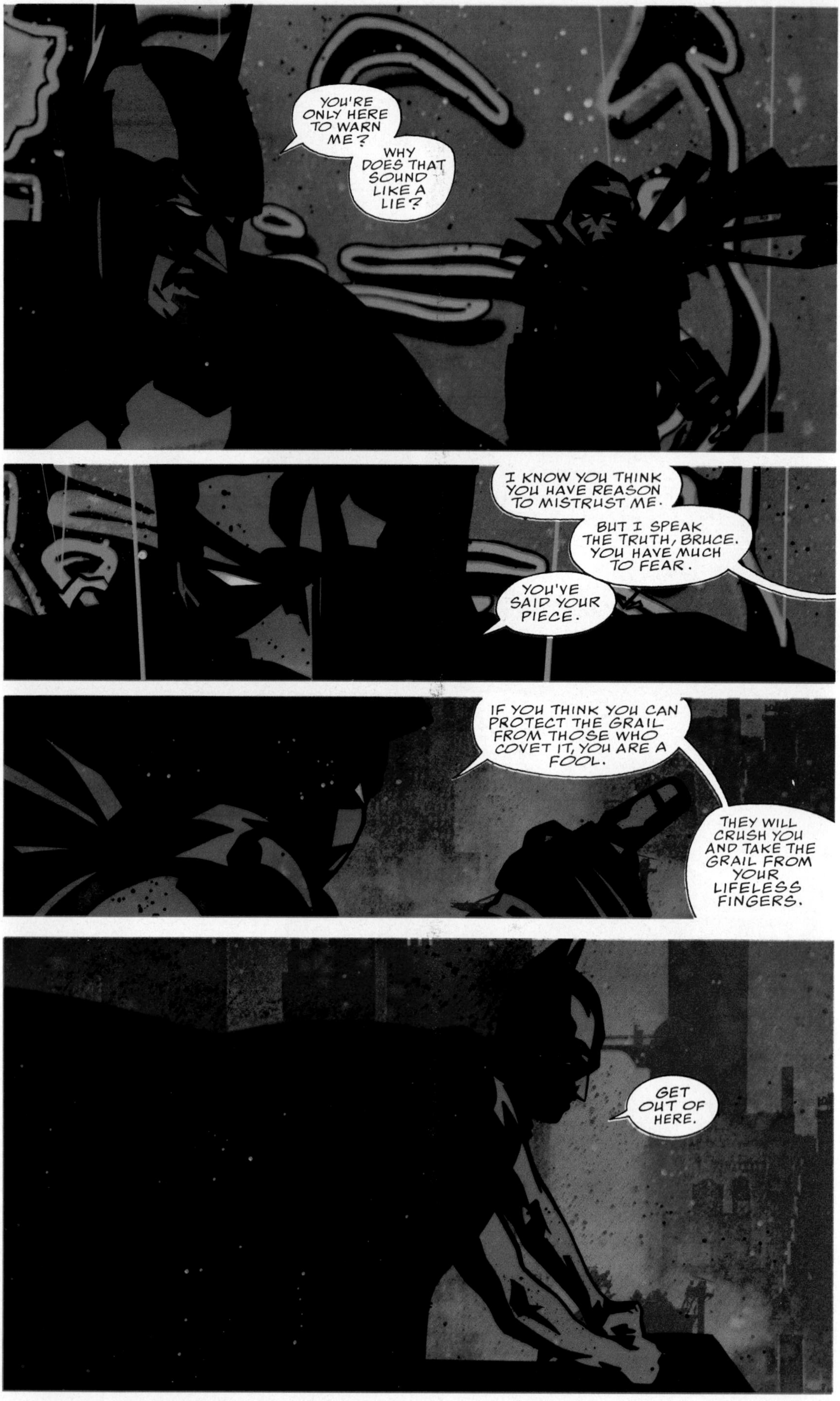
YOU'RE ONLY HERE TO WARN ME?
WHY DOES THAT SOUND LIKE A LIE?
I KNOW YOU THINK YOU HAVE REASON TO MISTRUST ME.
BUT I SPEAK THE TRUTH, BRUCE. YOU HAVE MUCH TO FEAR.
YOU'VE SAID YOUR PIECE.
IF YOU THINK YOU CAN PROTECT THE GRAIL FROM THOSE WHO COVET IT, YOU ARE A FOOL.
THEY WILL CRUSH YOU AND TAKE THE GRAIL FROM YOUR LIFELESS FINGERS.
GET OUT OF HERE.

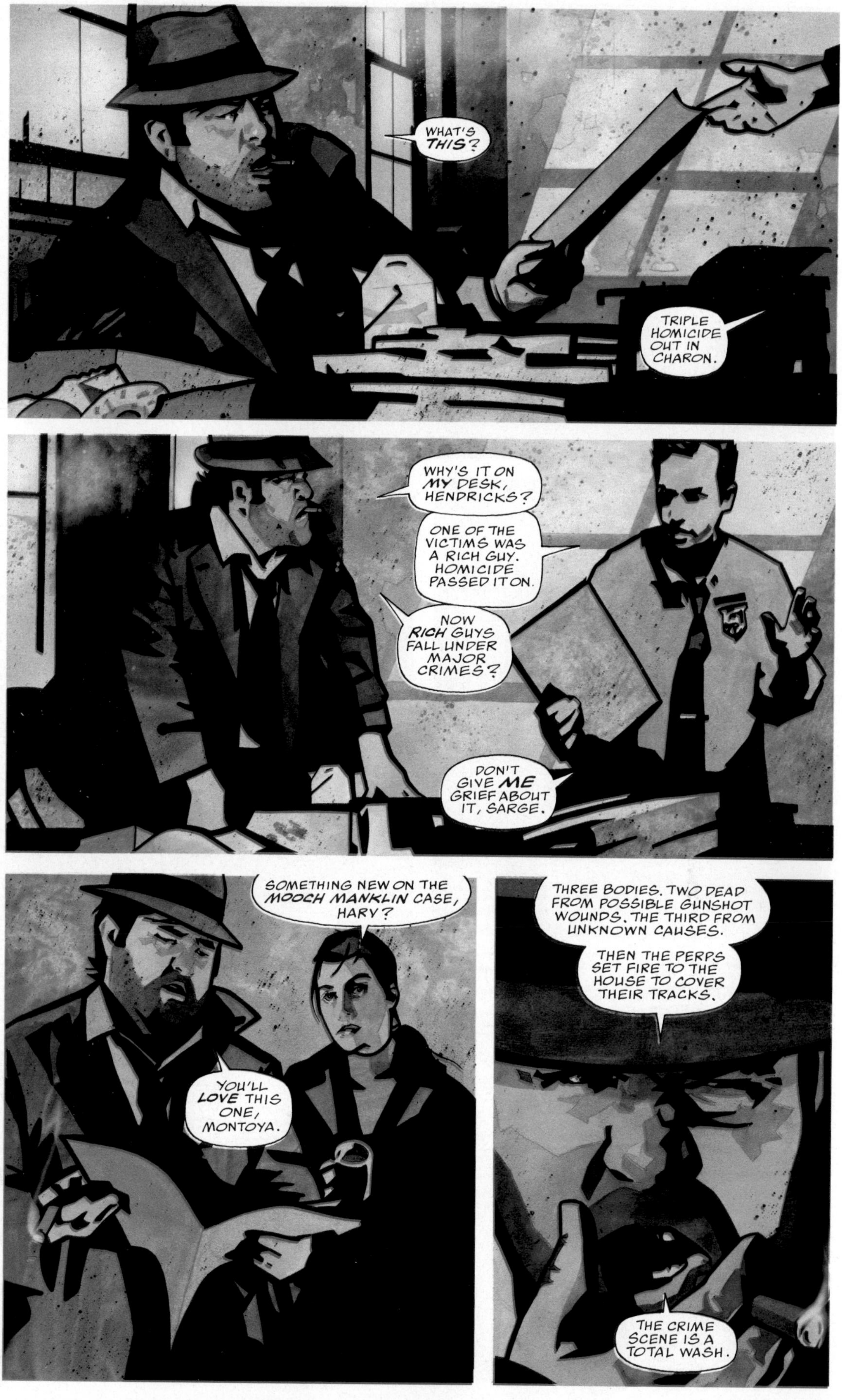
WHAT'S THIS?
TRIPLE HOMICIDE OUT IN CHARON.
WHY'S IT ON MY DESK, HENDRICKS?
ONE OF THE VICTIMS WAS A RICH GUY. HOMICIDE PASSED IT ON.
NOW RICH GUYS FALL UNDER MAJOR CRIMES?
DON'T GIVE ME GRIEF ABOUT IT, SARGE.
SOMETHING NEW ON THE MOOCH MANKLIN CASE, HARY?
YOU'LL LOVE THIS ONE, MONTOYA.
THREE BODIES. TWO DEAD FROM POSSIBLE GUNSHOT WOUNDS. THE THIRD FROM UNKNOWN CAUSES.
THEN THE PERPS SET FIRE TO THE HOUSE TO COVER THEIR TRACKS.
THE CRIME SCENE IS A TOTAL WASH.

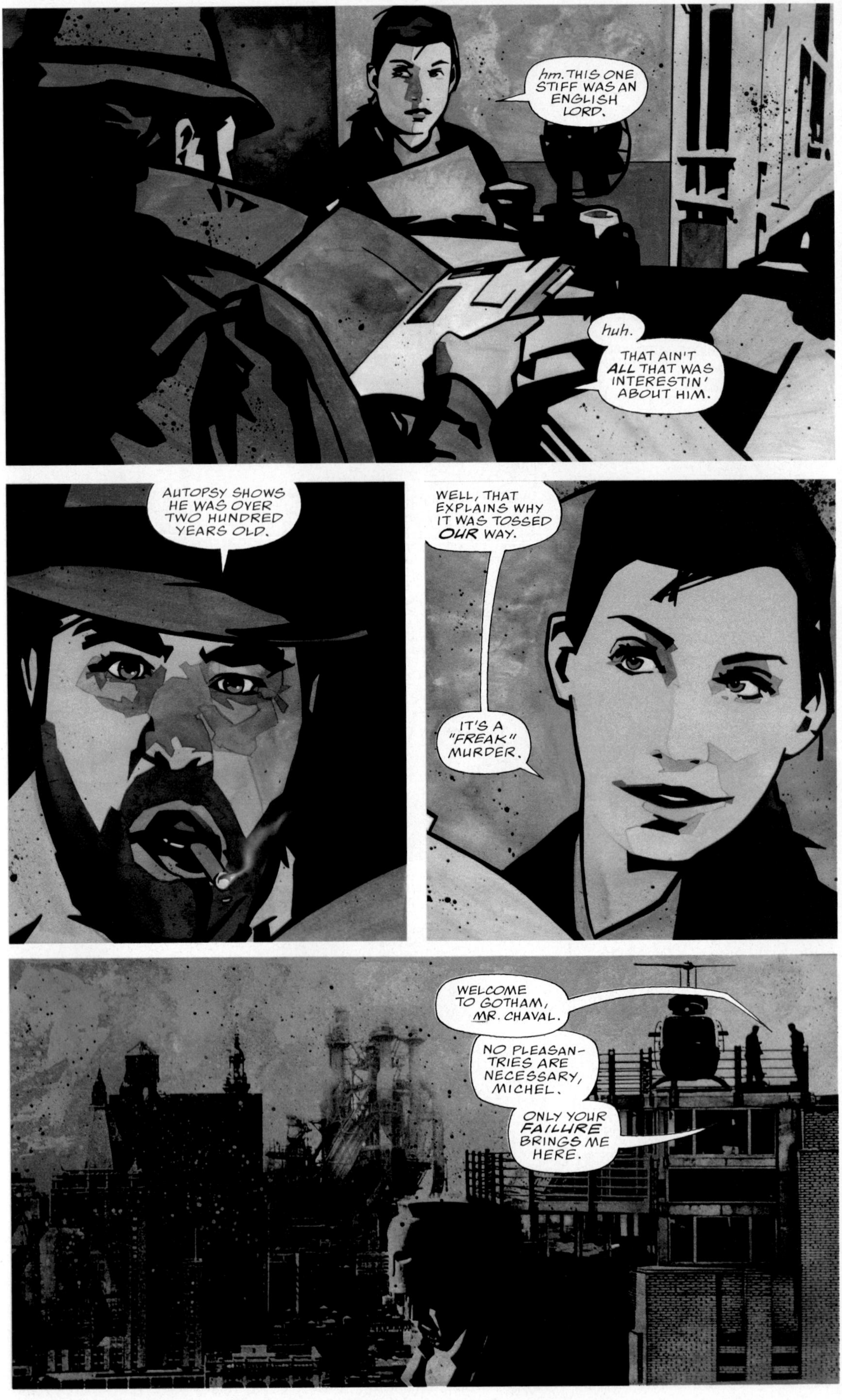
hm. THIS ONE STIFF WAS AN ENGLISH LORD.
huh.
THAT AIN'T ALL THAT WAS INTERESTIN' ABOUT HIM.
AUTOPSY SHOWS HE WAS OVER TWO HUNDRED YEARS OLD.
WELL, THAT EXPLAINS WHY IT WAS TOSSED OUR WAY.
IT'S A "FREAK" MURDER.
WELCOME TO GOTHAM, MR. CHAVAL.
NO PLEASANTRIES ARE NECESSARY, MICHEL.
ONLY YOUR FAILURE BRINGS ME HERE.

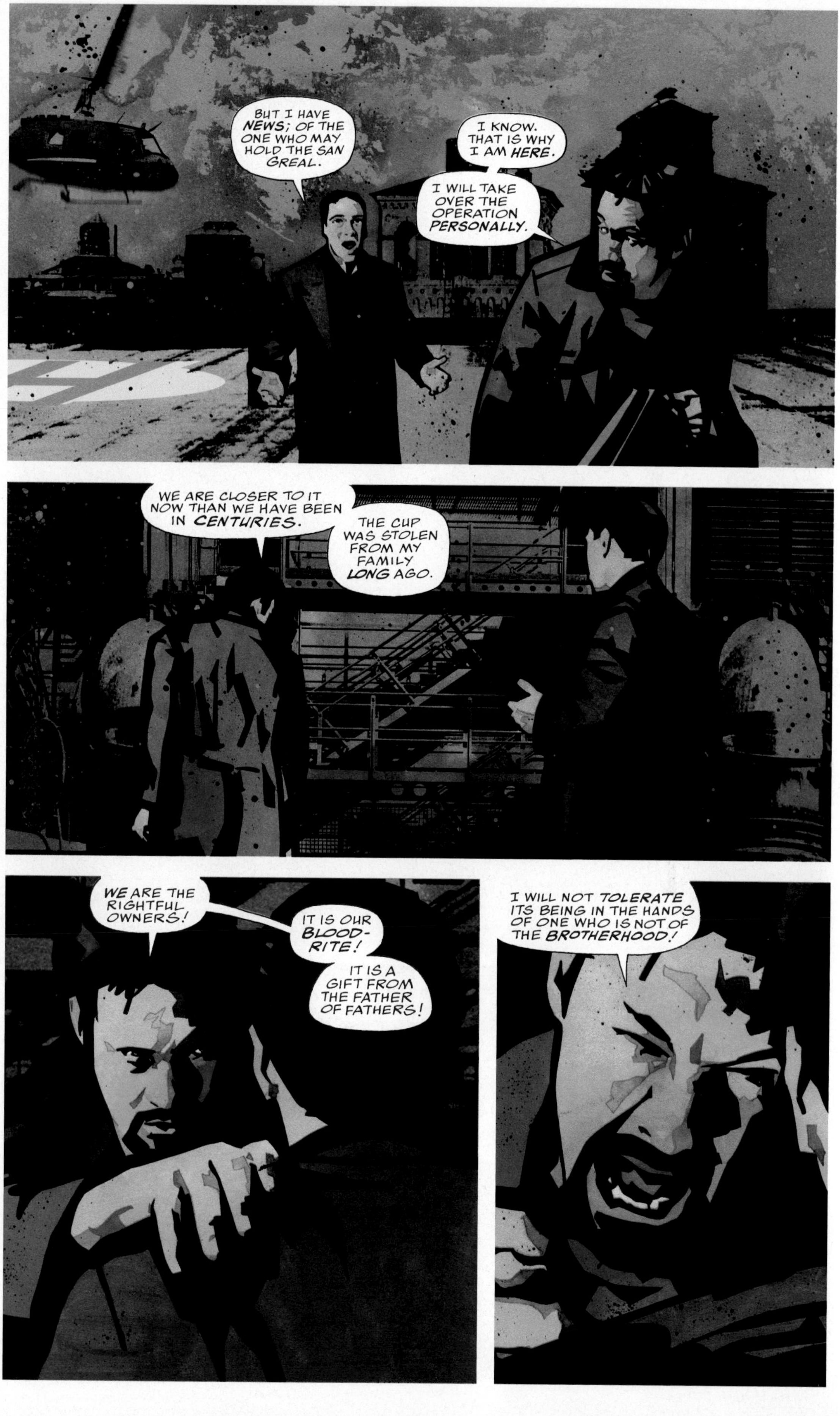
BUT I HAVE NEWS; OF THE ONE WHO MAY HOLD THE SAN GREAL.
I KNOW. THAT IS WHY I AM HERE.
I WILL TAKE OVER THE OPERATION PERSONALLY.
WE ARE CLOSER TO IT NOW THAN WE HAVE BEEN IN CENTURIES.
THE CUP WAS STOLEN FROM MY FAMILY LONG AGO.
WE ARE THE RIGHTFUL OWNERS!
IT IS OUR BLOOD-RITE!
IT IS A GIFT FROM THE FATHER OF FATHERS!
I WILL NOT TOLERATE ITS BEING IN THE HANDS OF ONE WHO IS NOT OF THE BROTHERHOOD!

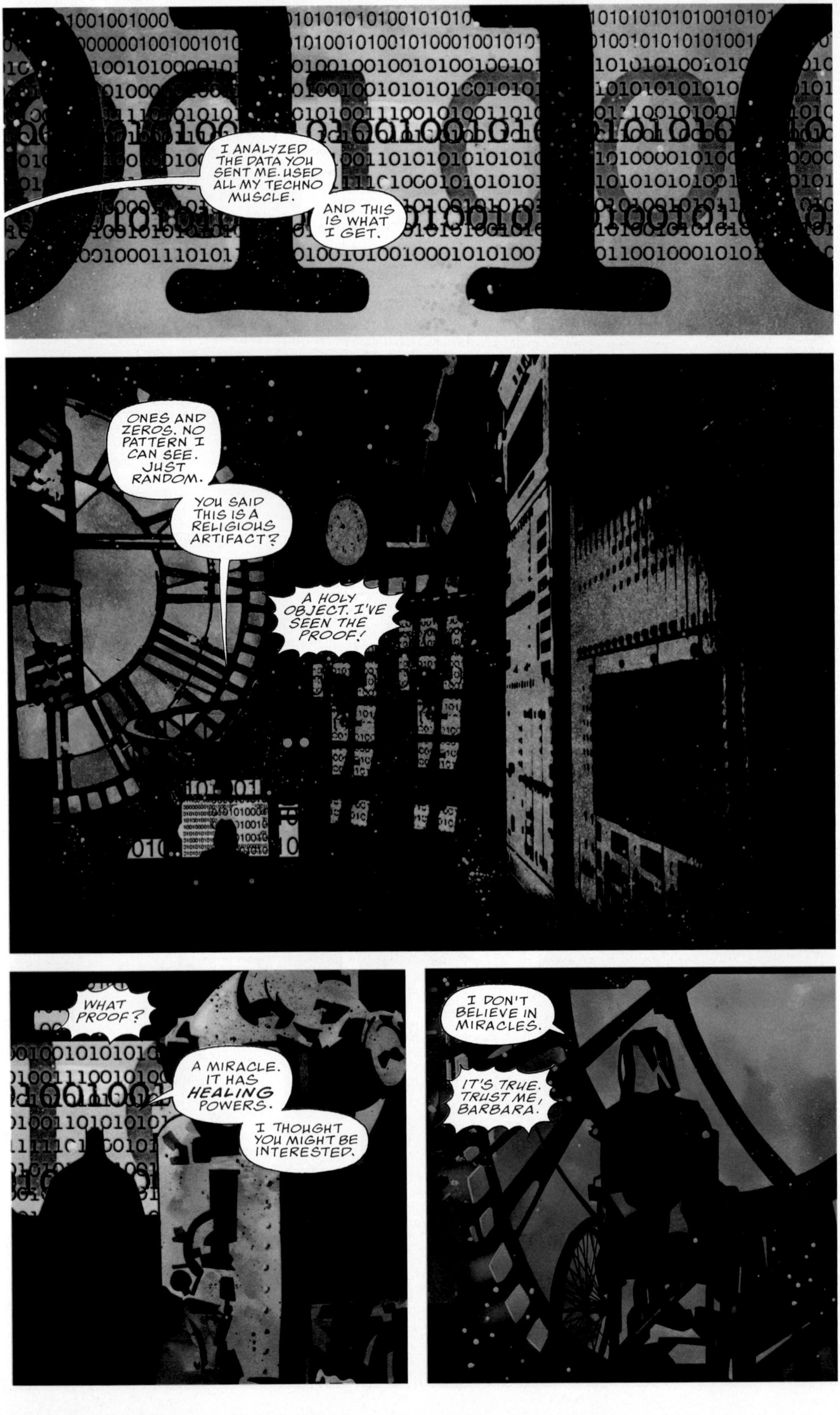
I ANALYZED THE DATA YOU SENT ME. USED ALL MY TECHNO MUSCLE.
AND THIS IS WHAT I GET.
ONES AND ZEROS. NO PATTERN I CAN SEE. JUST RANDOM.
YOU SAID THIS IS A RELIGIOUS ARTIFACT?
A HOLY OBJECT. I'VE SEEN THE PROOF!
WHAT PROOF?
A MIRACLE. IT HAS *HEALING* POWERS.
I THOUGHT YOU MIGHT BE INTERESTED.
I DON'T BELIEVE IN MIRACLES.
IT'S TRUE. TRUST ME, BARBARA!

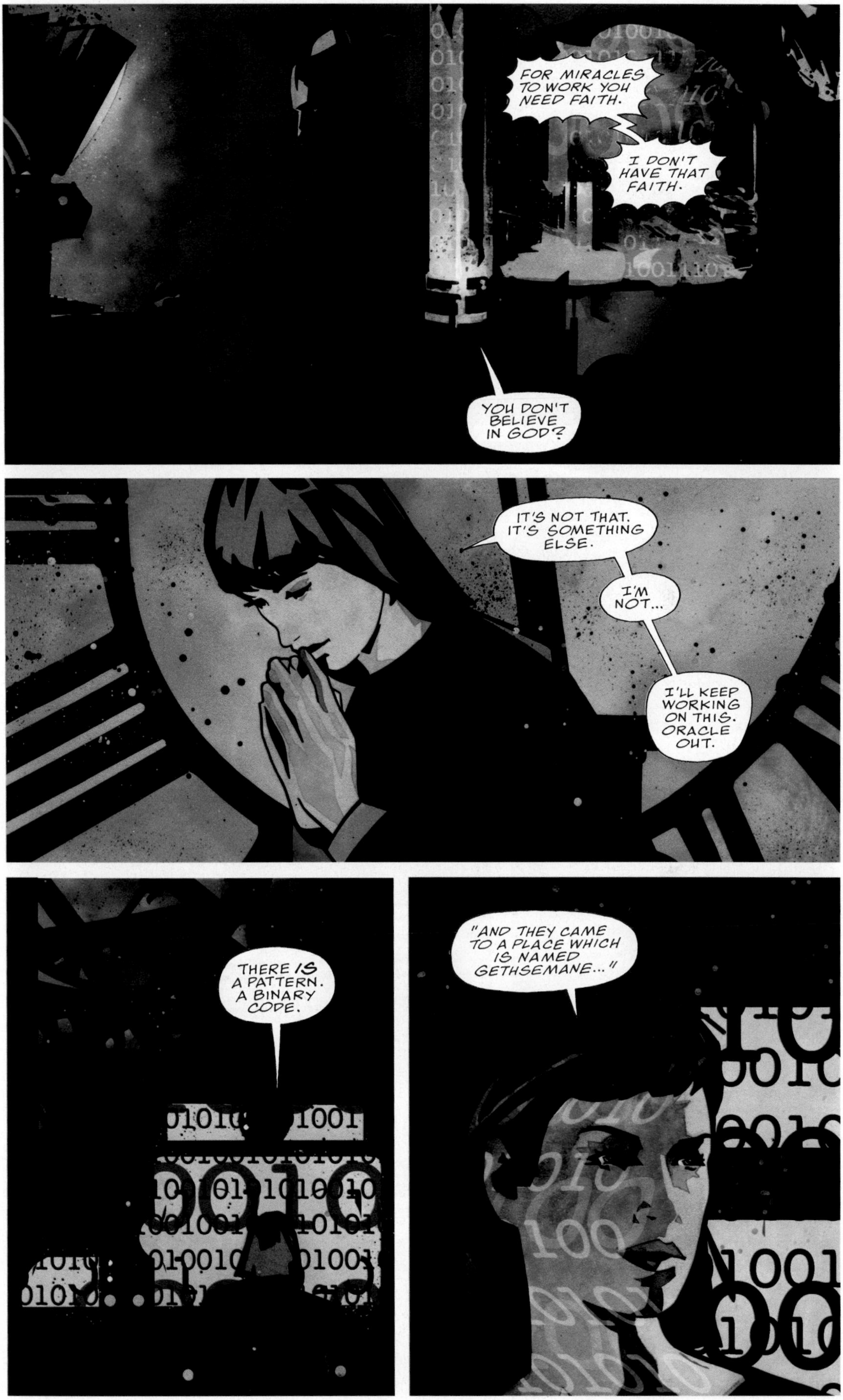
FOR MIRACLES TO WORK YOU NEED FAITH.
I DON'T HAVE THAT FAITH.
YOU DON'T BELIEVE IN GOD?
IT'S NOT THAT. IT'S SOMETHING ELSE.
I'M NOT...
I'LL KEEP WORKING ON THIS. ORACLE OUT.
THERE *IS* A PATTERN. A BINARY CODE.
"AND THEY CAME TO A PLACE WHICH IS NAMED GETHSEMANE..."

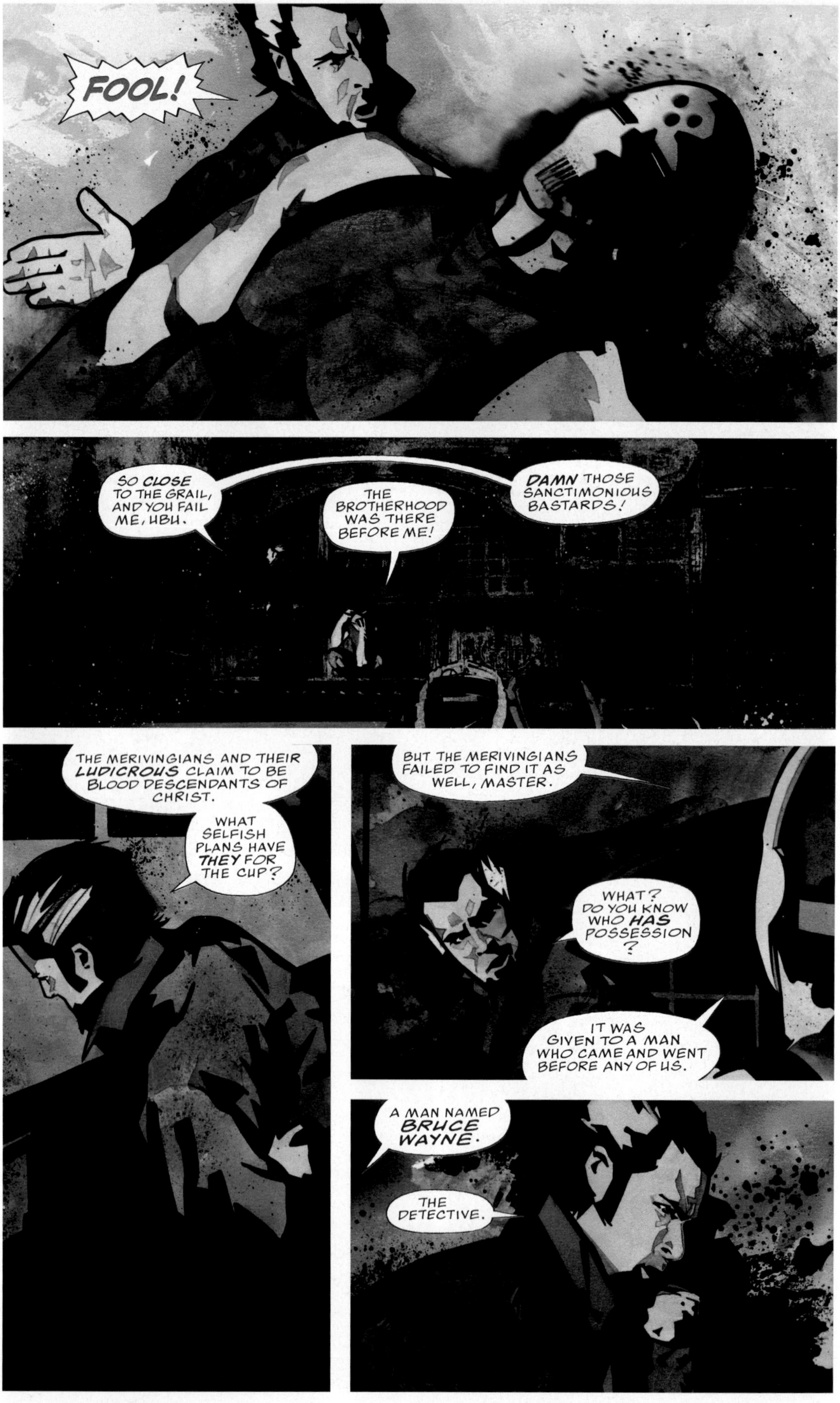
FOOL!
SO CLOSE TO THE GRAIL, AND YOU FAIL ME, UBU.
THE BROTHERHOOD WAS THERE BEFORE ME!
DAMN THOSE SANCTIMONIOUS BASTARDS!
THE MERIVINGIANS AND THEIR LUDICROUS CLAIM TO BE BLOOD DESCENDANTS OF CHRIST.
WHAT SELFISH PLANS HAVE THEY FOR THE CUP?
BUT THE MERIVINGIANS FAILED TO FIND IT AS WELL, MASTER.
WHAT? DO YOU KNOW WHO HAS POSSESSION?
IT WAS GIVEN TO A MAN WHO CAME AND WENT BEFORE ANY OF US.
A MAN NAMED BRUCE WAYNE.
THE DETECTIVE.

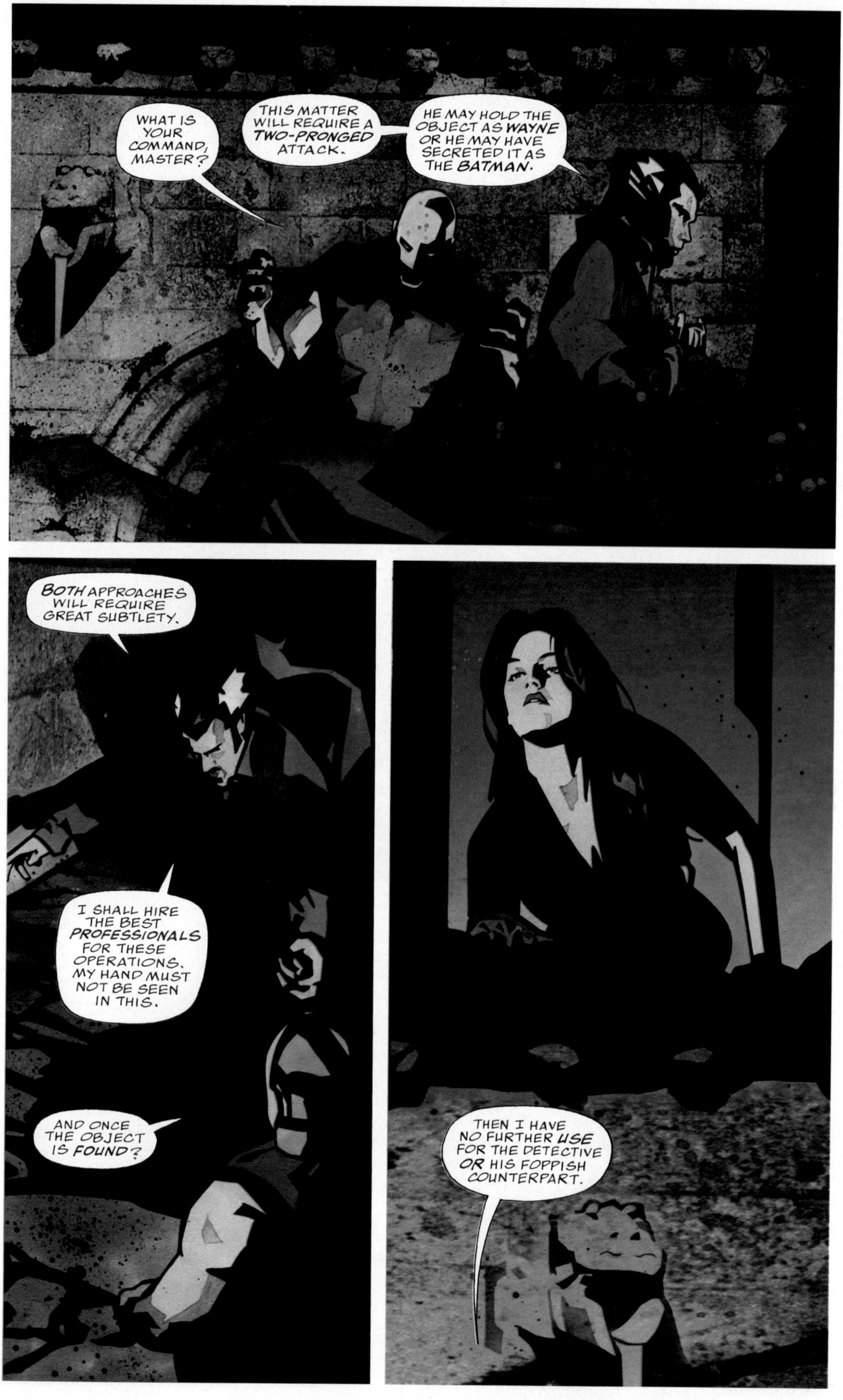
WHAT IS YOUR COMMAND, MASTER?
THIS MATTER WILL REQUIRE A TWO-PRONGED ATTACK.
HE MAY HOLD THE OBJECT AS WAYNE OR HE MAY HAVE SECRETED IT AS THE BATMAN.
BOTH APPROACHES WILL REQUIRE GREAT SUBTLETY.
I SHALL HIRE THE BEST PROFESSIONALS FOR THESE OPERATIONS. MY HAND MUST NOT BE SEEN IN THIS.
AND ONCE THE OBJECT IS FOUND?
THEN I HAVE NO FURTHER USE FOR THE DETECTIVE OR HIS FOPPISH COUNTERPART.

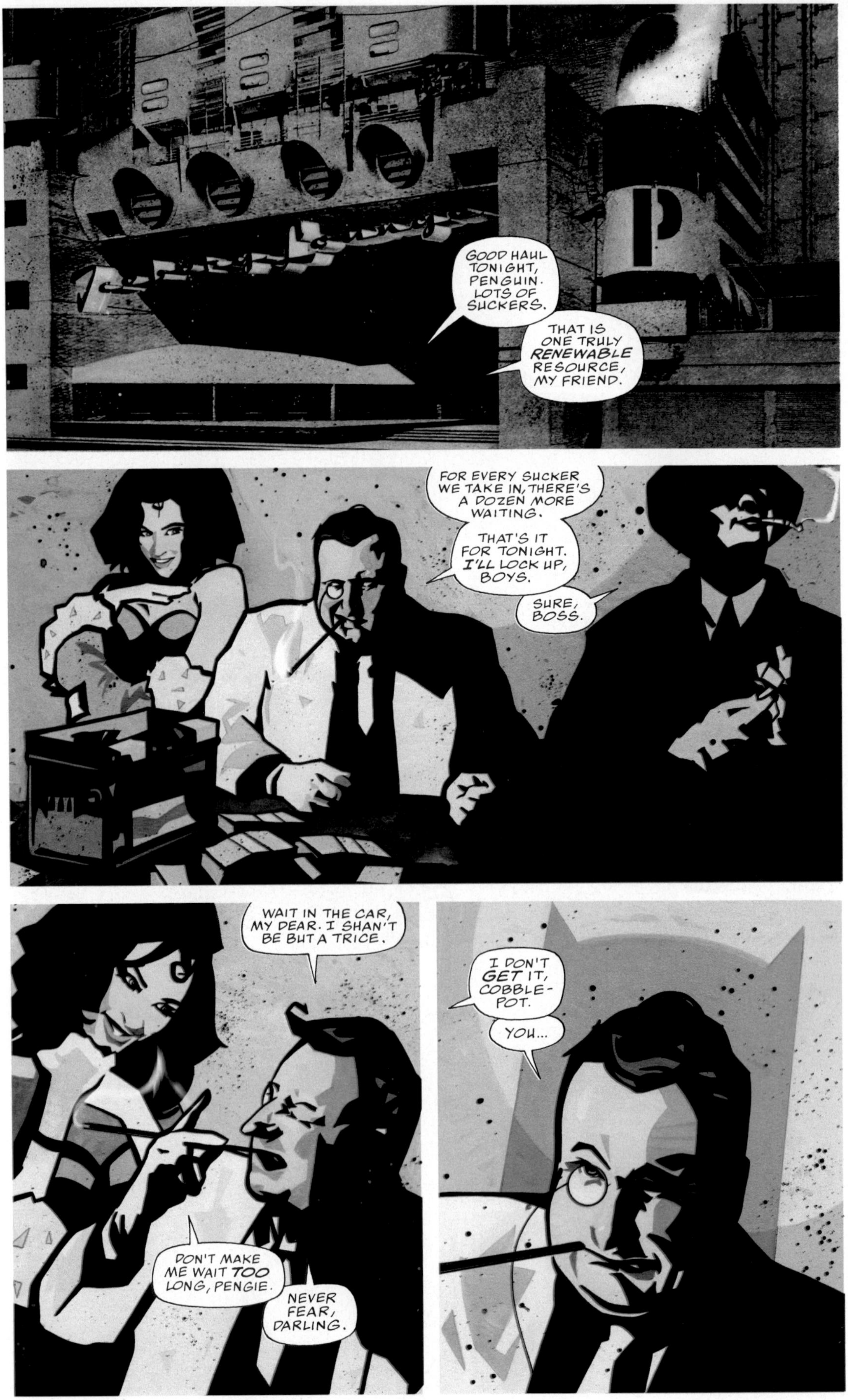
GOOD HAUL TONIGHT, PENGUIN. LOTS OF SUCKERS.
THAT IS ONE TRULY *RENEWABLE* RESOURCE, MY FRIEND.
FOR EVERY SUCKER WE TAKE IN, THERE'S A DOZEN MORE WAITING.
THAT'S IT FOR TONIGHT. *I'LL* LOCK UP, BOYS.
SURE, BOSS.
WAIT IN THE CAR, MY DEAR. I SHAN'T BE BUT A TRICE.
DON'T MAKE ME WAIT *TOO* LONG, PENGIE.
NEVER FEAR, DARLING.
I DON'T *GET* IT, COBBLE-POT.
YOU...

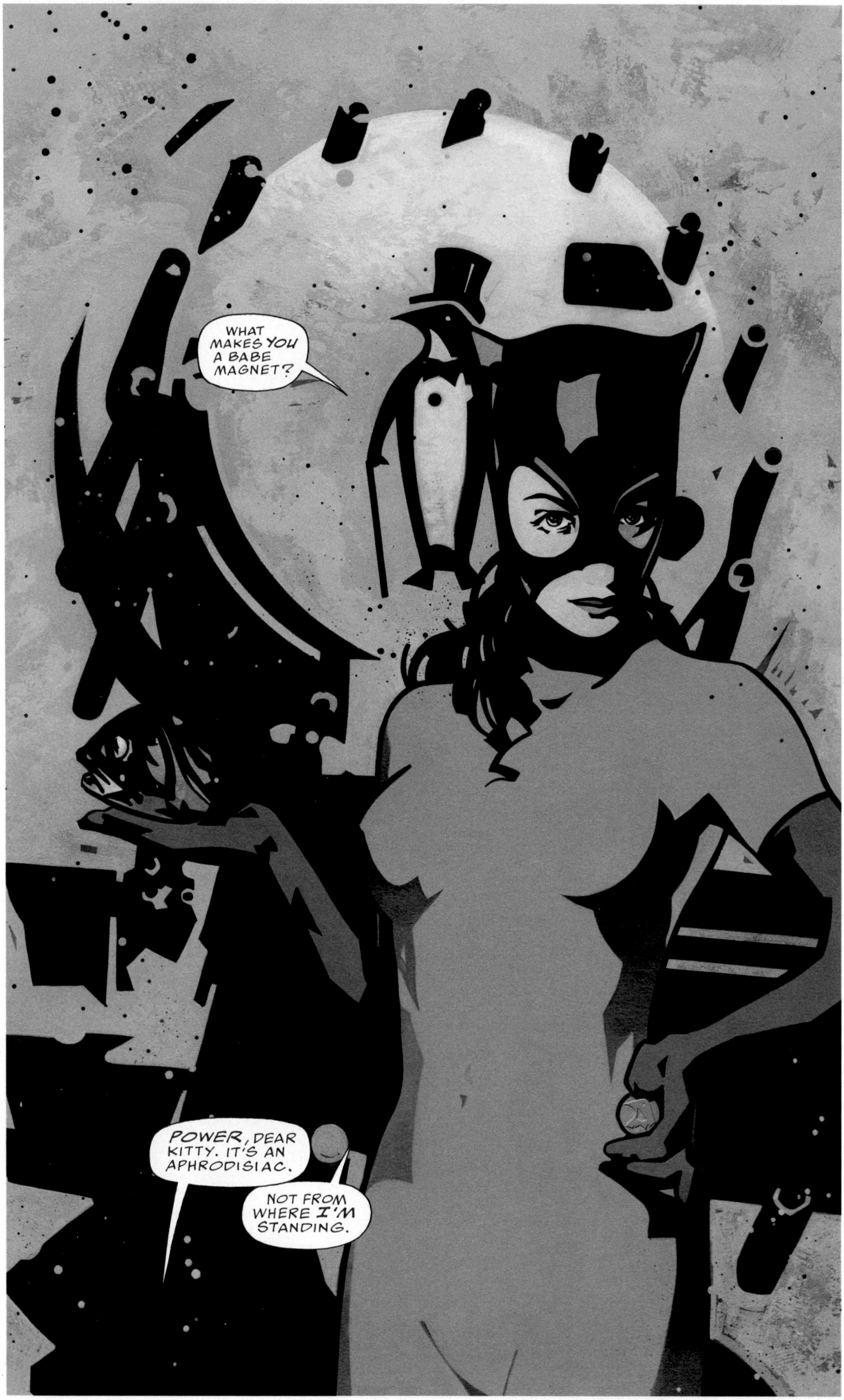
WHAT MAKES YOU A BABE MAGNET?
POWER, DEAR KITTY. IT'S AN APHRODISIAC.
NOT FROM WHERE I'M STANDING.

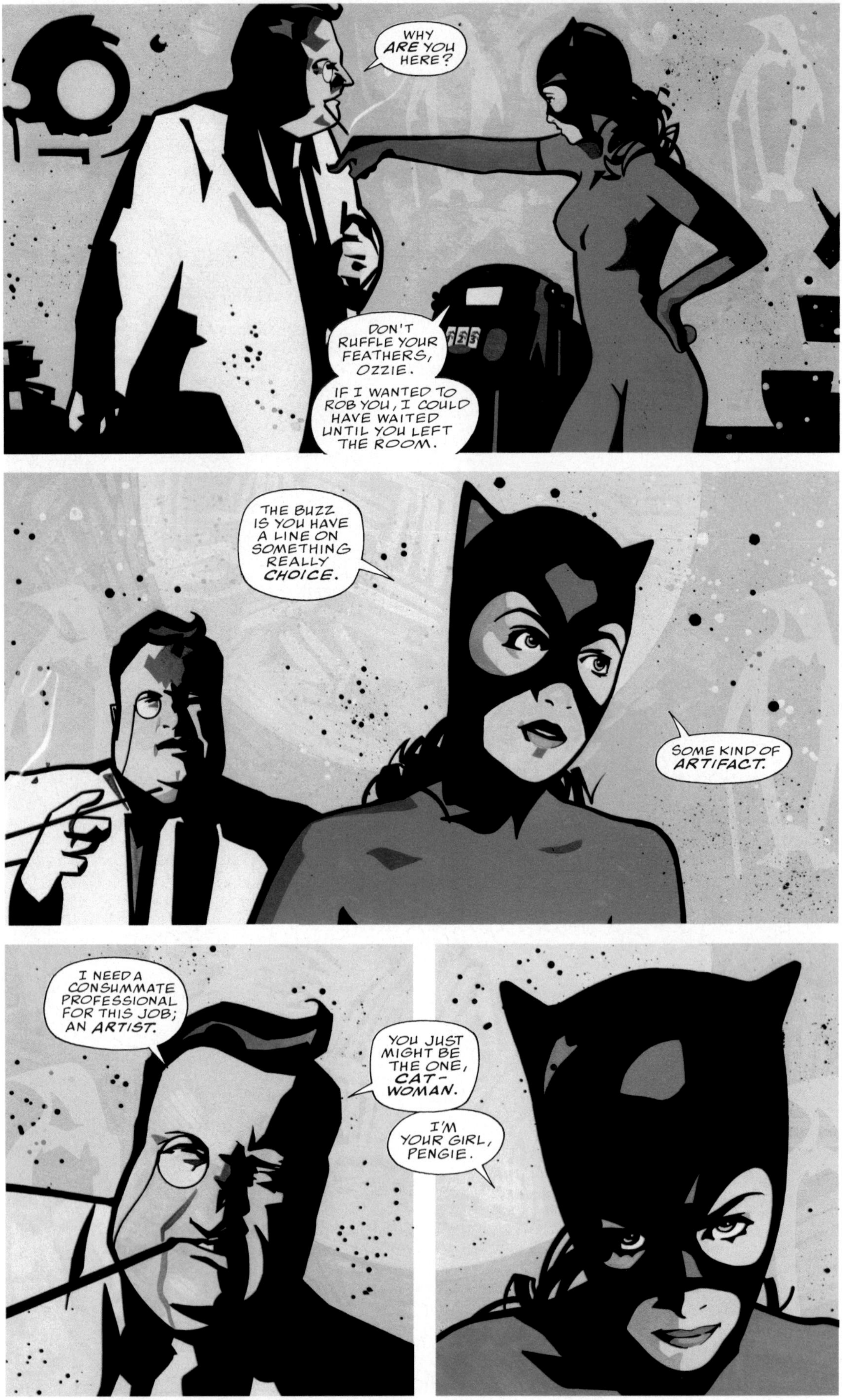
WHY ARE YOU HERE?
DON'T RUFFLE YOUR FEATHERS, OZZIE.
IF I WANTED TO ROB YOU, I COULD HAVE WAITED UNTIL YOU LEFT THE ROOM.
THE BUZZ IS YOU HAVE A LINE ON SOMETHING REALLY CHOICE.
SOME KIND OF ARTIFACT.
I NEED A CONSUMMATE PROFESSIONAL FOR THIS JOB; AN ARTIST.
YOU JUST MIGHT BE THE ONE, CAT-WOMAN.
I'M YOUR GIRL, PENGIE.

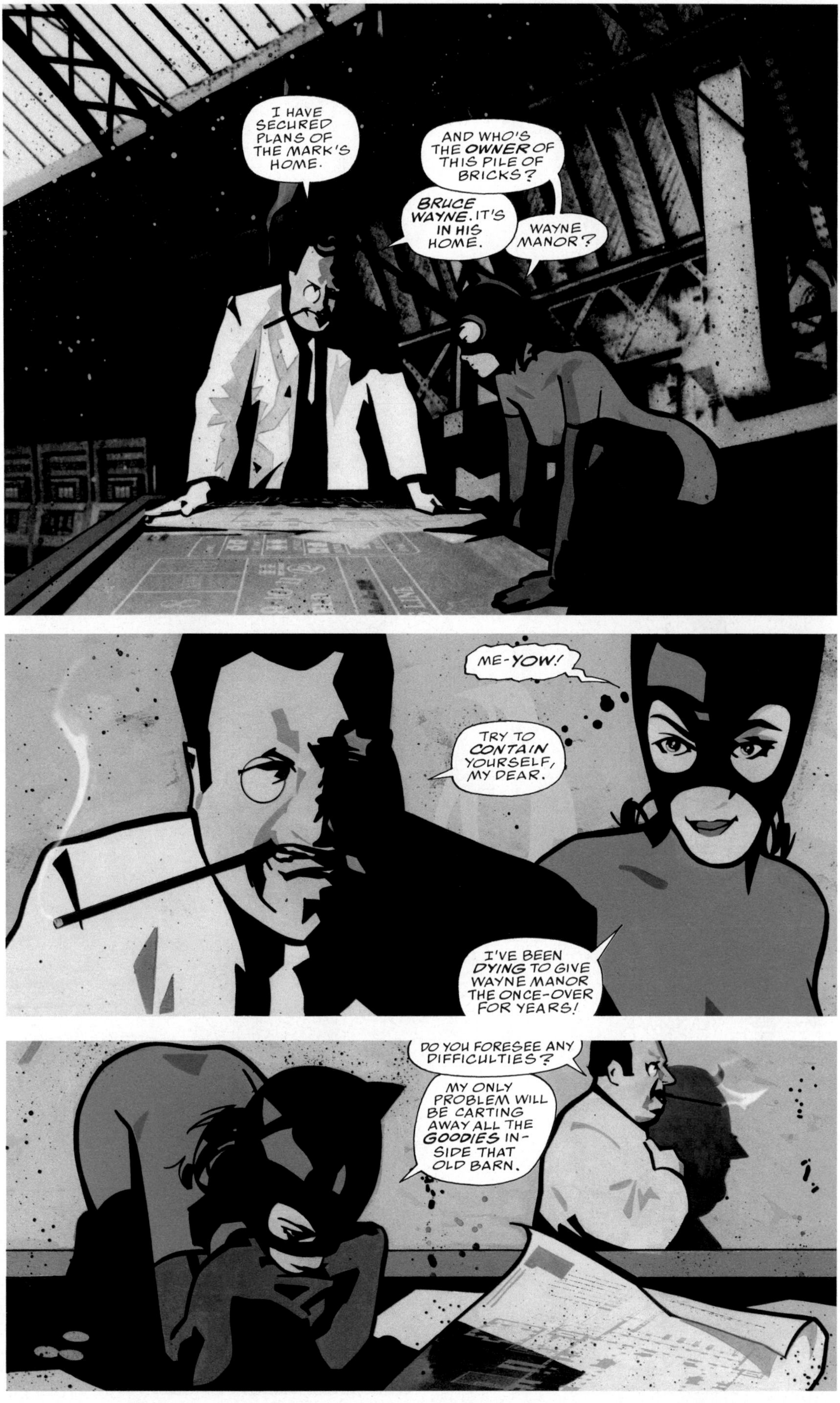
I HAVE SECURED PLANS OF THE MARK'S HOME.
AND WHO'S THE OWNER OF THIS PILE OF BRICKS?
BRUCE WAYNE. IT'S IN HIS HOME.
WAYNE MANOR?
ME-YOW!
TRY TO CONTAIN YOURSELF, MY DEAR.
I'VE BEEN DYING TO GIVE WAYNE MANOR THE ONCE-OVER FOR YEARS!
DO YOU FORESEE ANY DIFFICULTIES?
MY ONLY PROBLEM WILL BE CARTING AWAY ALL THE GOODIES IN-SIDE THAT OLD BARN.

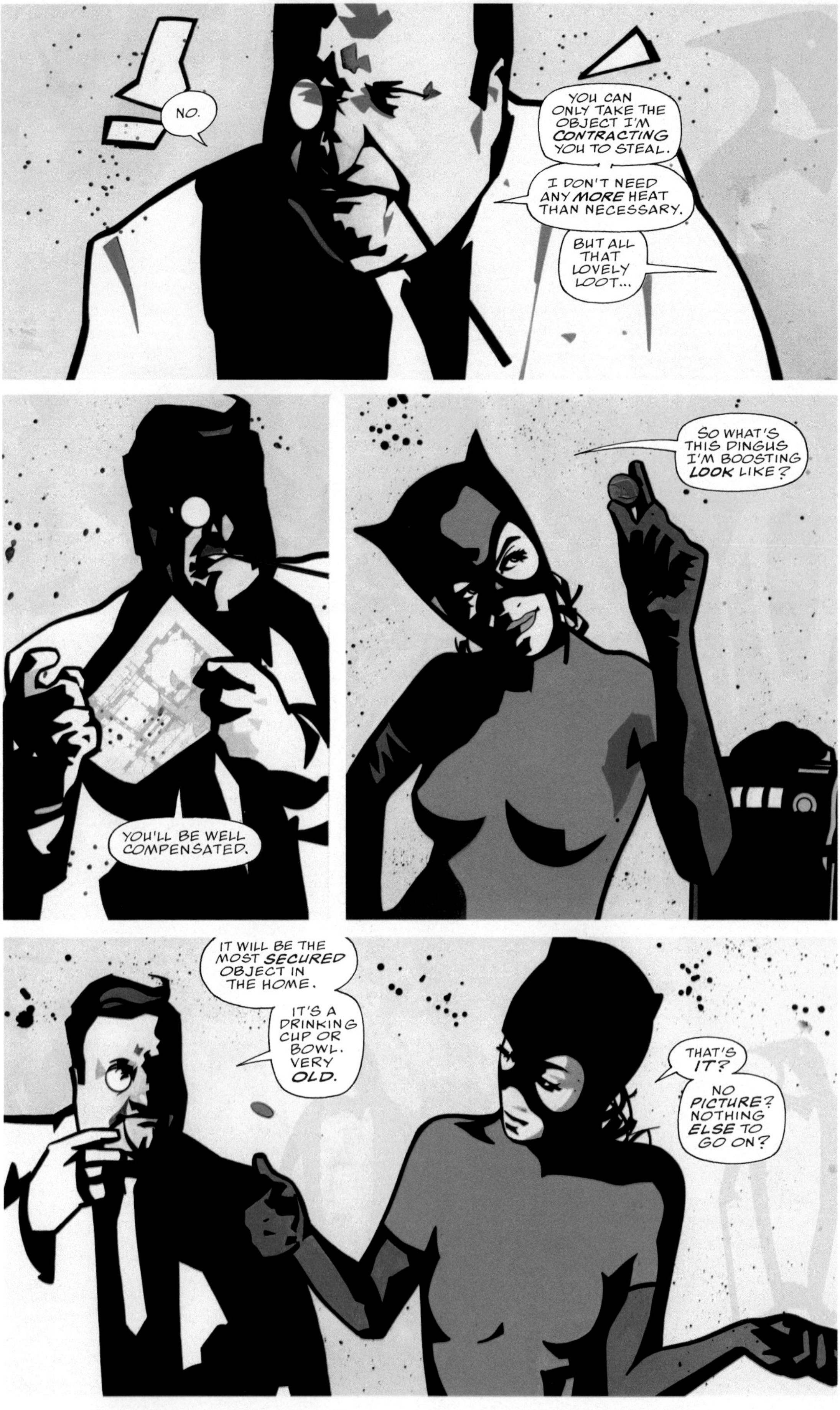
NO.
YOU CAN ONLY TAKE THE OBJECT I'M CONTRACTING YOU TO STEAL.
I DON'T NEED ANY MORE HEAT THAN NECESSARY.
BUT ALL THAT LOVELY LOOT...
YOU'LL BE WELL COMPENSATED.
SO WHAT'S THIS DINGUS I'M BOOSTING LOOK LIKE?
IT WILL BE THE MOST SECURED OBJECT IN THE HOME.
IT'S A DRINKING CUP OR BOWL. VERY OLD.
THAT'S IT?
NO PICTURE? NOTHING ELSE TO GO ON?

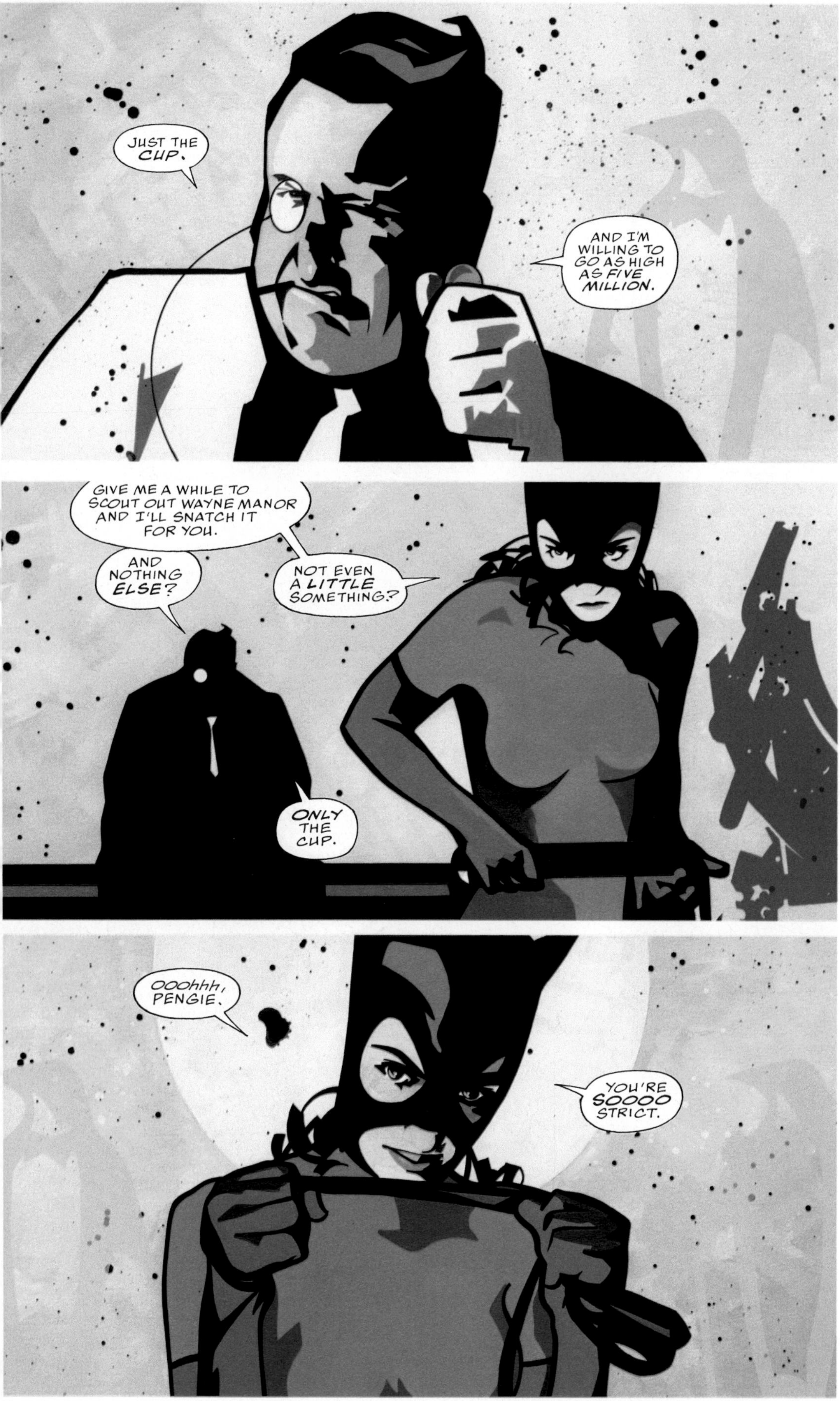
JUST THE CUP.
AND I'M WILLING TO GO AS HIGH AS FIVE MILLION.
GIVE ME A WHILE TO SCOUT OUT WAYNE MANOR AND I'LL SNATCH IT FOR YOU.
AND NOTHING ELSE?
NOT EVEN A LITTLE SOMETHING?
ONLY THE CUP.
OOOhhh, PENGIE.
YOU'RE SOOOO STRICT.

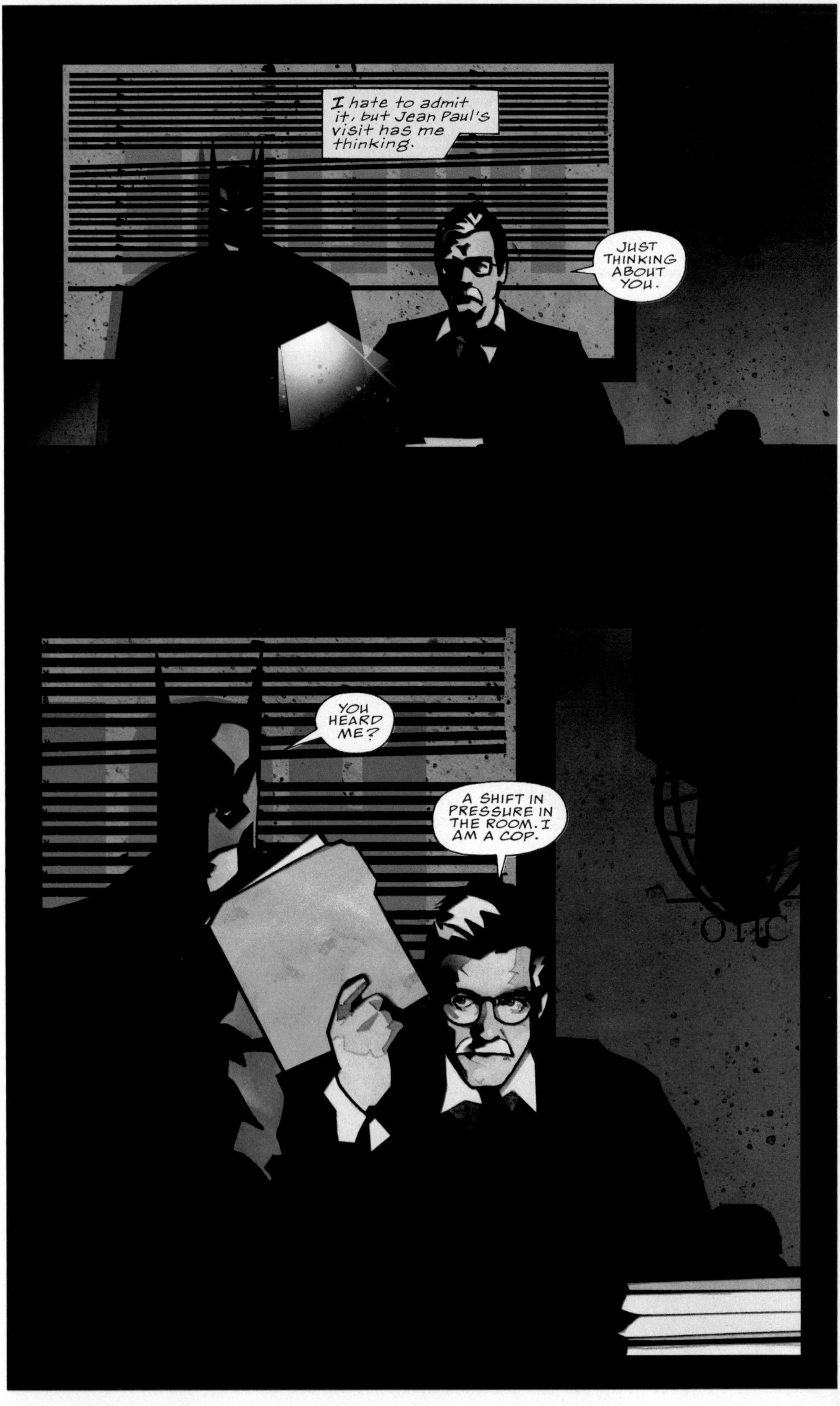
I hate to admit it, but Jean Paul's visit has me thinking.
JUST THINKING ABOUT YOU.
YOU HEARD ME?
A SHIFT IN PRESSURE IN THE ROOM. I AM A COP.

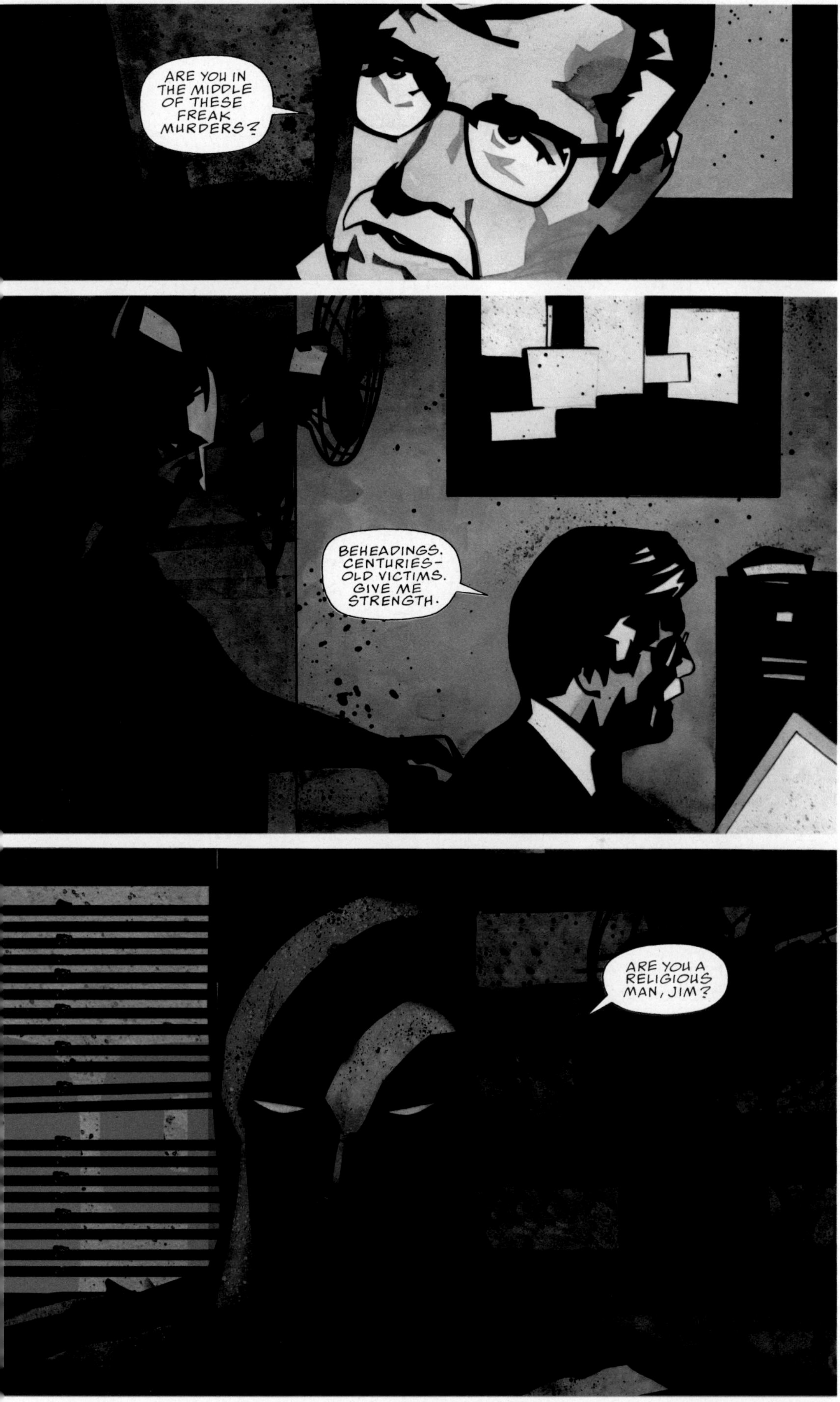
ARE YOU IN THE MIDDLE OF THESE FREAK MURDERS?
BEHEADINGS. CENTURIES-OLD VICTIMS. GIVE ME STRENGTH.
ARE YOU A RELIGIOUS MAN, JIM?

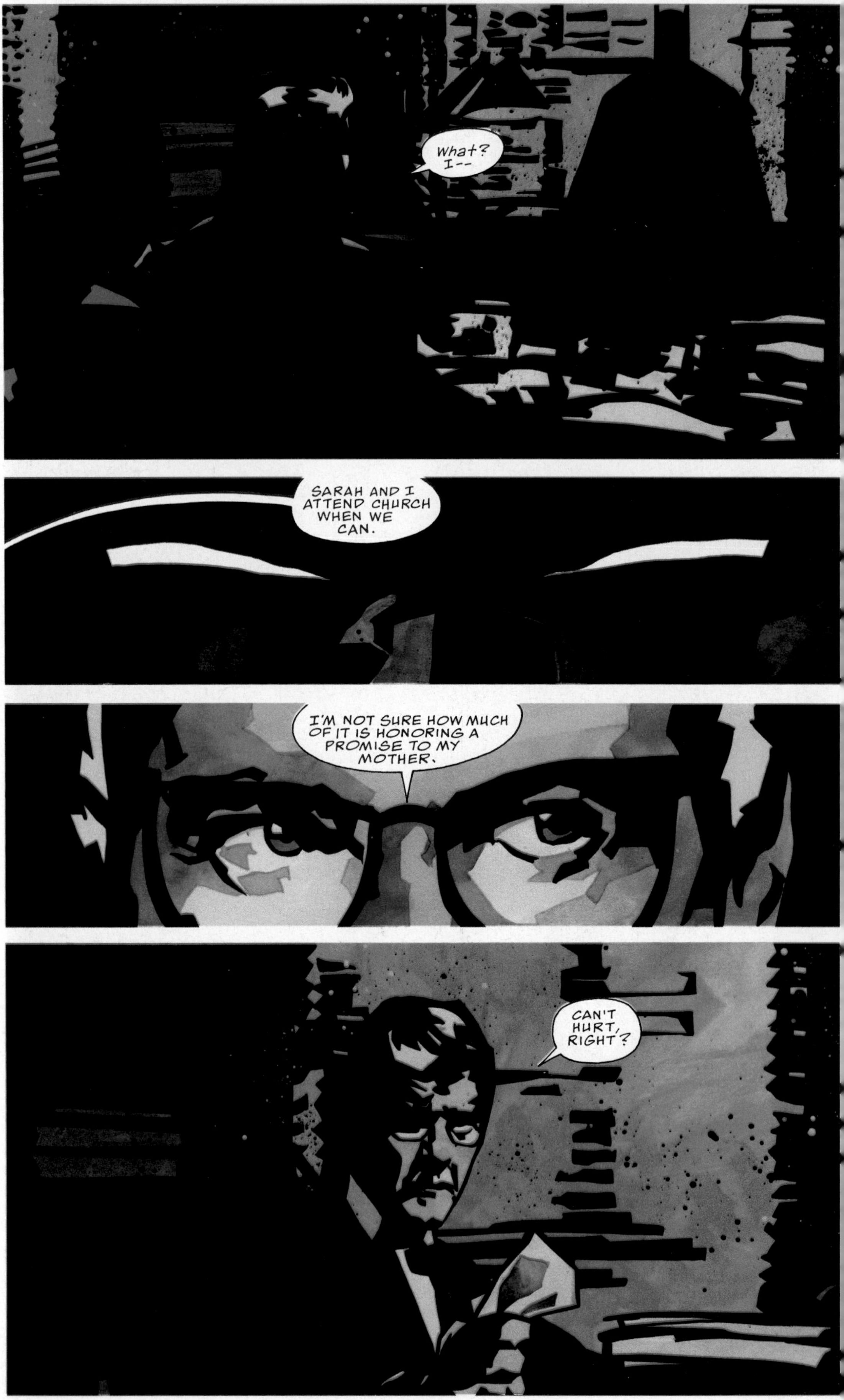
What? I--
SARAH AND I ATTEND CHURCH WHEN WE CAN.
I'M NOT SURE HOW MUCH OF IT IS HONORING A PROMISE TO MY MOTHER.
CAN'T HURT, RIGHT?

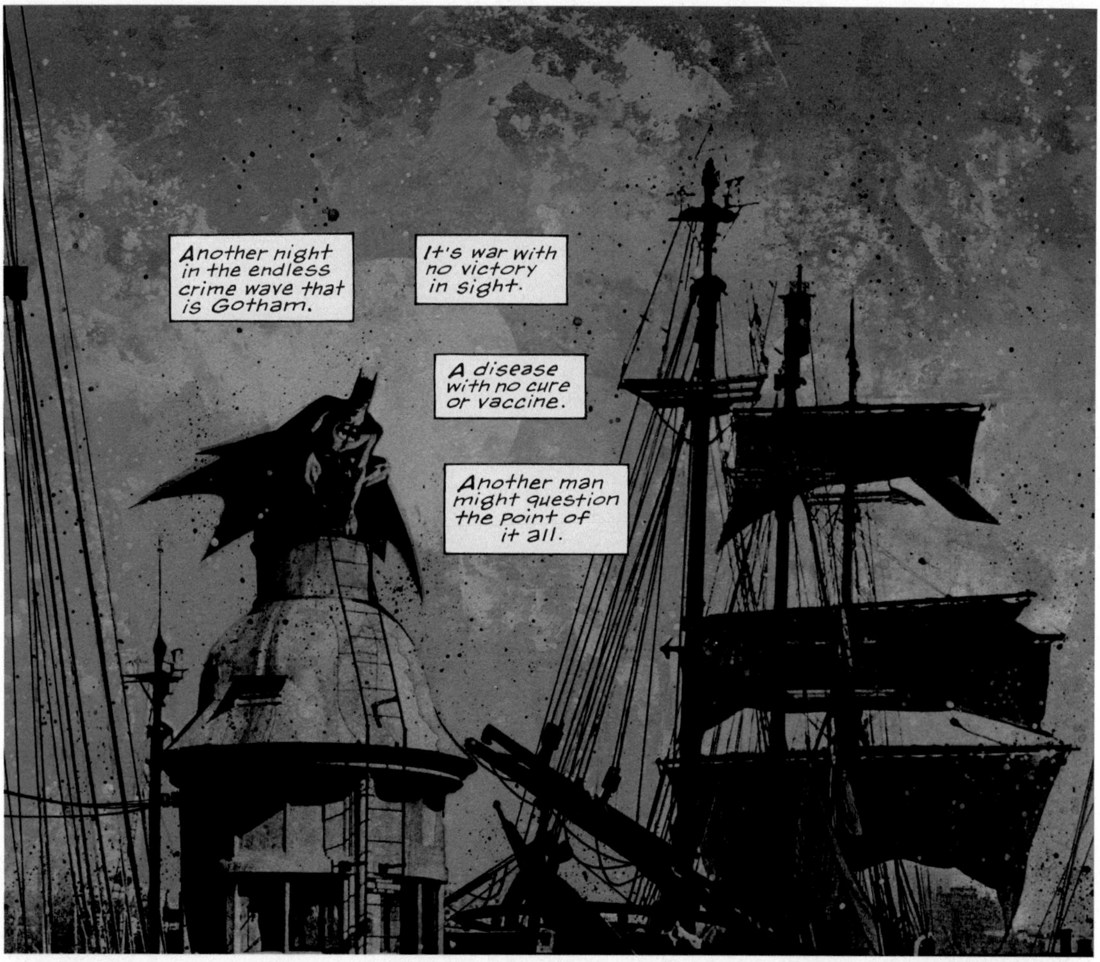
Another night in the endless crime wave that is Gotham.
It's war with no victory in sight.
A disease with no cure or vaccine.
Another man might question the point of it all.

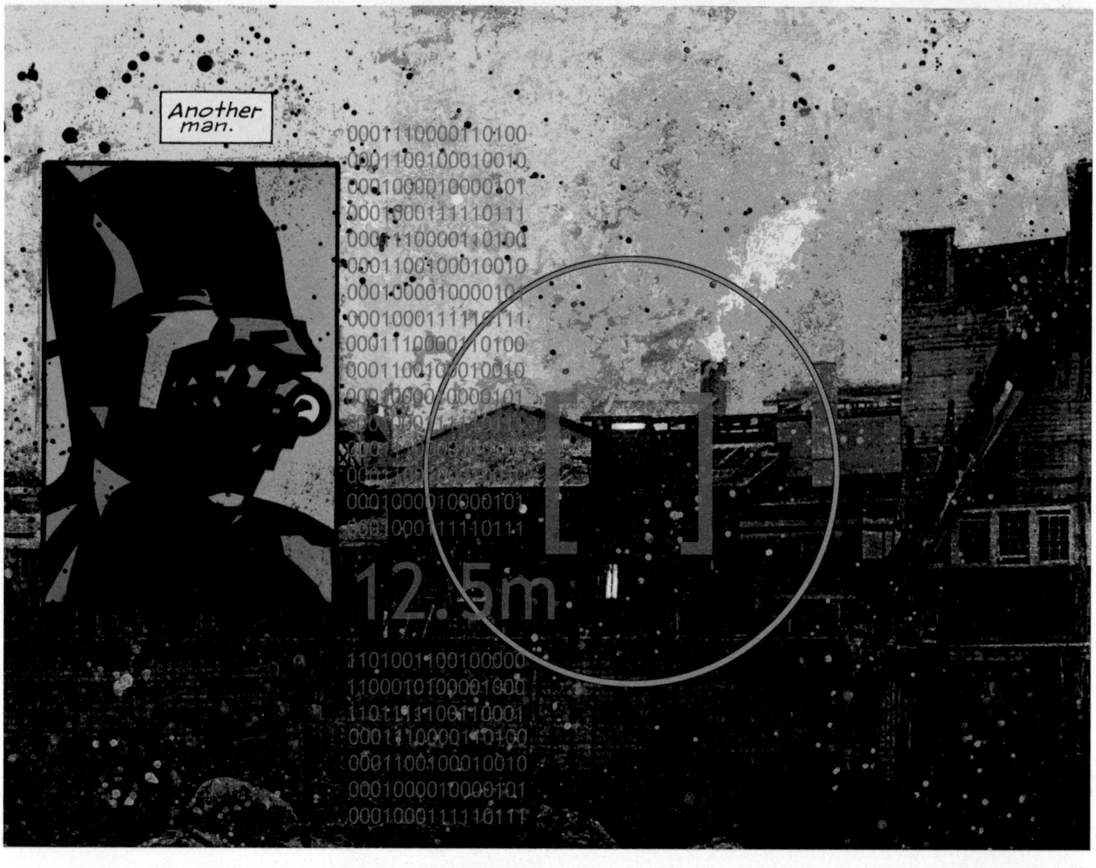
Another man.
0001110000110100
0001100100010010
0001000010000101
0001000111110111
12.5m
1101001100100000
1100010100001000
1101111100110001
0001110000110100
0001100100010010
0001000010000101
0001000111110111

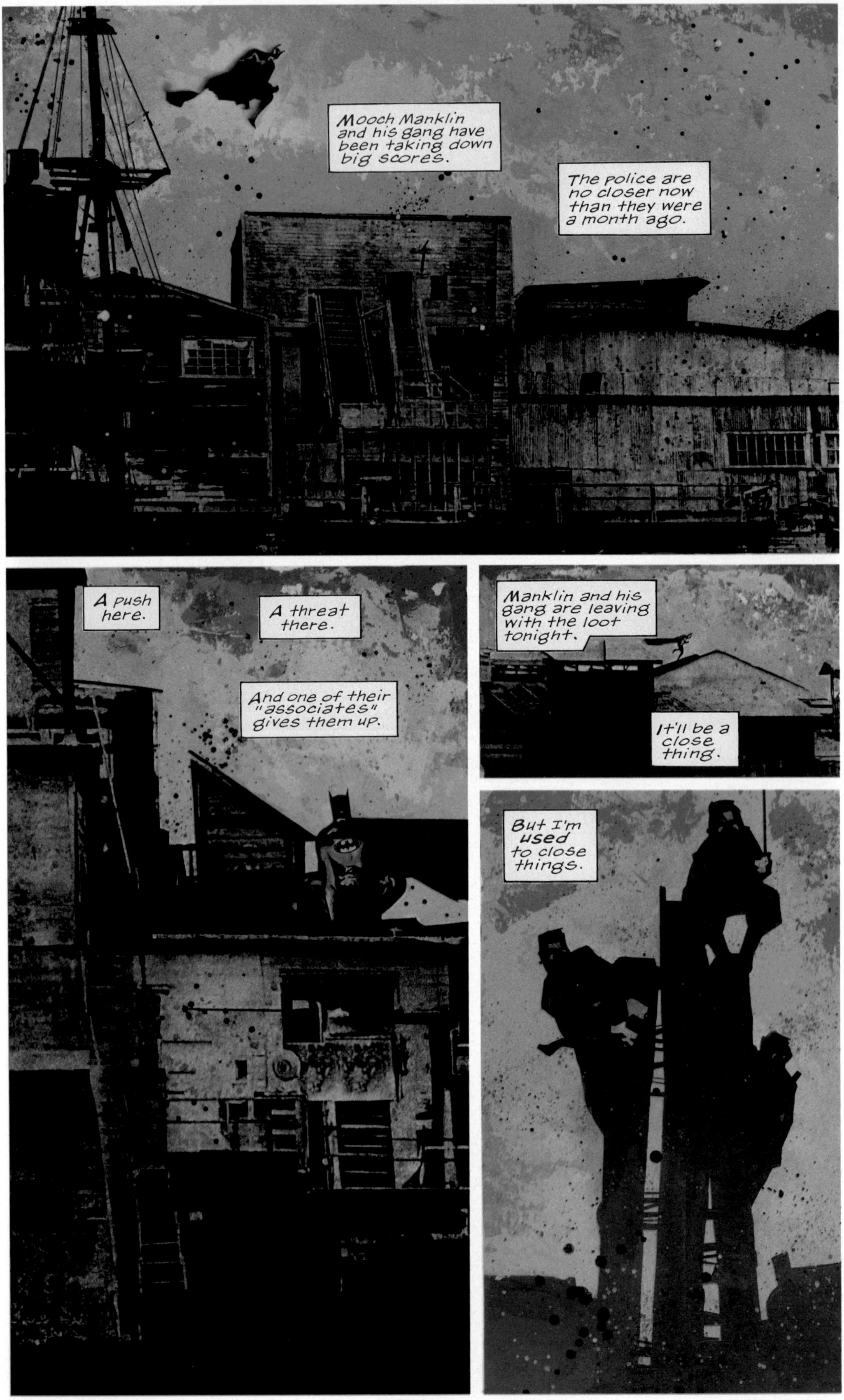
Mooch Manklin and his gang have been taking down big scores.
The police are no closer now than they were a month ago.
A push here.
A threat there.
And one of their "associates" gives them up.
Manklin and his gang are leaving with the loot tonight.
It'll be a close thing.
But I'm used to close things.

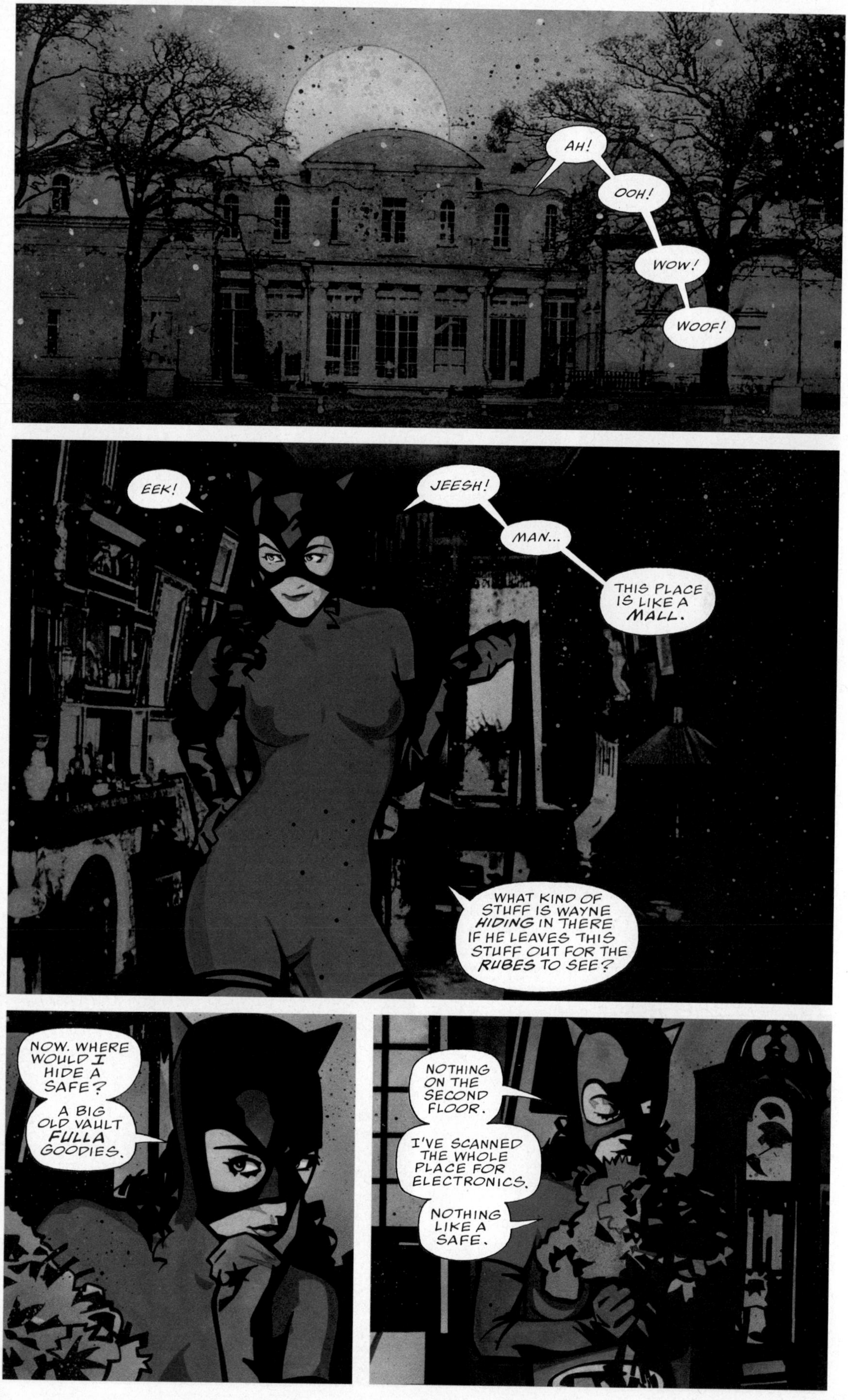
AH!
OOH!
WOW!
WOOF!
EEK!
JEESH!
MAN...
THIS PLACE IS LIKE A MALL.
WHAT KIND OF STUFF IS WAYNE HIDING IN THERE IF HE LEAVES THIS STUFF OUT FOR THE RUBES TO SEE?
NOW. WHERE WOULD I HIDE A SAFE?
A BIG OLD VAULT FULLA GOODIES.
NOTHING ON THE SECOND FLOOR.
I'VE SCANNED THE WHOLE PLACE FOR ELECTRONICS.
NOTHING LIKE A SAFE.

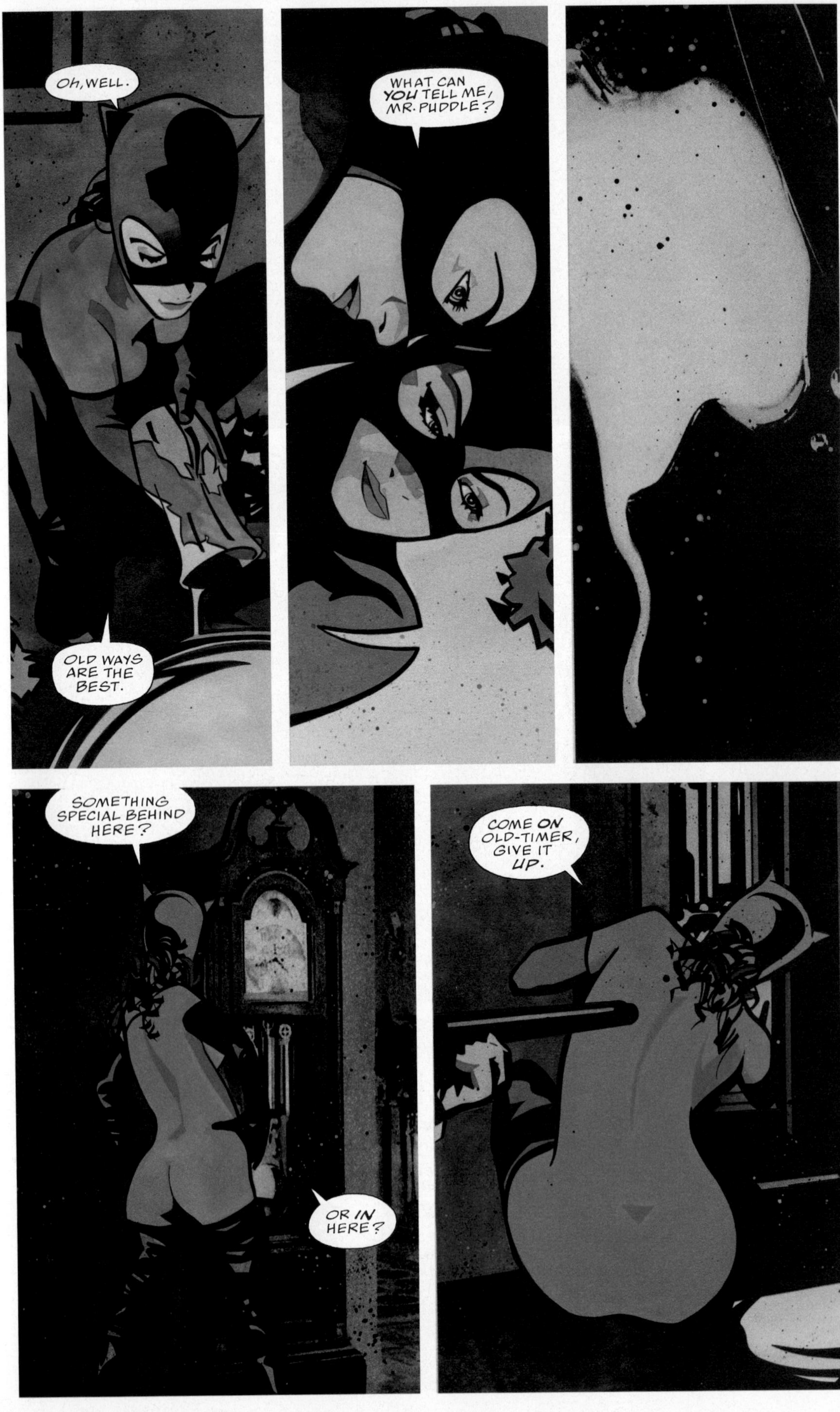
Oh, WELL.
OLD WAYS ARE THE BEST.
WHAT CAN YOU TELL ME, MR. PUDDLE?
SOMETHING SPECIAL BEHIND HERE?
OR IN HERE?
COME ON OLD-TIMER, GIVE IT UP.

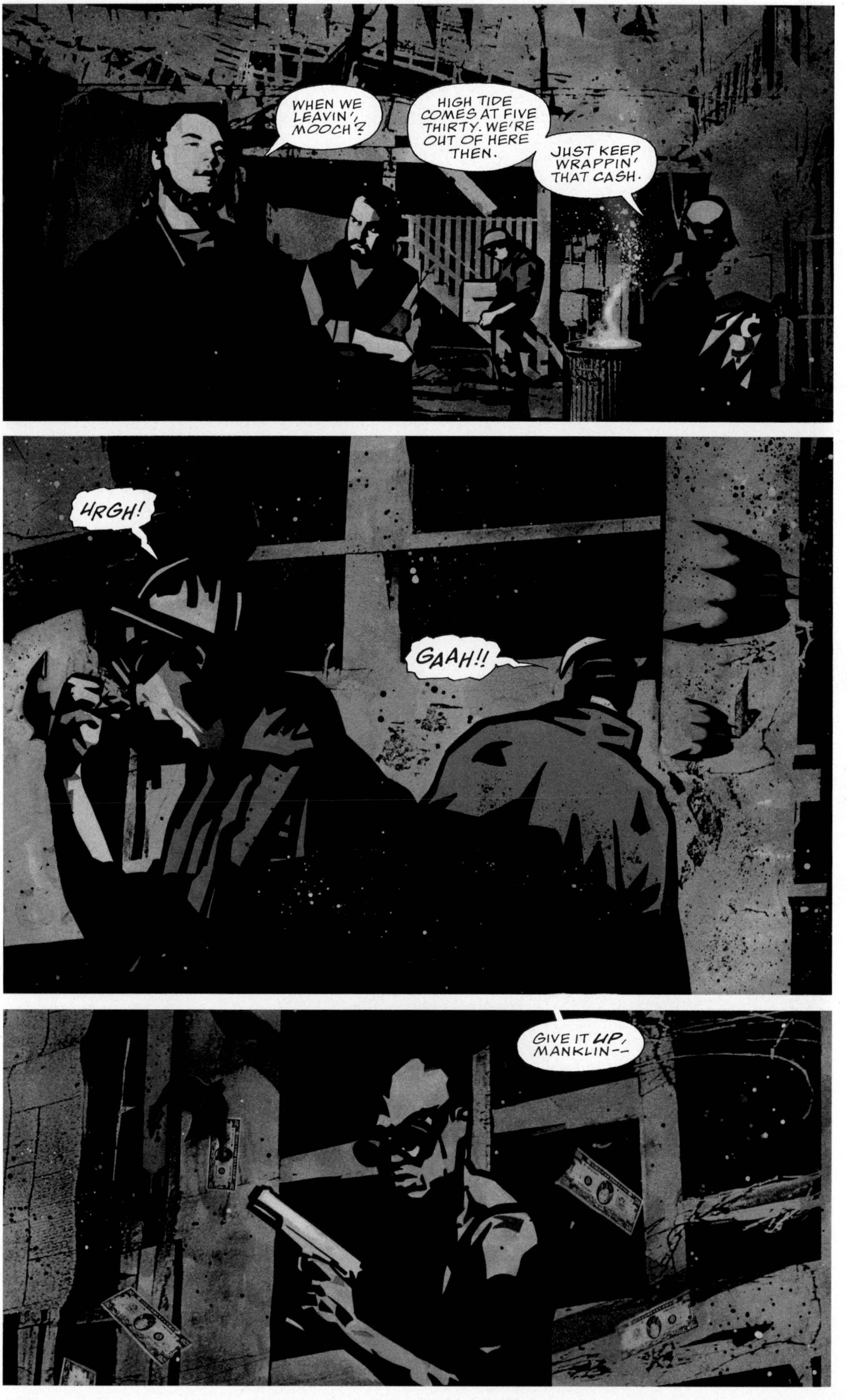
WHEN WE LEAVIN', MOOCH?
HIGH TIDE COMES AT FIVE THIRTY. WE'RE OUT OF HERE THEN.
JUST KEEP WRAPPIN' THAT CASH.
URGH!
GAAH!!
GIVE IT UP, MANKLIN--

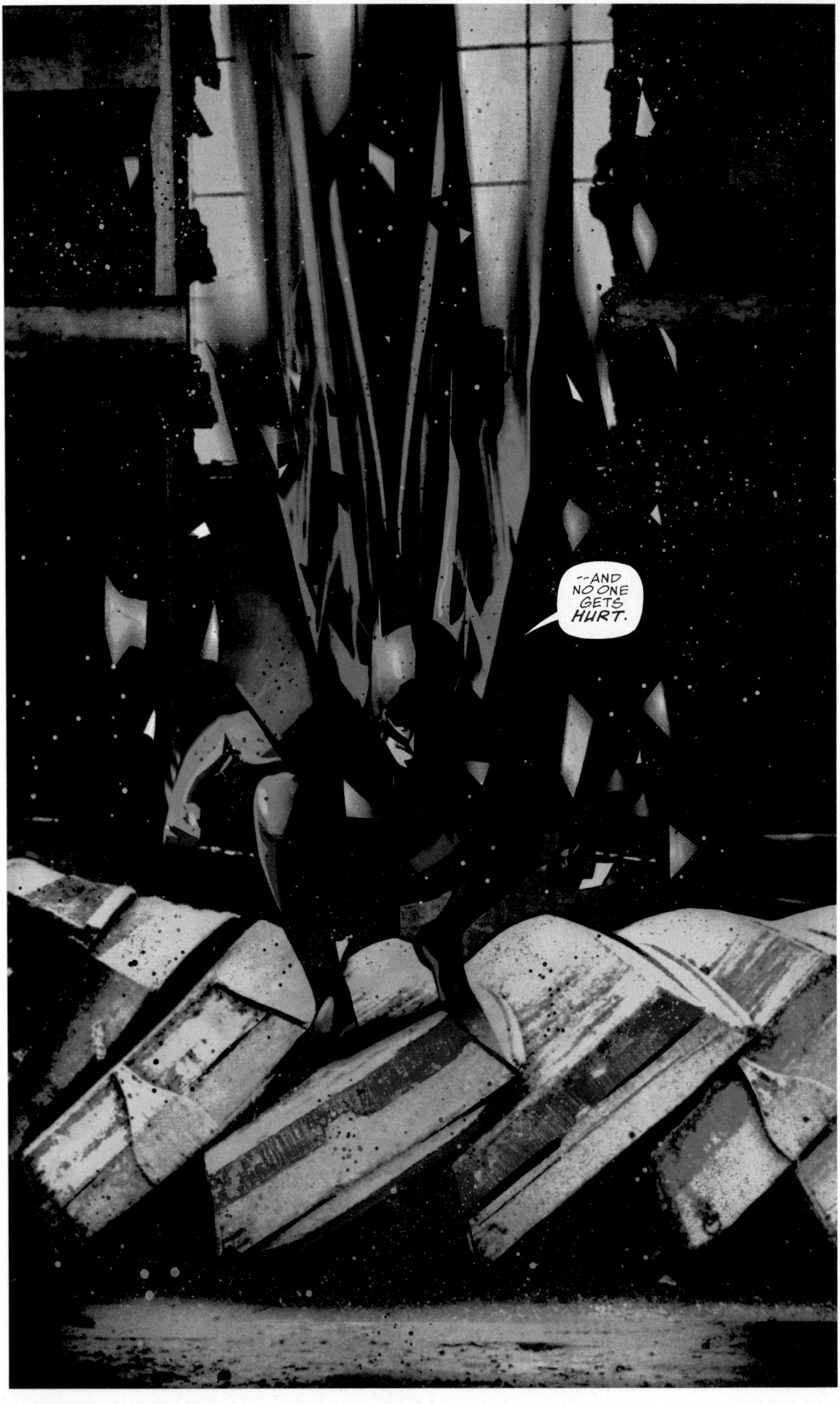
--AND NO ONE GETS HURT.

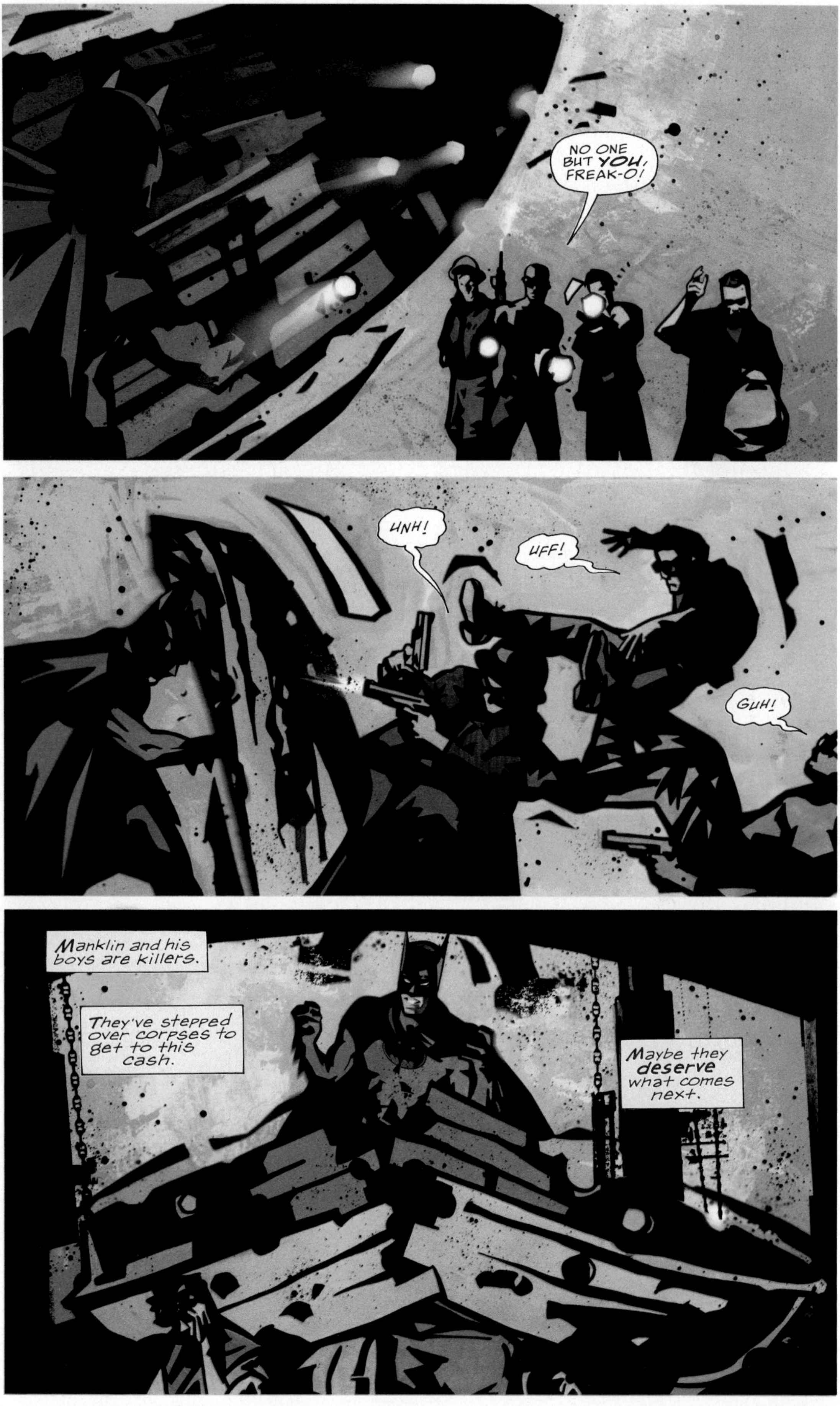
NO ONE BUT YOU, FREAK-O!
UNH!
UFF!
GUH!
Manklin and his boys are killers.
They've stepped over corpses to get to this cash.
Maybe they deserve what comes next.

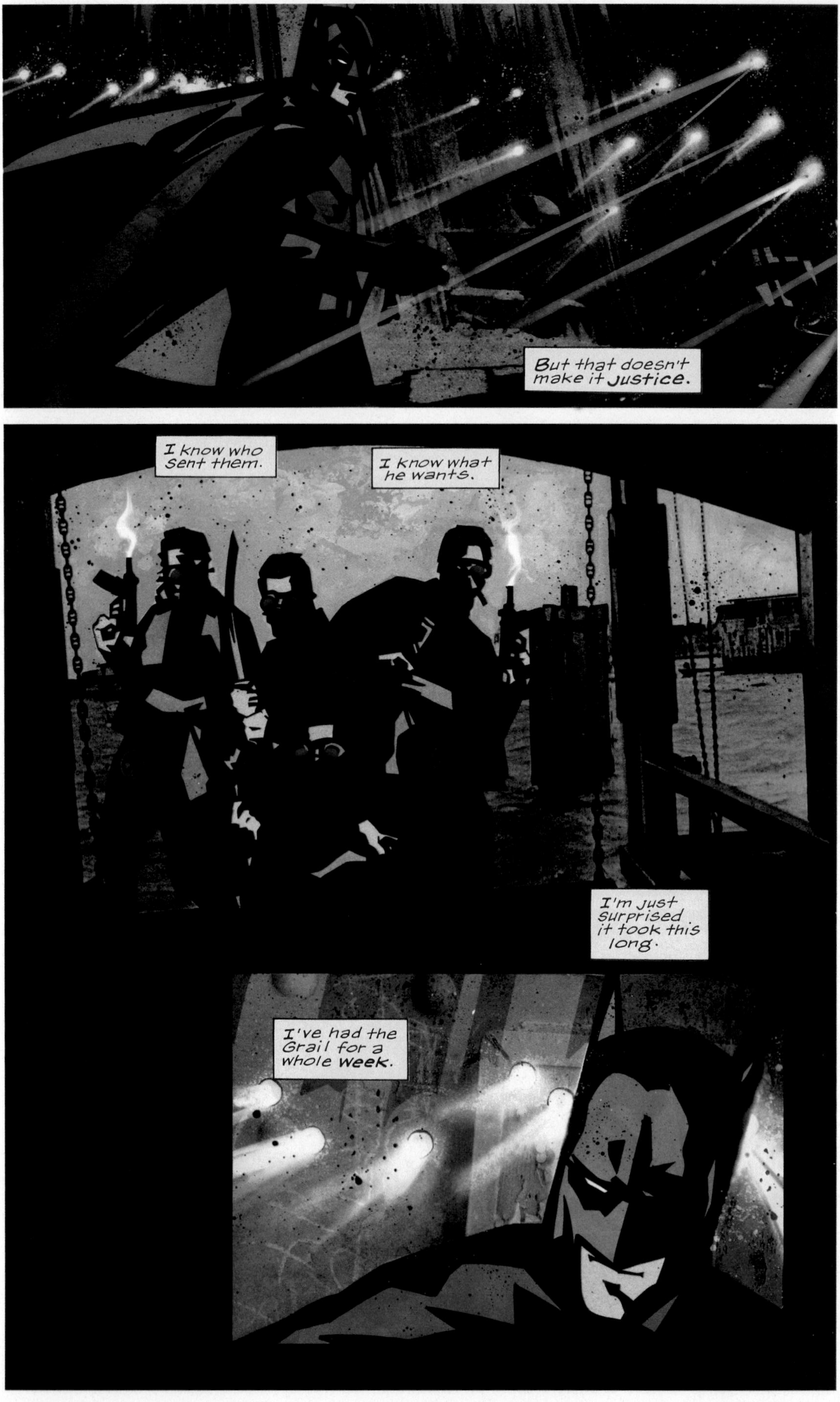

But that doesn't make it justice.
I know who sent them.
I know what he wants.
I'm just surprised it took this long.
I've had the Grail for a whole week.

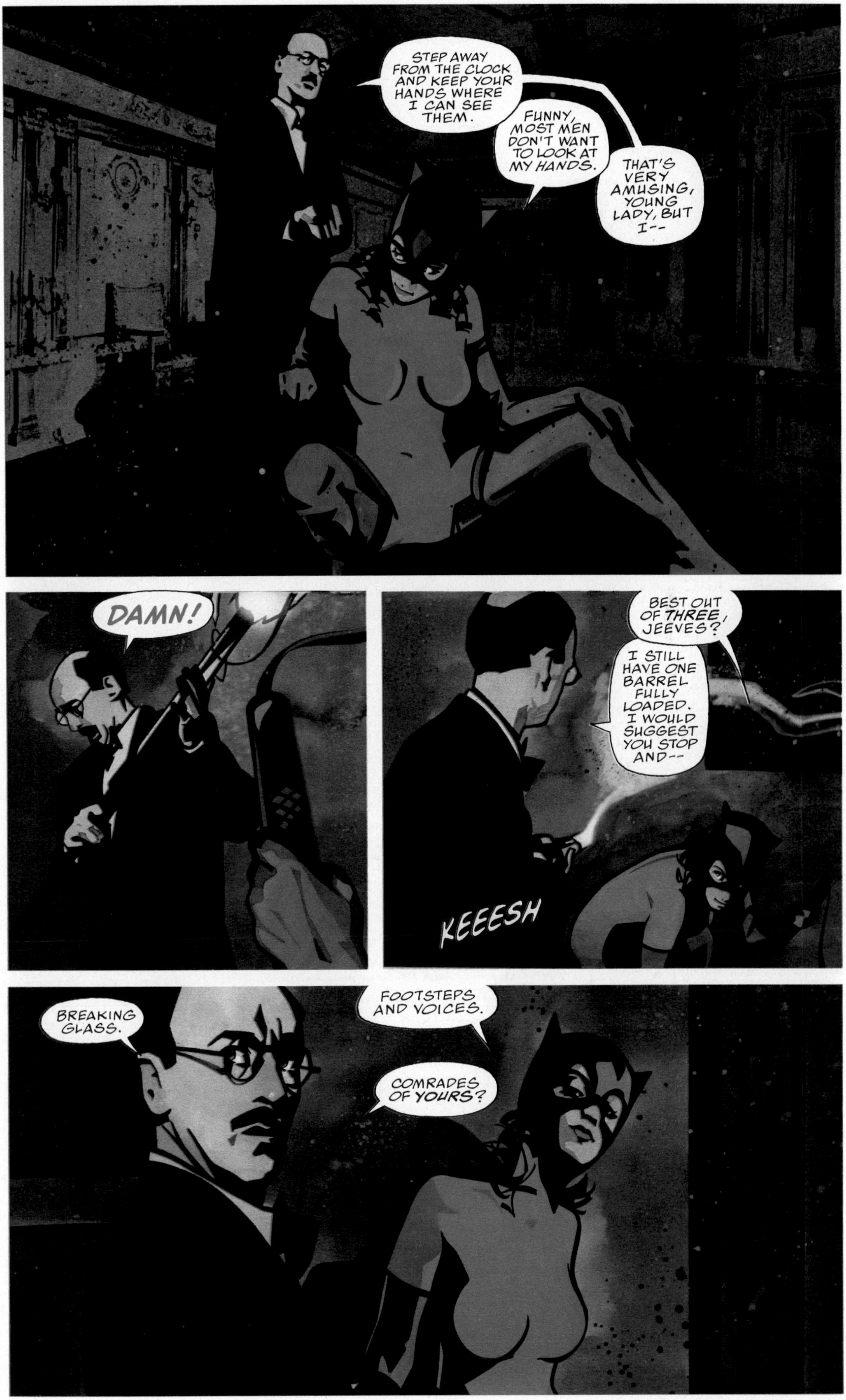
STEP AWAY FROM THE CLOCK AND KEEP YOUR HANDS WHERE I CAN SEE THEM.
FUNNY, MOST MEN DON'T WANT TO LOOK AT MY *HANDS*.
THAT'S VERY AMUSING, YOUNG LADY, BUT I--
DAMN!
BEST OUT OF *THREE*, JEEVES?
I STILL HAVE ONE BARREL FULLY LOADED. I WOULD SUGGEST YOU STOP AND--
KEEESH
BREAKING GLASS.
FOOTSTEPS AND VOICES.
COMRADES OF *YOURS*?

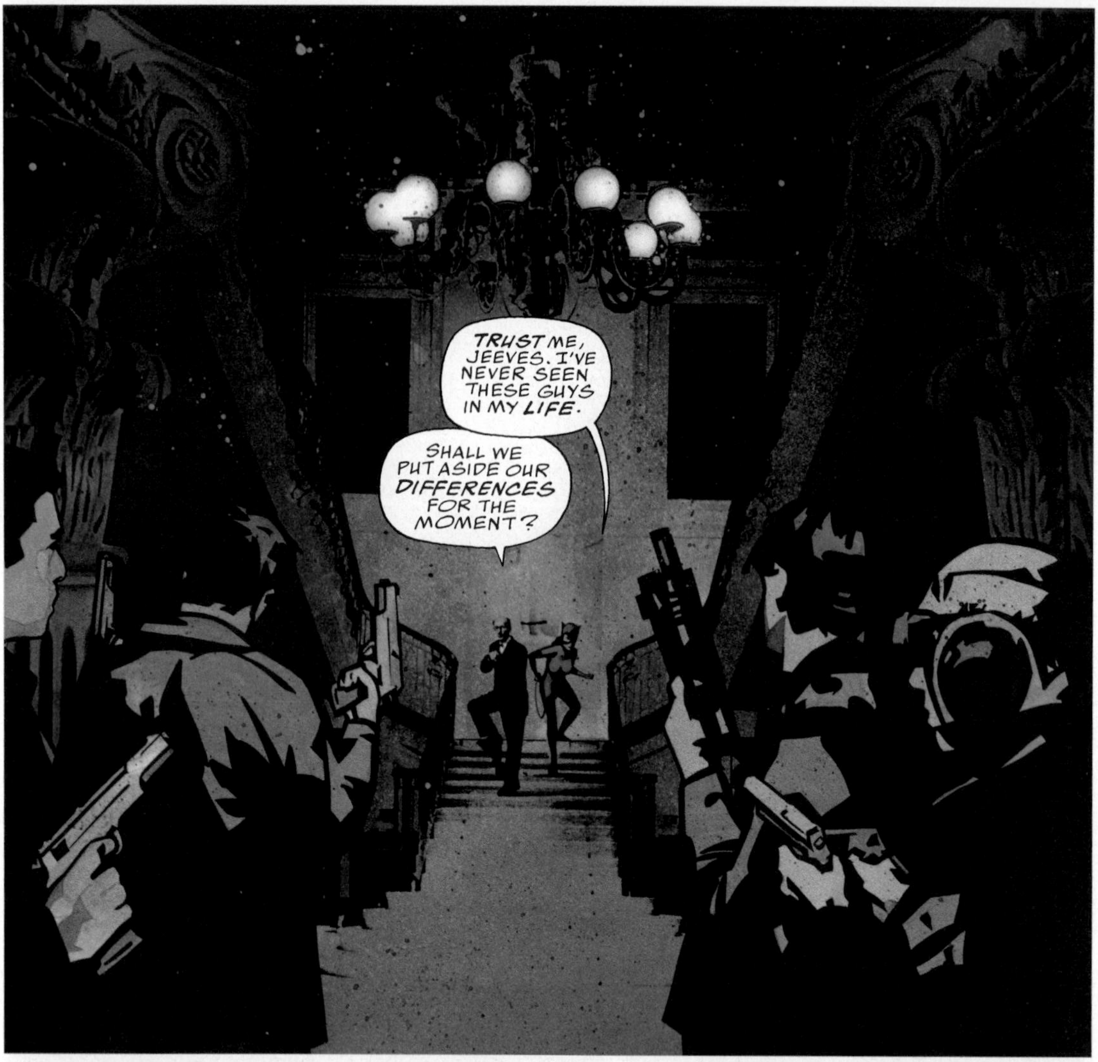
TRUST ME, JEEVES. I'VE NEVER SEEN THESE GUYS IN MY LIFE.
SHALL WE PUT ASIDE OUR DIFFERENCES FOR THE MOMENT?

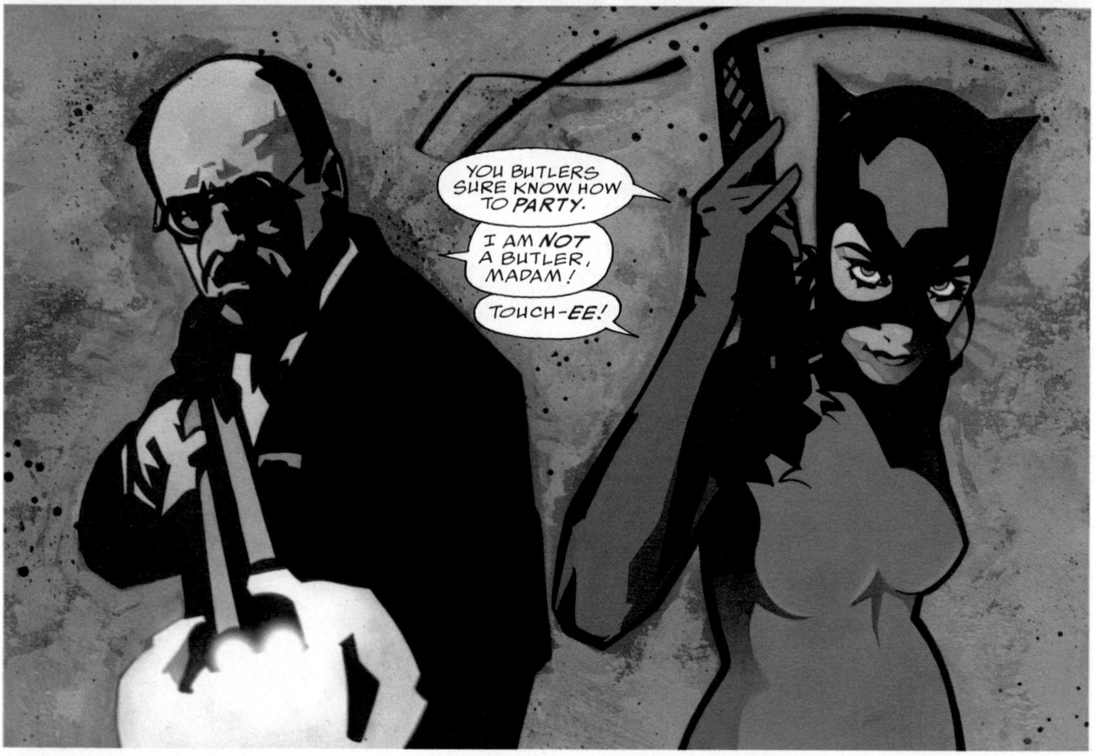
YOU BUTLERS SURE KNOW HOW TO PARTY.
I AM NOT A BUTLER, MADAM!
TOUCH-EE!

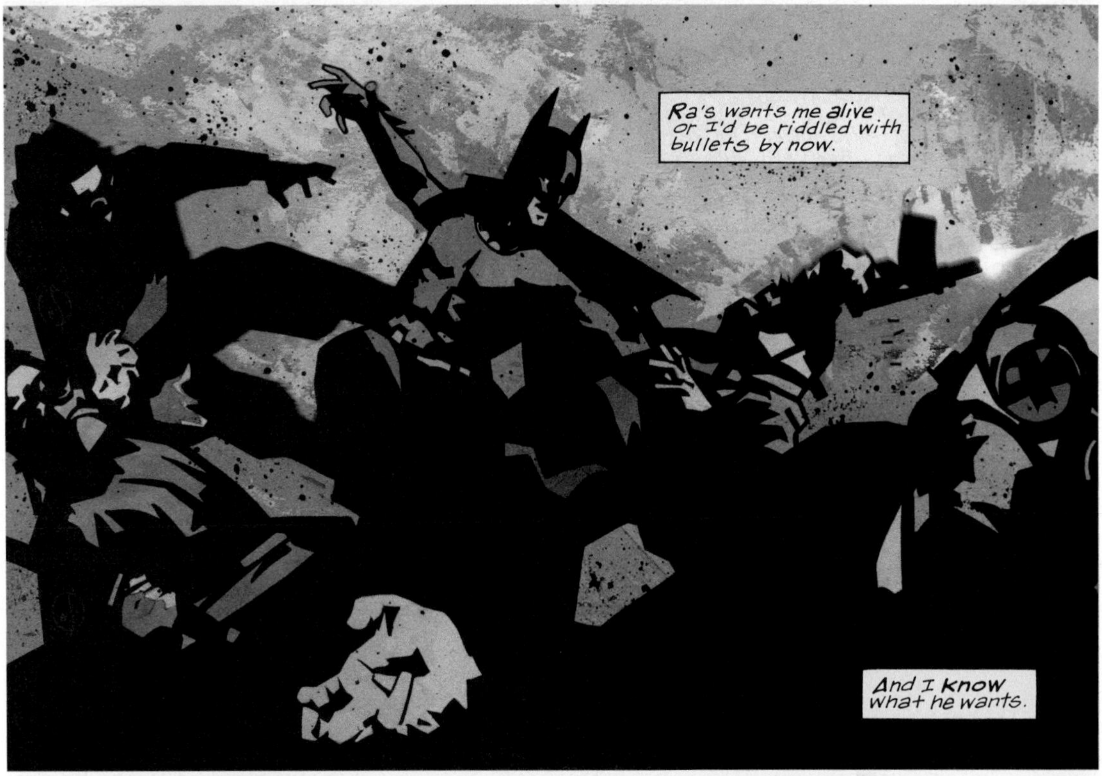
Ra's wants me alive or I'd be riddled with bullets by now.
And I know what he wants.

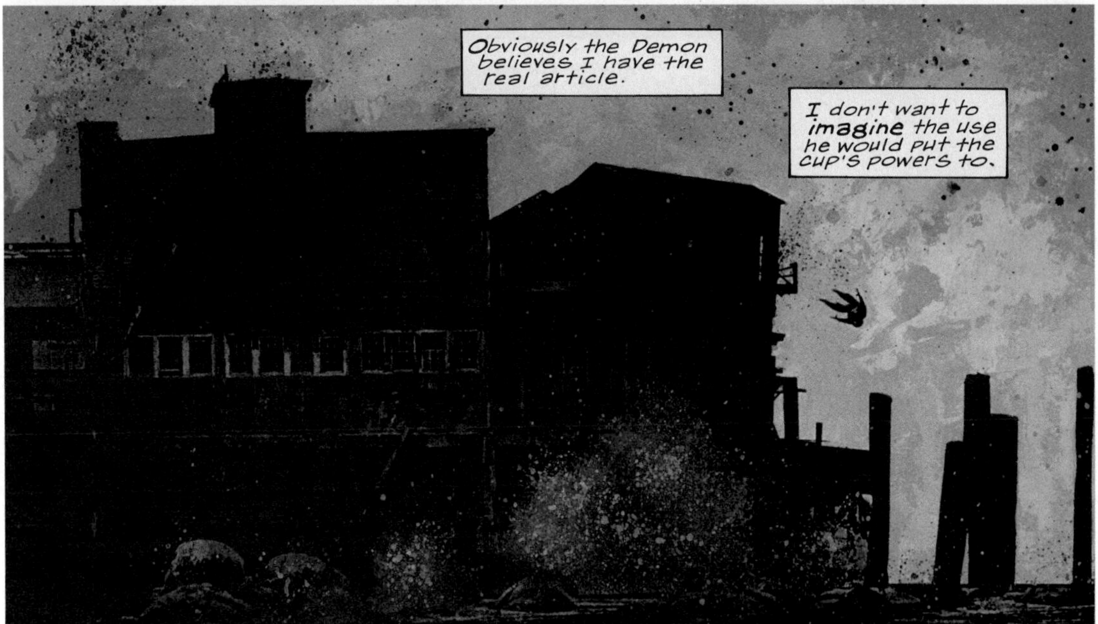
Obviously the Demon believes I have the real article.
I don't want to imagine the use he would put the cup's powers to.

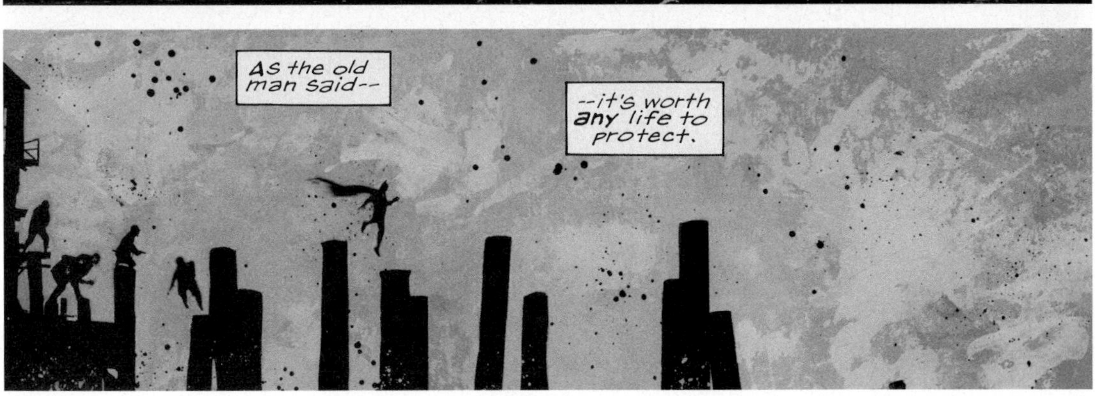
As the old man said--
--it's worth any life to protect.

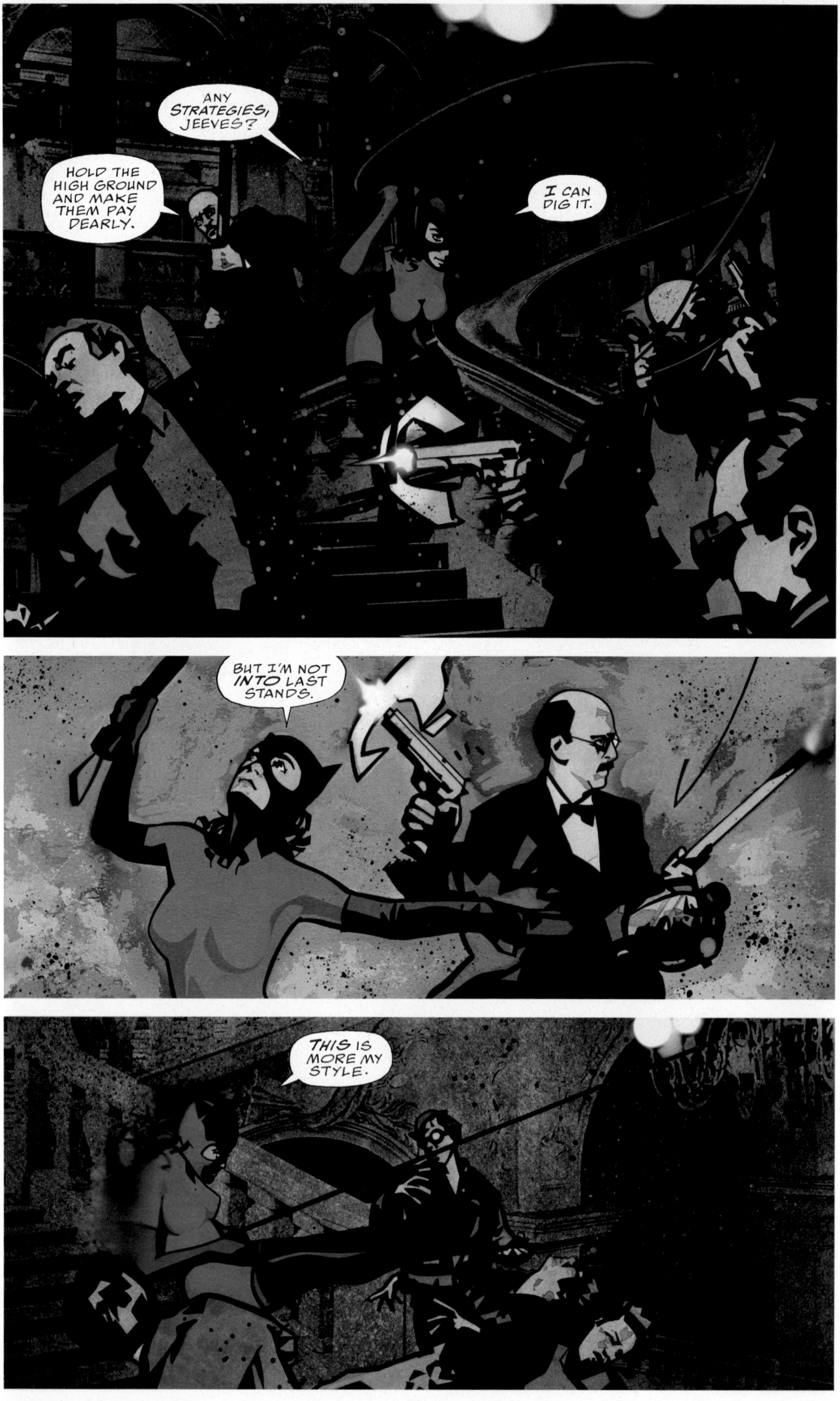
ANY STRATEGIES, JEEVES?
HOLD THE HIGH GROUND AND MAKE THEM PAY DEARLY.
I CAN DIG IT.
BUT I'M NOT INTO LAST STANDS.
THIS IS MORE MY STYLE.

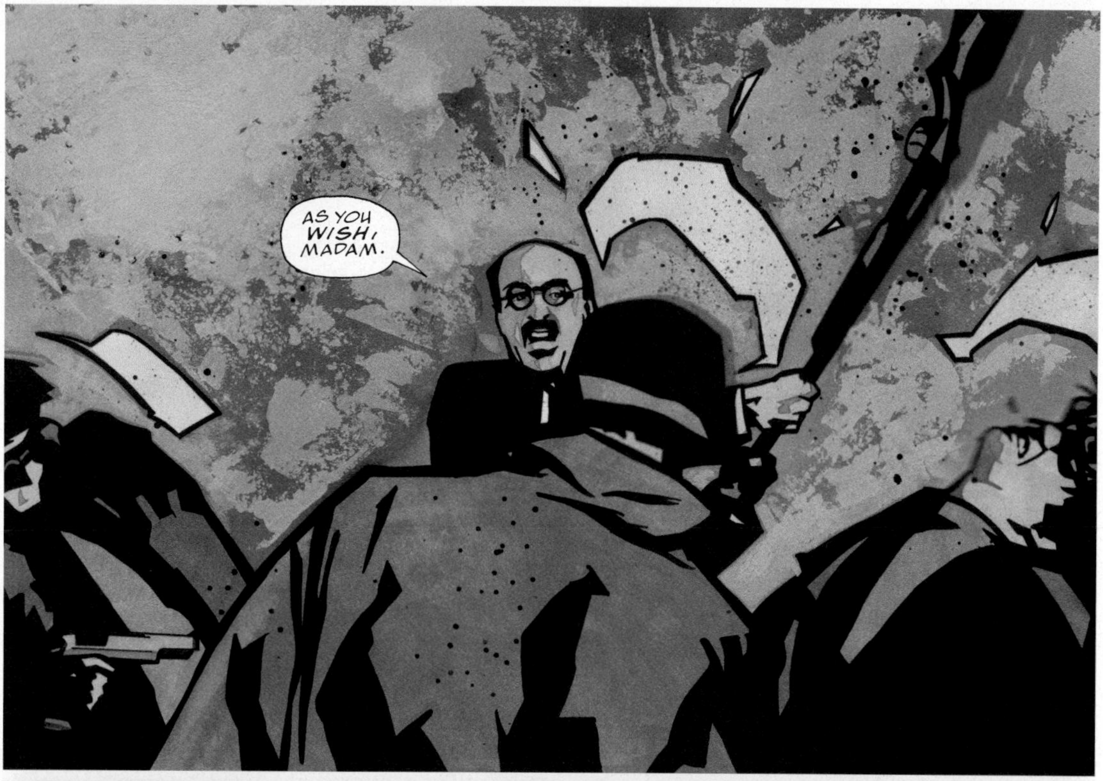
AS YOU WISH, MADAM.

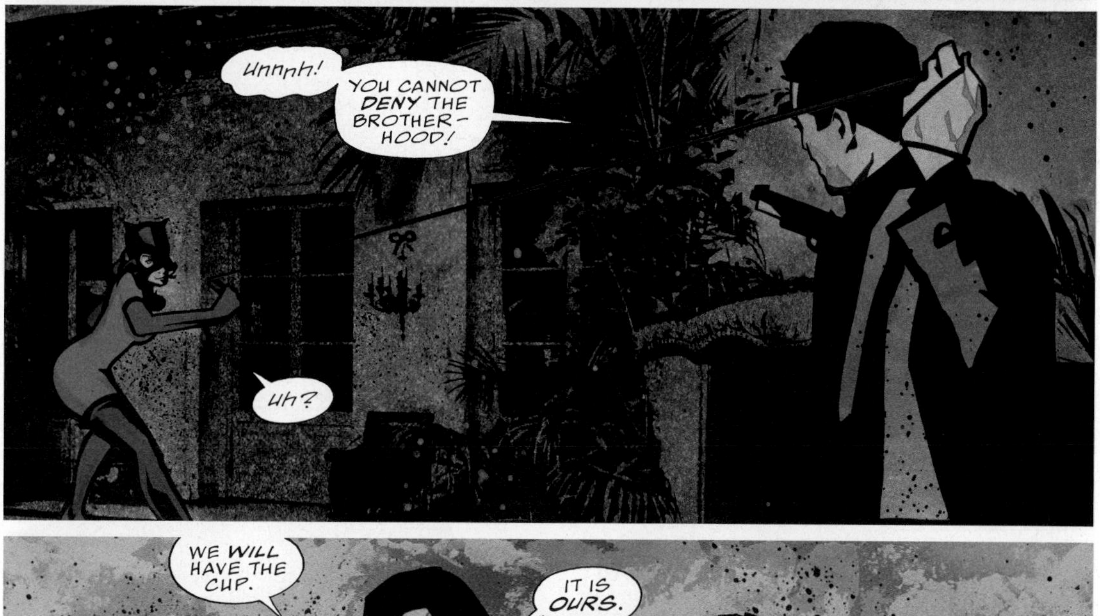
Unnnh!
YOU CANNOT DENY THE BROTHER-HOOD!
Uh?

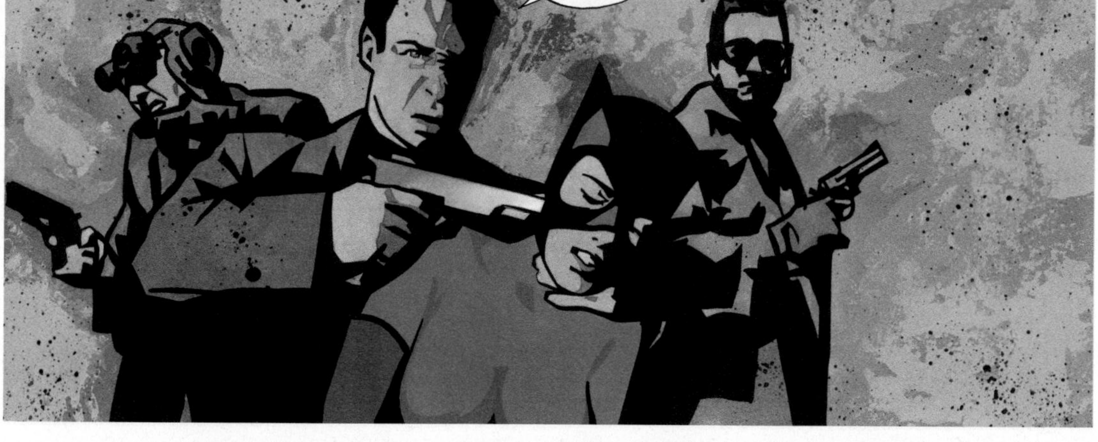
WE WILL HAVE THE CUP.
IT IS OURS.

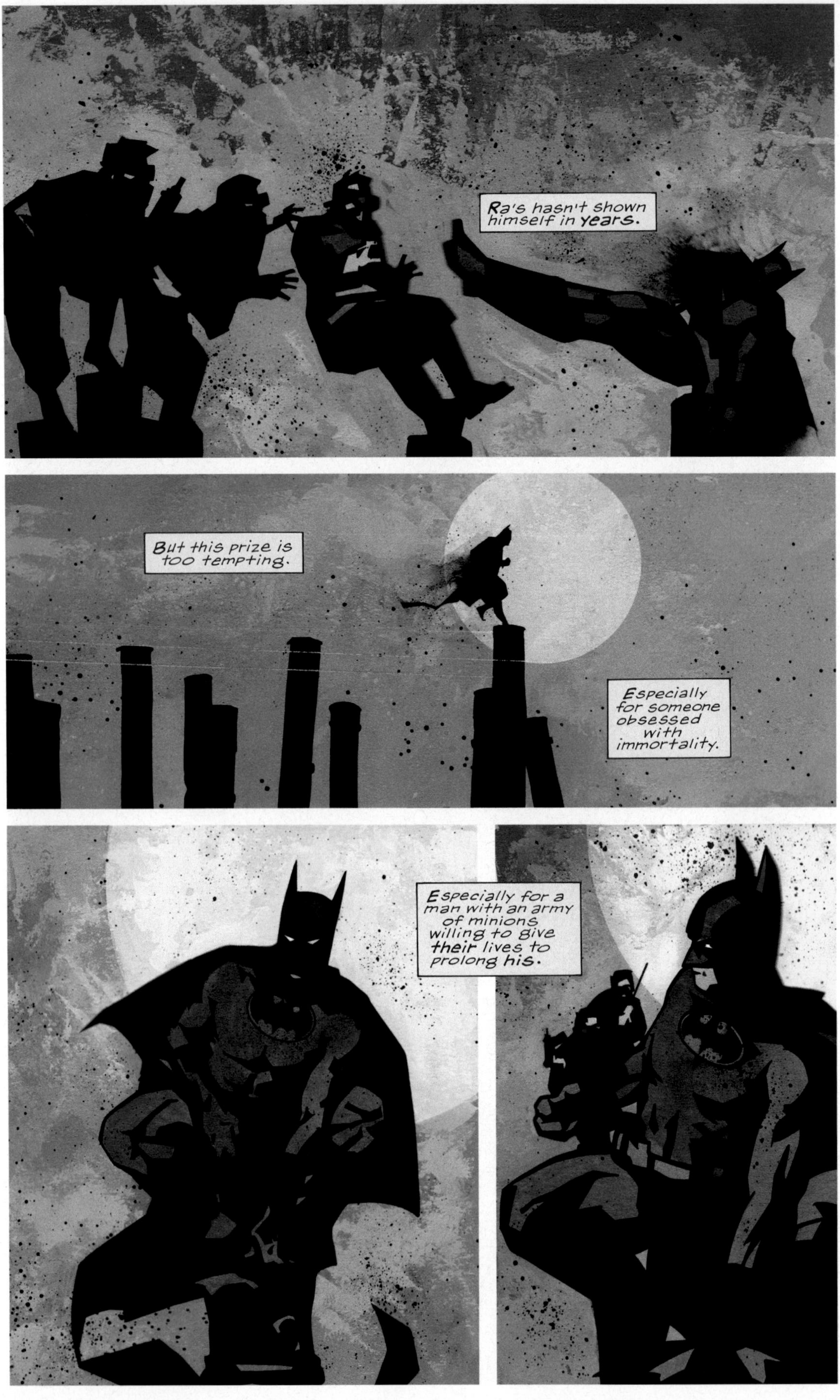
Ra's hasn't shown himself in years.
But this prize is too tempting.
Especially for someone obsessed with immortality.
Especially for a man with an army of minions willing to give their lives to prolong his.

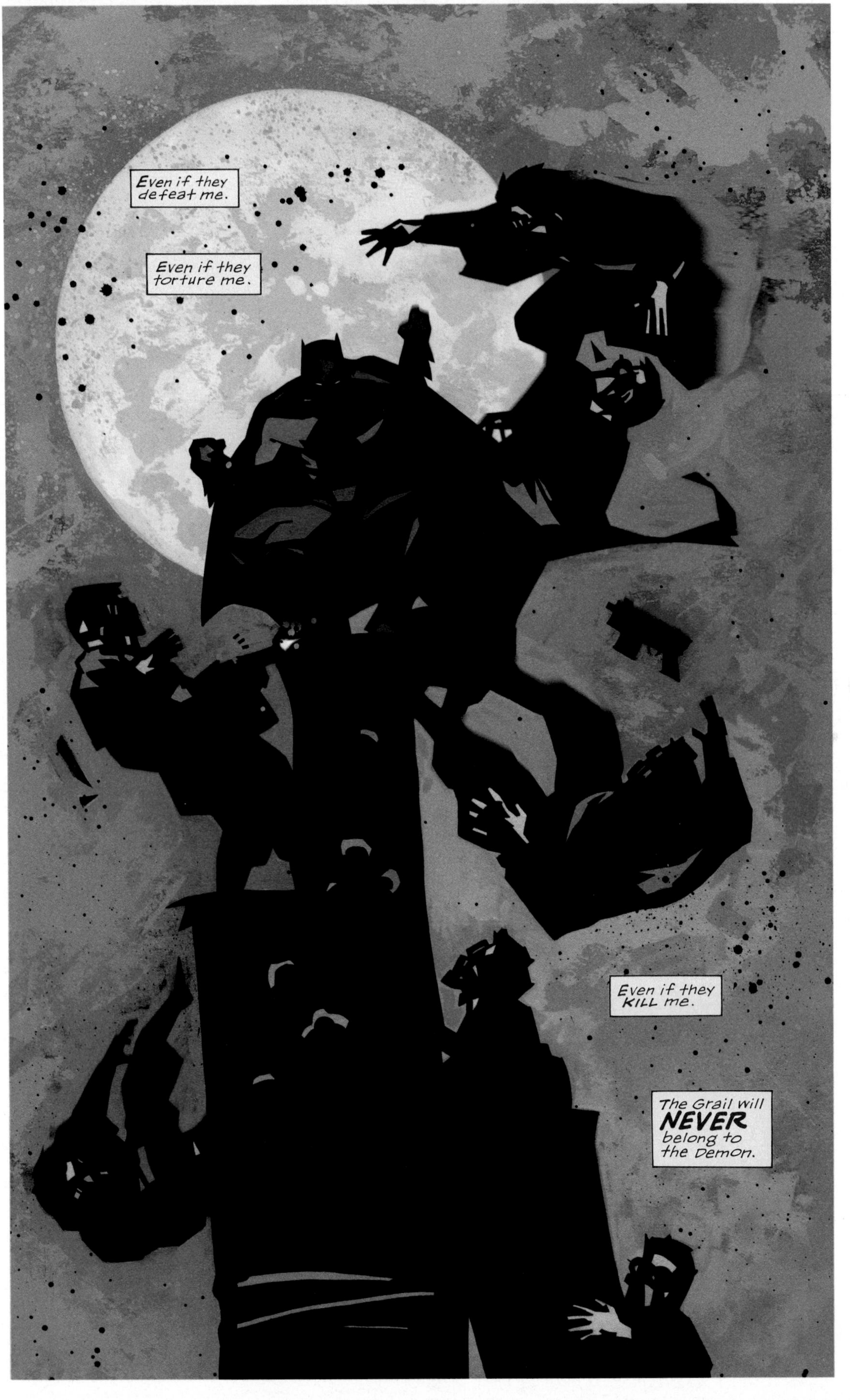
Even if they defeat me.
Even if they torture me.
Even if they KILL me.
The Grail will NEVER belong to the Demon.

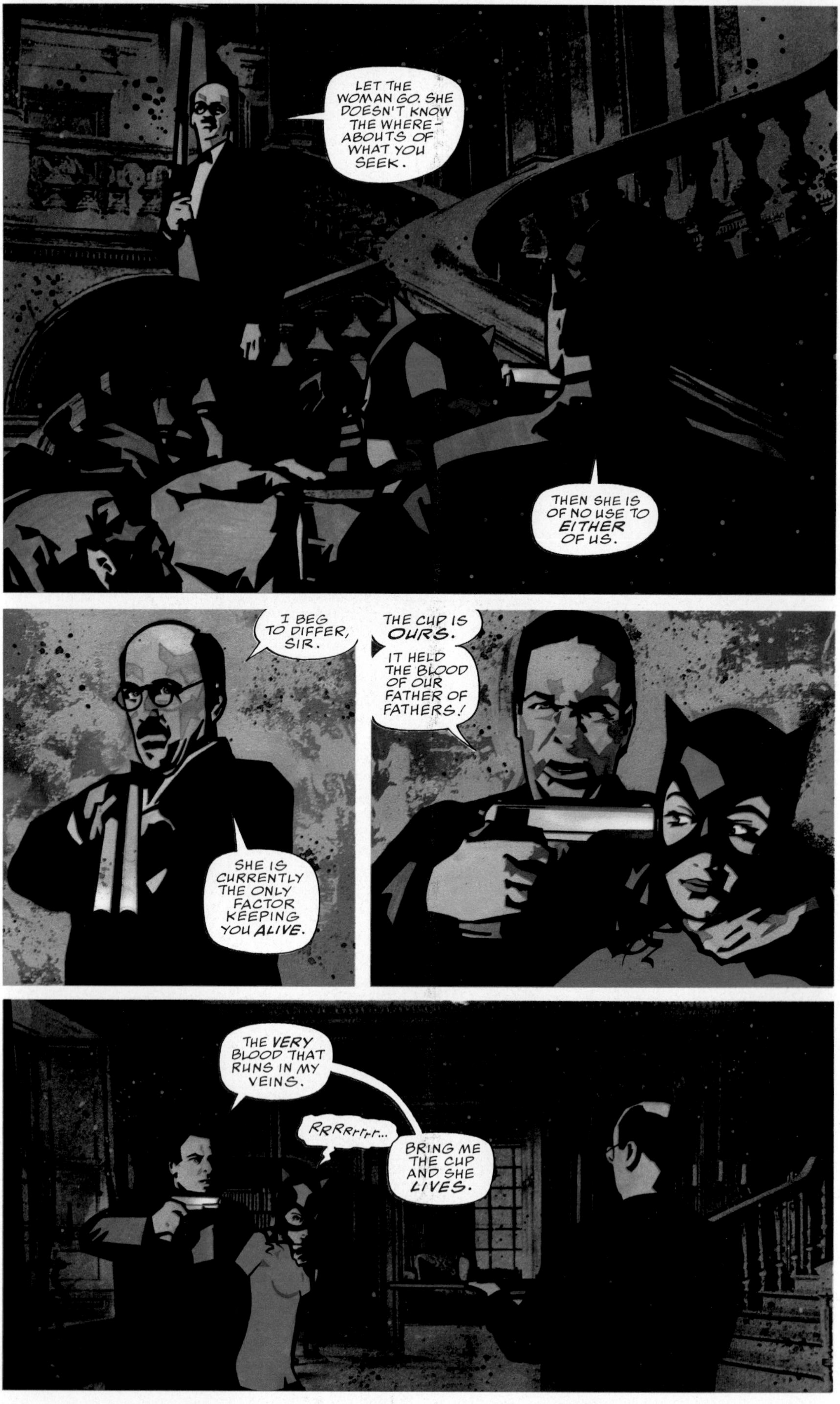
LET THE WOMAN GO. SHE DOESN'T KNOW THE WHERE-ABOUTS OF WHAT YOU SEEK.
THEN SHE IS OF NO USE TO EITHER OF US.
I BEG TO DIFFER, SIR.
SHE IS CURRENTLY THE ONLY FACTOR KEEPING YOU ALIVE.
THE CUP IS OURS.
IT HELD THE BLOOD OF OUR FATHER OF FATHERS!
THE VERY BLOOD THAT RUNS IN MY VEINS.
RRRRrrr-r...
BRING ME THE CUP AND SHE LIVES.

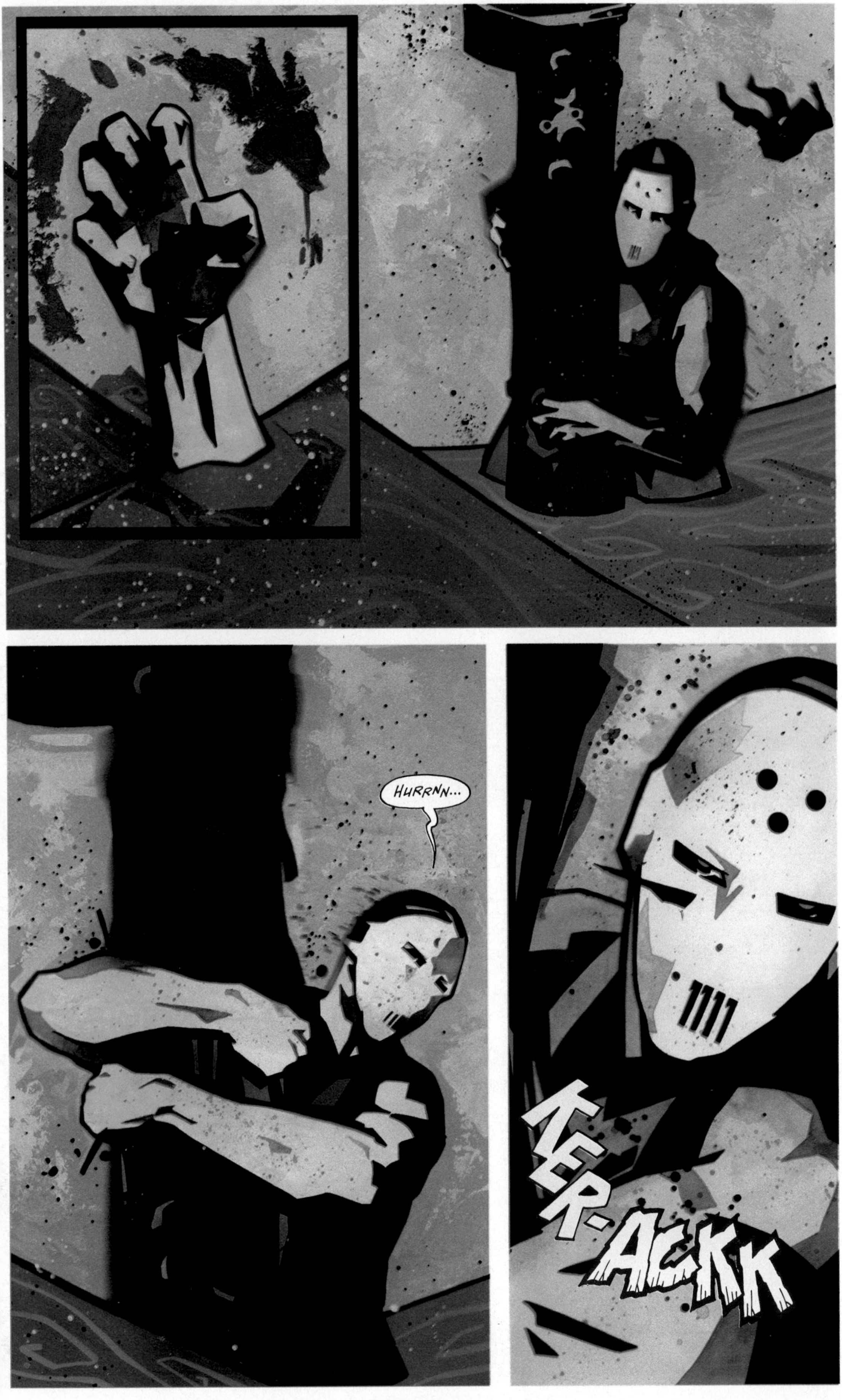
HURRNN...
KER-ACKK

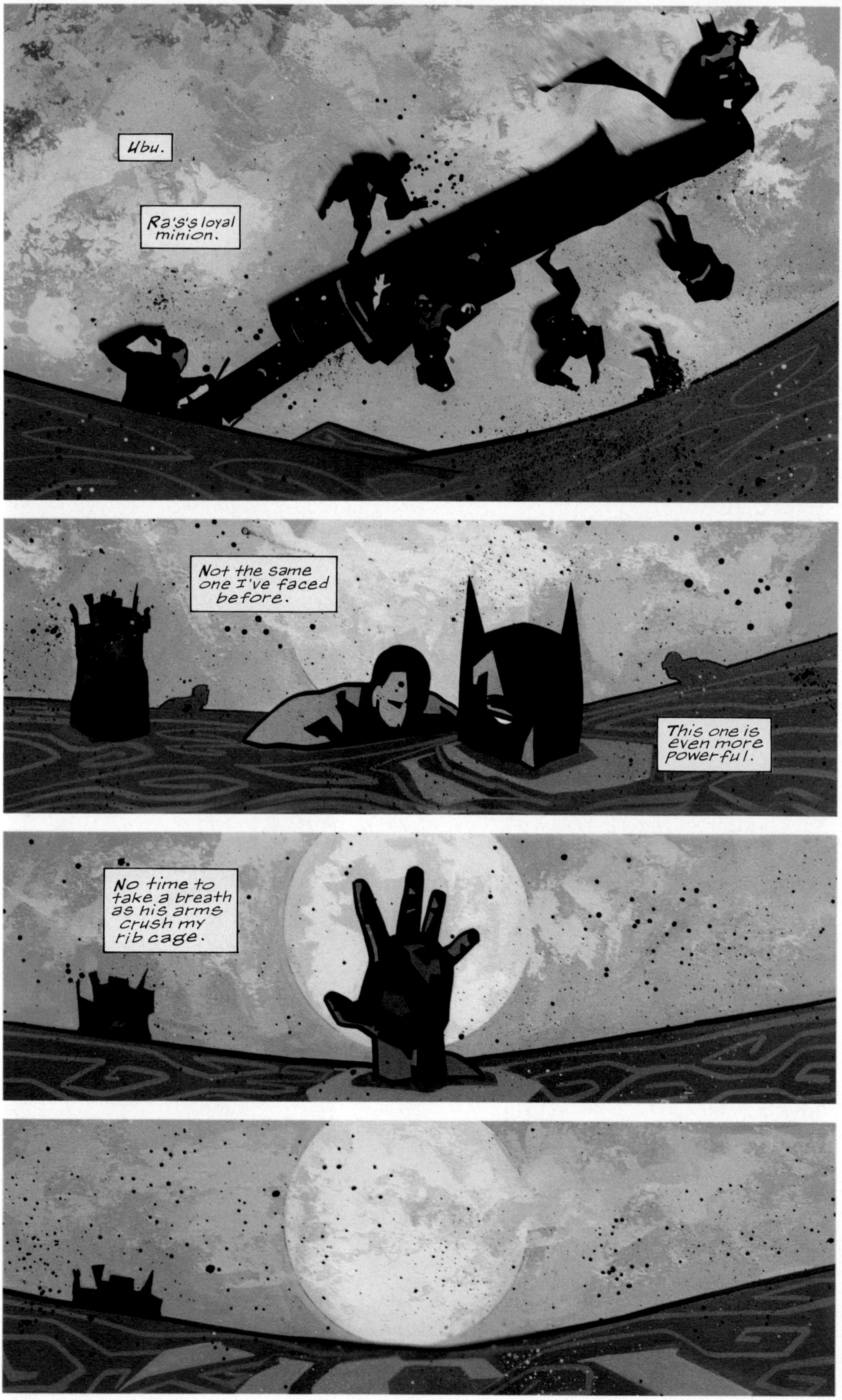
Ubu.
Ra's's loyal minion.
Not the same one I've faced before.
This one is even more powerful.
No time to take a breath as his arms crush my rib cage.

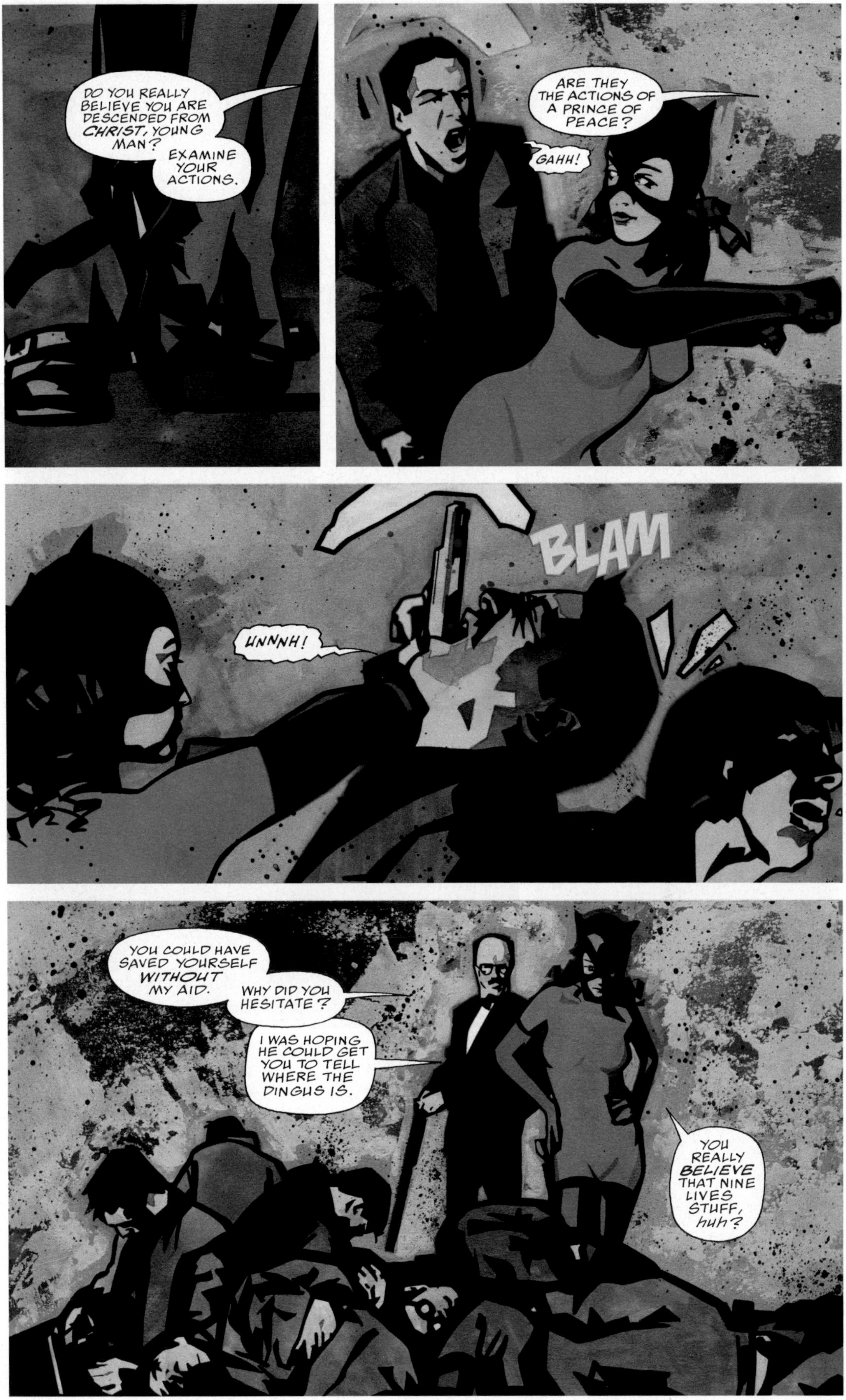
DO YOU REALLY BELIEVE YOU ARE DESCENDED FROM CHRIST, YOUNG MAN?
EXAMINE YOUR ACTIONS.
ARE THEY THE ACTIONS OF A PRINCE OF PEACE?
GAHH!
BLAM
UNNNH!
YOU COULD HAVE SAVED YOURSELF WITHOUT MY AID.
WHY DID YOU HESITATE?
I WAS HOPING HE COULD GET YOU TO TELL WHERE THE DINGUS IS.
YOU REALLY BELIEVE THAT NINE LIVES STUFF, huh?

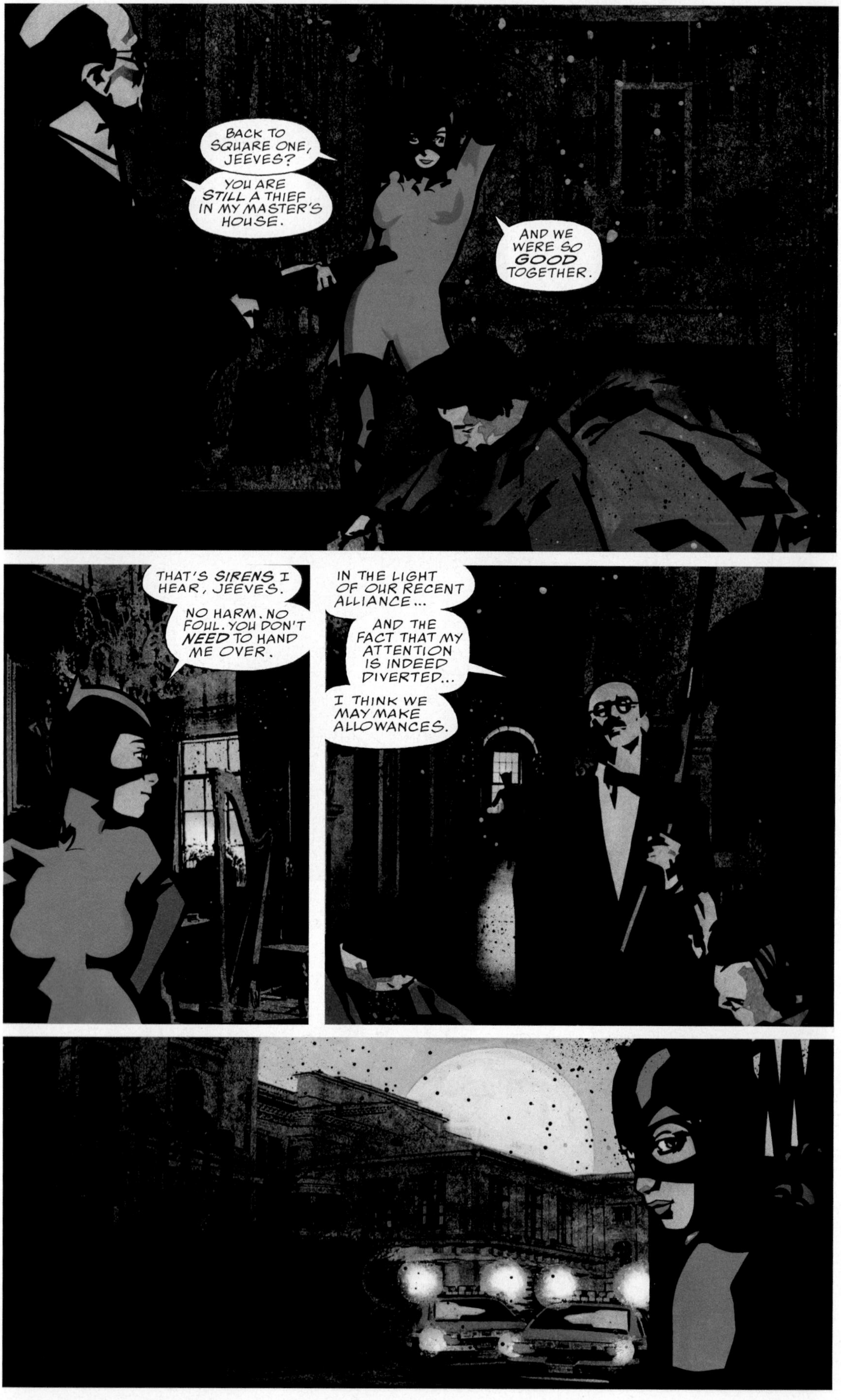
BACK TO SQUARE ONE, JEEVES?
YOU ARE STILL A THIEF IN MY MASTER'S HOUSE.
AND WE WERE SO GOOD TOGETHER.
THAT'S SIRENS I HEAR, JEEVES.
NO HARM. NO FOUL. YOU DON'T NEED TO HAND ME OVER.
IN THE LIGHT OF OUR RECENT ALLIANCE...
AND THE FACT THAT MY ATTENTION IS INDEED DIVERTED...
I THINK WE MAY MAKE ALLOWANCES.

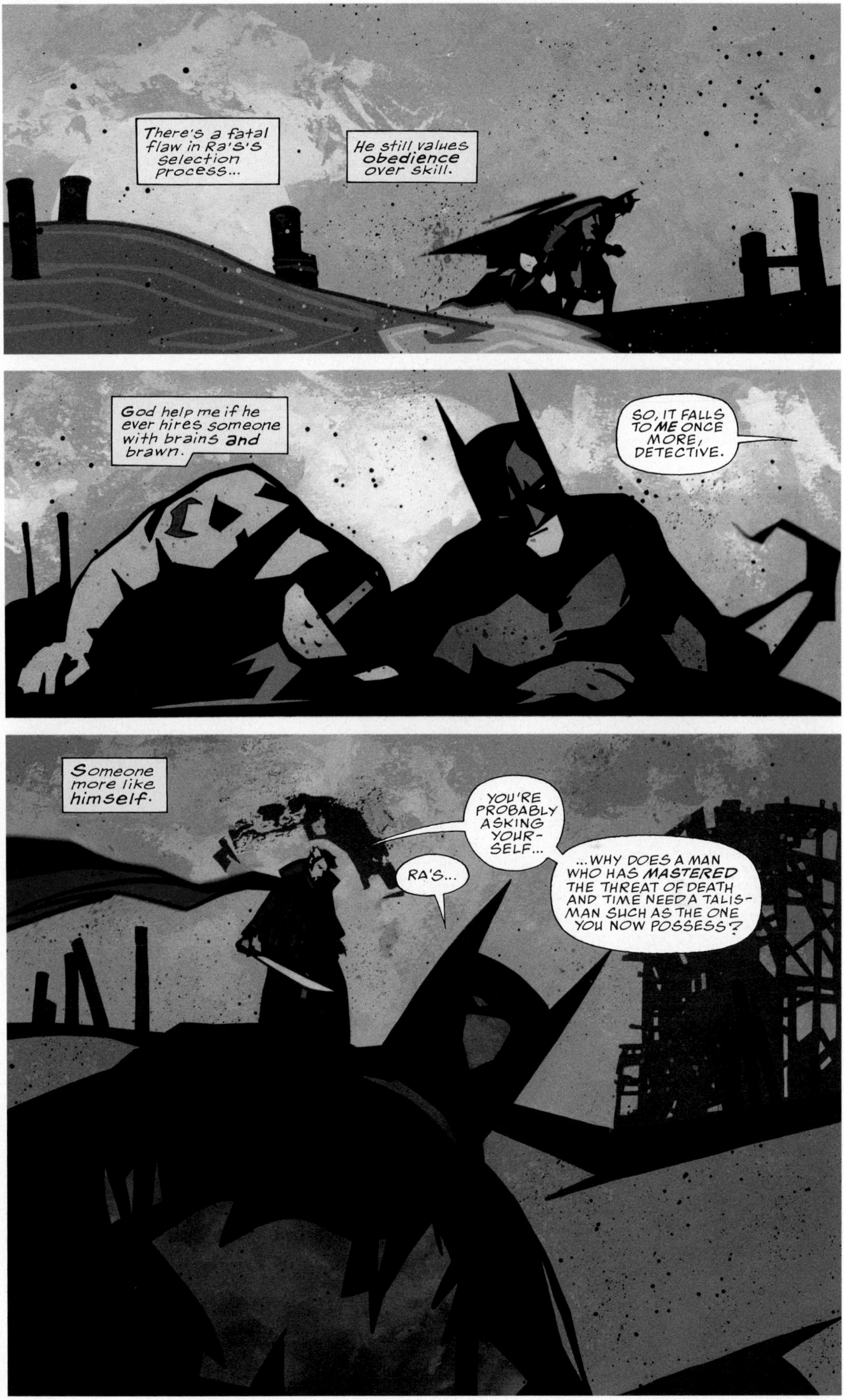
There's a fatal flaw in Ra's's selection process...
He still values obedience over skill.
God help me if he ever hires someone with brains and brawn.
SO, IT FALLS TO ME ONCE MORE, DETECTIVE.
Someone more like himself.
YOU'RE PROBABLY ASKING YOURSELF...
RA'S...
...WHY DOES A MAN WHO HAS MASTERED THE THREAT OF DEATH AND TIME NEED A TALISMAN SUCH AS THE ONE YOU NOW POSSESS?

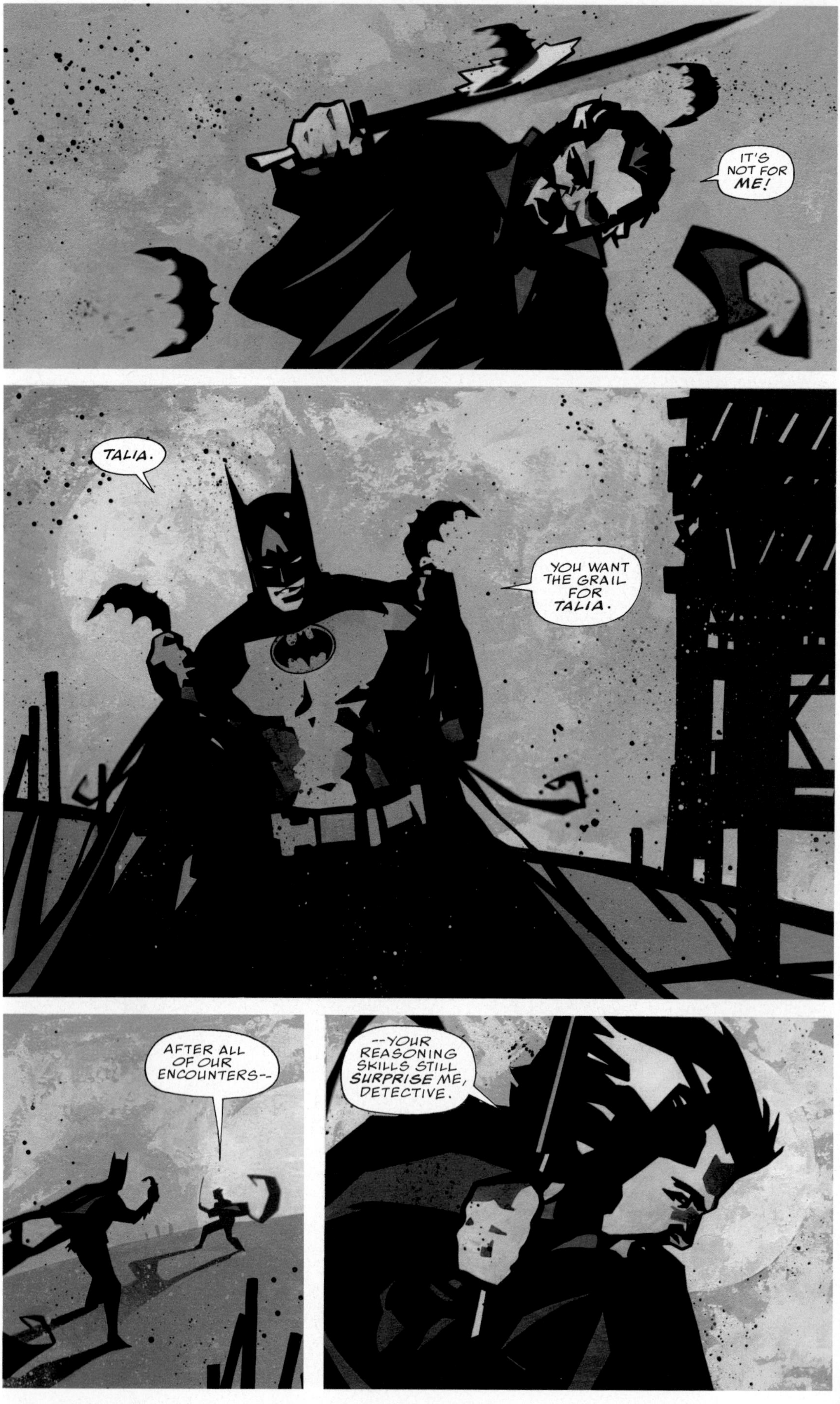
IT'S NOT FOR ME!
TALIA.
YOU WANT THE GRAIL FOR TALIA.
AFTER ALL OF OUR ENCOUNTERS--
--YOUR REASONING SKILLS STILL SURPRISE ME, DETECTIVE.

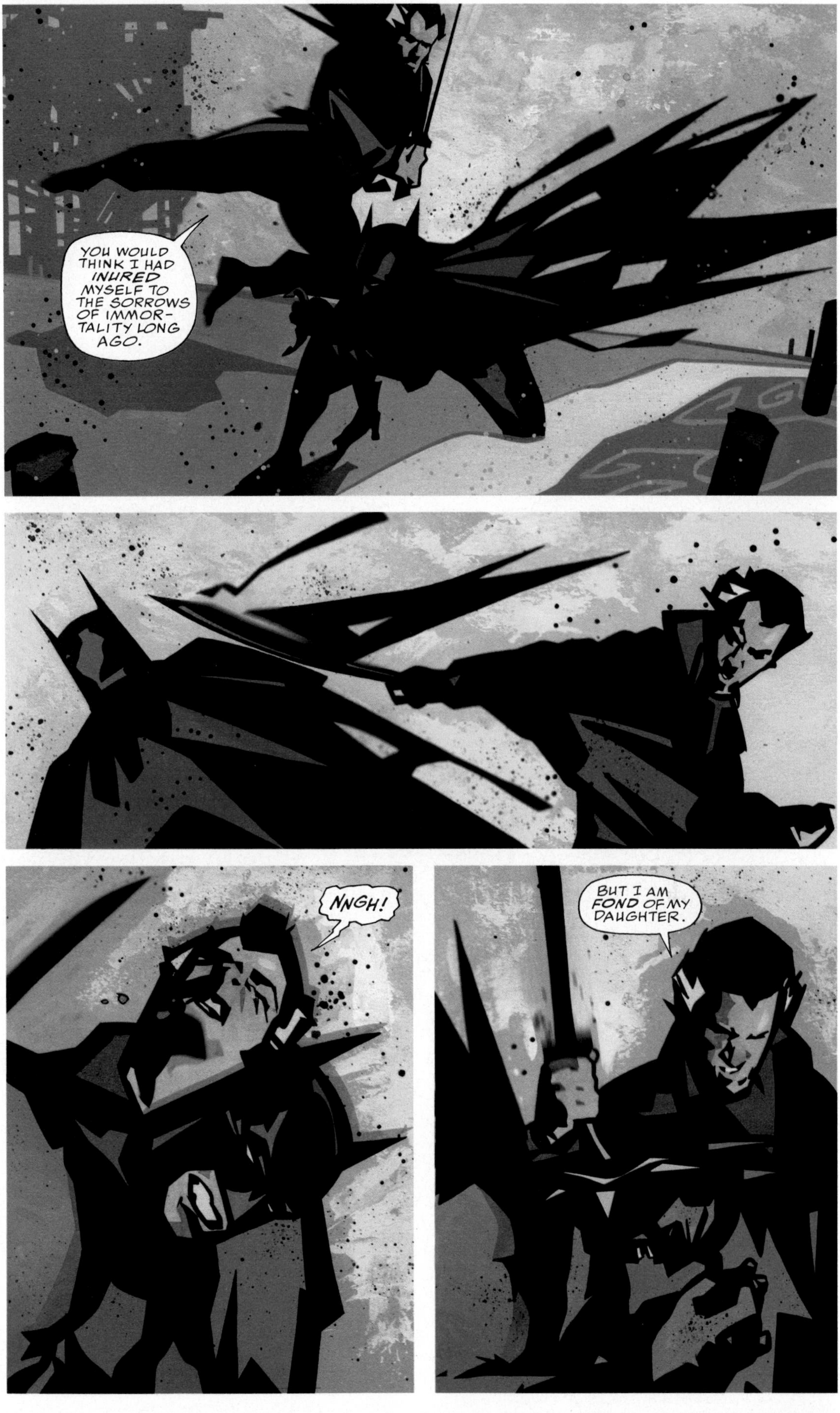
YOU WOULD THINK I HAD INURED MYSELF TO THE SORROWS OF IMMOR-TALITY LONG AGO.
NNGH!
BUT I AM FOND OF MY DAUGHTER.

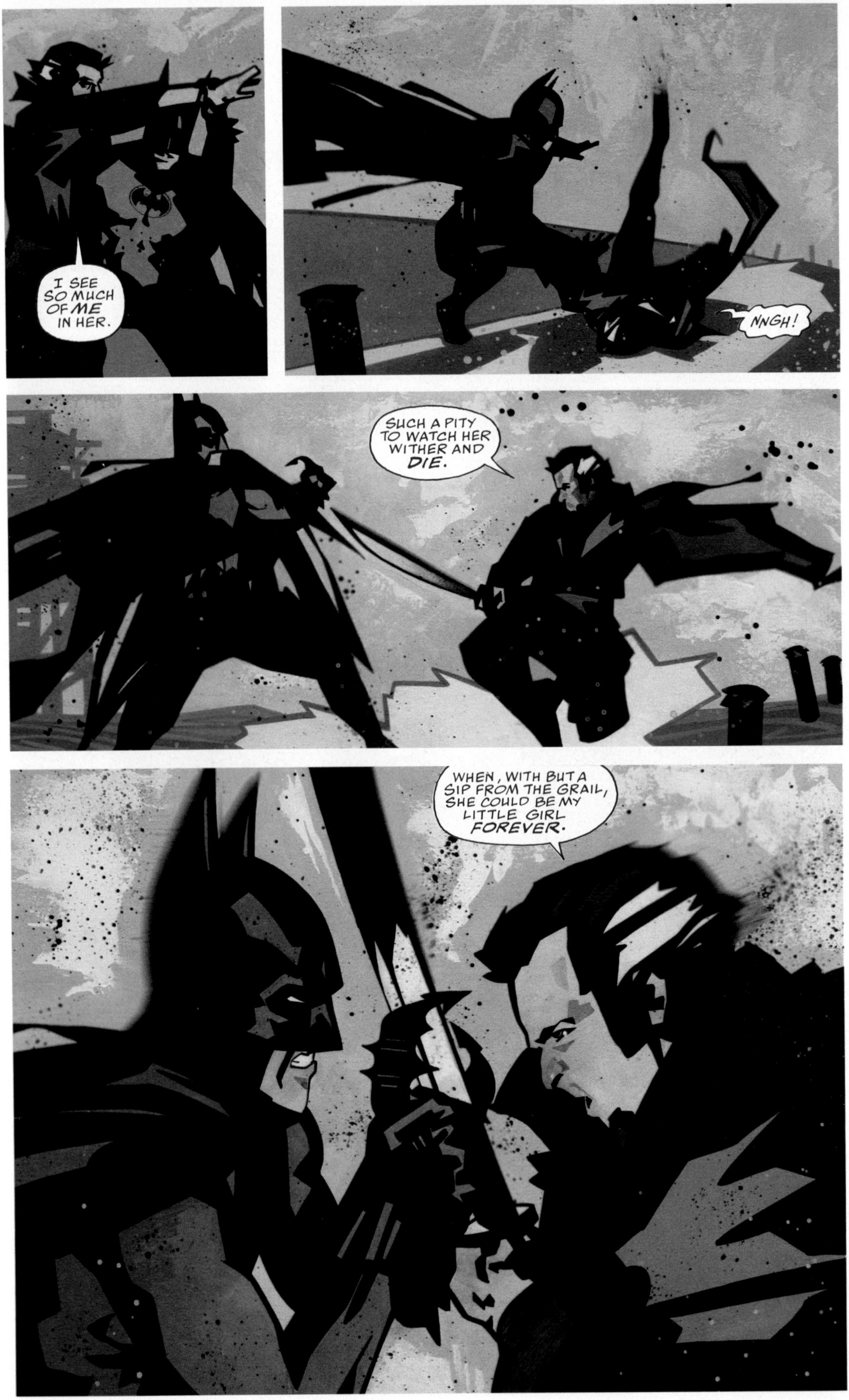
I SEE SO MUCH OF ME IN HER.
NNGH!
SUCH A PITY TO WATCH HER WITHER AND DIE.
WHEN, WITH BUT A SIP FROM THE GRAIL, SHE COULD BE MY LITTLE GIRL FOREVER.

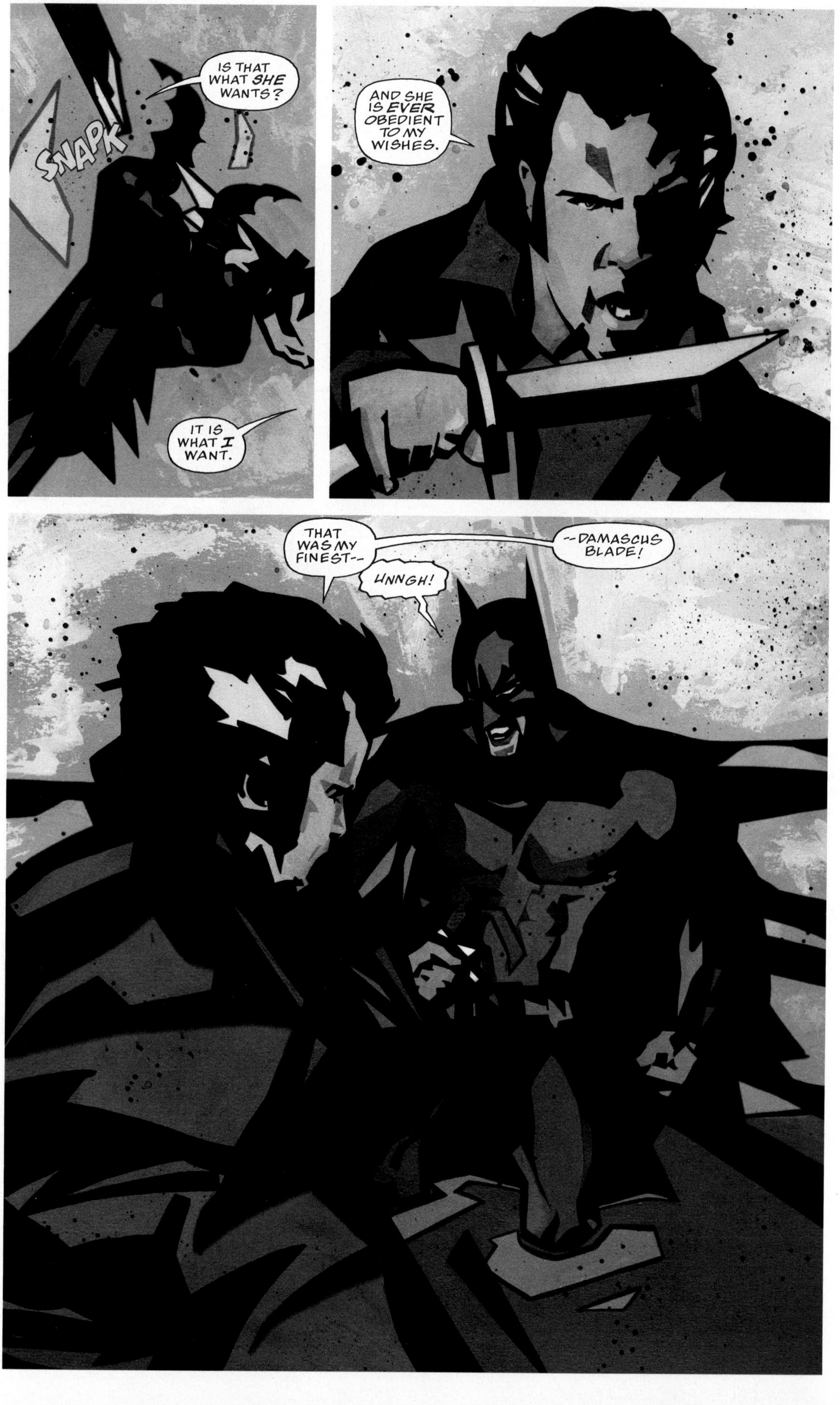

IS THAT WHAT SHE WANTS?
SNAPK
IT IS WHAT I WANT.
AND SHE IS EVER OBEDIENT TO MY WISHES.
THAT WAS MY FINEST--
UNNGH!
--DAMASCUS BLADE!

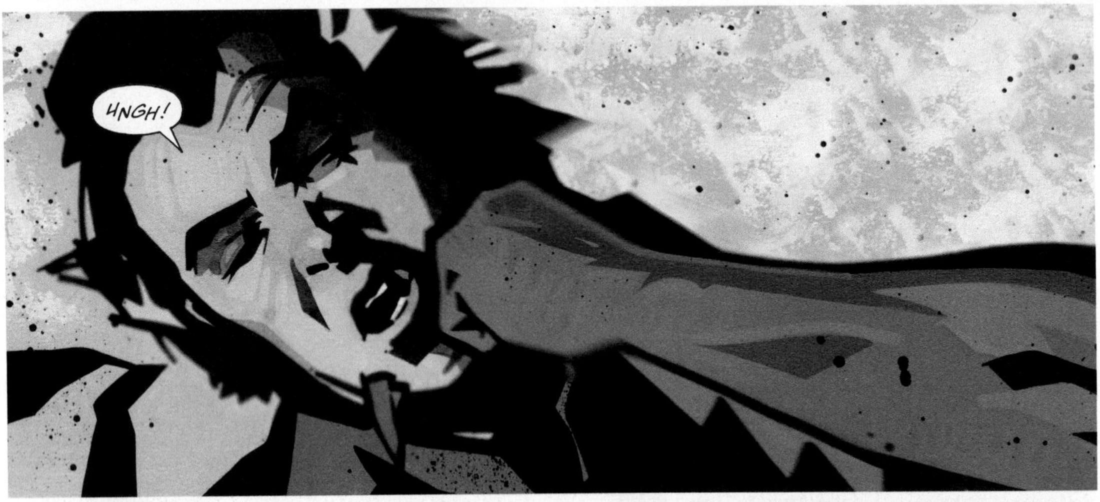
UNGH!

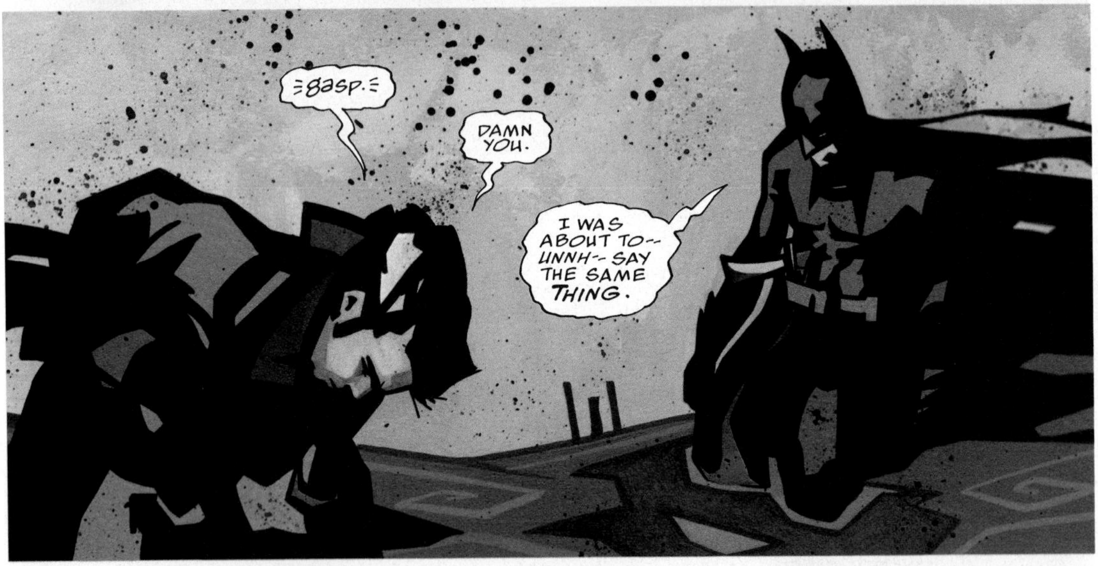
gasp.
DAMN YOU.
I WAS ABOUT TO-- UNNH-- SAY THE SAME THING.

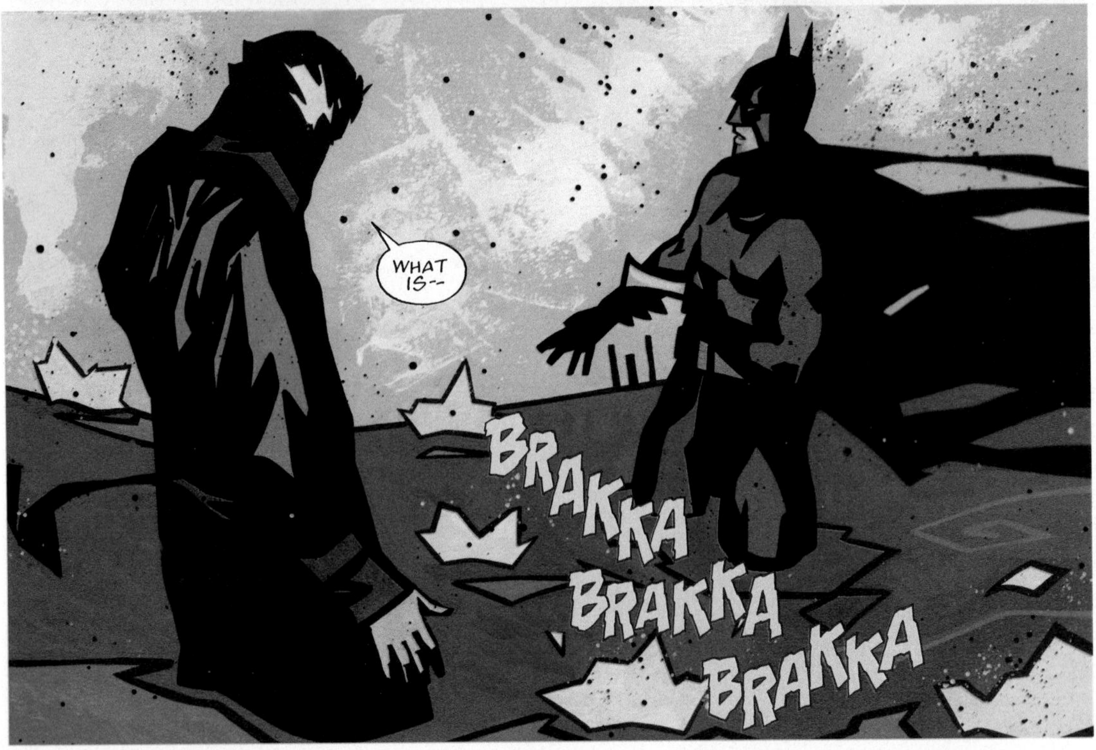
WHAT IS--
BRAKKA
BRAKKA
BRAKKA

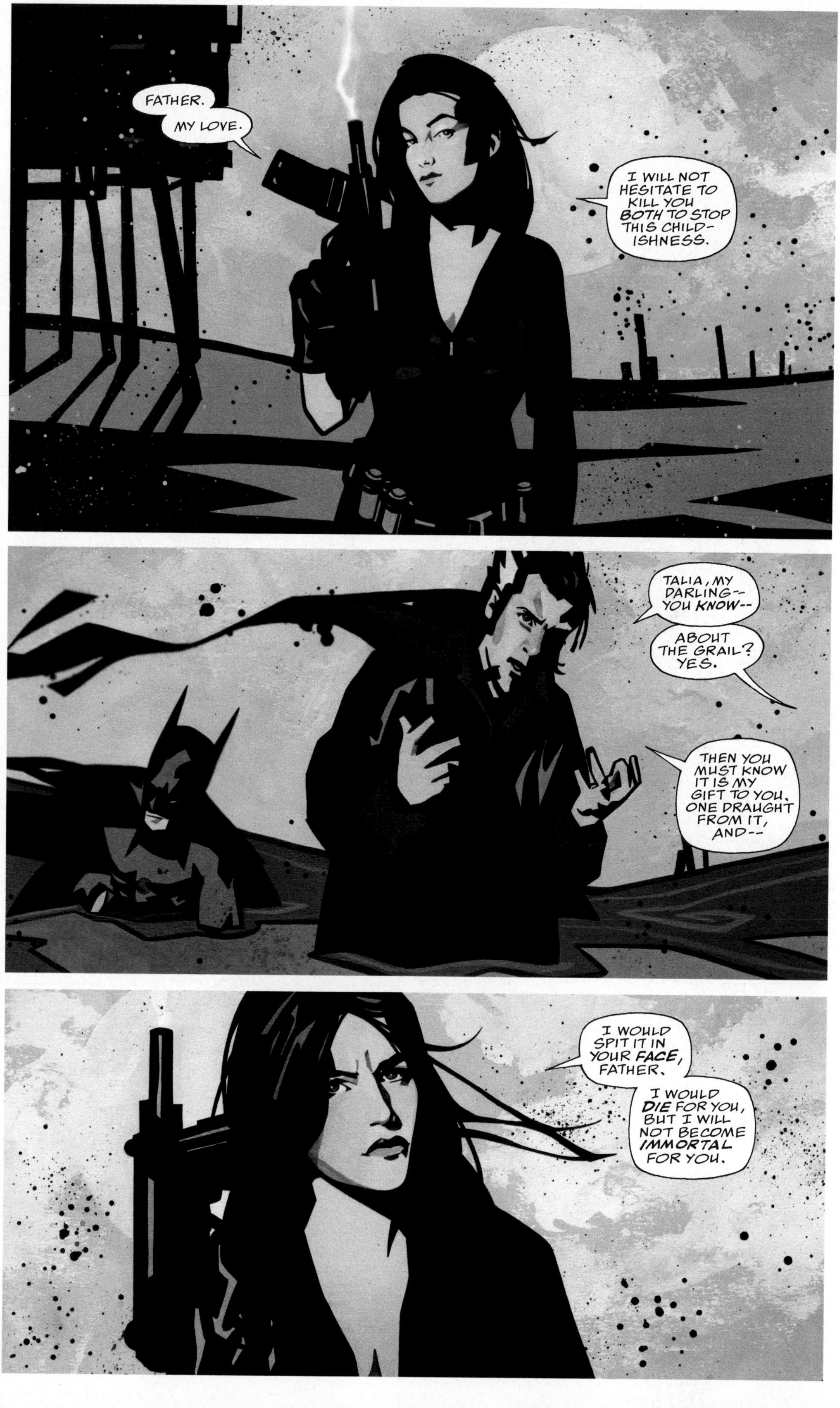
FATHER.
MY LOVE.
I WILL NOT HESITATE TO KILL YOU BOTH TO STOP THIS CHILD-ISHNESS.
TALIA, MY DARLING-- YOU KNOW--
ABOUT THE GRAIL? YES.
THEN YOU MUST KNOW IT IS MY GIFT TO YOU. ONE DRAUGHT FROM IT, AND--
I WOULD SPIT IT IN YOUR FACE, FATHER.
I WOULD DIE FOR YOU, BUT I WILL NOT BECOME IMMORTAL FOR YOU.

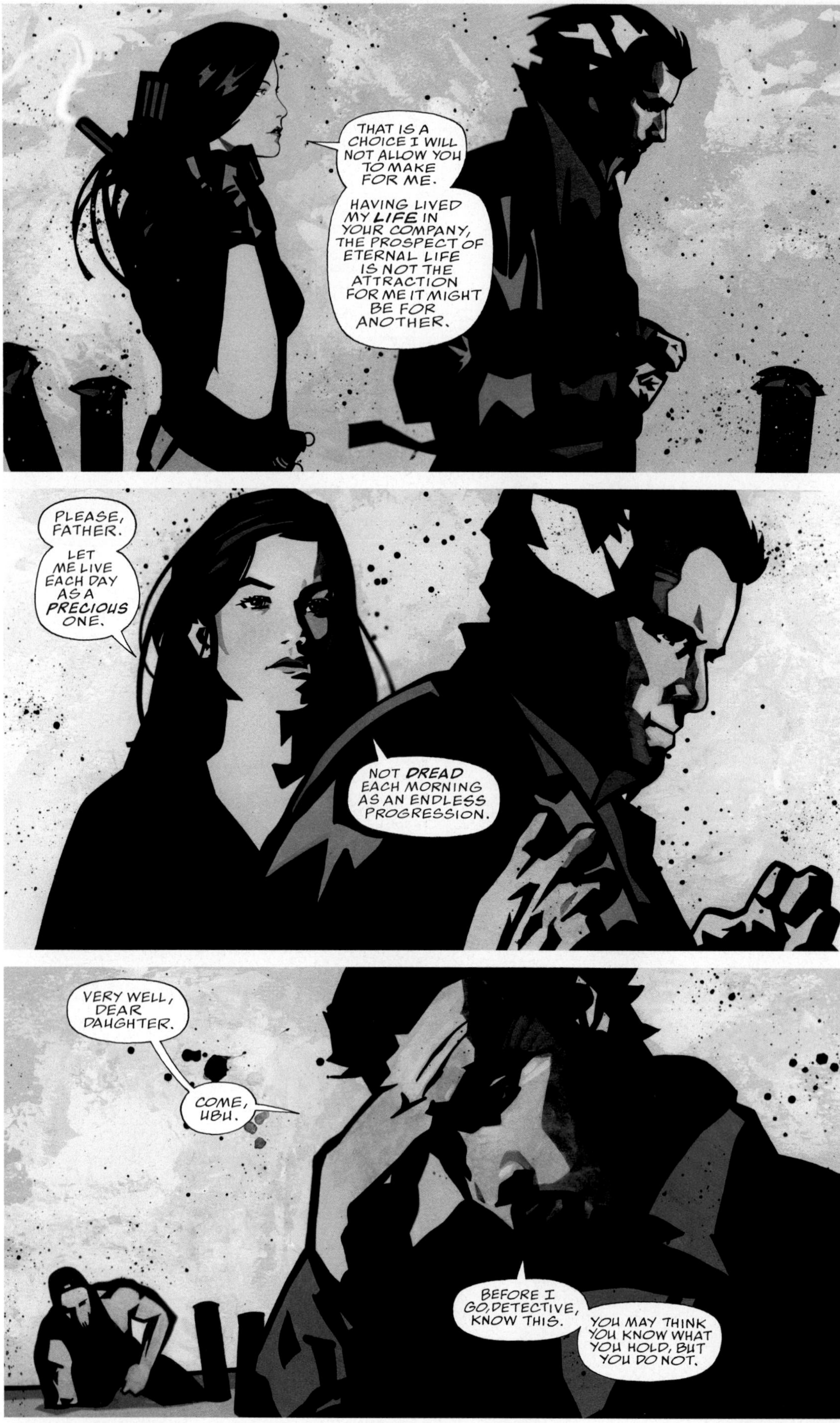

THAT IS A CHOICE I WILL NOT ALLOW YOU TO MAKE FOR ME.
HAVING LIVED MY LIFE IN YOUR COMPANY, THE PROSPECT OF ETERNAL LIFE IS NOT THE ATTRACTION FOR ME IT MIGHT BE FOR ANOTHER.
PLEASE, FATHER.
LET ME LIVE EACH DAY AS A PRECIOUS ONE.
NOT DREAD EACH MORNING AS AN ENDLESS PROGRESSION.
VERY WELL, DEAR DAUGHTER.
COME, UBU.
BEFORE I GO, DETECTIVE, KNOW THIS.
YOU MAY THINK YOU KNOW WHAT YOU HOLD, BUT YOU DO NOT.

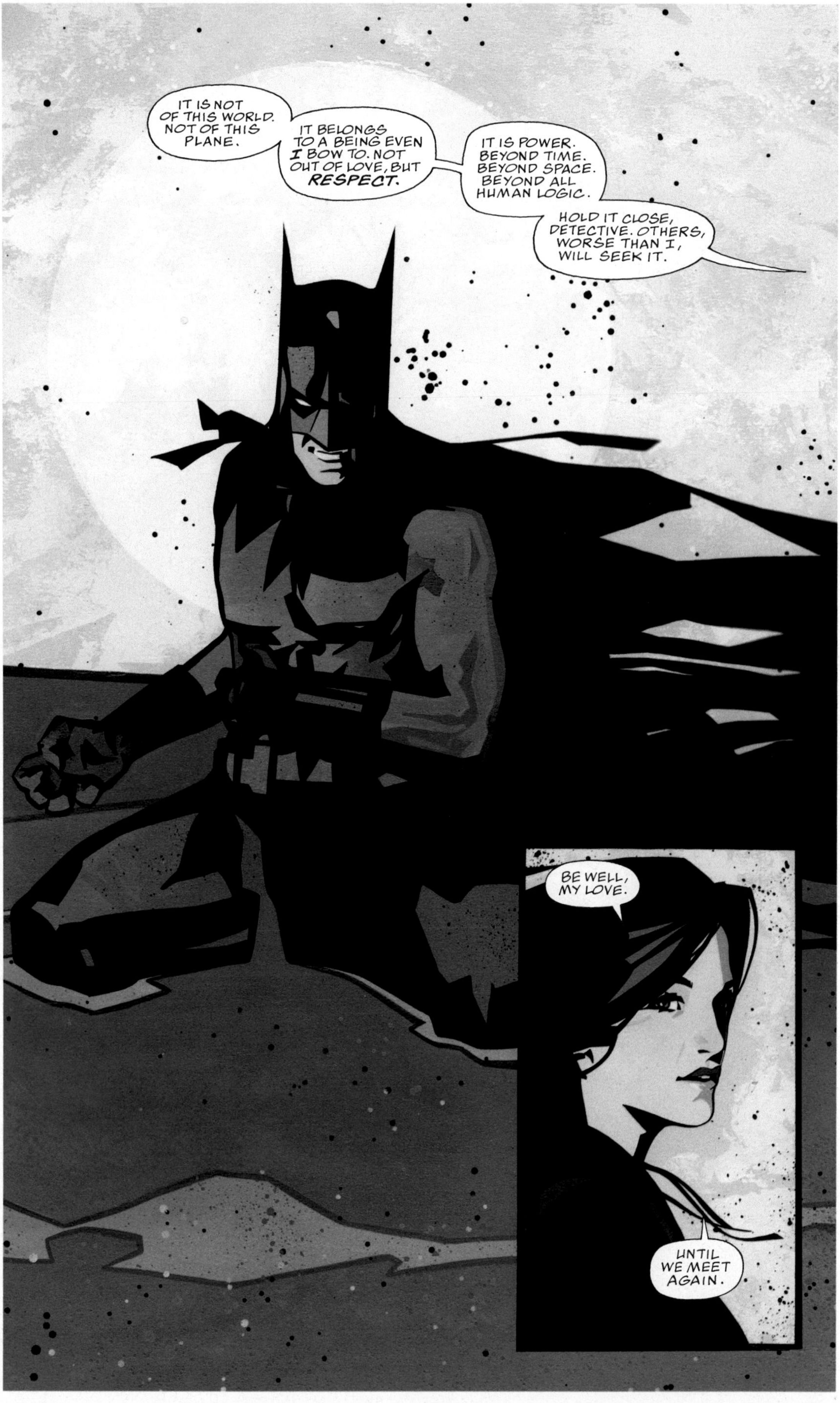
IT IS NOT OF THIS WORLD. NOT OF THIS PLANE.
IT BELONGS TO A BEING EVEN I BOW TO. NOT OUT OF LOVE, BUT RESPECT.
IT IS POWER. BEYOND TIME. BEYOND SPACE. BEYOND ALL HUMAN LOGIC.
HOLD IT CLOSE, DETECTIVE. OTHERS, WORSE THAN I, WILL SEEK IT.
BE WELL, MY LOVE.
UNTIL WE MEET AGAIN.

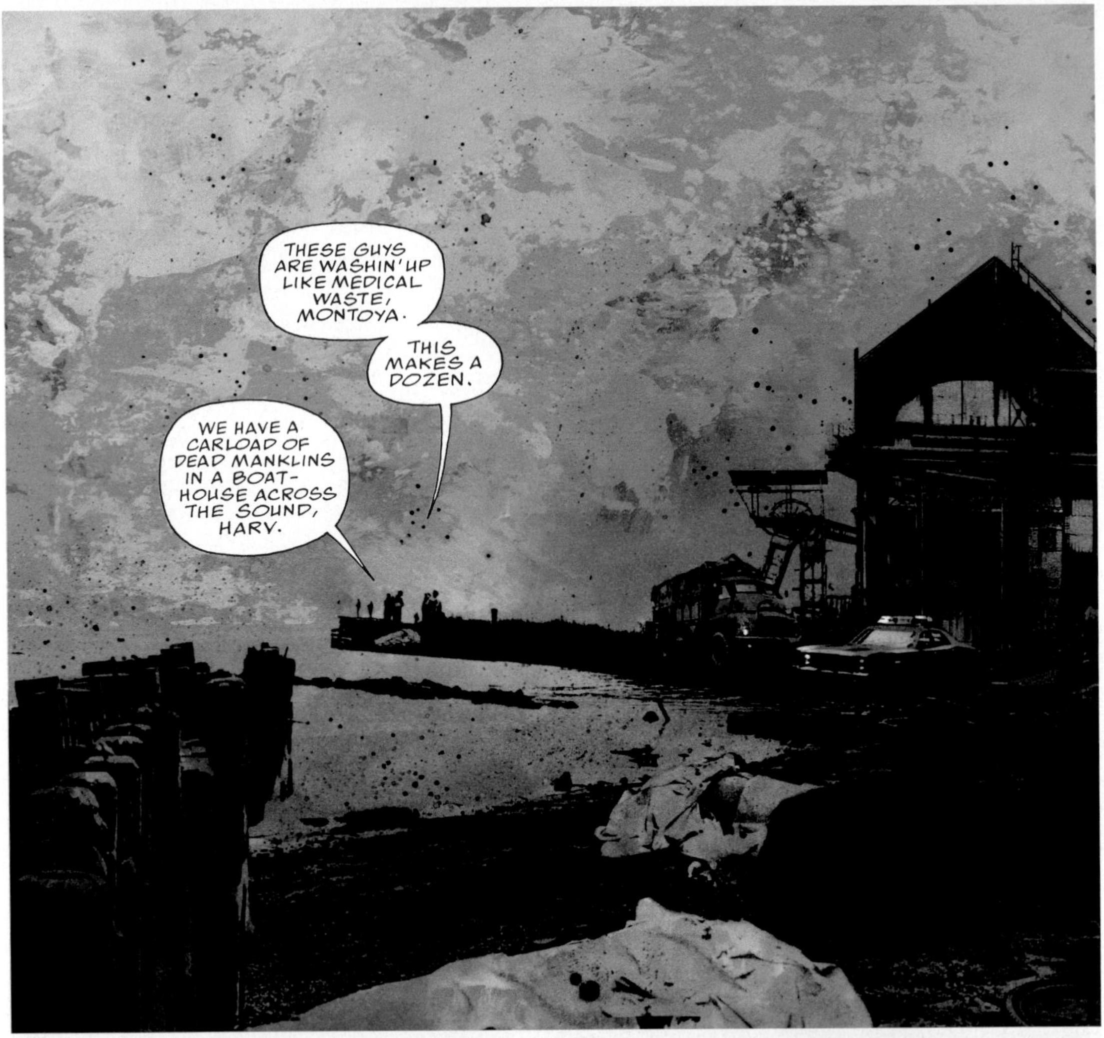
THESE GUYS ARE WASHIN' UP LIKE MEDICAL WASTE, MONTOYA.
THIS MAKES A DOZEN.
WE HAVE A CARLOAD OF DEAD MANKLINS IN A BOAT-HOUSE ACROSS THE SOUND, HARV.

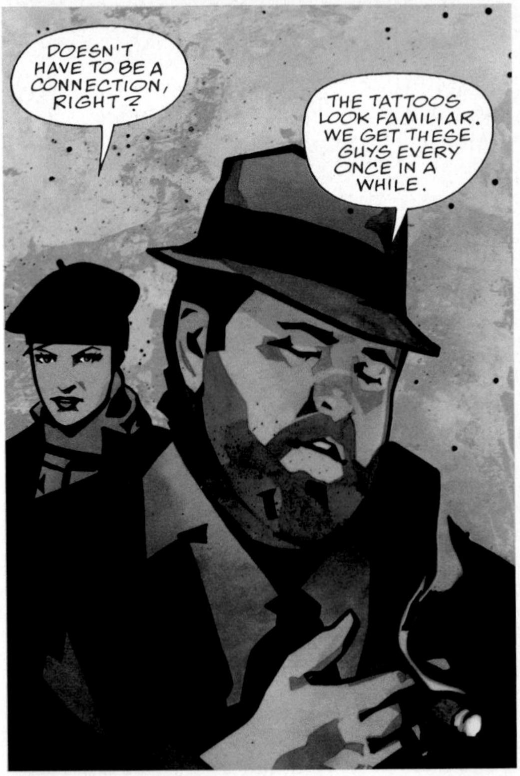
DOESN'T HAVE TO BE A CONNECTION, RIGHT?
THE TATTOOS LOOK FAMILIAR. WE GET THESE GUYS EVERY ONCE IN A WHILE.

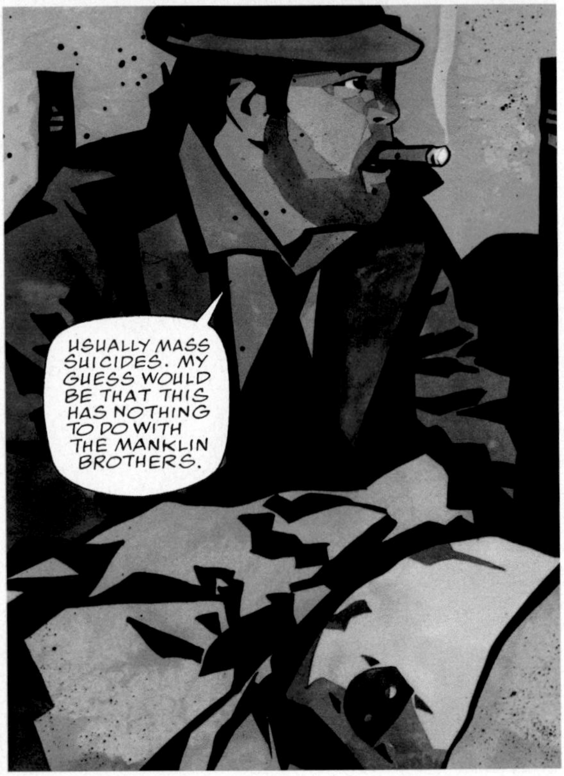
USUALLY MASS SUICIDES. MY GUESS WOULD BE THAT THIS HAS NOTHING TO DO WITH THE MANKLIN BROTHERS.

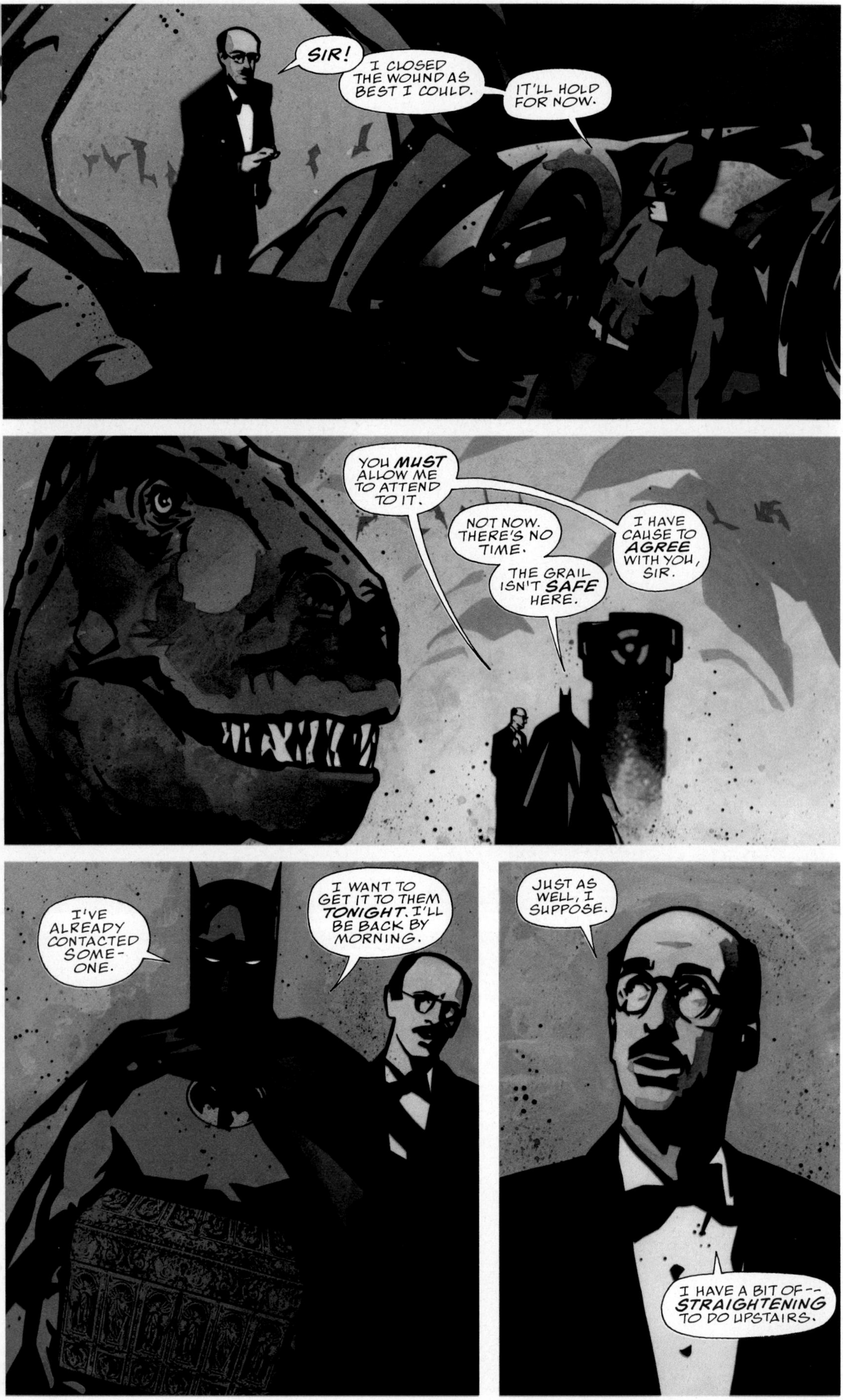
SIR!
I CLOSED THE WOUND AS BEST I COULD.
IT'LL HOLD FOR NOW.
YOU MUST ALLOW ME TO ATTEND TO IT.
NOT NOW. THERE'S NO TIME.
THE GRAIL ISN'T SAFE HERE.
I HAVE CAUSE TO AGREE WITH YOU, SIR.
I'VE ALREADY CONTACTED SOME-ONE.
I WANT TO GET IT TO THEM TONIGHT. I'LL BE BACK BY MORNING.
JUST AS WELL, I SUPPOSE.
I HAVE A BIT OF--STRAIGHTENING TO DO UPSTAIRS.

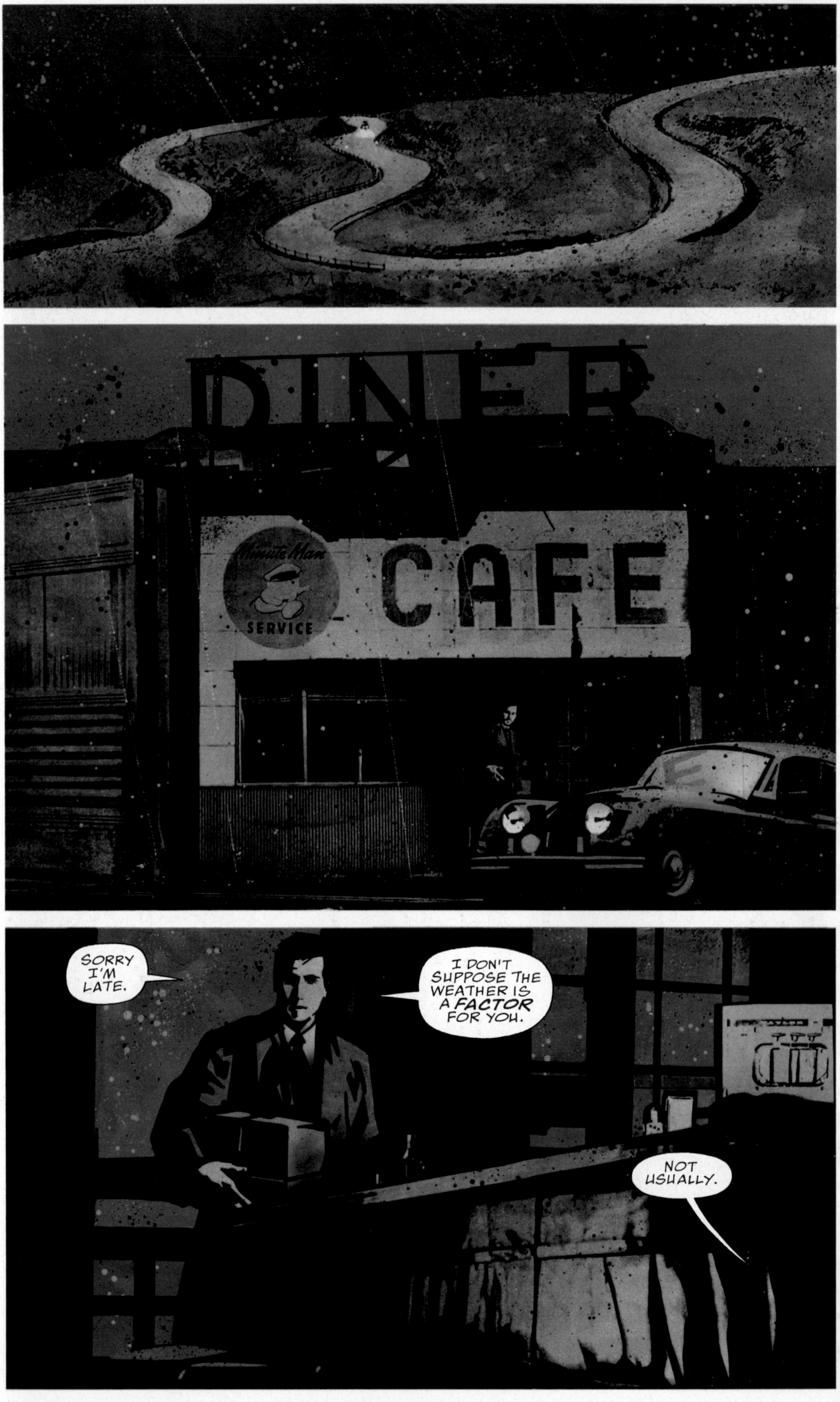
DINER
Minute Man
SERVICE
CAFE
SORRY I'M LATE.
I DON'T SUPPOSE THE WEATHER IS A *FACTOR* FOR YOU.
NOT USUALLY.

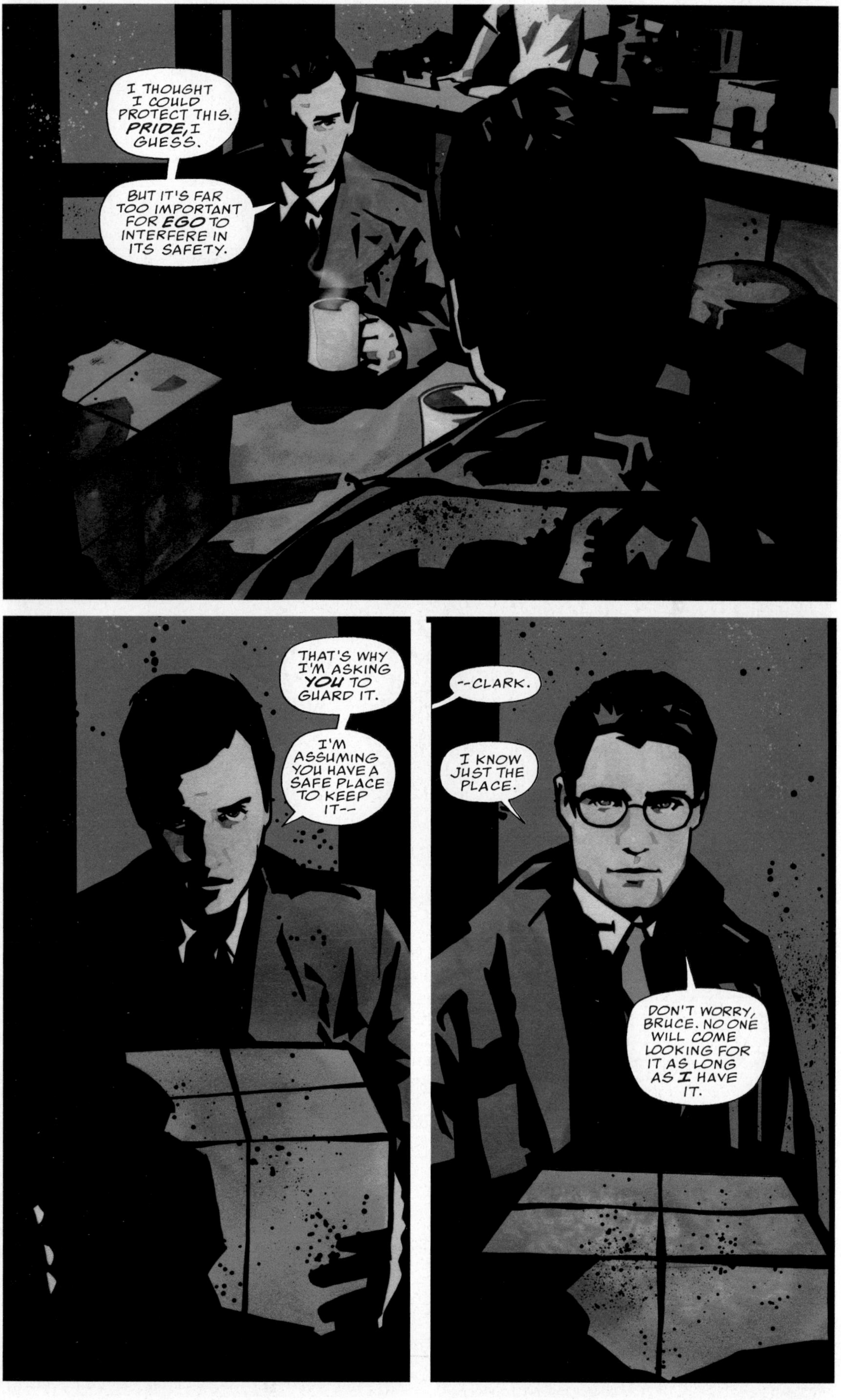
I THOUGHT I COULD PROTECT THIS. PRIDE, I GUESS.
BUT IT'S FAR TOO IMPORTANT FOR EGO TO INTERFERE IN ITS SAFETY.
THAT'S WHY I'M ASKING YOU TO GUARD IT.
I'M ASSUMING YOU HAVE A SAFE PLACE TO KEEP IT--
--CLARK.
I KNOW JUST THE PLACE.
DON'T WORRY, BRUCE. NO ONE WILL COME LOOKING FOR IT AS LONG AS I HAVE IT.

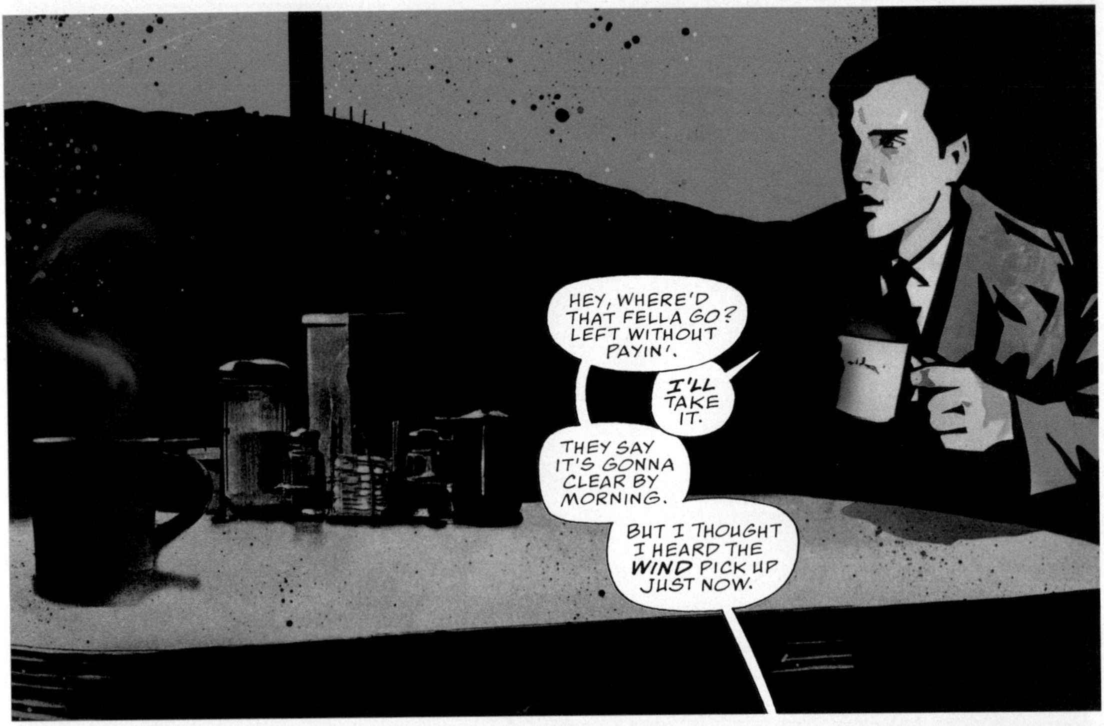
HEY, WHERE'D THAT FELLA GO? LEFT WITHOUT PAYIN'.
I'LL TAKE IT.
THEY SAY IT'S GONNA CLEAR BY MORNING.
BUT I THOUGHT I HEARD THE WIND PICK UP JUST NOW.

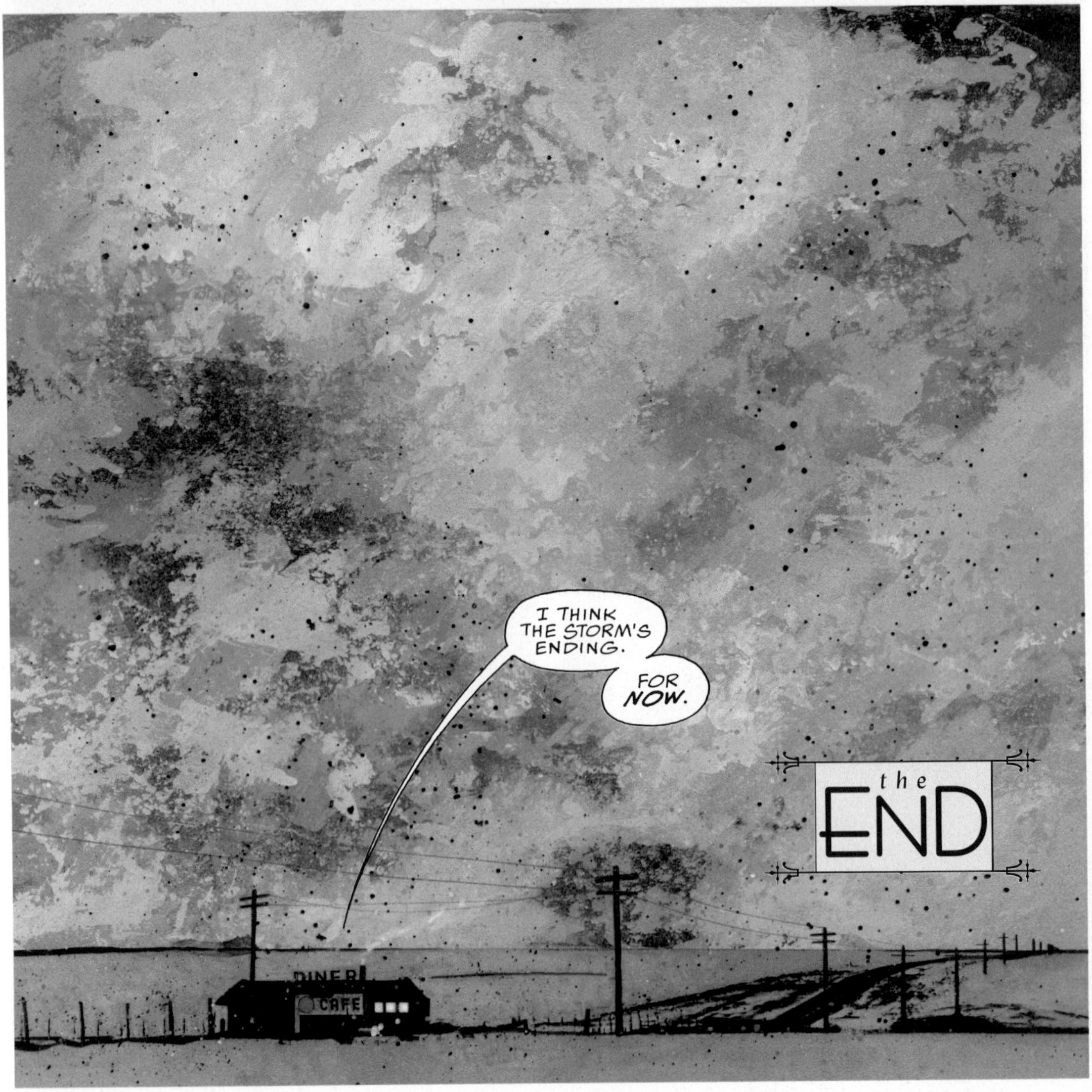
I THINK THE STORM'S ENDING.
FOR NOW.
the END
DINER
CAFE

PART II · THE ANKH

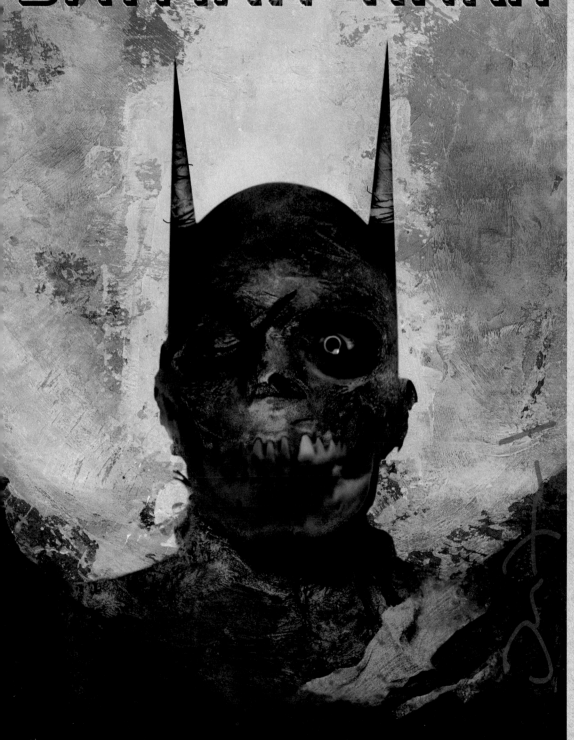

BATMAN THE ANKH

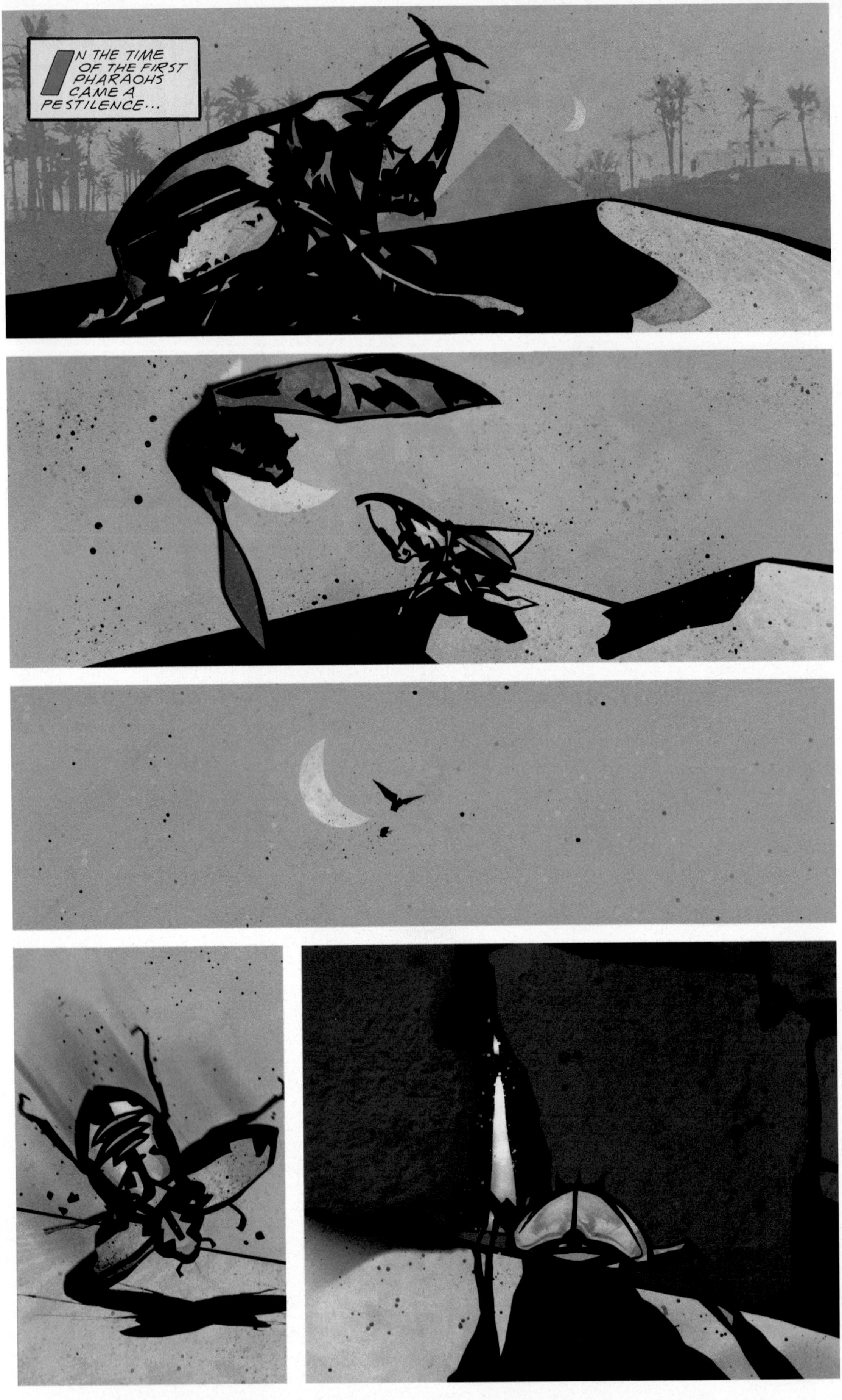
IN THE TIME OF THE FIRST PHARAOHS CAME A PESTILENCE...

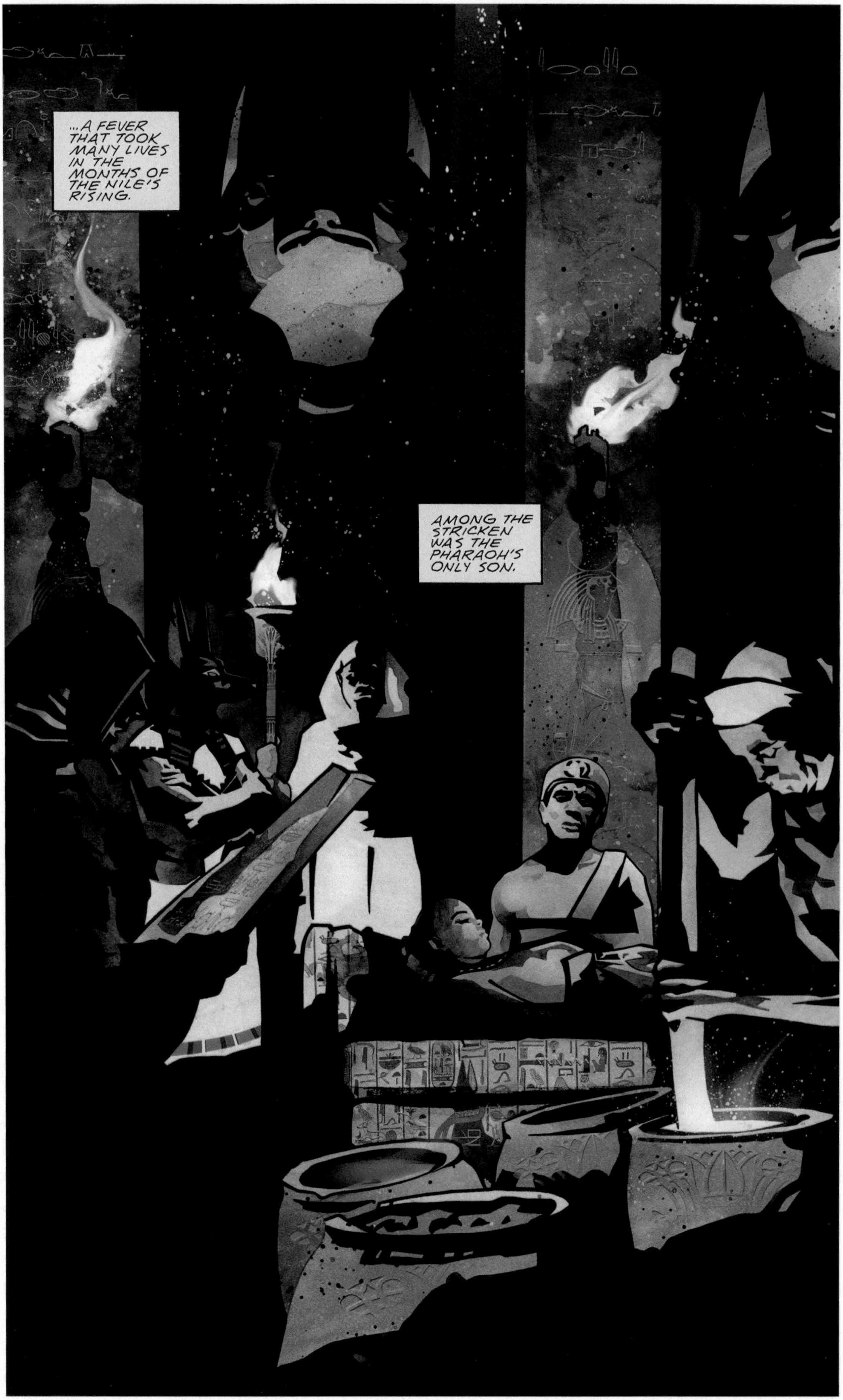
...A FEVER THAT TOOK MANY LIVES IN THE MONTHS OF THE NILE'S RISING.
AMONG THE STRICKEN WAS THE PHARAOH'S ONLY SON.

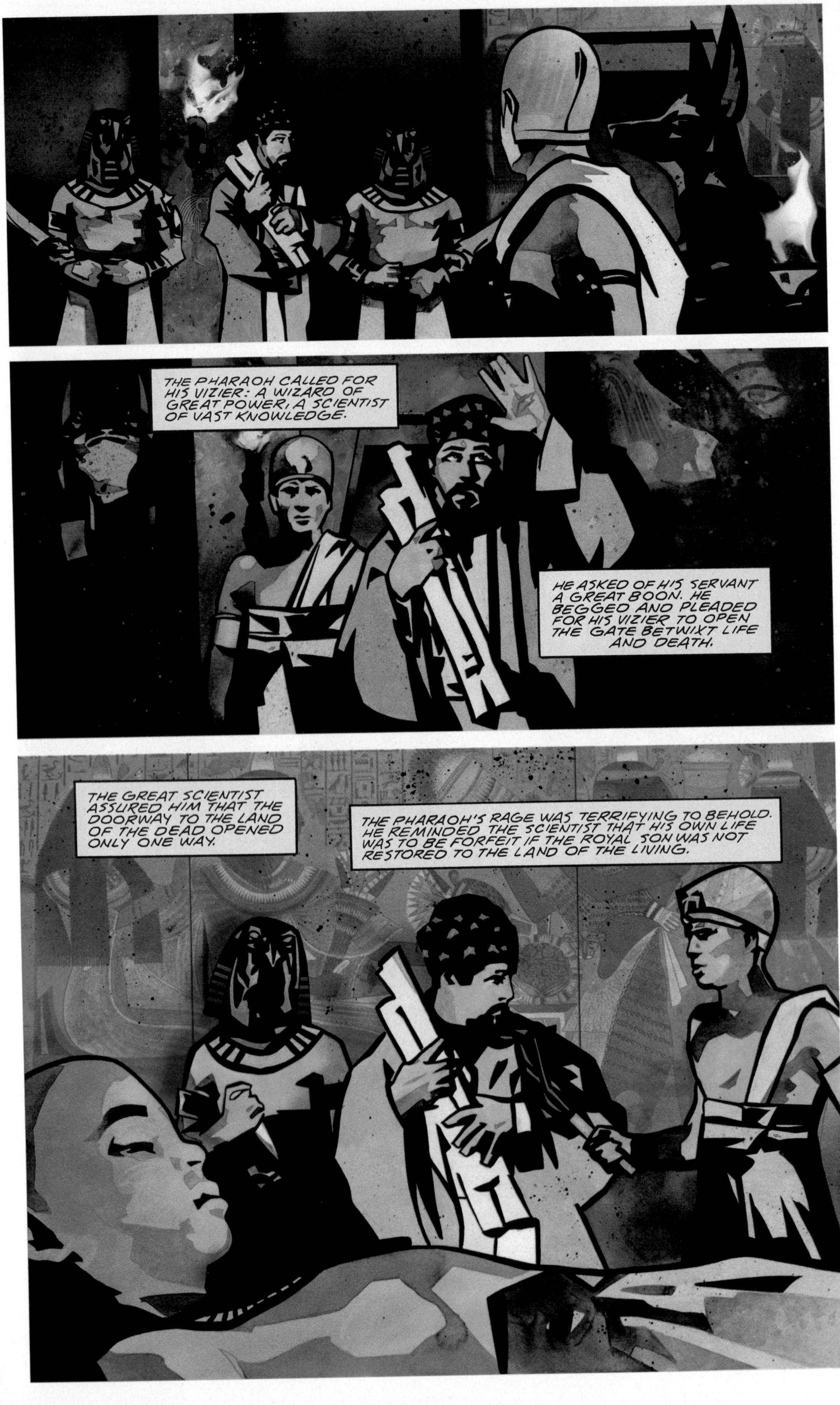
THE PHARAOH CALLED FOR HIS VIZIER: A WIZARD OF GREAT POWER, A SCIENTIST OF VAST KNOWLEDGE.
HE ASKED OF HIS SERVANT A GREAT BOON. HE BEGGED AND PLEADED FOR HIS VIZIER TO OPEN THE GATE BETWIXT LIFE AND DEATH.
THE GREAT SCIENTIST ASSURED HIM THAT THE DOORWAY TO THE LAND OF THE DEAD OPENED ONLY ONE WAY.
THE PHARAOH'S RAGE WAS TERRIFYING TO BEHOLD. HE REMINDED THE SCIENTIST THAT HIS OWN LIFE WAS TO BE FORFEIT IF THE ROYAL SON WAS NOT RESTORED TO THE LAND OF THE LIVING.

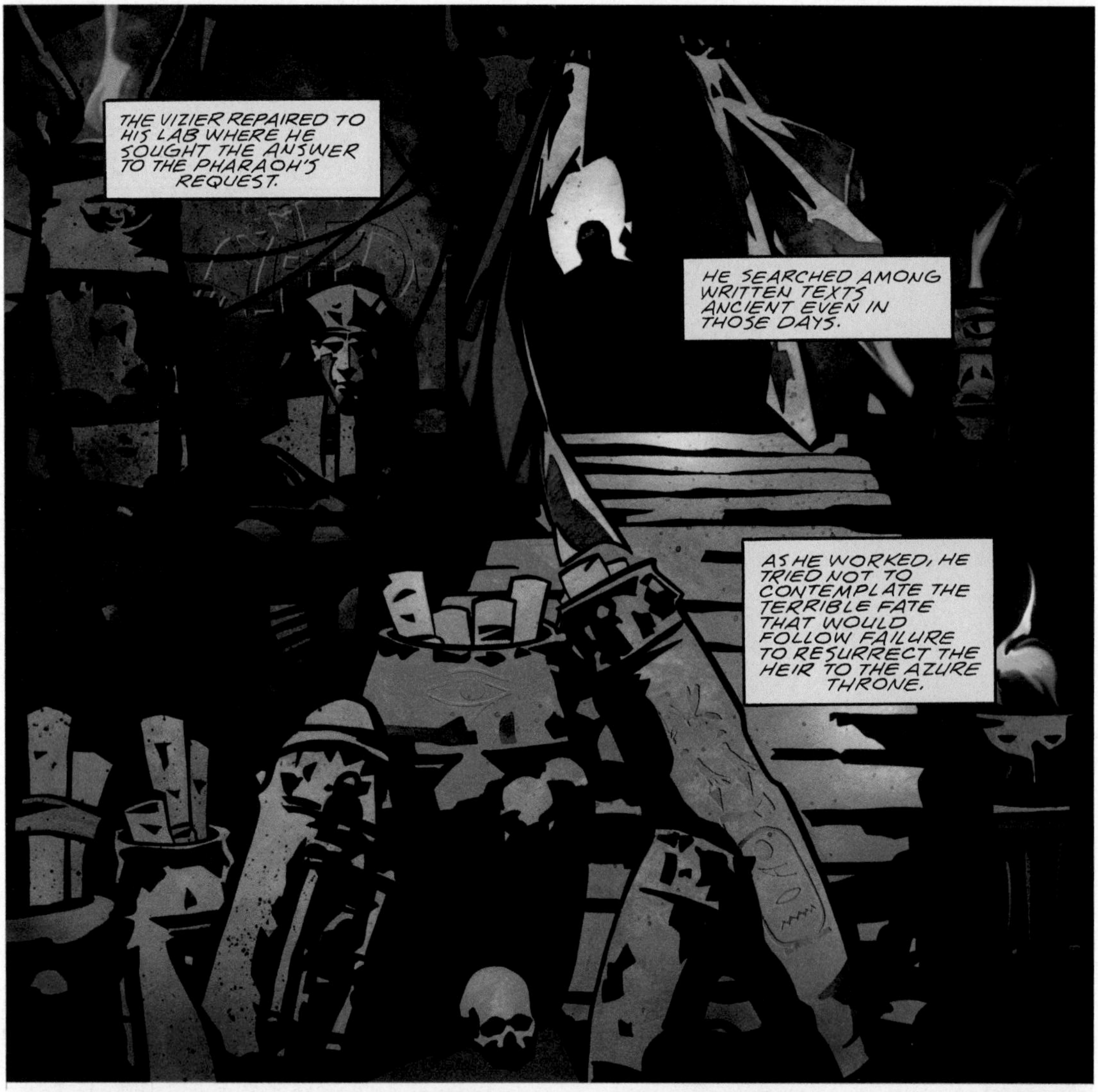
THE VIZIER REPAIRED TO HIS LAB WHERE HE SOUGHT THE ANSWER TO THE PHARAOH'S REQUEST.
HE SEARCHED AMONG WRITTEN TEXTS ANCIENT EVEN IN THOSE DAYS.
AS HE WORKED, HE TRIED NOT TO CONTEMPLATE THE TERRIBLE FATE THAT WOULD FOLLOW FAILURE TO RESURRECT THE HEIR TO THE AZURE THRONE.

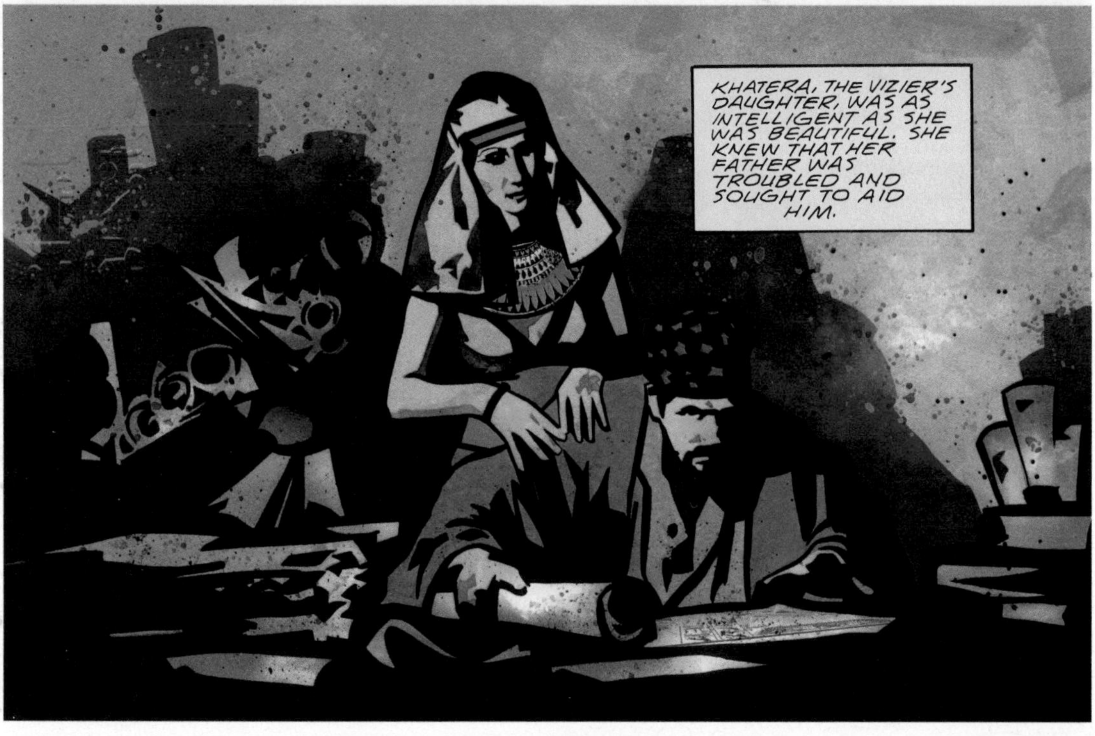
KHATERA, THE VIZIER'S DAUGHTER, WAS AS INTELLIGENT AS SHE WAS BEAUTIFUL. SHE KNEW THAT HER FATHER WAS TROUBLED AND SOUGHT TO AID HIM.

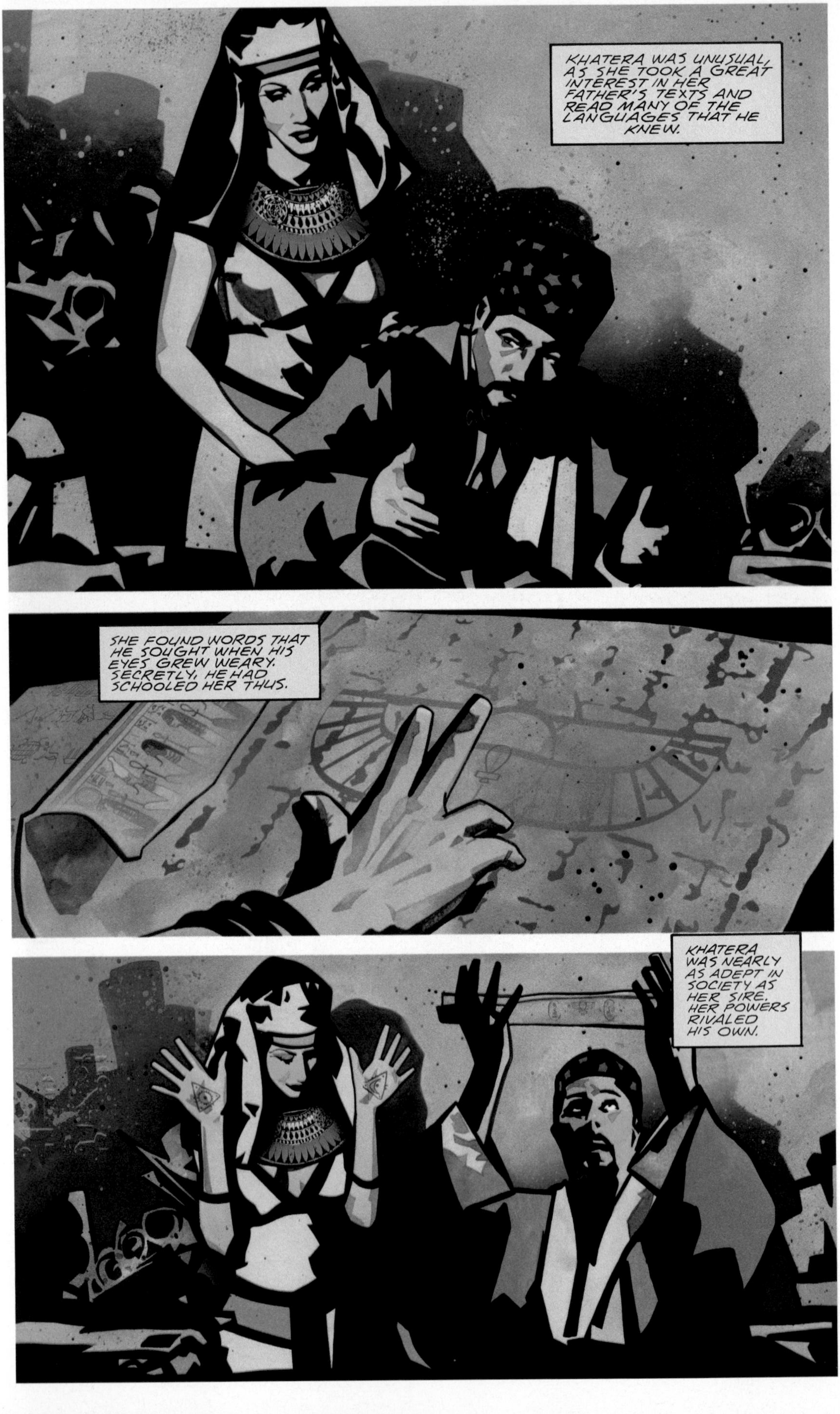
KHATERA WAS UNUSUAL, AS SHE TOOK A GREAT INTEREST IN HER FATHER'S TEXTS AND READ MANY OF THE LANGUAGES THAT HE KNEW.
SHE FOUND WORDS THAT HE SOUGHT WHEN HIS EYES GREW WEARY. SECRETLY, HE HAD SCHOOLED HER THUS.
KHATERA WAS NEARLY AS ADEPT IN SOCIETY AS HER SIRE. HER POWERS RIVALED HIS OWN.

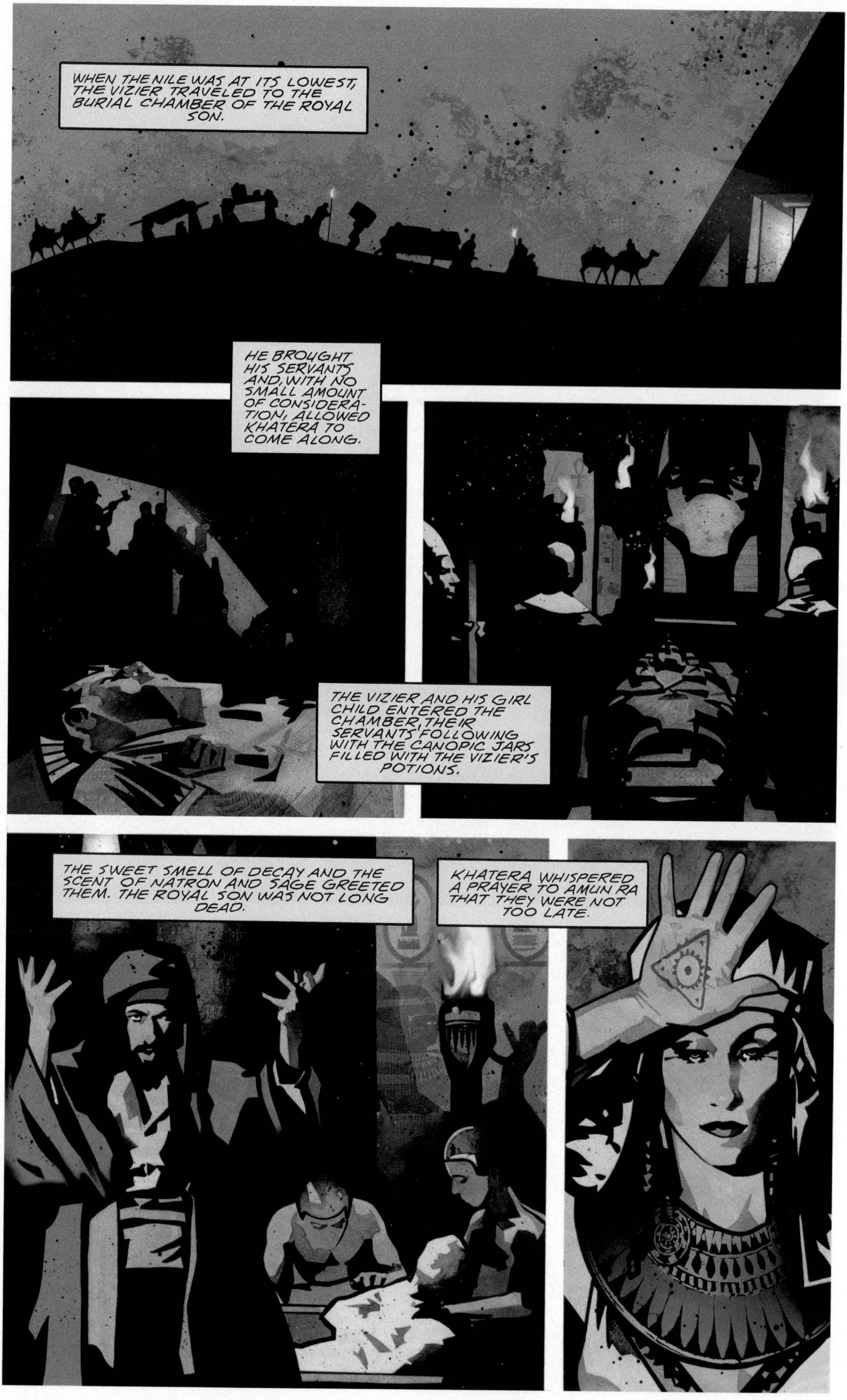
WHEN THE NILE WAS AT ITS LOWEST, THE VIZIER TRAVELED TO THE BURIAL CHAMBER OF THE ROYAL SON.
HE BROUGHT HIS SERVANTS AND, WITH NO SMALL AMOUNT OF CONSIDERATION, ALLOWED KHATERA TO COME ALONG.
THE VIZIER AND HIS GIRL CHILD ENTERED THE CHAMBER, THEIR SERVANTS FOLLOWING WITH THE CANOPIC JARS FILLED WITH THE VIZIER'S POTIONS.
THE SWEET SMELL OF DECAY AND THE SCENT OF NATRON AND SAGE GREETED THEM. THE ROYAL SON WAS NOT LONG DEAD.
KHATERA WHISPERED A PRAYER TO AMUN RA THAT THEY WERE NOT TOO LATE.

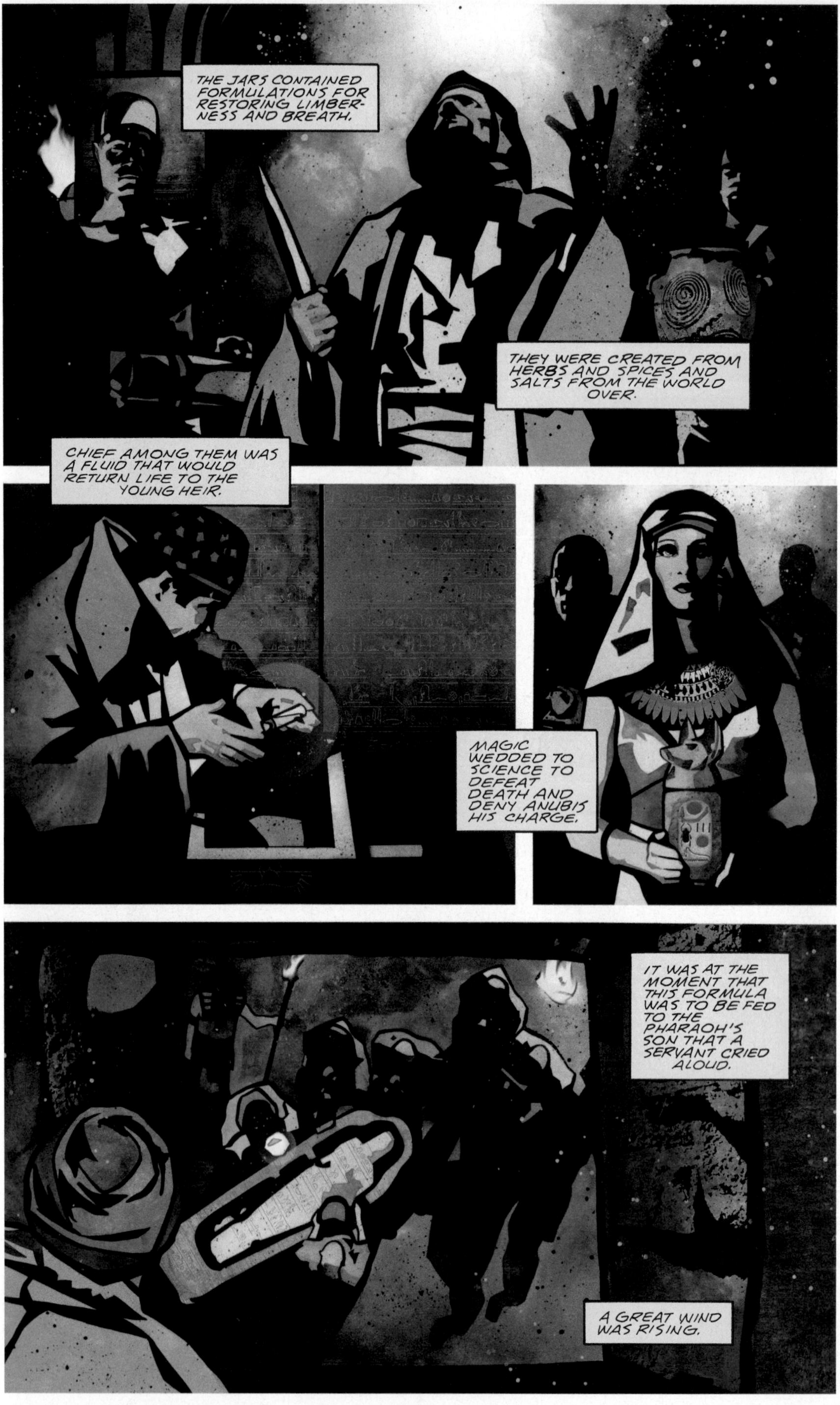
THE JARS CONTAINED FORMULATIONS FOR RESTORING LIMBER-NESS AND BREATH.
THEY WERE CREATED FROM HERBS AND SPICES AND SALTS FROM THE WORLD OVER.
CHIEF AMONG THEM WAS A FLUID THAT WOULD RETURN LIFE TO THE YOUNG HEIR.
MAGIC WEDDED TO SCIENCE TO DEFEAT DEATH AND DENY ANUBIS HIS CHARGE.
IT WAS AT THE MOMENT THAT THIS FORMULA WAS TO BE FED TO THE PHARAOH'S SON THAT A SERVANT CRIED ALOUD.
A GREAT WIND WAS RISING.

A FEARSOME STORM OF SAND WAS RUSHING ACROSS THE DESERT FROM THE SOUTH.

IT HELD WITHIN IT THE ANGER OF THE GODS. THE SERVANTS MURMURED IN TERROR.

TO SAVE THEIR MASTER FROM THE FURY OF THE STORM, THE BURIAL VAULT WAS SEALED.

WITHIN SECONDS, THOSE SERVANTS LAY DEAD, FELLED BY THE RAGING WINDS.

THE VIZIER AND HIS FOLLOWERS WERE LEFT BURIED, SAFE FROM THE RAVAGES OF THE SANDSTORM ABOVE.

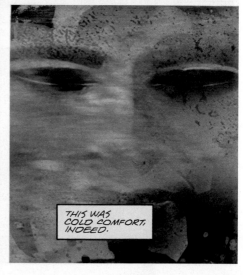

THIS WAS COLD COMFORT, INDEED.

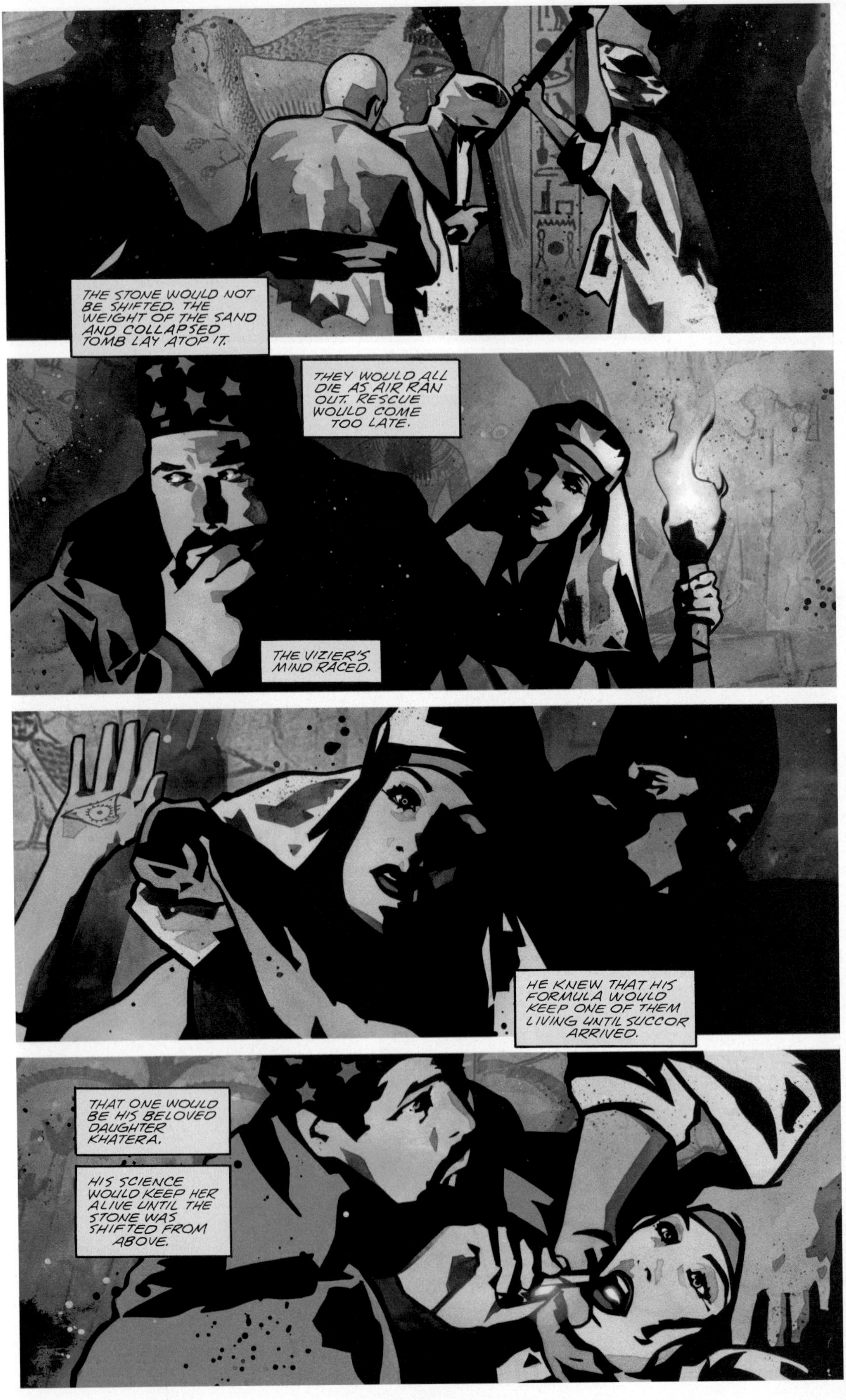
THE STONE WOULD NOT BE SHIFTED. THE WEIGHT OF THE SAND AND COLLAPSED TOMB LAY ATOP IT.
THEY WOULD ALL DIE AS AIR RAN OUT. RESCUE WOULD COME TOO LATE.
THE VIZIER'S MIND RACED.
HE KNEW THAT HIS FORMULA WOULD KEEP ONE OF THEM LIVING UNTIL SUCCOR ARRIVED.
THAT ONE WOULD BE HIS BELOVED DAUGHTER KHATERA.
HIS SCIENCE WOULD KEEP HER ALIVE UNTIL THE STONE WAS SHIFTED FROM ABOVE.

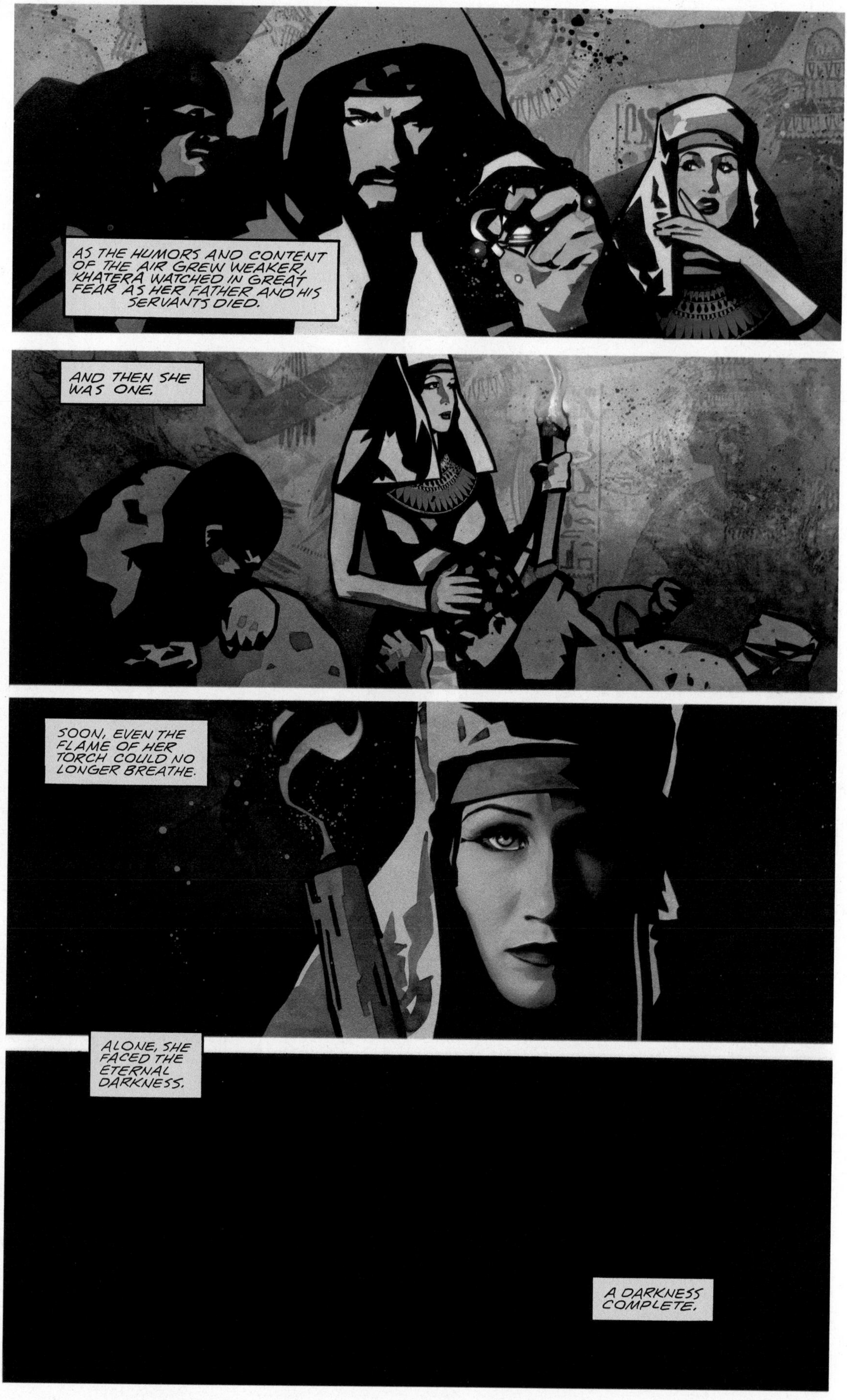
AS THE HUMORS AND CONTENT OF THE AIR GREW WEAKER, KHATERA WATCHED IN GREAT FEAR AS HER FATHER AND HIS SERVANTS DIED.
AND THEN SHE WAS ONE.
SOON, EVEN THE FLAME OF HER TORCH COULD NO LONGER BREATHE.
ALONE, SHE FACED THE ETERNAL DARKNESS.
A DARKNESS COMPLETE.

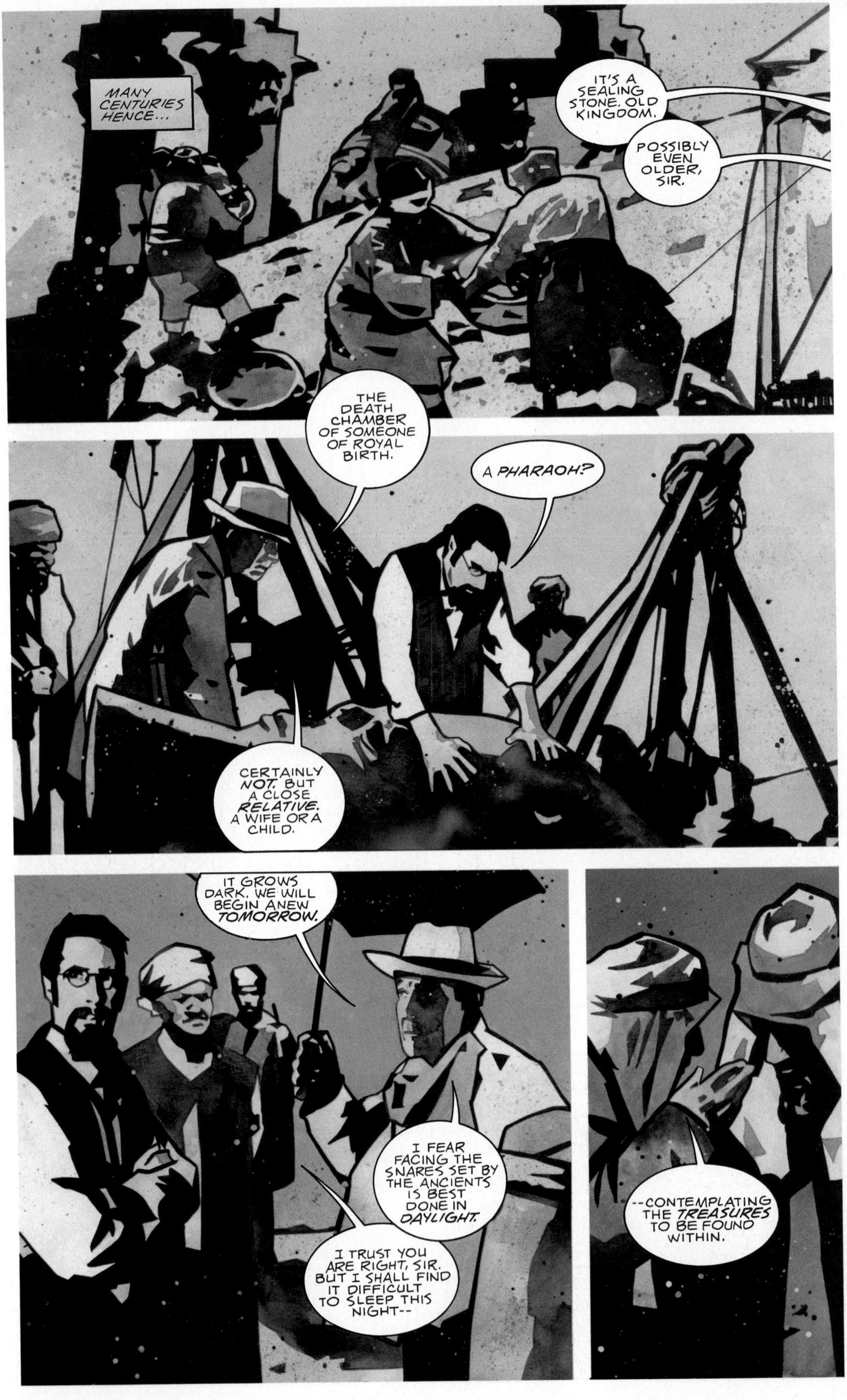
MANY CENTURIES HENCE...
IT'S A SEALING STONE. OLD KINGDOM.
POSSIBLY EVEN OLDER, SIR.
THE DEATH CHAMBER OF SOMEONE OF ROYAL BIRTH.
A PHARAOH?
CERTAINLY NOT. BUT A CLOSE RELATIVE. A WIFE OR A CHILD.
IT GROWS DARK. WE WILL BEGIN ANEW TOMORROW.
I FEAR FACING THE SNARES SET BY THE ANCIENTS IS BEST DONE IN DAYLIGHT.
I TRUST YOU ARE RIGHT, SIR. BUT I SHALL FIND IT DIFFICULT TO SLEEP THIS NIGHT--
--CONTEMPLATING THE TREASURES TO BE FOUND WITHIN.

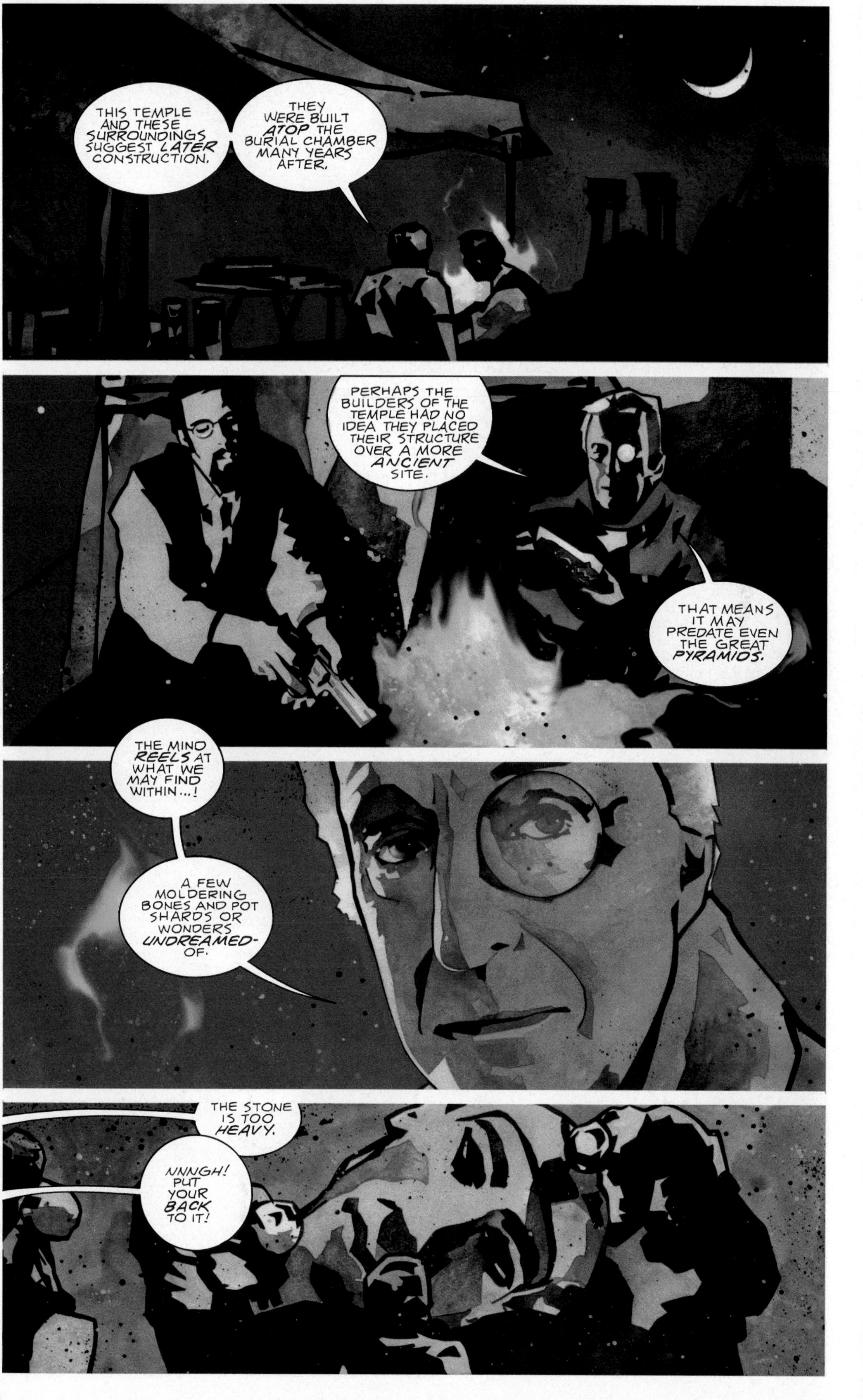
THIS TEMPLE AND THESE SURROUNDINGS SUGGEST LATER CONSTRUCTION.
THEY WERE BUILT ATOP THE BURIAL CHAMBER MANY YEARS AFTER.
PERHAPS THE BUILDERS OF THE TEMPLE HAD NO IDEA THEY PLACED THEIR STRUCTURE OVER A MORE ANCIENT SITE.
THAT MEANS IT MAY PREDATE EVEN THE GREAT PYRAMIDS.
THE MIND REELS AT WHAT WE MAY FIND WITHIN...!
A FEW MOLDERING BONES AND POT SHARDS OR WONDERS UNDREAMED-OF.
THE STONE IS TOO HEAVY.
NNNGH! PUT YOUR BACK TO IT!

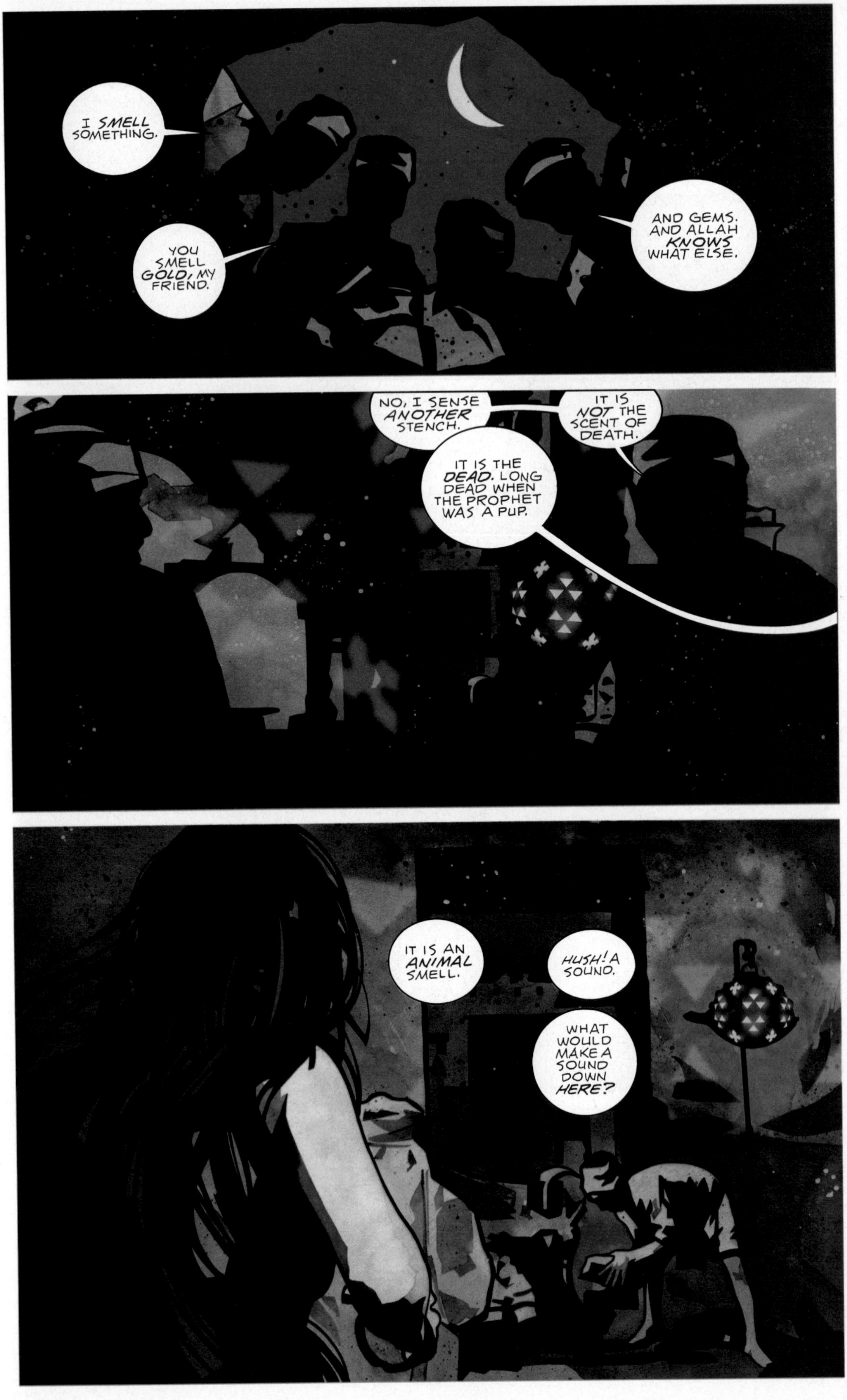
I SMELL SOMETHING.
YOU SMELL GOLD, MY FRIEND.
AND GEMS. AND ALLAH KNOWS WHAT ELSE.
NO, I SENSE ANOTHER STENCH.
IT IS NOT THE SCENT OF DEATH.
IT IS THE DEAD. LONG DEAD WHEN THE PROPHET WAS A PUP.
IT IS AN ANIMAL SMELL.
HUSH! A SOUND.
WHAT WOULD MAKE A SOUND DOWN HERE?

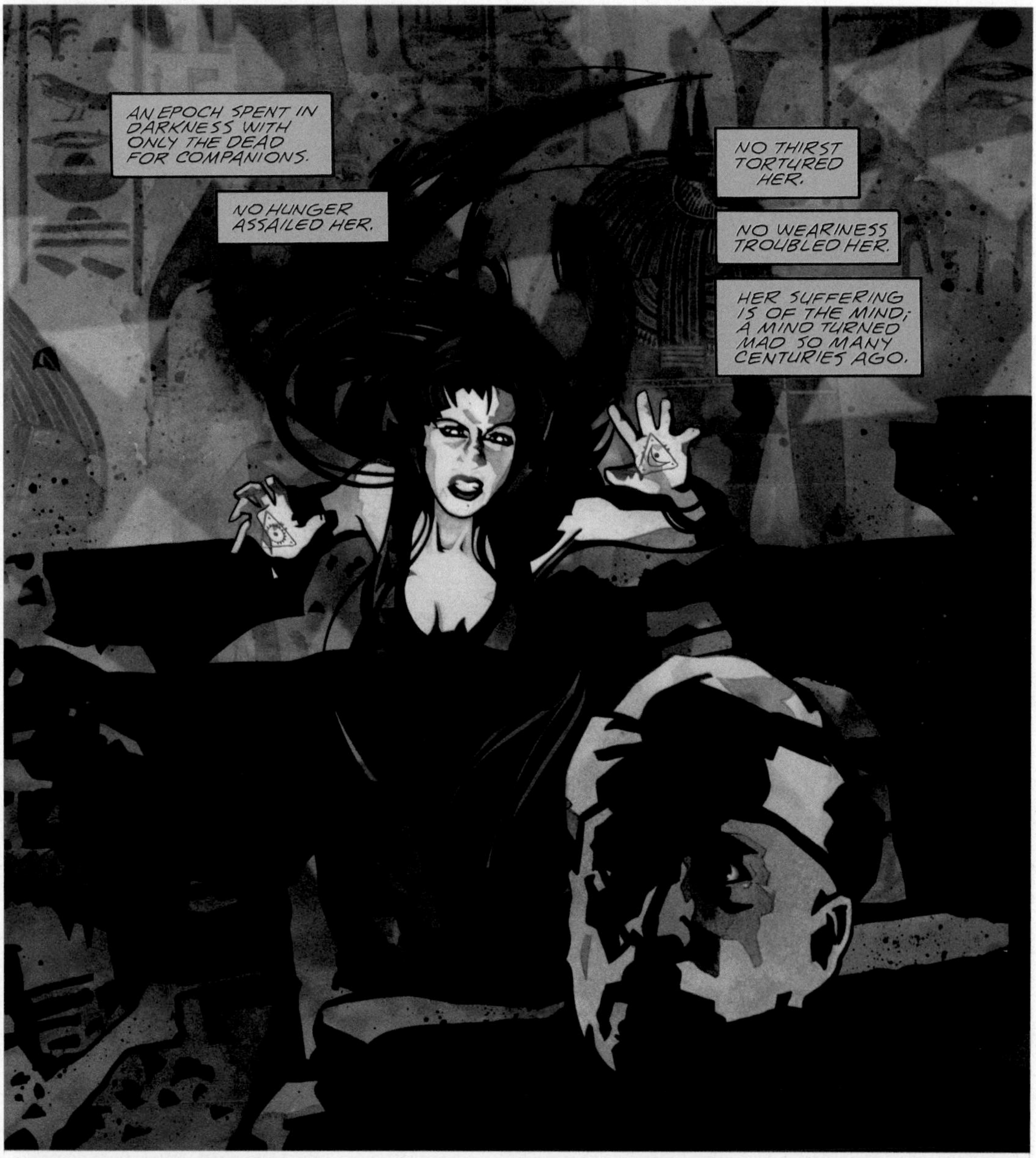
AN EPOCH SPENT IN DARKNESS WITH ONLY THE DEAD FOR COMPANIONS.
NO HUNGER ASSAILED HER.
NO THIRST TORTURED HER.
NO WEARINESS TROUBLED HER.
HER SUFFERING IS OF THE MIND; A MIND TURNED MAD SO MANY CENTURIES AGO.

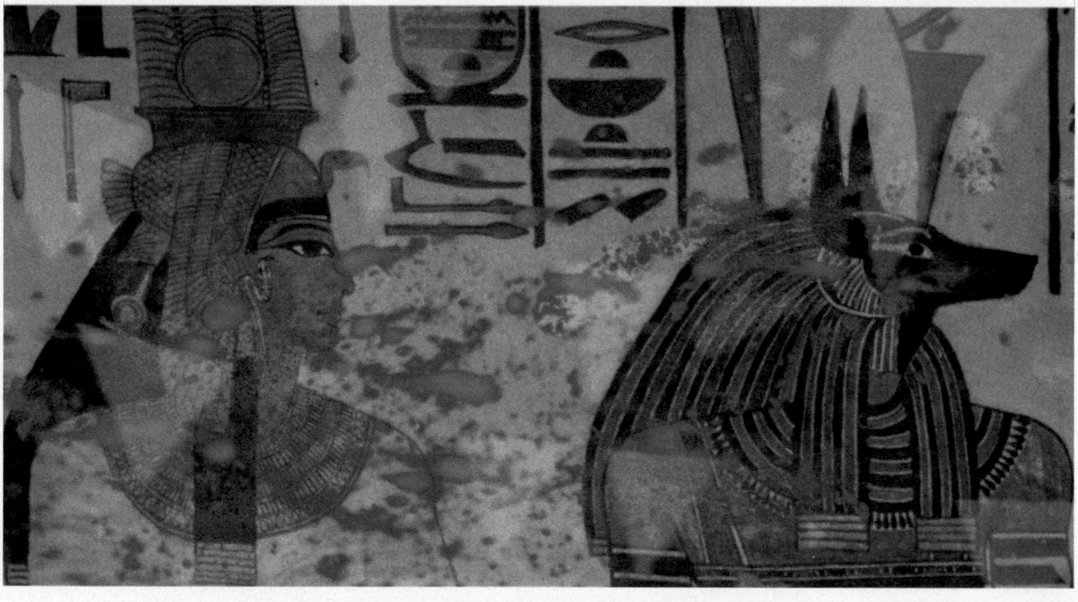

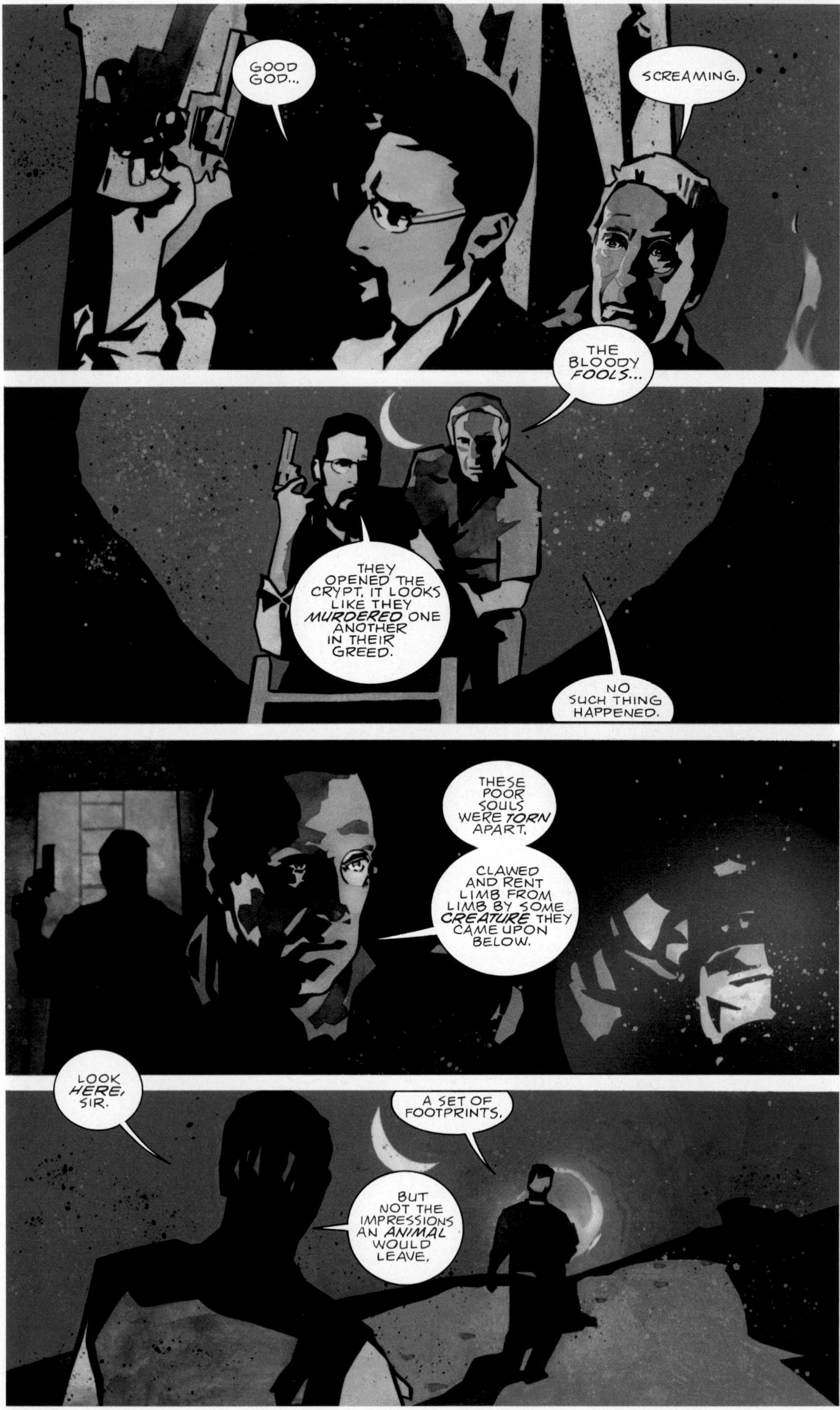

GOOD GOD...
SCREAMING.
THE BLOODY *FOOLS*...
THEY OPENED THE CRYPT, IT LOOKS LIKE THEY *MURDERED* ONE ANOTHER IN THEIR GREED.
NO SUCH THING HAPPENED.
THESE POOR SOULS WERE *TORN* APART.
CLAWED AND RENT LIMB FROM LIMB BY SOME *CREATURE* THEY CAME UPON BELOW.
LOOK *HERE*, SIR.
A SET OF FOOTPRINTS.
BUT NOT THE IMPRESSIONS AN *ANIMAL* WOULD LEAVE.

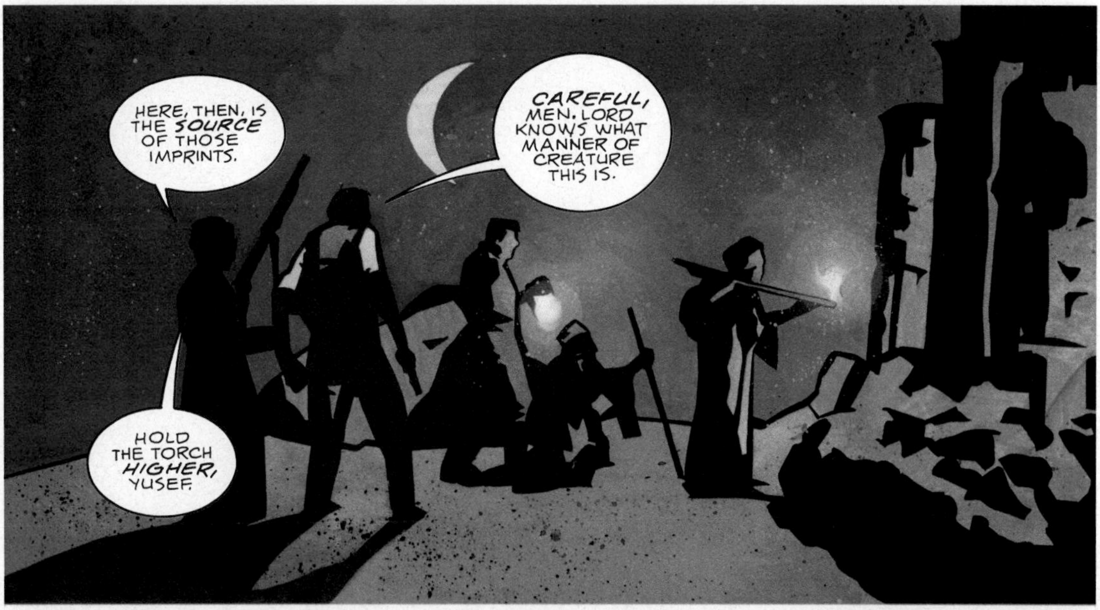
HERE, THEN, IS THE SOURCE OF THOSE IMPRINTS.
CAREFUL, MEN. LORD KNOWS WHAT MANNER OF CREATURE THIS IS.
HOLD THE TORCH HIGHER, YUSEF.

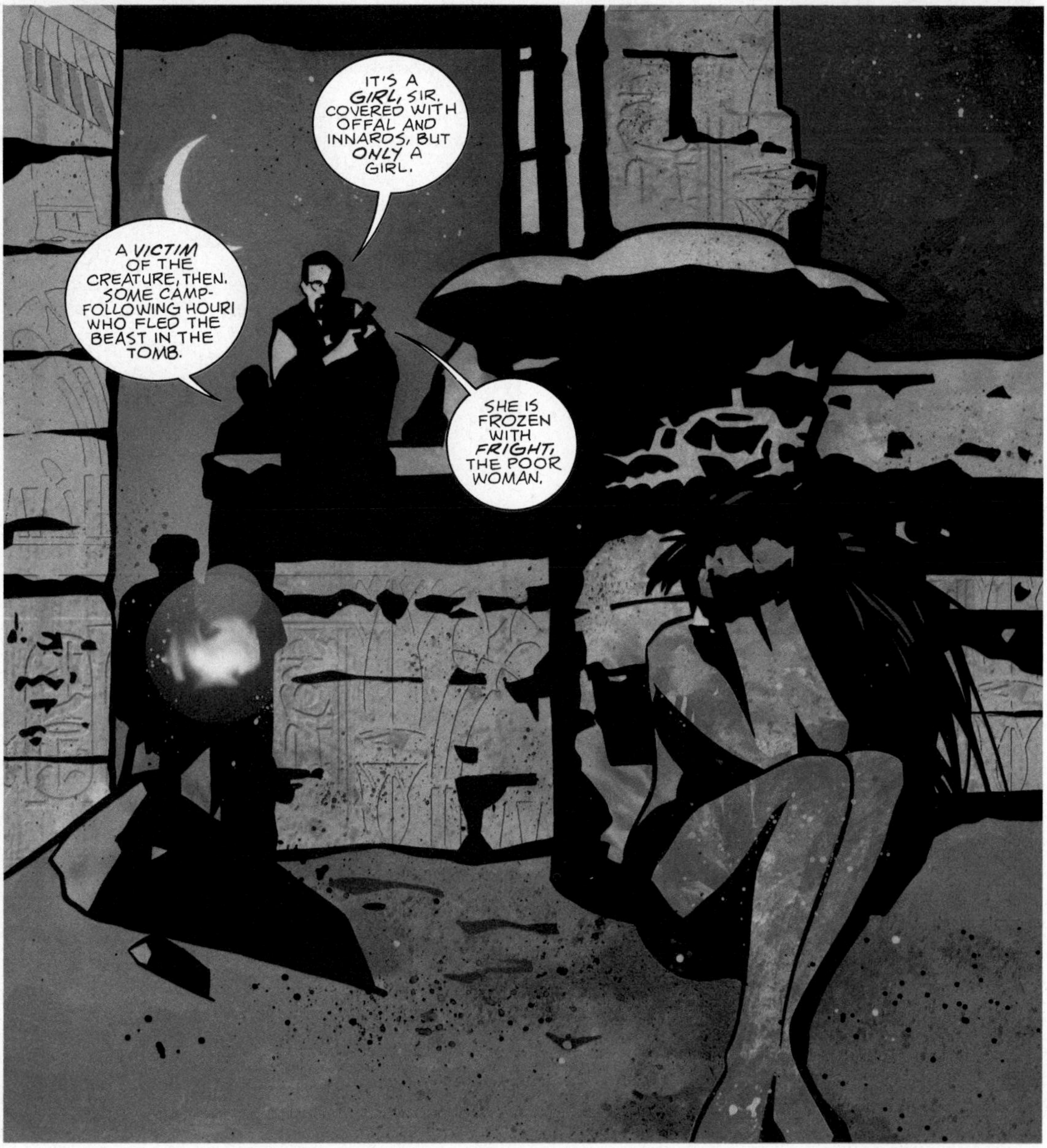
IT'S A GIRL, SIR. COVERED WITH OFFAL AND INNARDS, BUT ONLY A GIRL.
A VICTIM OF THE CREATURE, THEN. SOME CAMP-FOLLOWING HOURI WHO FLED THE BEAST IN THE TOMB.
SHE IS FROZEN WITH FRIGHT, THE POOR WOMAN.

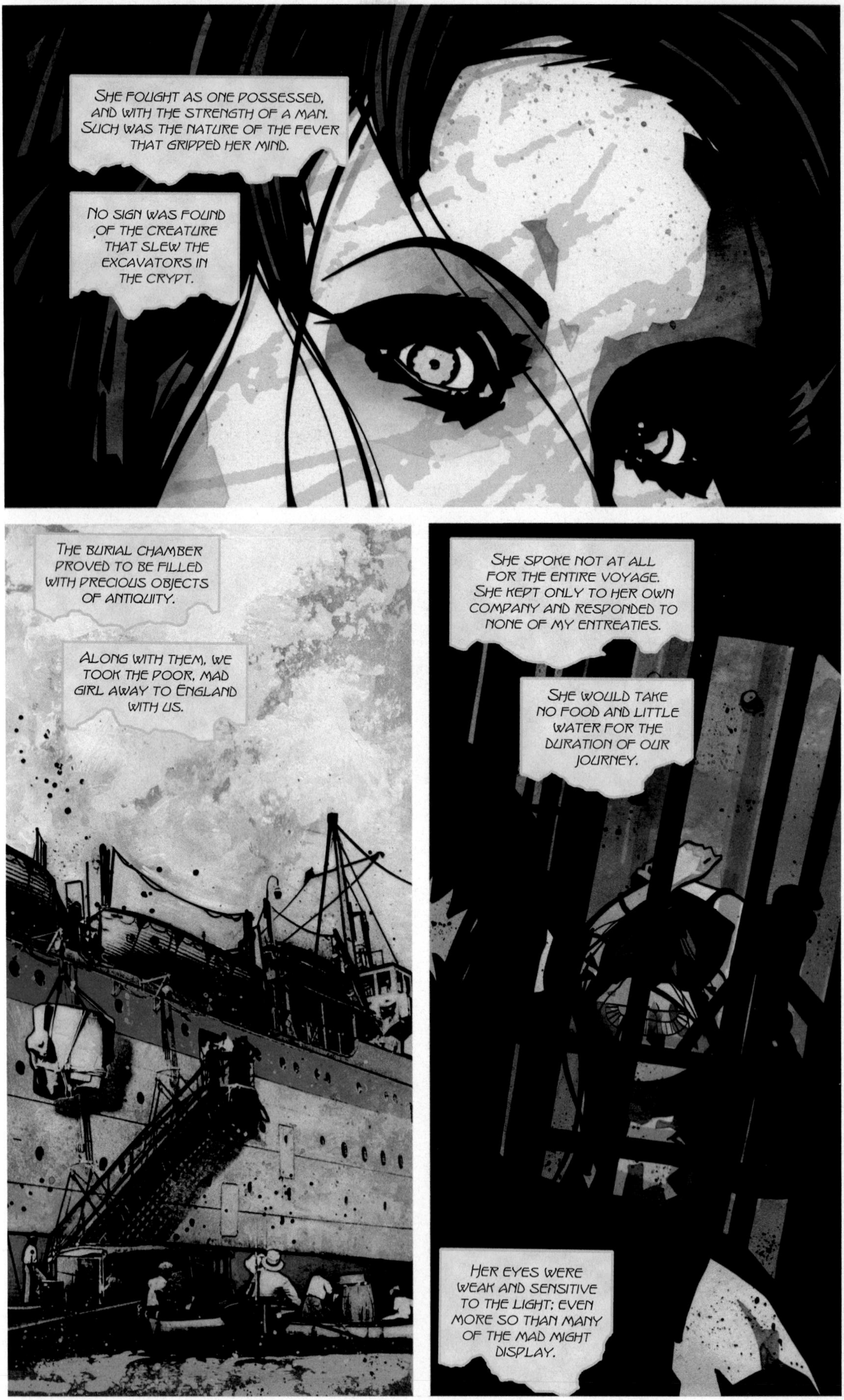
SHE FOUGHT AS ONE POSSESSED, AND WITH THE STRENGTH OF A MAN. SUCH WAS THE NATURE OF THE FEVER THAT GRIPPED HER MIND.
NO SIGN WAS FOUND OF THE CREATURE THAT SLEW THE EXCAVATORS IN THE CRYPT.
THE BURIAL CHAMBER PROVED TO BE FILLED WITH PRECIOUS OBJECTS OF ANTIQUITY.
ALONG WITH THEM, WE TOOK THE POOR, MAD GIRL AWAY TO ENGLAND WITH US.
SHE SPOKE NOT AT ALL FOR THE ENTIRE VOYAGE. SHE KEPT ONLY TO HER OWN COMPANY AND RESPONDED TO NONE OF MY ENTREATIES.
SHE WOULD TAKE NO FOOD AND LITTLE WATER FOR THE DURATION OF OUR JOURNEY.
HER EYES WERE WEAK AND SENSITIVE TO THE LIGHT; EVEN MORE SO THAN MANY OF THE MAD MIGHT DISPLAY.

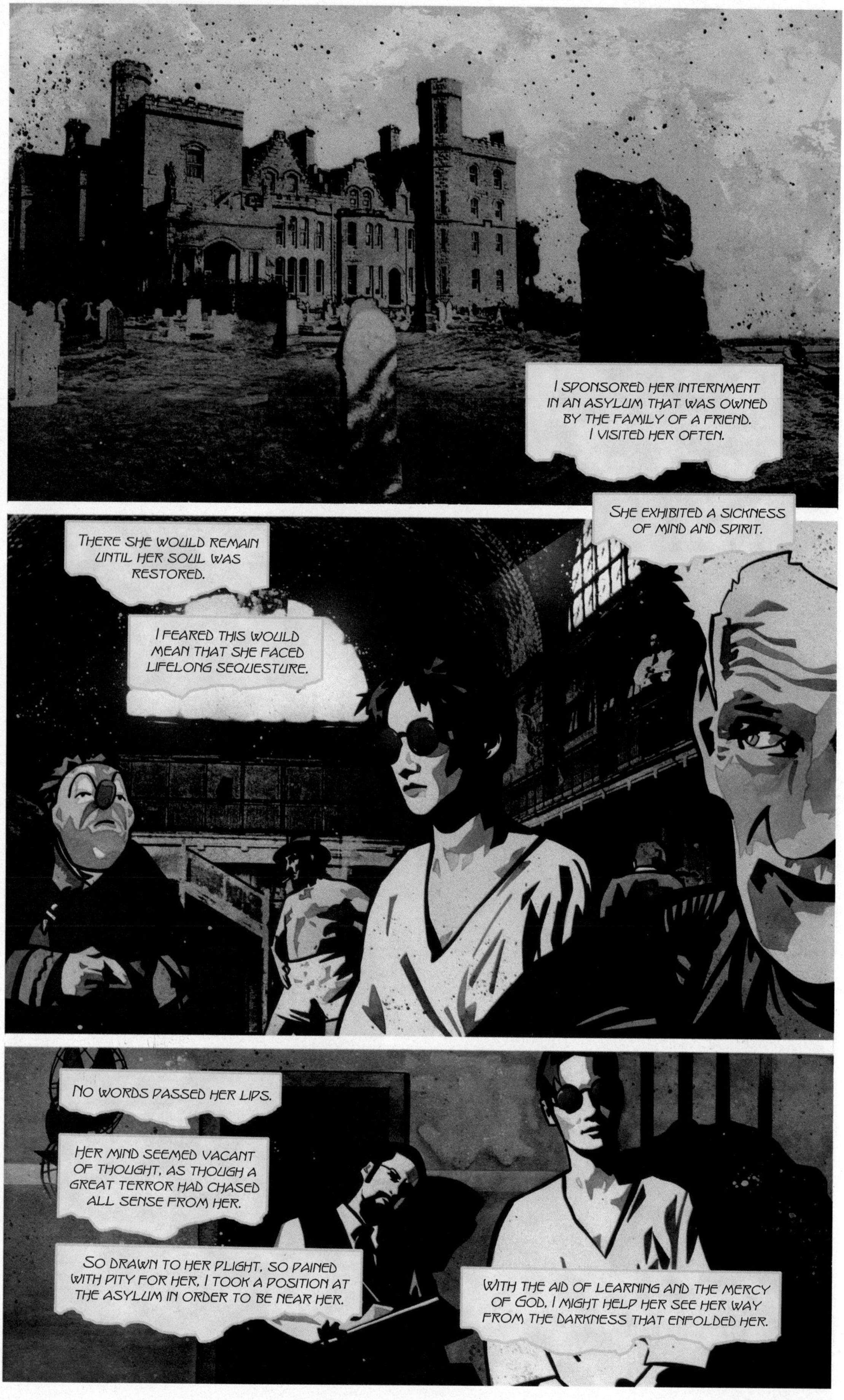
I SPONSORED HER INTERNMENT IN AN ASYLUM THAT WAS OWNED BY THE FAMILY OF A FRIEND. I VISITED HER OFTEN.
THERE SHE WOULD REMAIN UNTIL HER SOUL WAS RESTORED.
SHE EXHIBITED A SICKNESS OF MIND AND SPIRIT.
I FEARED THIS WOULD MEAN THAT SHE FACED LIFELONG SEQUESTURE.
NO WORDS PASSED HER LIPS.
HER MIND SEEMED VACANT OF THOUGHT, AS THOUGH A GREAT TERROR HAD CHASED ALL SENSE FROM HER.
SO DRAWN TO HER PLIGHT, SO PAINED WITH PITY FOR HER, I TOOK A POSITION AT THE ASYLUM IN ORDER TO BE NEAR HER.
WITH THE AID OF LEARNING AND THE MERCY OF GOD, I MIGHT HELP HER SEE HER WAY FROM THE DARKNESS THAT ENFOLDED HER.

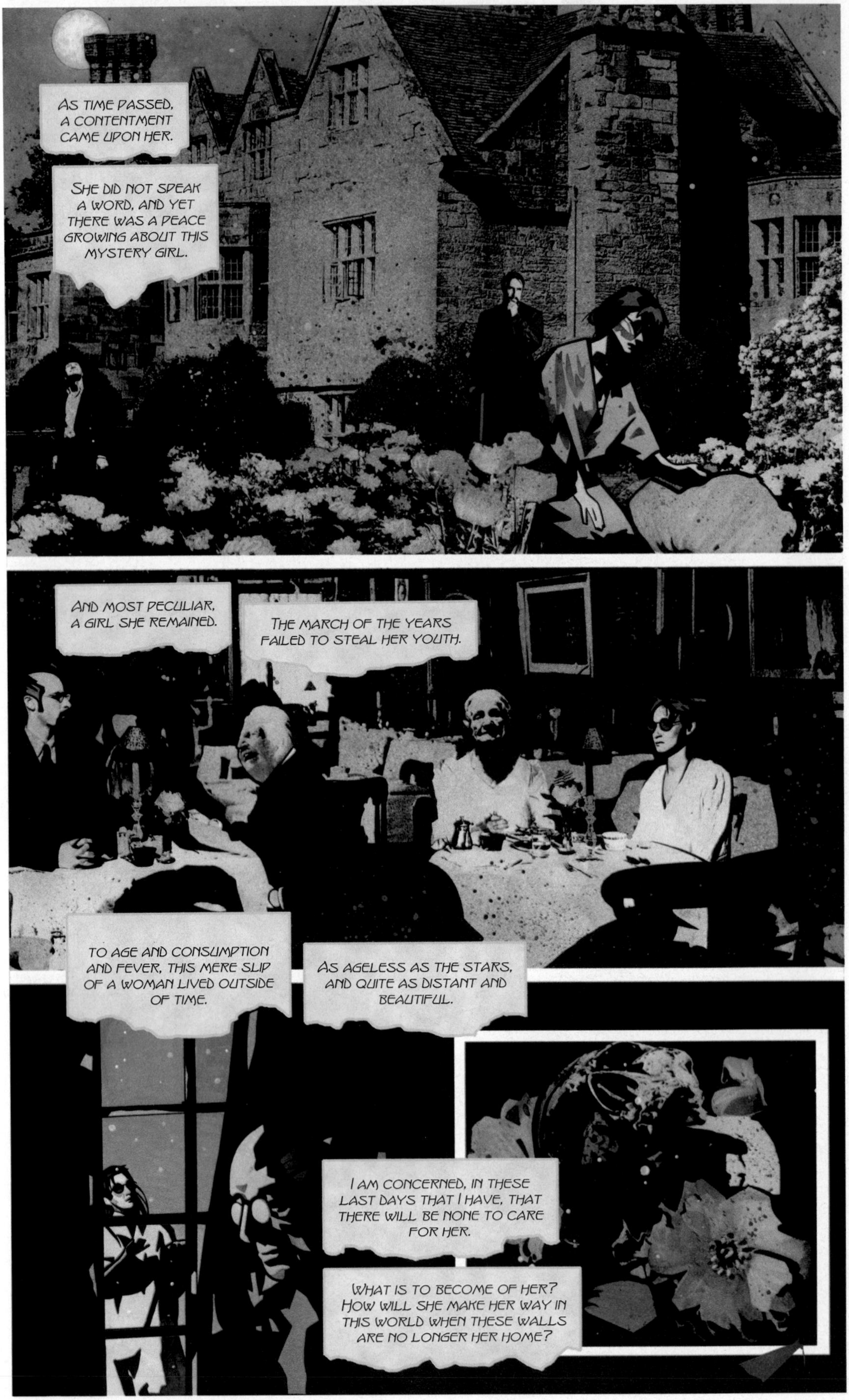
AS TIME PASSED, A CONTENTMENT CAME UPON HER.
SHE DID NOT SPEAK A WORD, AND YET THERE WAS A PEACE GROWING ABOUT THIS MYSTERY GIRL.
AND MOST PECULIAR, A GIRL SHE REMAINED.
THE MARCH OF THE YEARS FAILED TO STEAL HER YOUTH.
TO AGE AND CONSUMPTION AND FEVER, THIS MERE SLIP OF A WOMAN LIVED OUTSIDE OF TIME.
AS AGELESS AS THE STARS, AND QUITE AS DISTANT AND BEAUTIFUL.
I AM CONCERNED, IN THESE LAST DAYS THAT I HAVE, THAT THERE WILL BE NONE TO CARE FOR HER.
WHAT IS TO BECOME OF HER? HOW WILL SHE MAKE HER WAY IN THIS WORLD WHEN THESE WALLS ARE NO LONGER HER HOME?

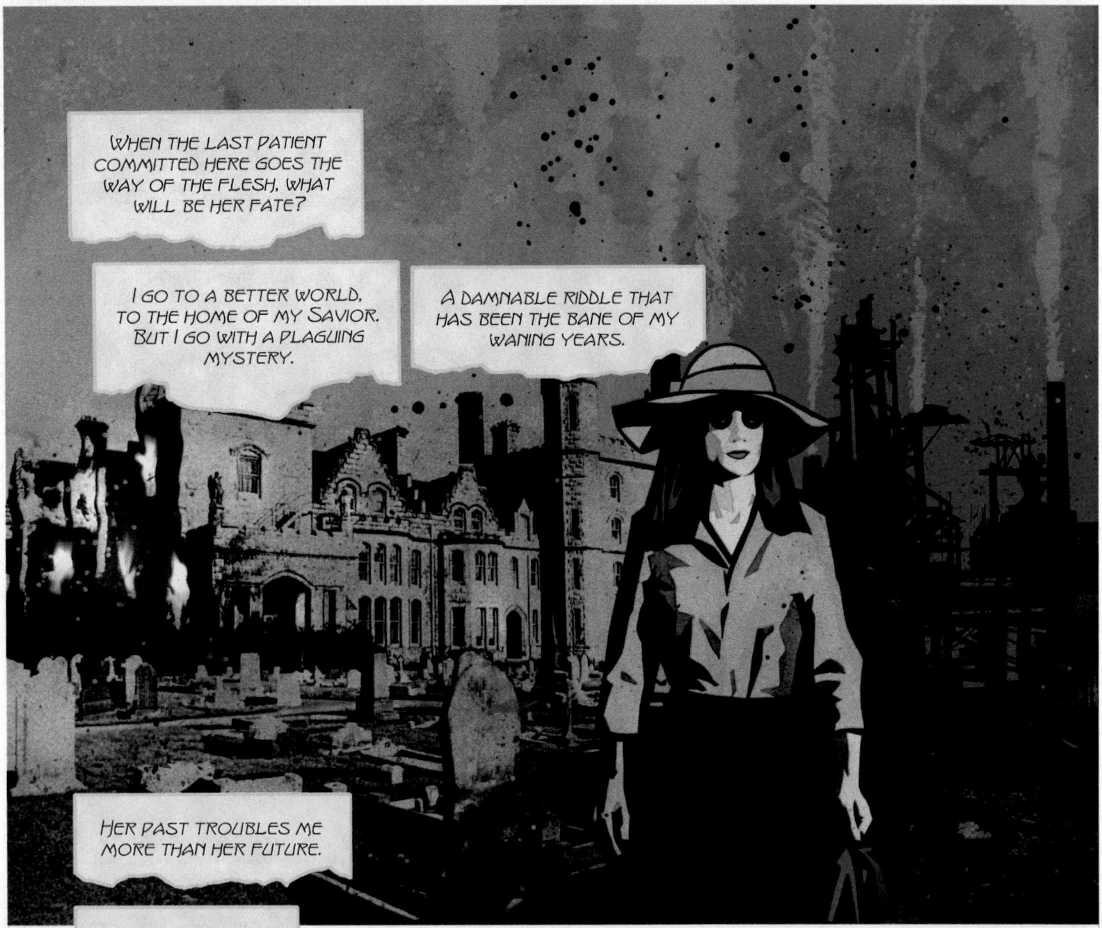
WHEN THE LAST PATIENT COMMITTED HERE GOES THE WAY OF THE FLESH, WHAT WILL BE HER FATE?
I GO TO A BETTER WORLD, TO THE HOME OF MY SAVIOR. BUT I GO WITH A PLAGUING MYSTERY.
A DAMNABLE RIDDLE THAT HAS BEEN THE BANE OF MY WANING YEARS.
HER PAST TROUBLES ME MORE THAN HER FUTURE.

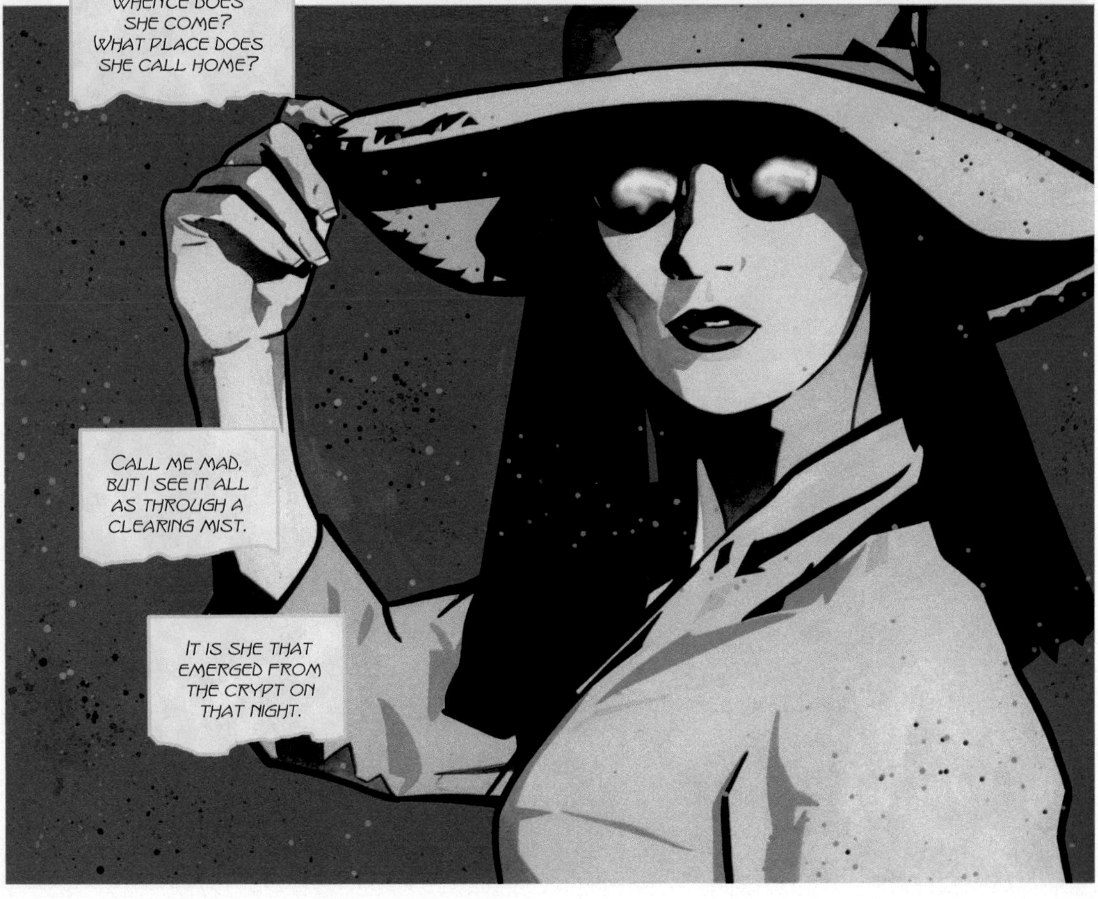
WHENCE DOES SHE COME? WHAT PLACE DOES SHE CALL HOME?
CALL ME MAD, BUT I SEE IT ALL AS THROUGH A CLEARING MIST.
IT IS SHE THAT EMERGED FROM THE CRYPT ON THAT NIGHT.

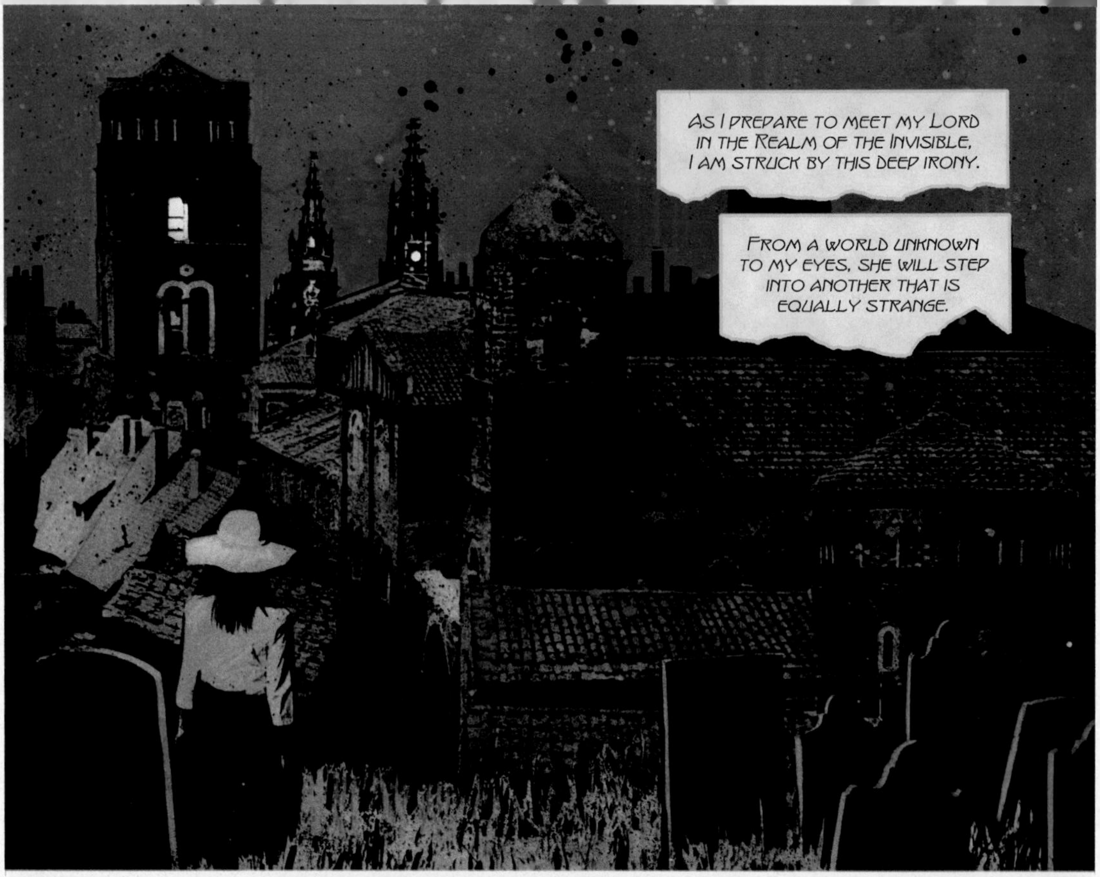
AS I PREPARE TO MEET MY LORD IN THE REALM OF THE INVISIBLE, I AM STRUCK BY THIS DEEP IRONY.
FROM A WORLD UNKNOWN TO MY EYES, SHE WILL STEP INTO ANOTHER THAT IS EQUALLY STRANGE.

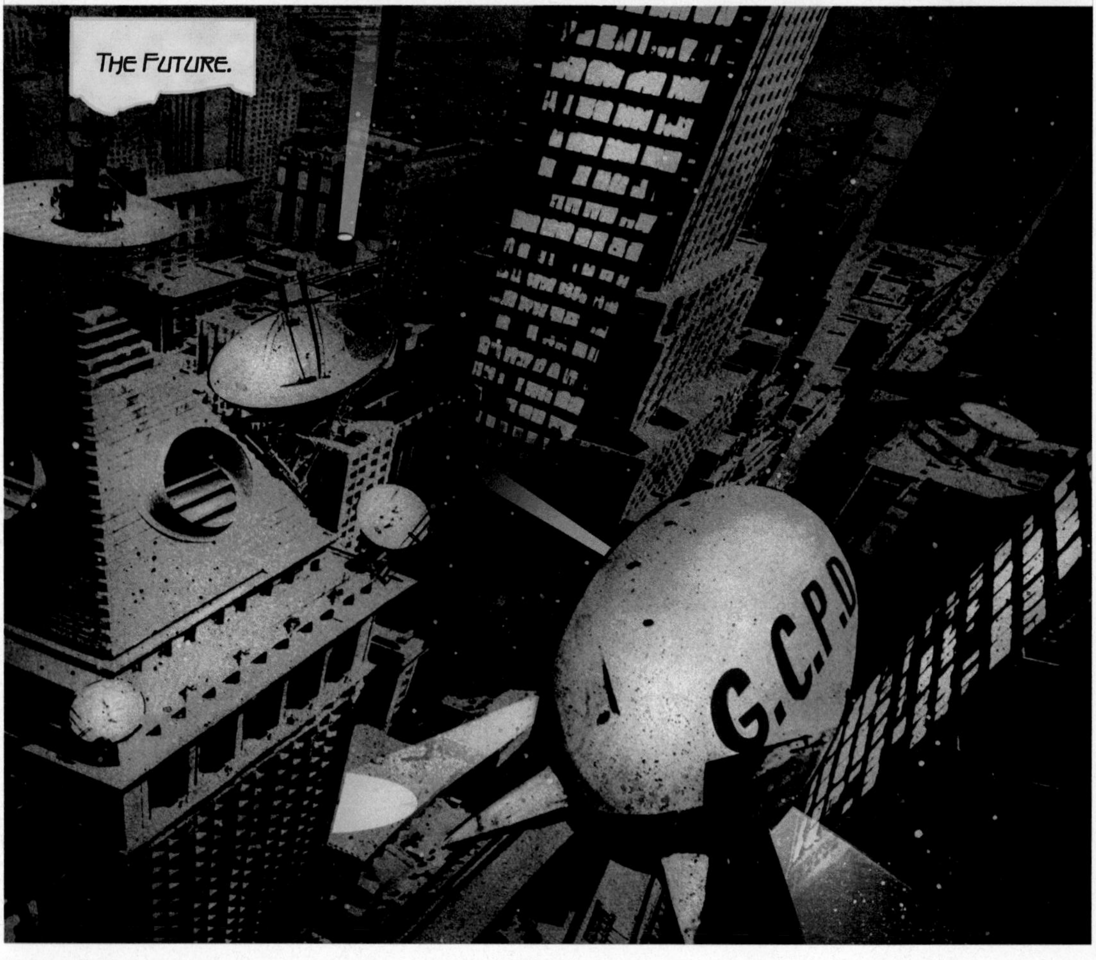
THE FUTURE.
G.C.P.D.

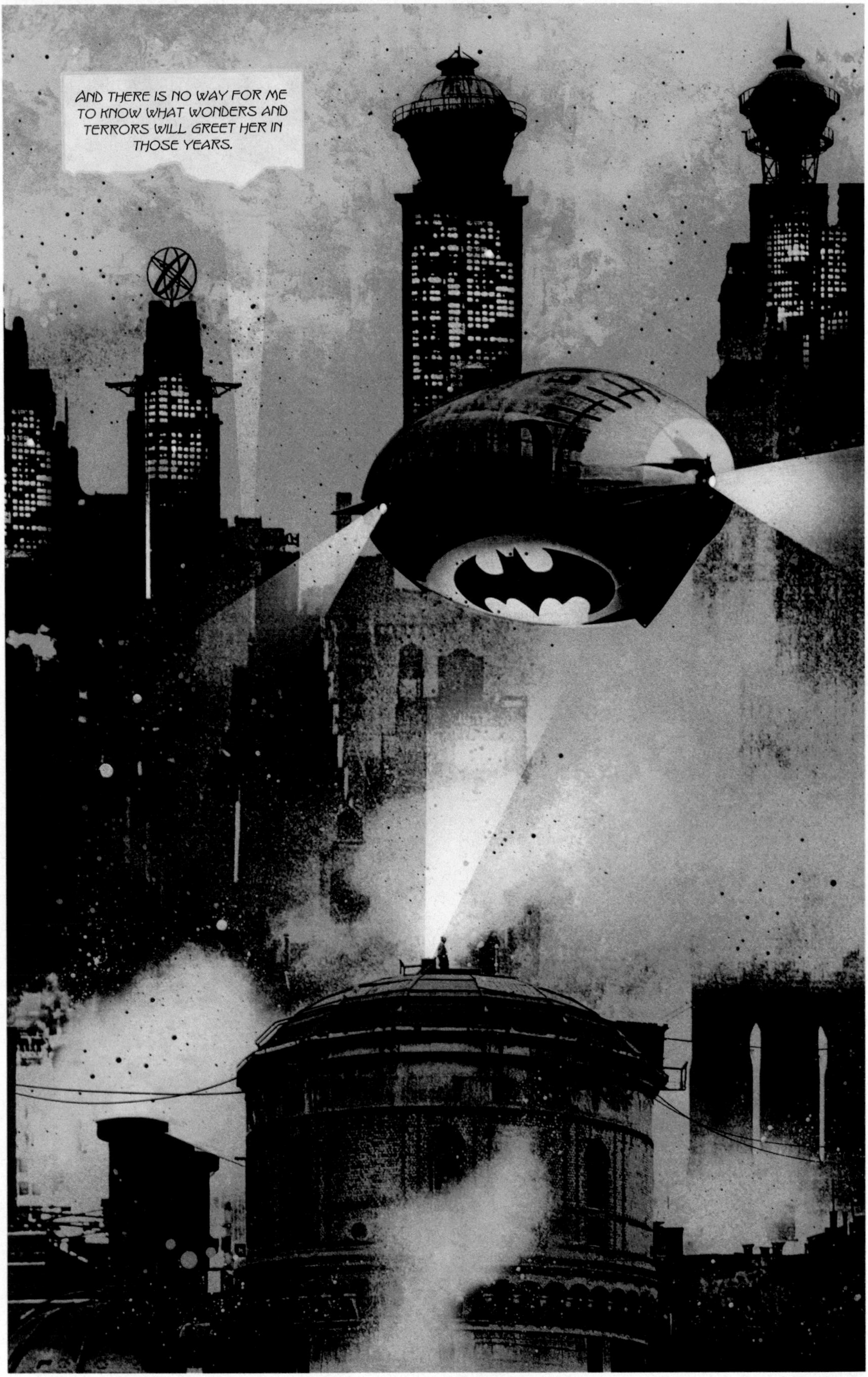
AND THERE IS NO WAY FOR ME TO KNOW WHAT WONDERS AND TERRORS WILL GREET HER IN THOSE YEARS.

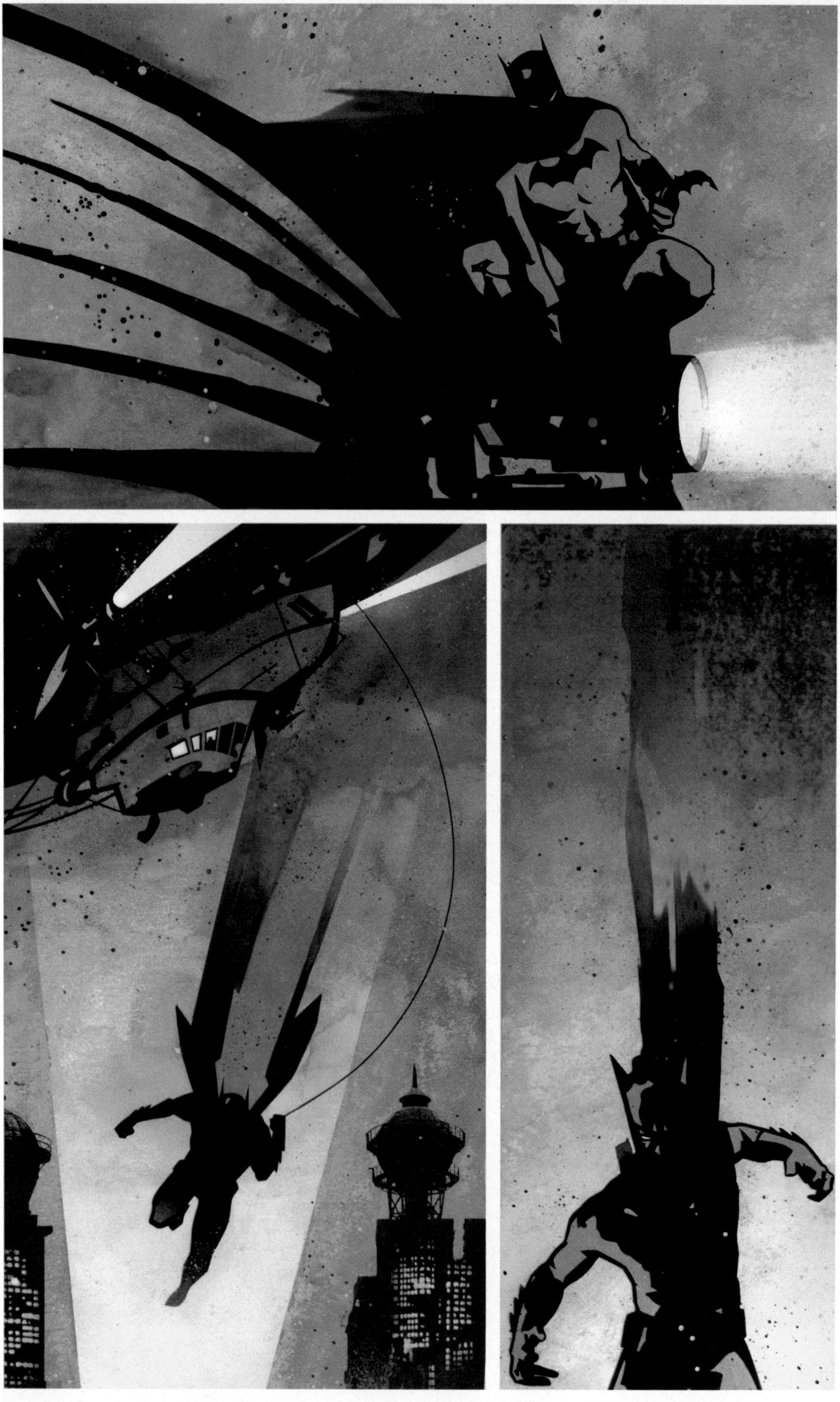

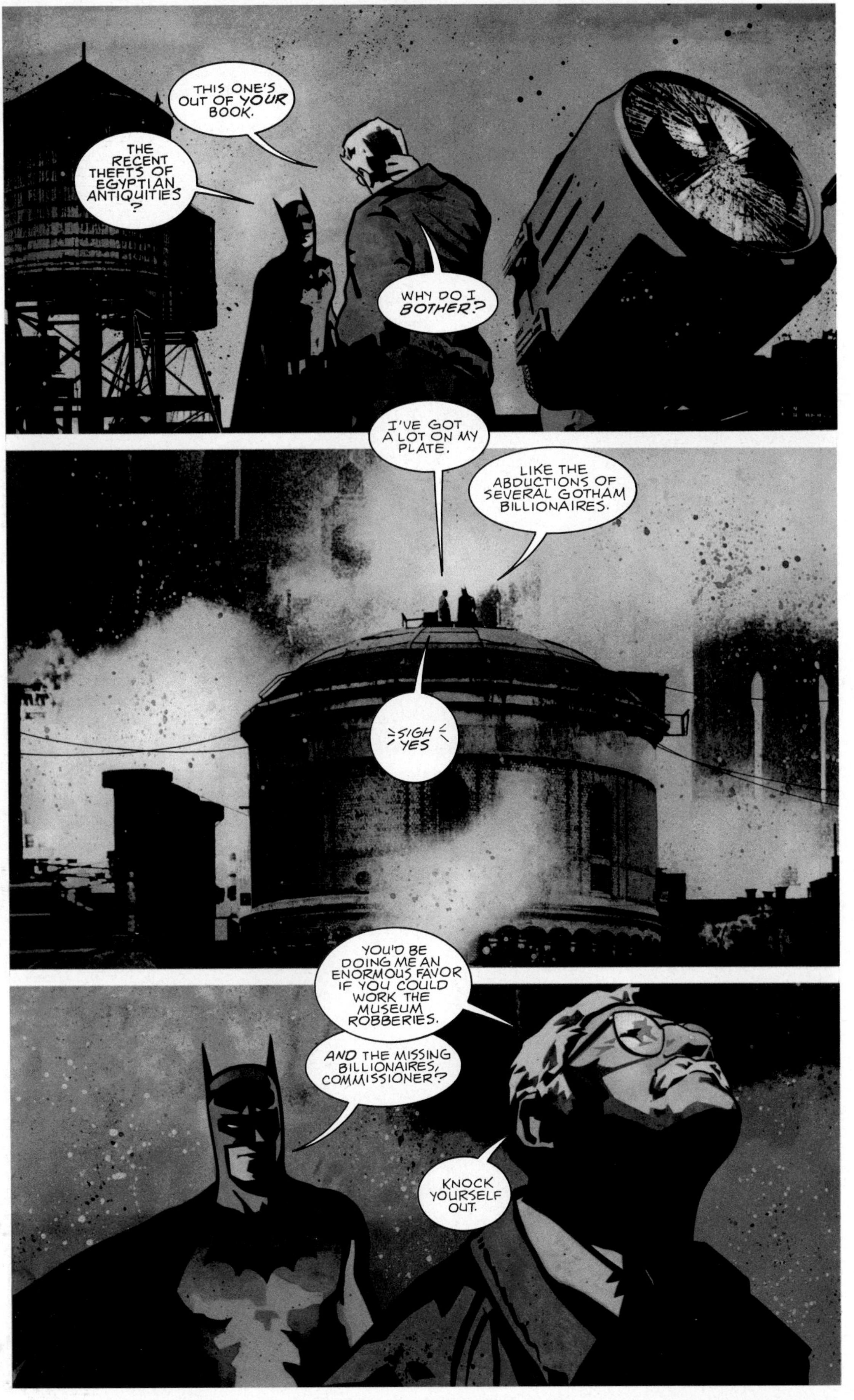
THIS ONE'S OUT OF YOUR BOOK.
THE RECENT THEFTS OF EGYPTIAN ANTIQUITIES?
WHY DO I BOTHER?
I'VE GOT A LOT ON MY PLATE.
LIKE THE ABDUCTIONS OF SEVERAL GOTHAM BILLIONAIRES.
SIGH YES
YOU'D BE DOING ME AN ENORMOUS FAVOR IF YOU COULD WORK THE MUSEUM ROBBERIES.
AND THE MISSING BILLIONAIRES, COMMISSIONER?
KNOCK YOURSELF OUT.

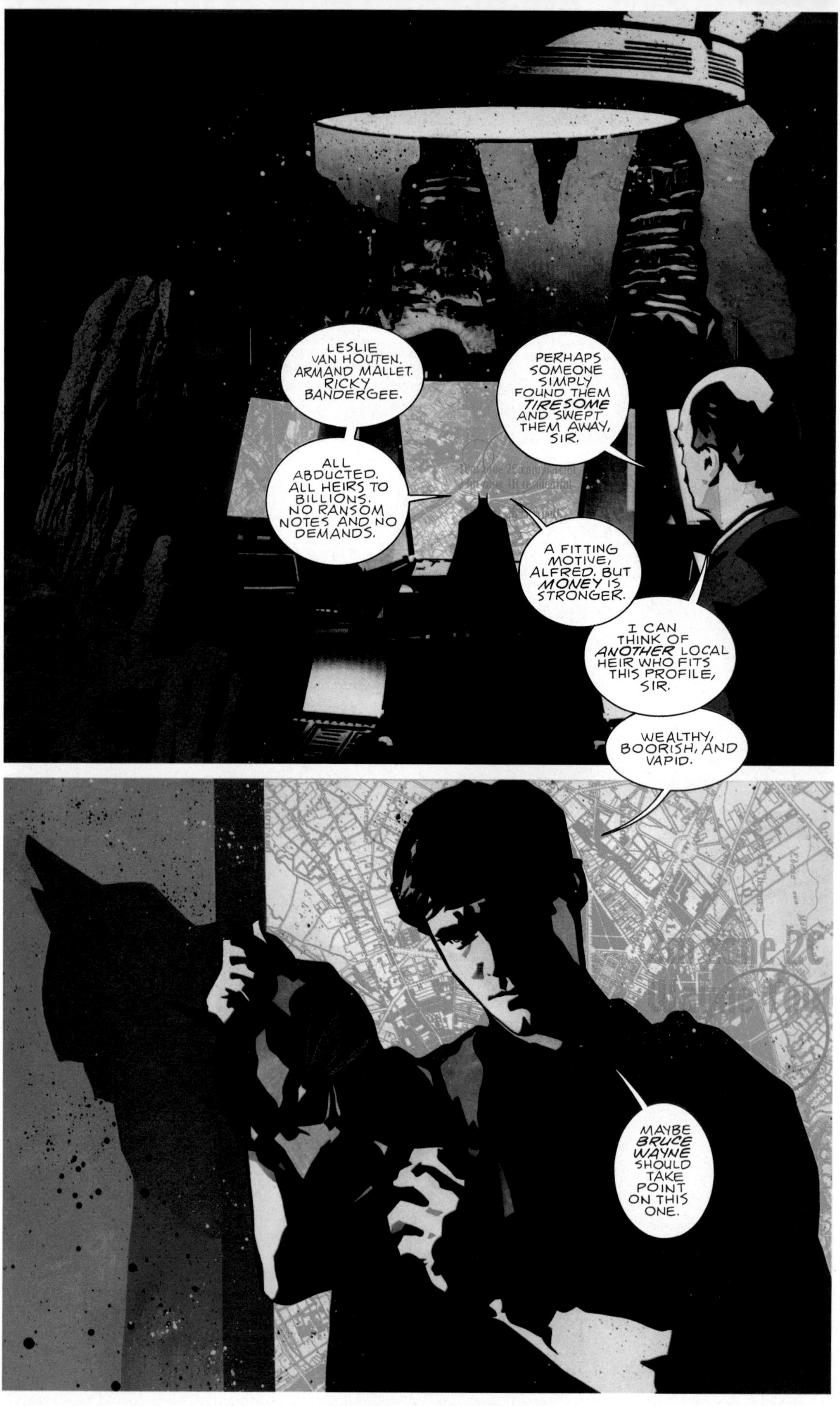
LESLIE VAN HOUTEN. ARMAND MALLET. RICKY BANDERGEE.
ALL ABDUCTED. ALL HEIRS TO BILLIONS. NO RANSOM NOTES AND NO DEMANDS.
PERHAPS SOMEONE SIMPLY FOUND THEM TIRESOME AND SWEPT THEM AWAY, SIR.
A FITTING MOTIVE, ALFRED. BUT MONEY IS STRONGER.
I CAN THINK OF ANOTHER LOCAL HEIR WHO FITS THIS PROFILE, SIR.
WEALTHY, BOORISH, AND VAPID.
MAYBE BRUCE WAYNE SHOULD TAKE POINT ON THIS ONE.

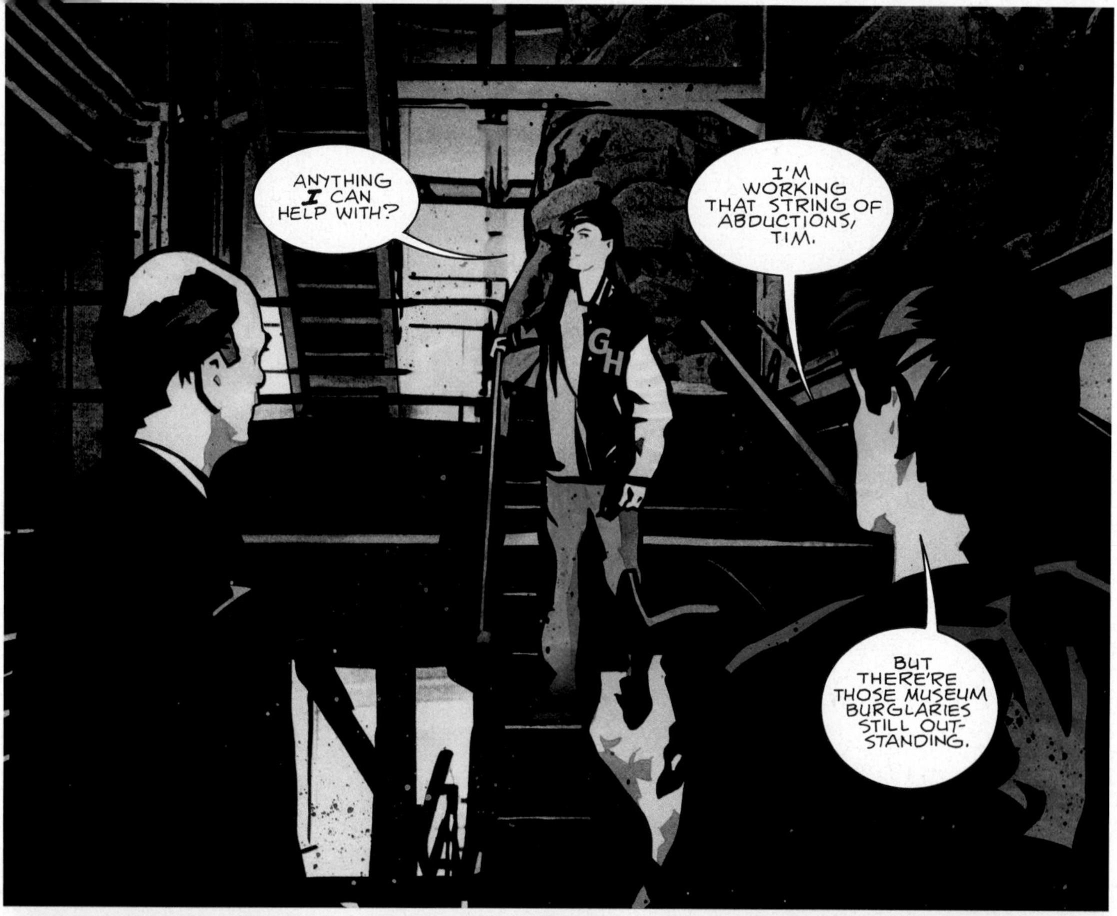
ANYTHING I CAN HELP WITH?
I'M WORKING THAT STRING OF ABDUCTIONS, TIM.
BUT THERE'RE THOSE MUSEUM BURGLARIES STILL OUT-STANDING.

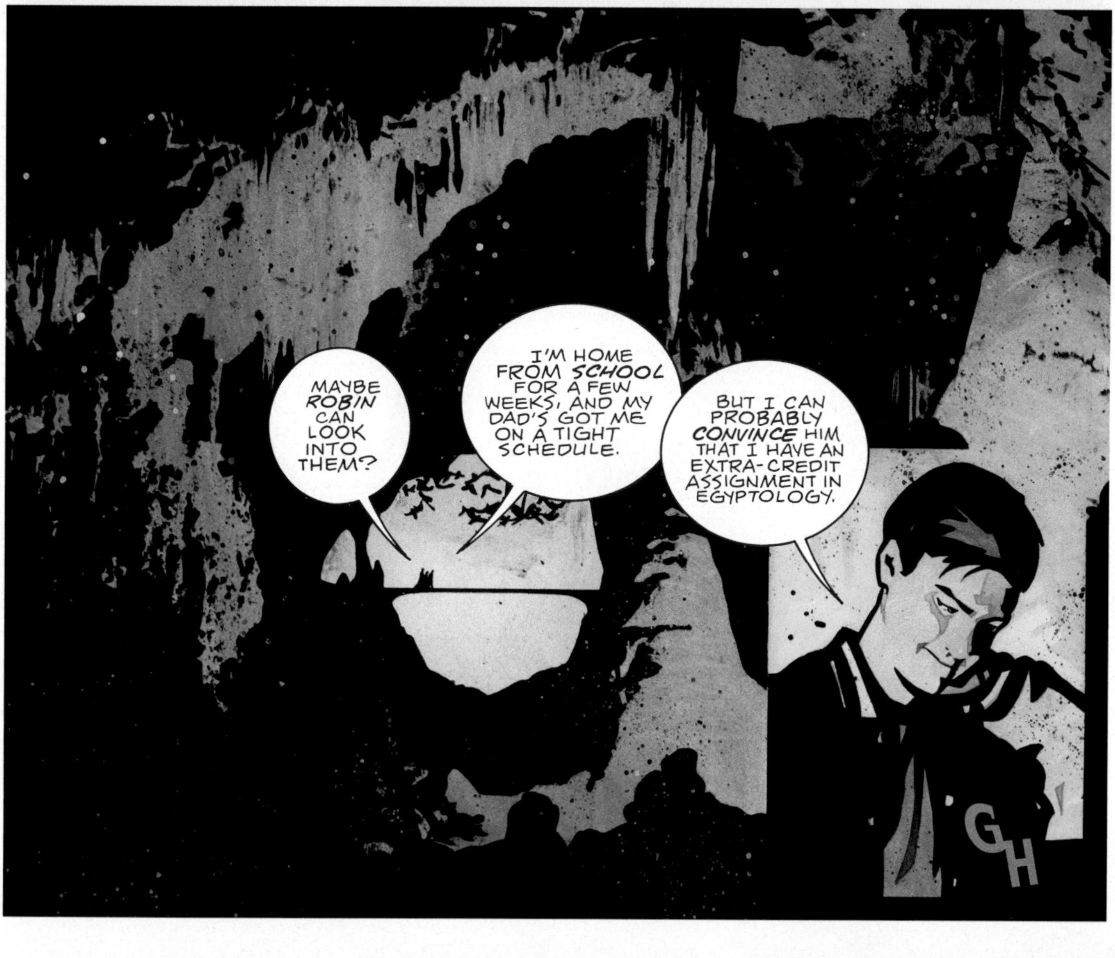
MAYBE ROBIN CAN LOOK INTO THEM?
I'M HOME FROM SCHOOL FOR A FEW WEEKS, AND MY DAD'S GOT ME ON A TIGHT SCHEDULE.
BUT I CAN PROBABLY CONVINCE HIM THAT I HAVE AN EXTRA-CREDIT ASSIGNMENT IN EGYPTOLOGY.

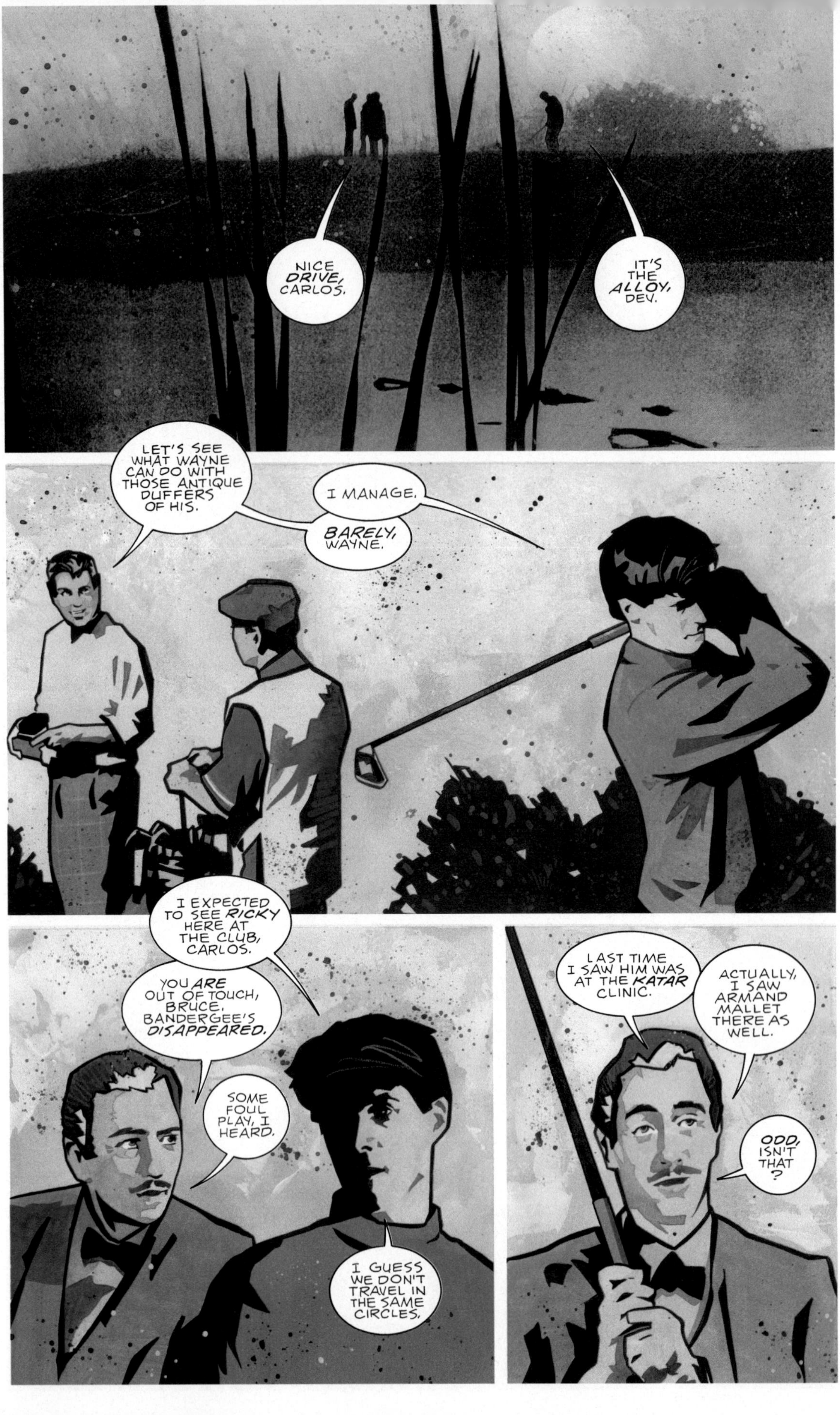
NICE DRIVE, CARLOS.
IT'S THE ALLOY, DEV.
LET'S SEE WHAT WAYNE CAN DO WITH THOSE ANTIQUE DUFFERS OF HIS.
I MANAGE.
BARELY, WAYNE.
I EXPECTED TO SEE RICKY HERE AT THE CLUB, CARLOS.
YOU ARE OUT OF TOUCH, BRUCE. BANDERGEE'S DISAPPEARED.
SOME FOUL PLAY, I HEARD.
I GUESS WE DON'T TRAVEL IN THE SAME CIRCLES.
LAST TIME I SAW HIM WAS AT THE KATAR CLINIC.
ACTUALLY, I SAW ARMAND MALLET THERE AS WELL.
ODD, ISN'T THAT?

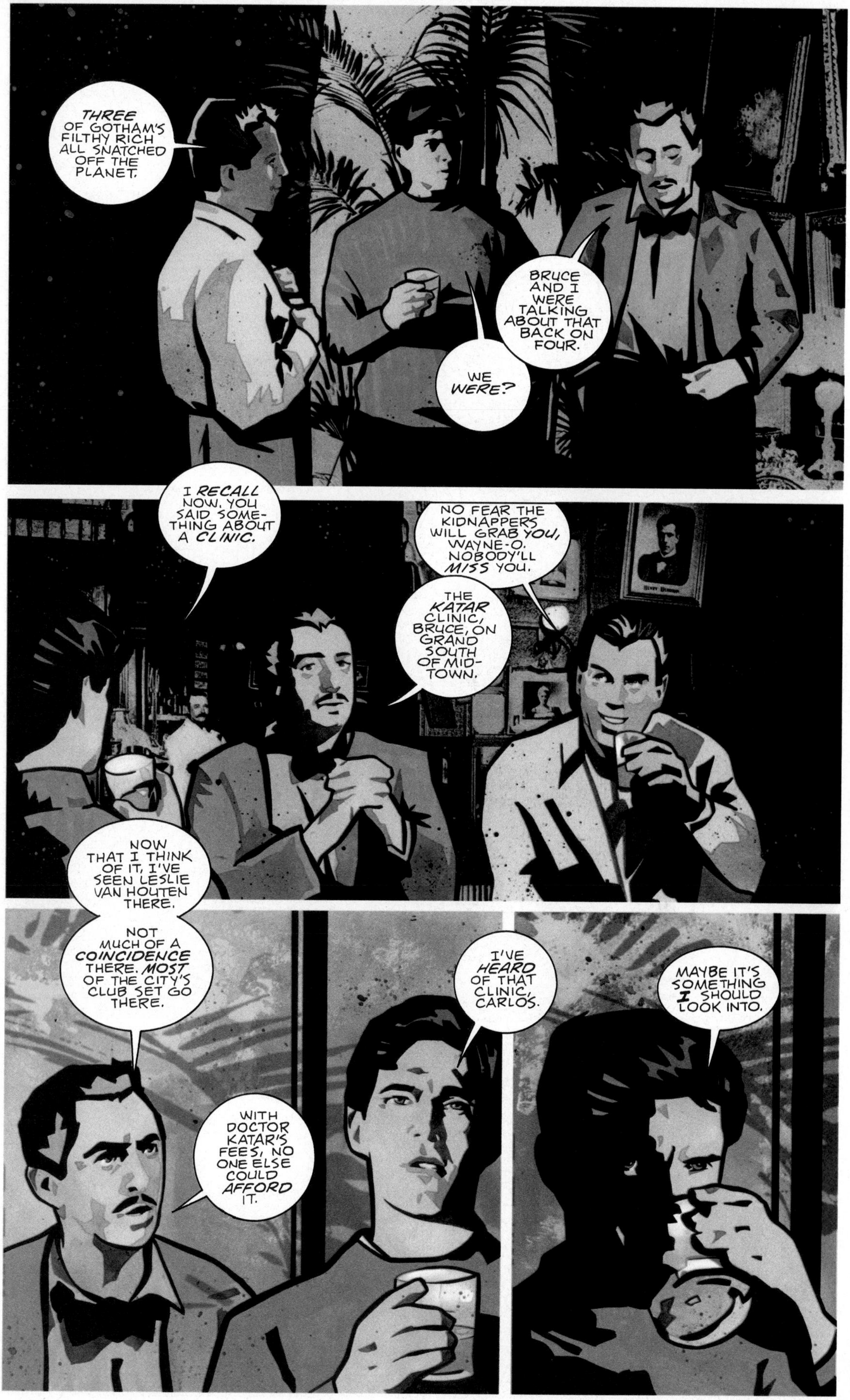
THREE OF GOTHAM'S FILTHY RICH ALL SNATCHED OFF THE PLANET.
BRUCE AND I WERE TALKING ABOUT THAT BACK ON FOUR.
WE WERE?
I RECALL NOW. YOU SAID SOME-THING ABOUT A CLINIC.
NO FEAR THE KIDNAPPERS WILL GRAB YOU, WAYNE-O. NOBODY'LL MISS YOU.
THE KATAR CLINIC, BRUCE, ON GRAND SOUTH OF MID-TOWN.
NOW THAT I THINK OF IT, I'VE SEEN LESLIE VAN HOUTEN THERE.
NOT MUCH OF A COINCIDENCE THERE. MOST OF THE CITY'S CLUB SET GO THERE.
WITH DOCTOR KATAR'S FEES, NO ONE ELSE COULD AFFORD IT.
I'VE HEARD OF THAT CLINIC, CARLOS.
MAYBE IT'S SOMETHING I SHOULD LOOK INTO.

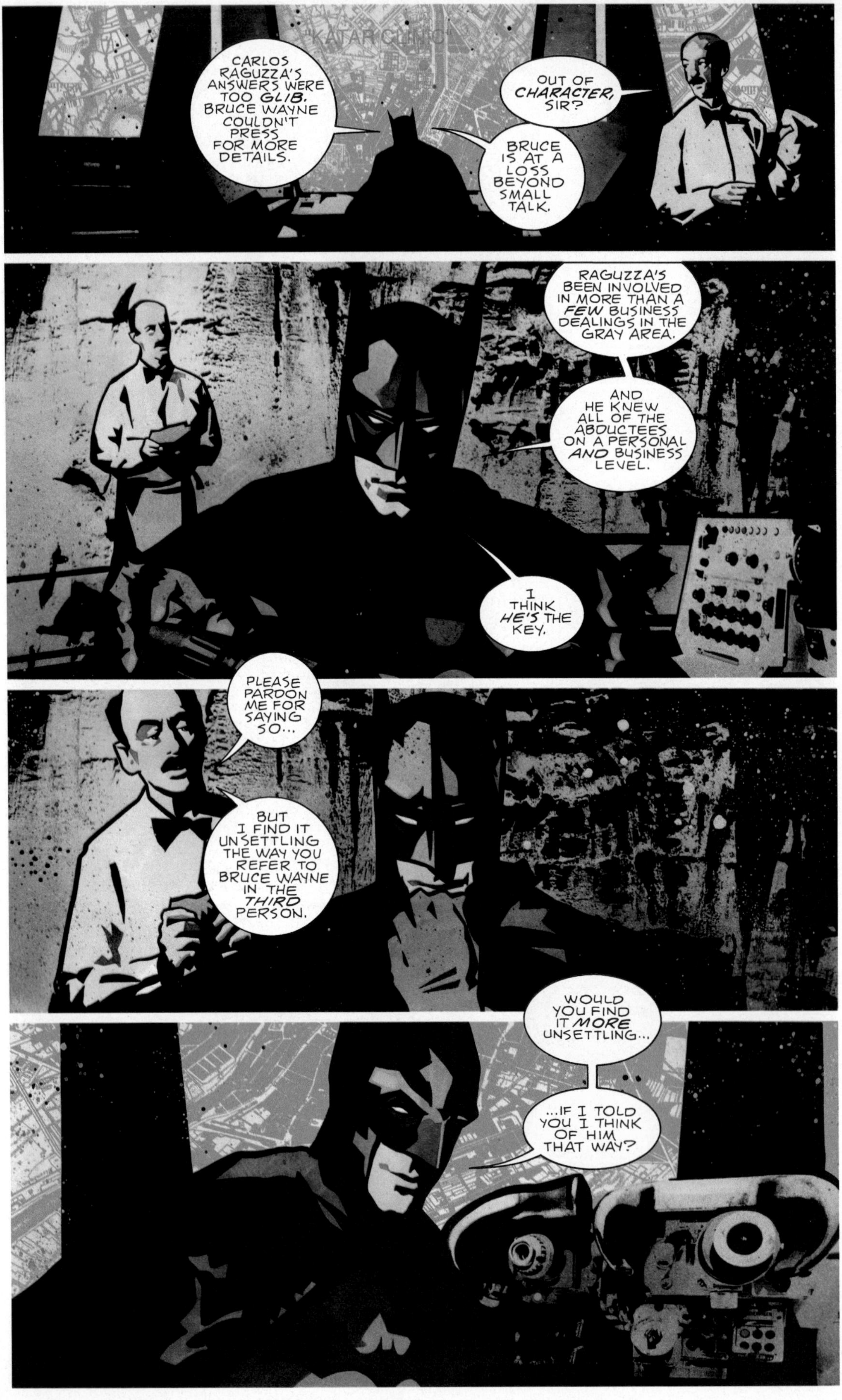
"KATAR CLINIC"
CARLOS RAGUZZA'S ANSWERS WERE TOO GLIB. BRUCE WAYNE COULDN'T PRESS FOR MORE DETAILS.
OUT OF CHARACTER, SIR?
BRUCE IS AT A LOSS BEYOND SMALL TALK.
RAGUZZA'S BEEN INVOLVED IN MORE THAN A FEW BUSINESS DEALINGS IN THE GRAY AREA.
AND HE KNEW ALL OF THE ABDUCTEES ON A PERSONAL AND BUSINESS LEVEL.
I THINK HE'S THE KEY.
PLEASE PARDON ME FOR SAYING SO...
BUT I FIND IT UNSETTLING THE WAY YOU REFER TO BRUCE WAYNE IN THE THIRD PERSON.
WOULD YOU FIND IT MORE UNSETTLING...
...IF I TOLD YOU I THINK OF HIM THAT WAY?

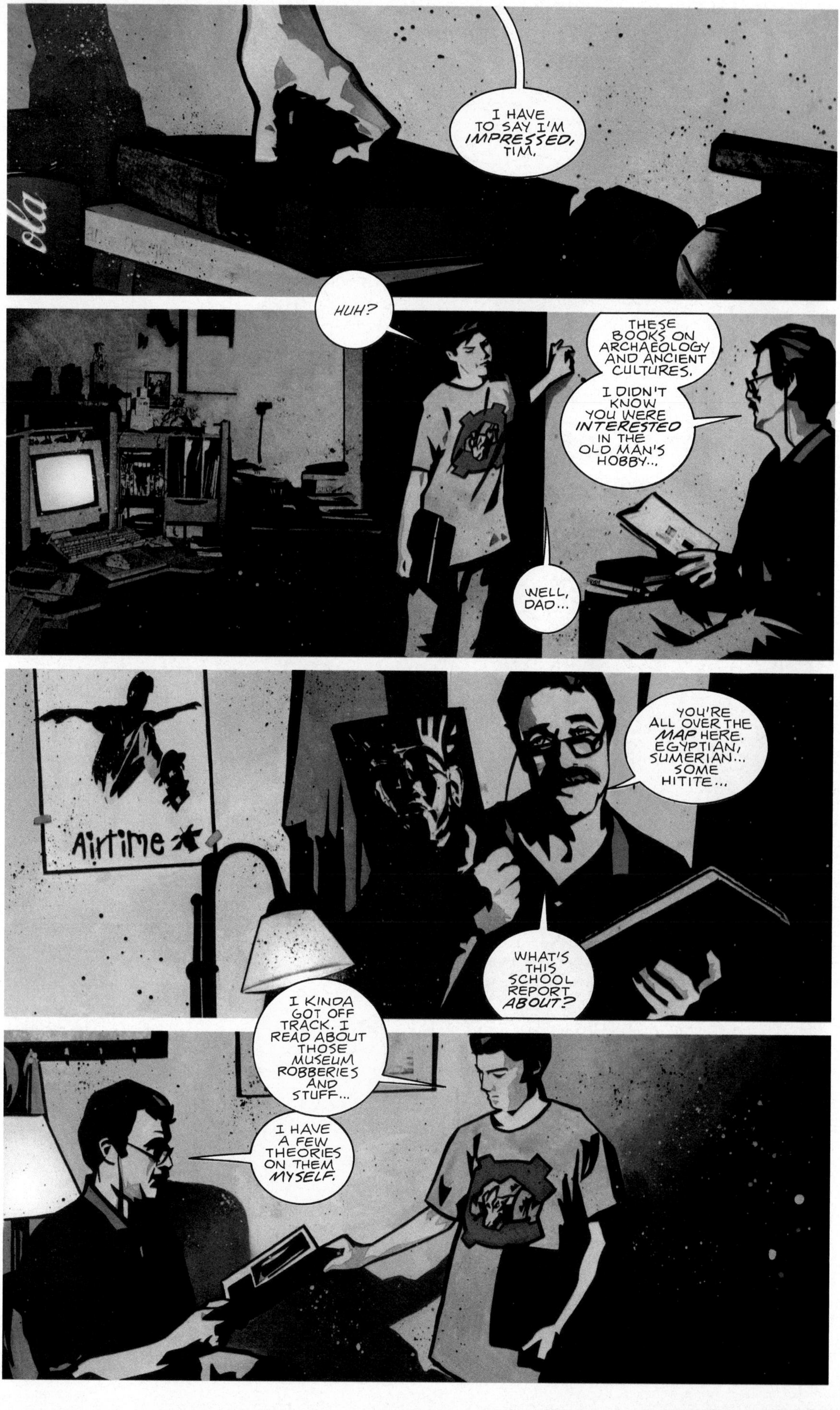
ola
I HAVE TO SAY I'M *IMPRESSED*, TIM.
HUH?
THESE BOOKS ON ARCHAEOLOGY AND ANCIENT CULTURES.
I DIDN'T KNOW YOU WERE *INTERESTED* IN THE OLD MAN'S HOBBY...
WELL, DAD...
Airtime
YOU'RE ALL OVER THE *MAP* HERE. EGYPTIAN, SUMERIAN... SOME HITITE...
WHAT'S THIS SCHOOL REPORT *ABOUT?*
I KINDA GOT OFF TRACK. I READ ABOUT THOSE MUSEUM ROBBERIES AND STUFF...
I HAVE A FEW THEORIES ON THEM *MYSELF*.

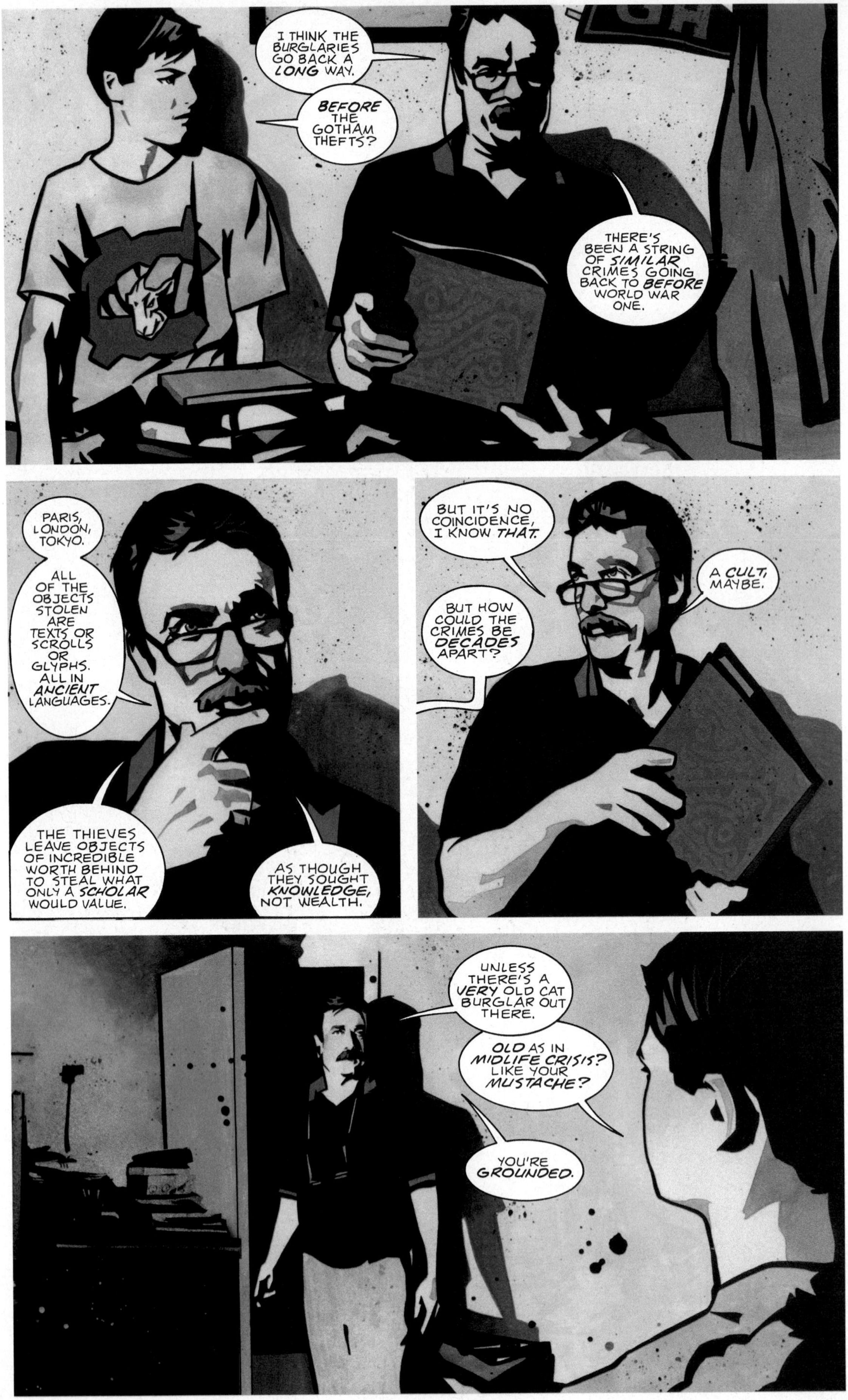
I THINK THE BURGLARIES GO BACK A LONG WAY.
BEFORE THE GOTHAM THEFTS?
THERE'S BEEN A STRING OF SIMILAR CRIMES GOING BACK TO BEFORE WORLD WAR ONE.
PARIS, LONDON, TOKYO.
ALL OF THE OBJECTS STOLEN ARE TEXTS OR SCROLLS OR GLYPHS. ALL IN ANCIENT LANGUAGES.
THE THIEVES LEAVE OBJECTS OF INCREDIBLE WORTH BEHIND TO STEAL WHAT ONLY A SCHOLAR WOULD VALUE.
AS THOUGH THEY SOUGHT KNOWLEDGE, NOT WEALTH.
BUT IT'S NO COINCIDENCE, I KNOW THAT.
A CULT, MAYBE.
BUT HOW COULD THE CRIMES BE DECADES APART?
UNLESS THERE'S A VERY OLD CAT BURGLAR OUT THERE.
OLD AS IN MIDLIFE CRISIS? LIKE YOUR MUSTACHE?
YOU'RE GROUNDED.

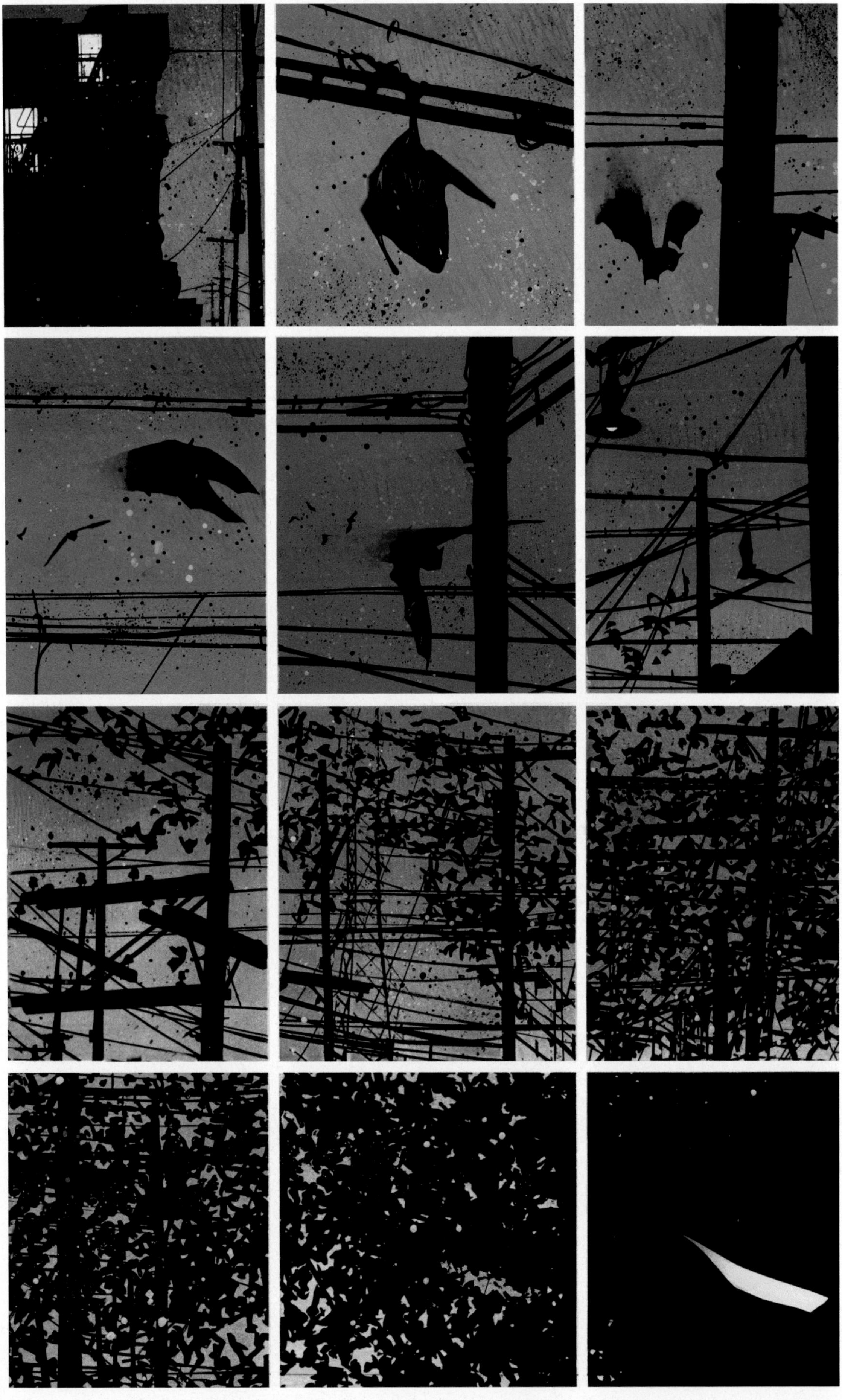

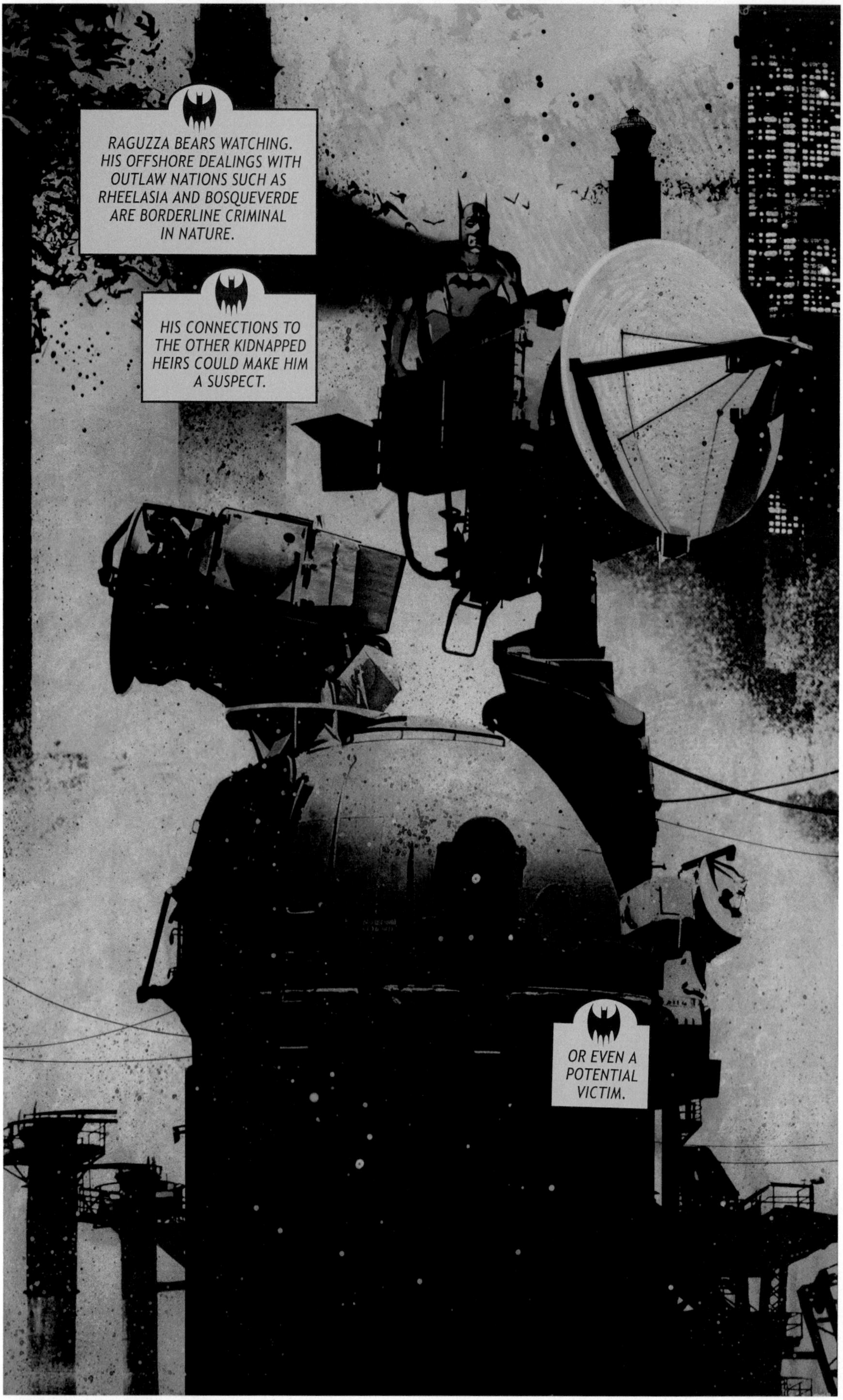
RAGUZZA BEARS WATCHING. HIS OFFSHORE DEALINGS WITH OUTLAW NATIONS SUCH AS RHEELASIA AND BOSQUEVERDE ARE BORDERLINE CRIMINAL IN NATURE.
HIS CONNECTIONS TO THE OTHER KIDNAPPED HEIRS COULD MAKE HIM A SUSPECT.
OR EVEN A POTENTIAL VICTIM.

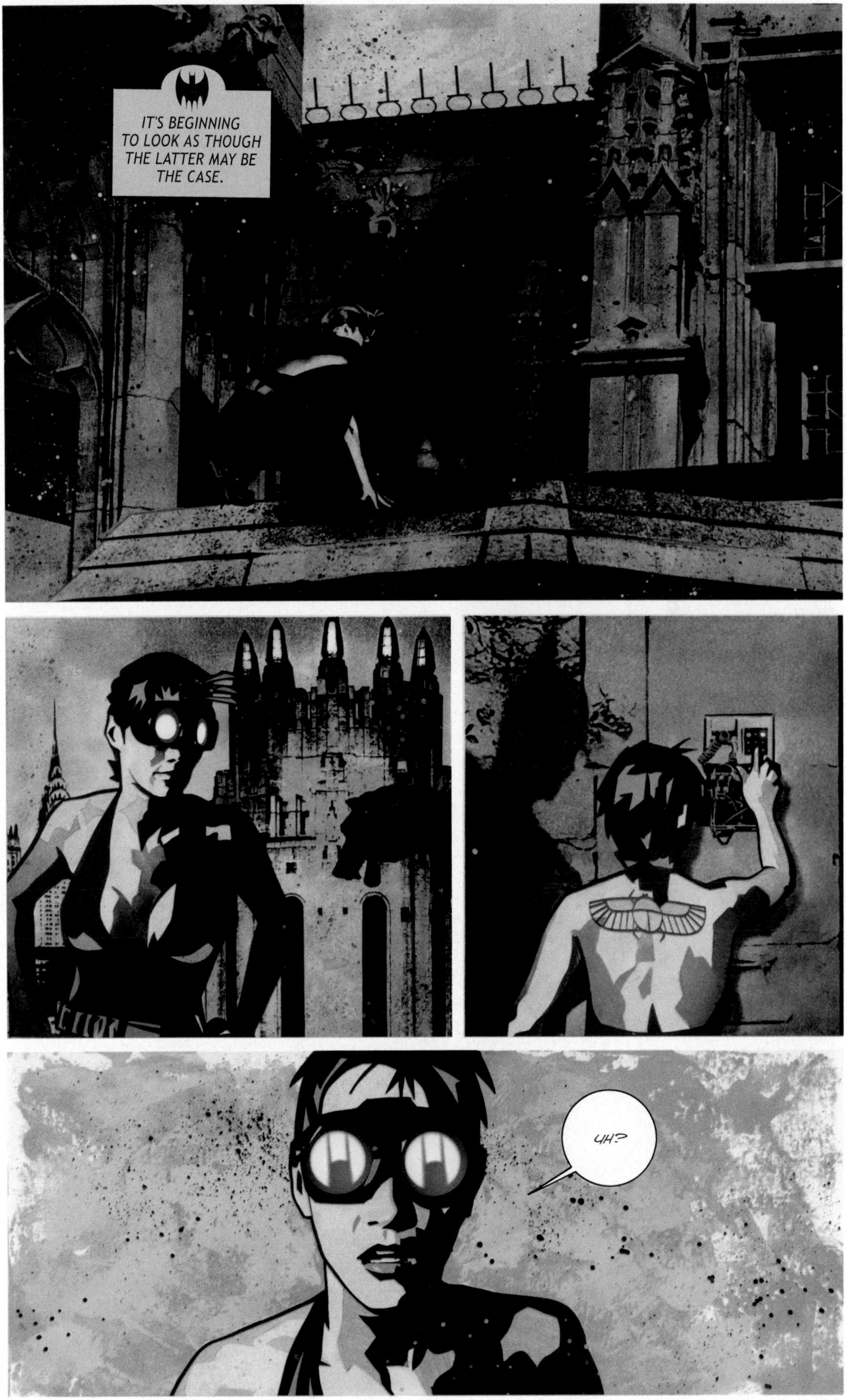
IT'S BEGINNING TO LOOK AS THOUGH THE LATTER MAY BE THE CASE.
UH?

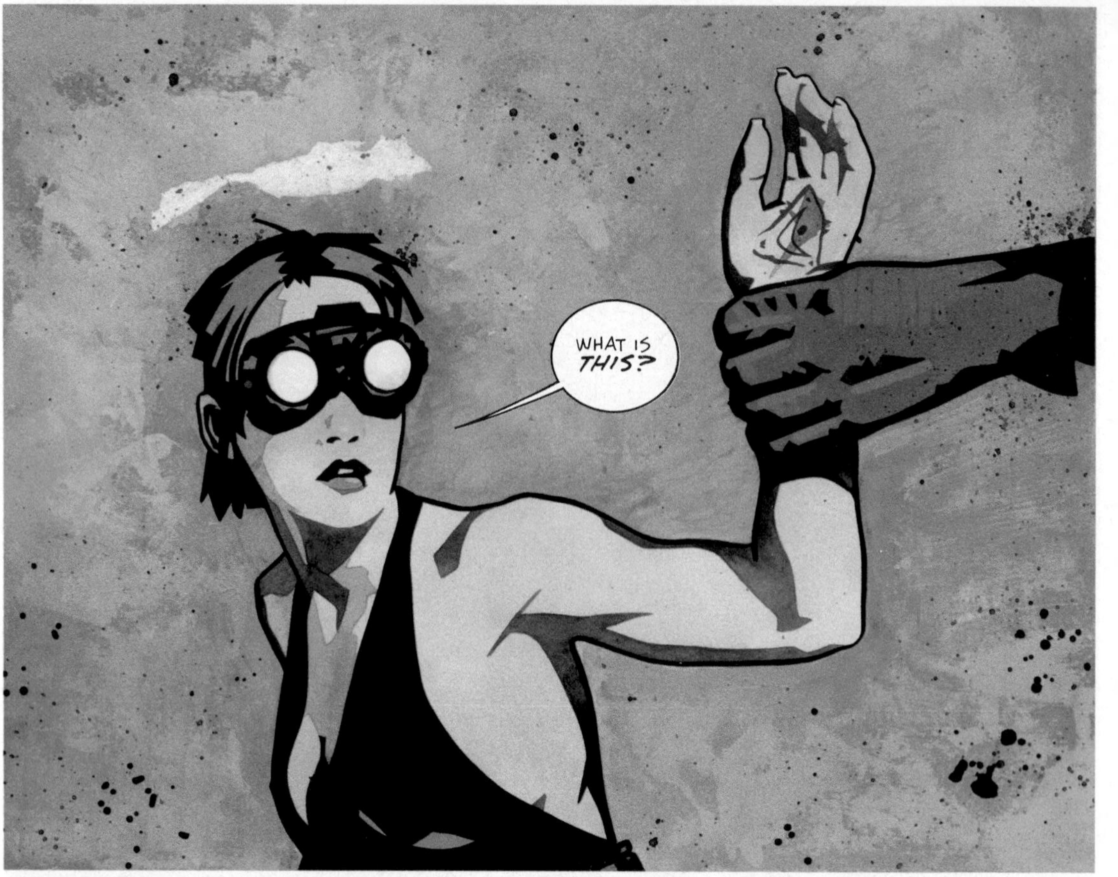
WHAT IS THIS?

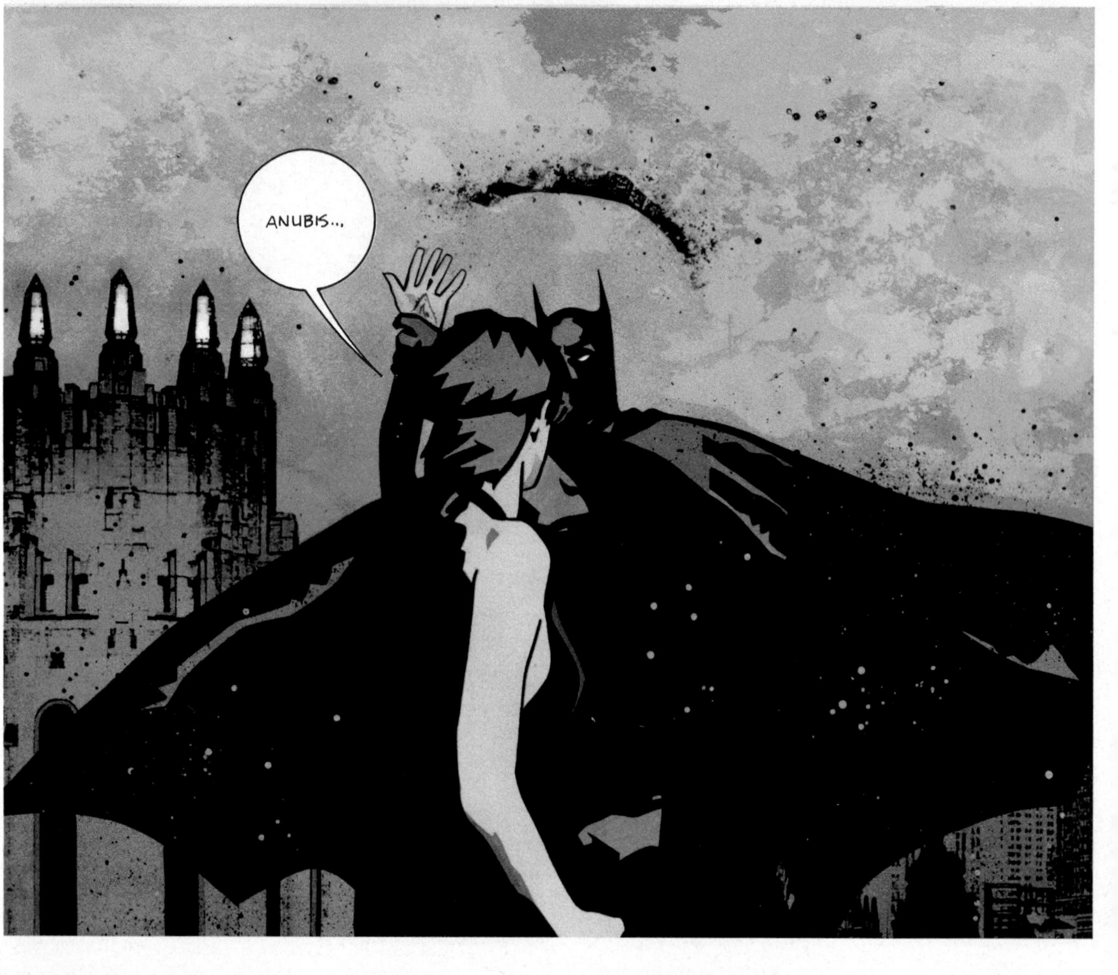
ANUBIS...

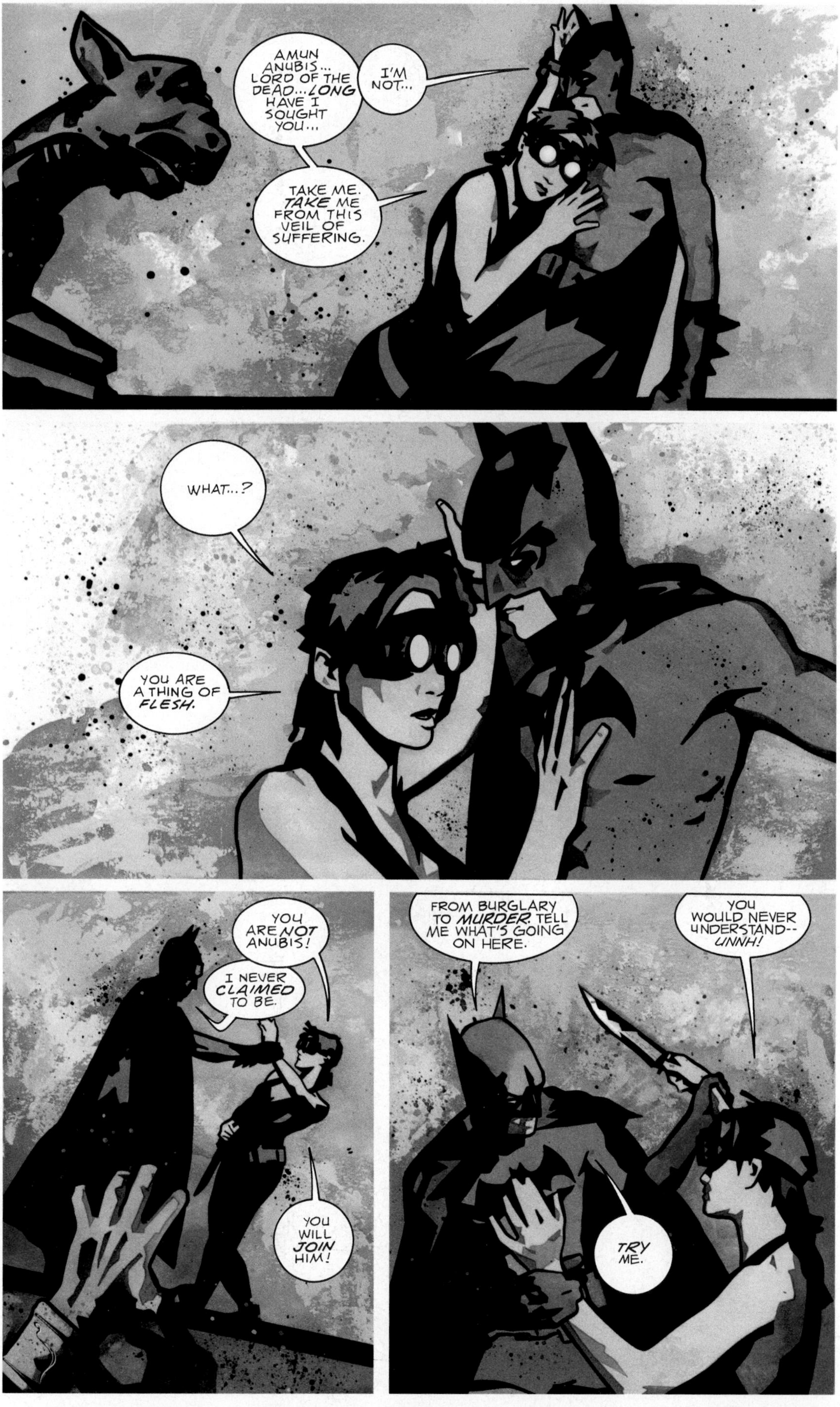
AMUN ANUBIS... LORD OF THE DEAD...LONG HAVE I SOUGHT YOU...
I'M NOT...
TAKE ME. TAKE ME FROM THIS VEIL OF SUFFERING.
WHAT...?
YOU ARE A THING OF FLESH.
YOU ARE NOT ANUBIS!
I NEVER CLAIMED TO BE.
YOU WILL JOIN HIM!
FROM BURGLARY TO MURDER. TELL ME WHAT'S GOING ON HERE.
YOU WOULD NEVER UNDERSTAND-- UNNH!
TRY ME.

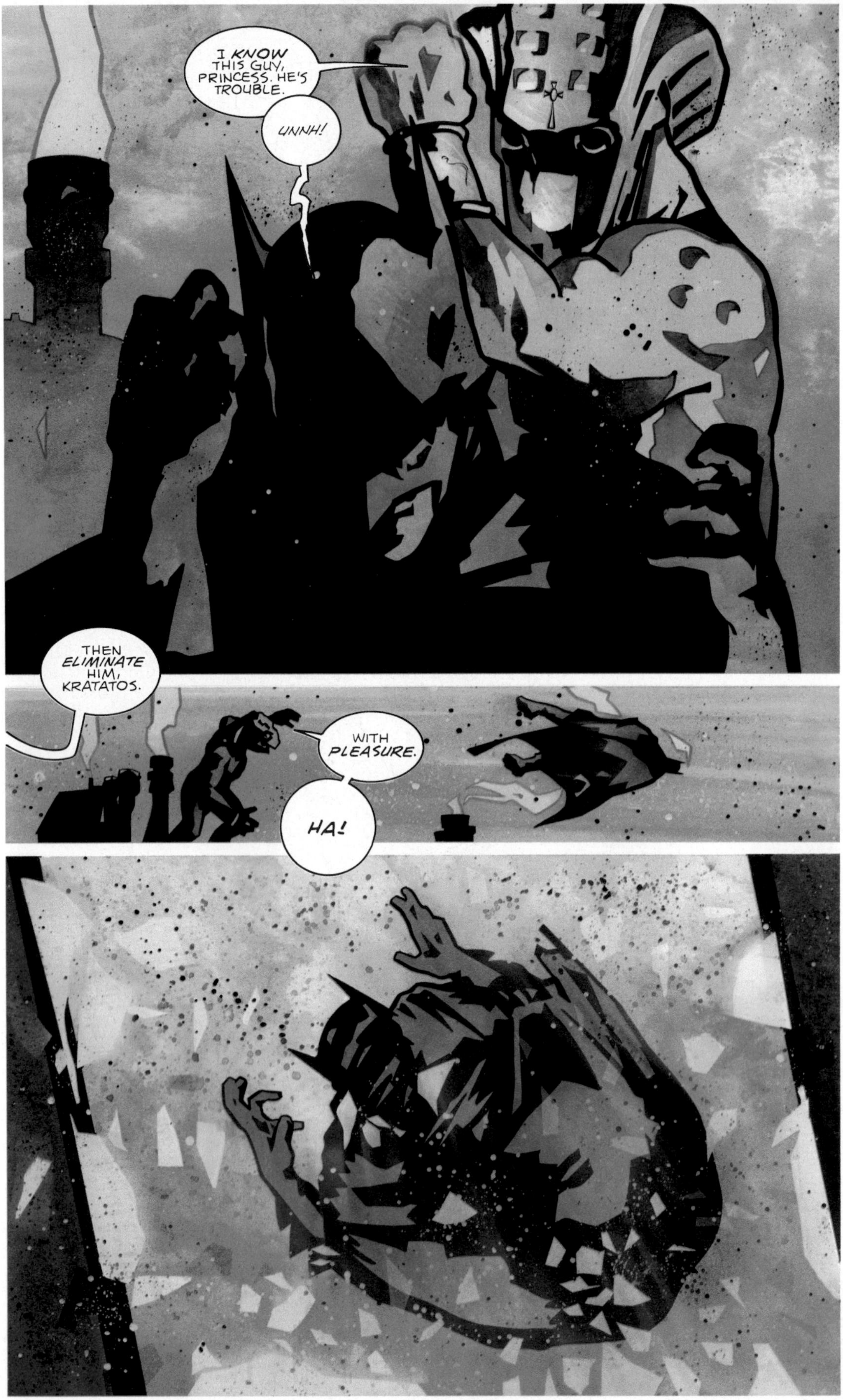
I KNOW THIS GUY, PRINCESS. HE'S TROUBLE.
UNNH!
THEN ELIMINATE HIM, KRATATOS.
WITH PLEASURE.
HA!

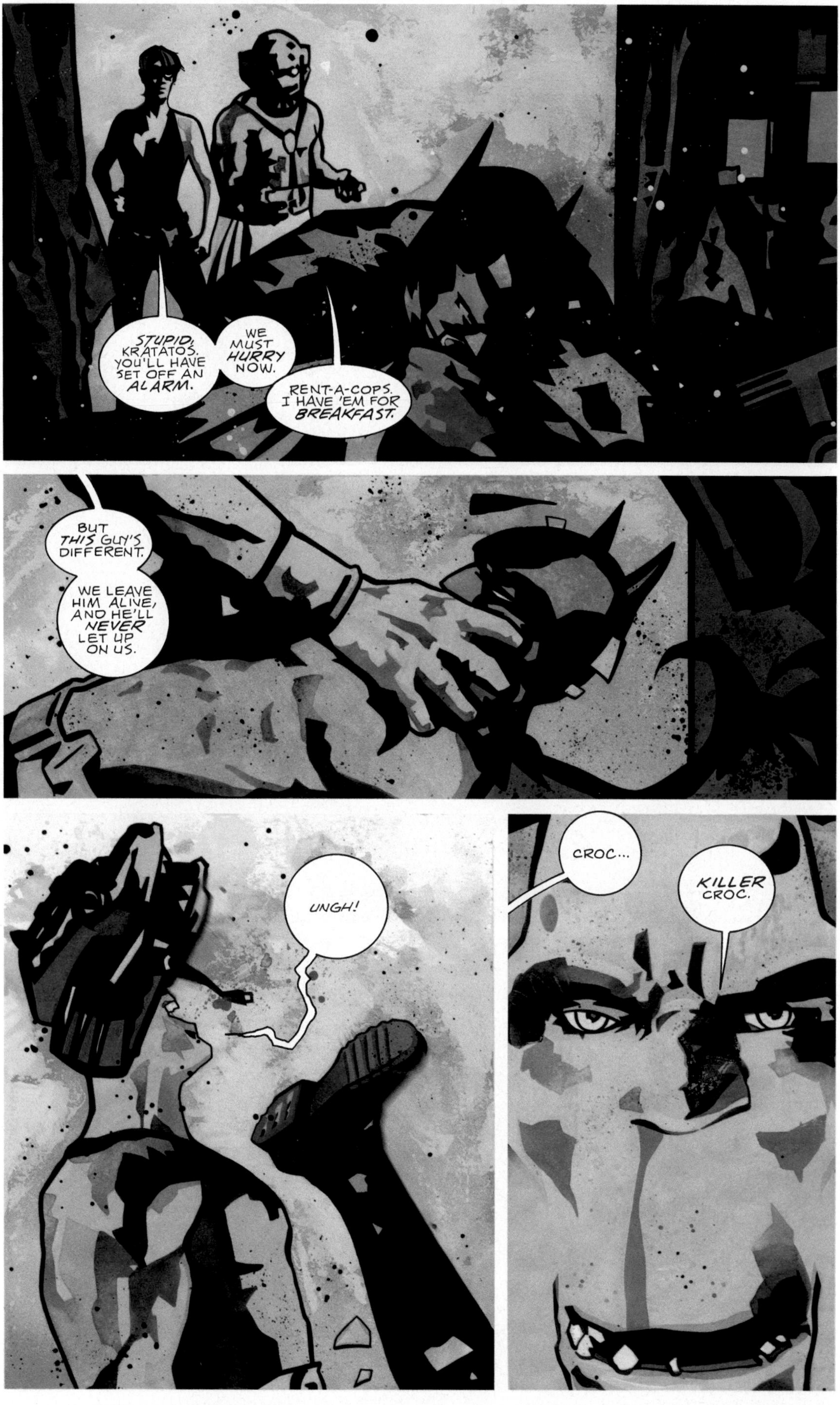
STUPID, KRATATOS. YOU'LL HAVE SET OFF AN ALARM.
WE MUST HURRY NOW.
RENT-A-COPS. I HAVE 'EM FOR BREAKFAST.
BUT THIS GUY'S DIFFERENT.
WE LEAVE HIM ALIVE, AND HE'LL NEVER LET UP ON US.
UNGH!
CROC...
KILLER CROC.

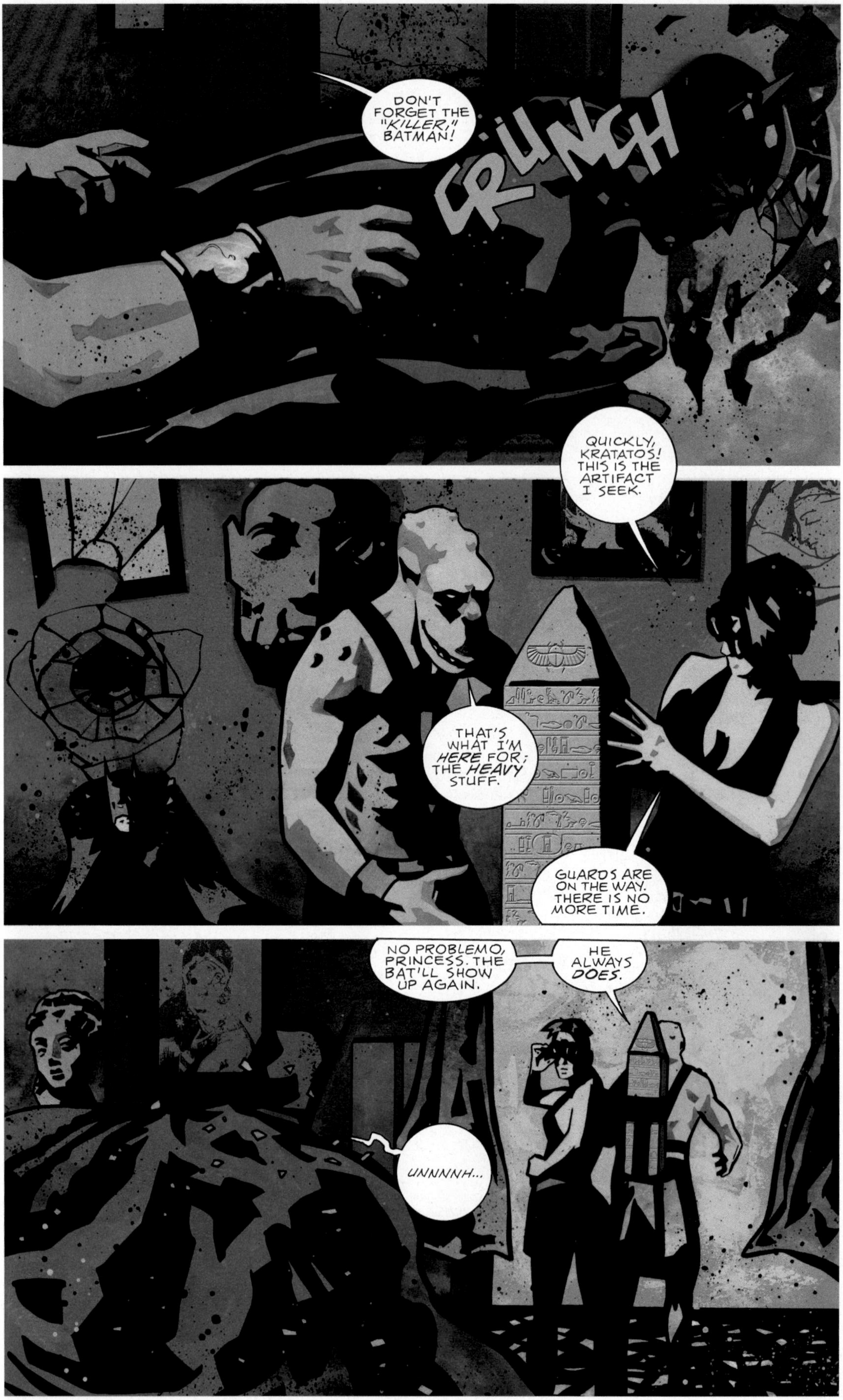
DON'T FORGET THE "KILLER," BATMAN!
CRUNCH
QUICKLY, KRATATOS! THIS IS THE ARTIFACT I SEEK.
THAT'S WHAT I'M HERE FOR; THE HEAVY STUFF.
GUARDS ARE ON THE WAY. THERE IS NO MORE TIME.
NO PROBLEMO, PRINCESS. THE BAT'LL SHOW UP AGAIN.
HE ALWAYS DOES.
UNNNNH...

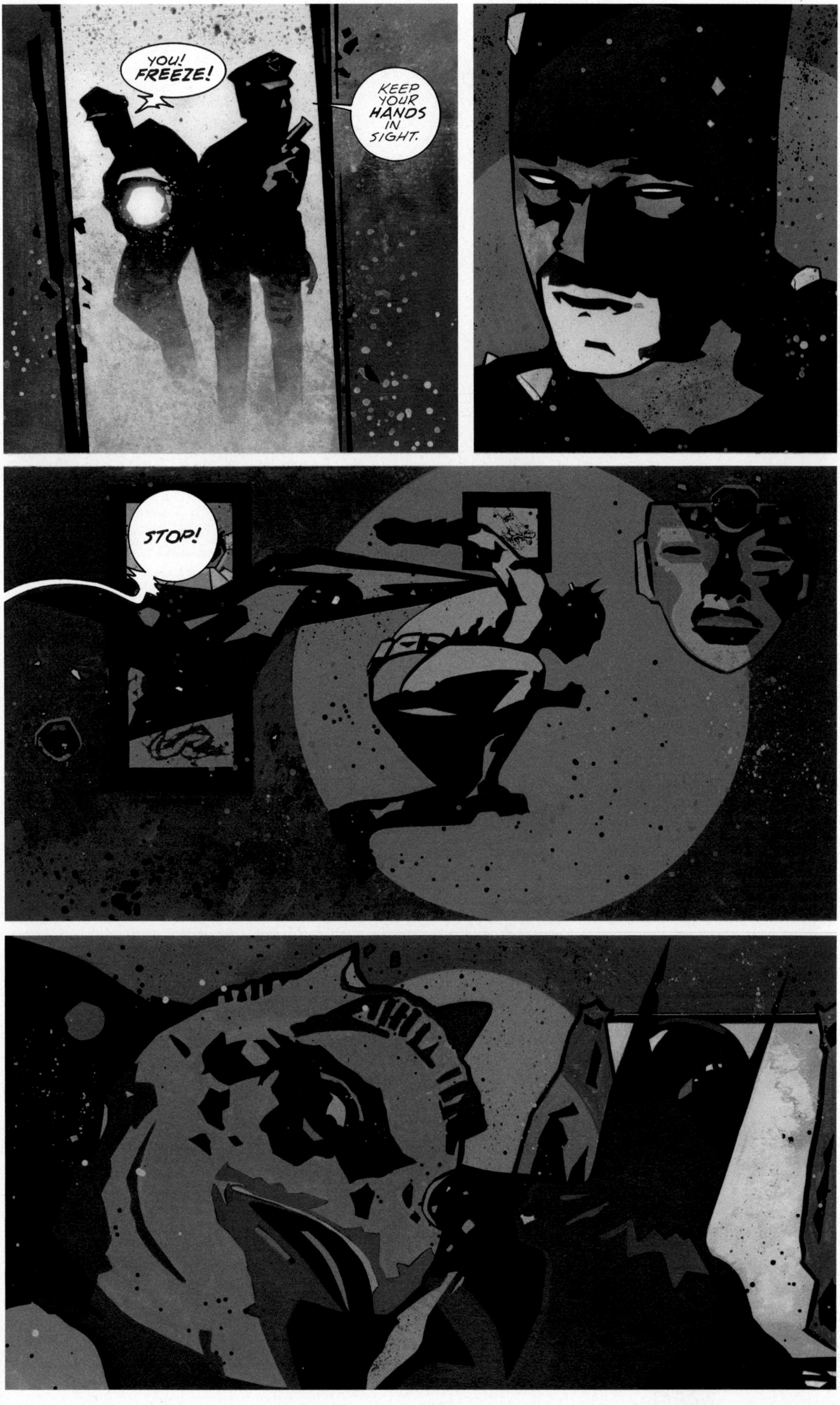
YOU! FREEZE!
KEEP YOUR HANDS IN SIGHT.
STOP!

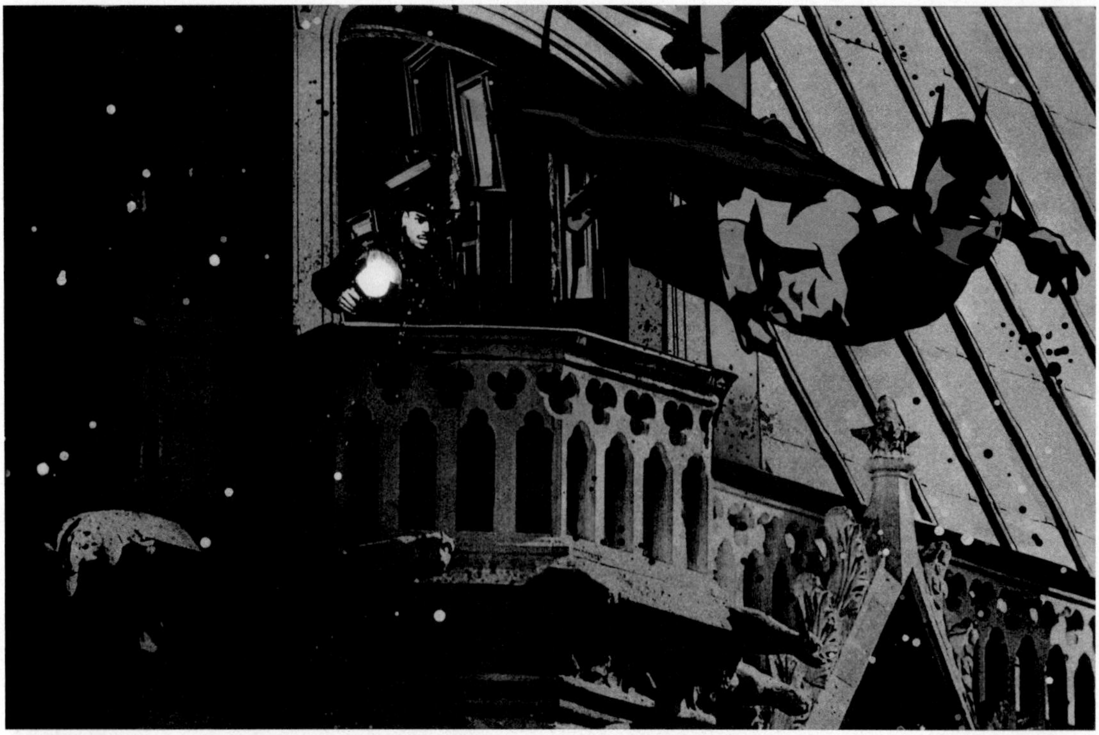
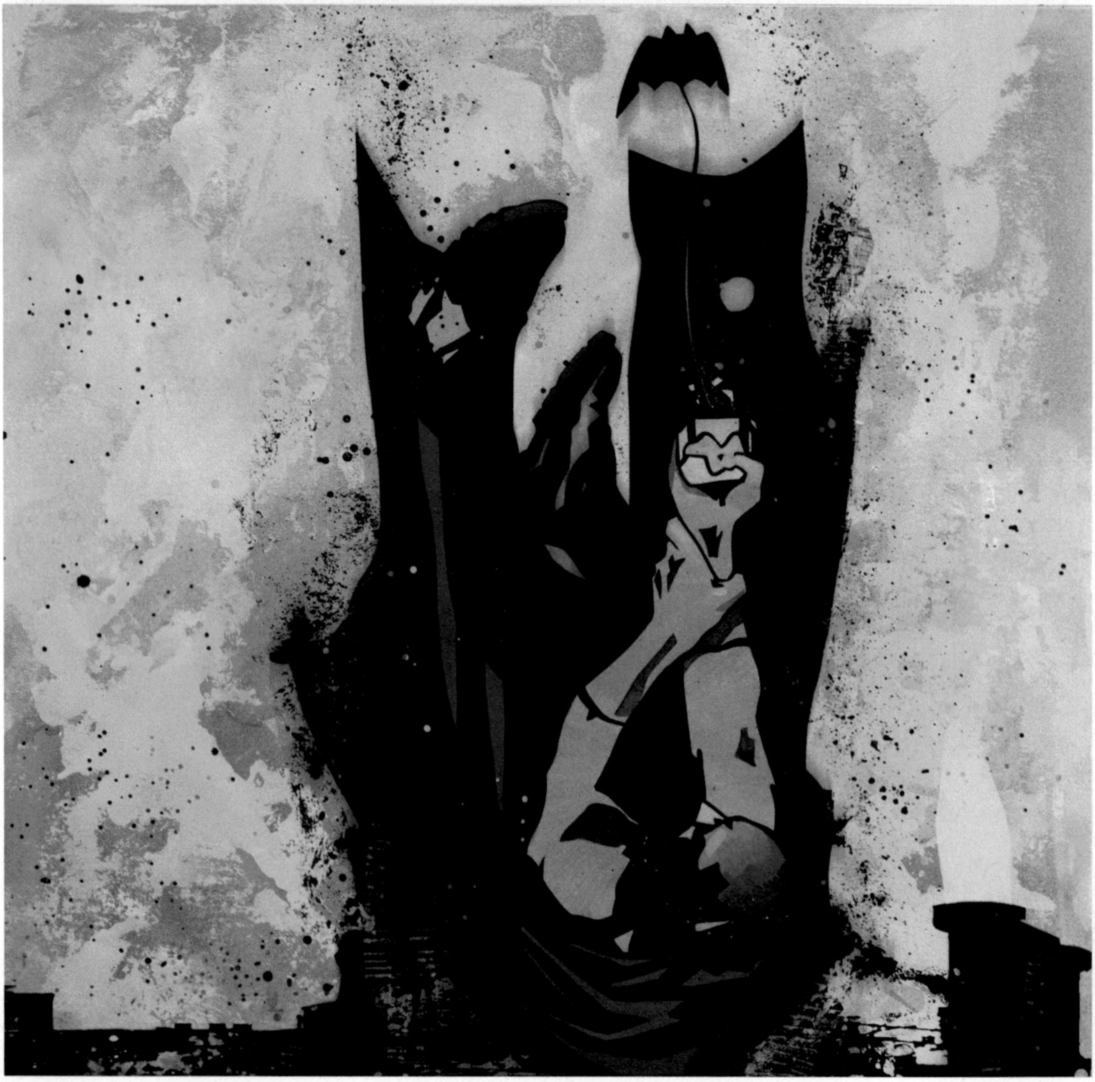

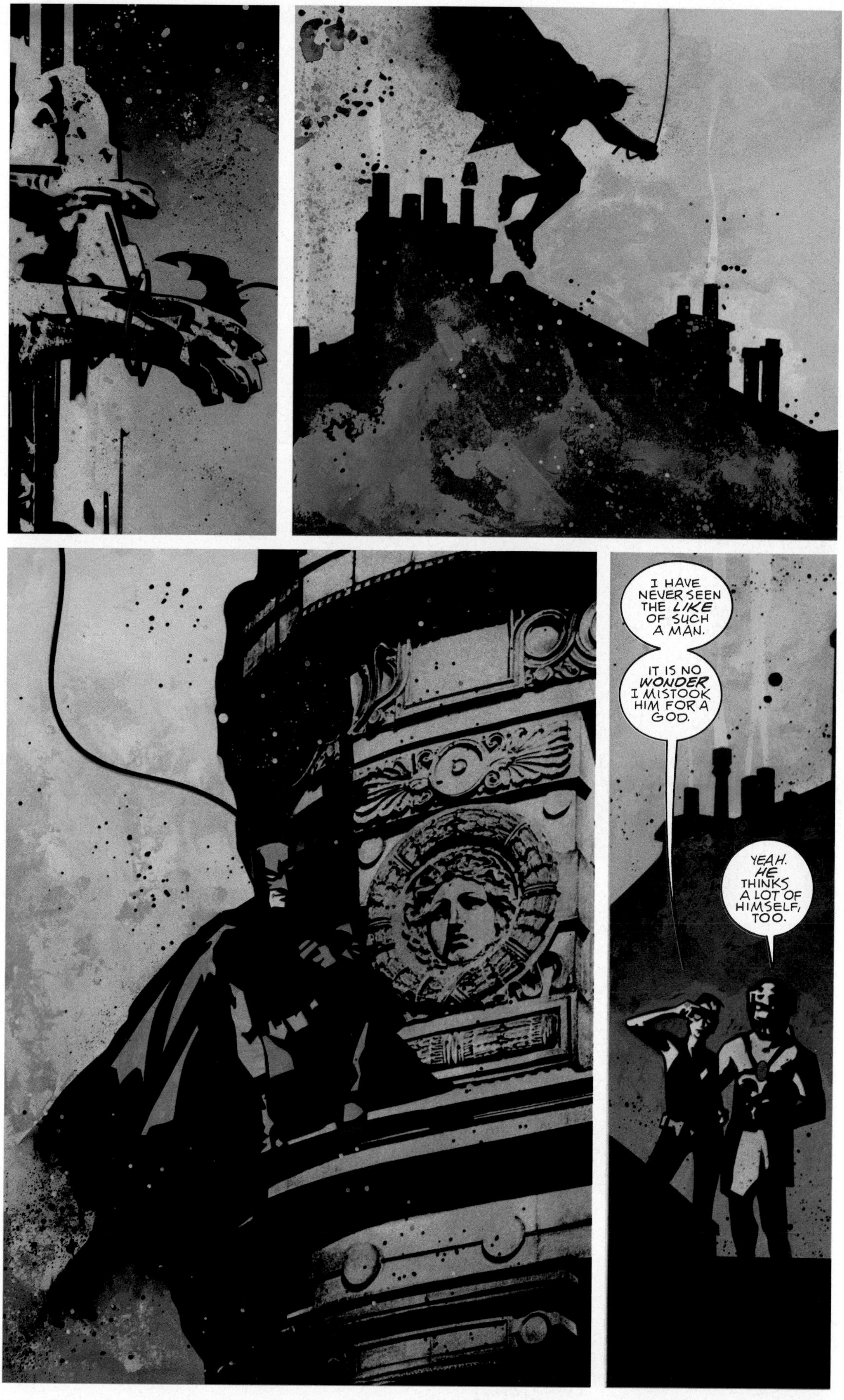
I HAVE NEVER SEEN THE LIKE OF SUCH A MAN.
IT IS NO WONDER I MISTOOK HIM FOR A GOD.
YEAH. HE THINKS A LOT OF HIMSELF, TOO.

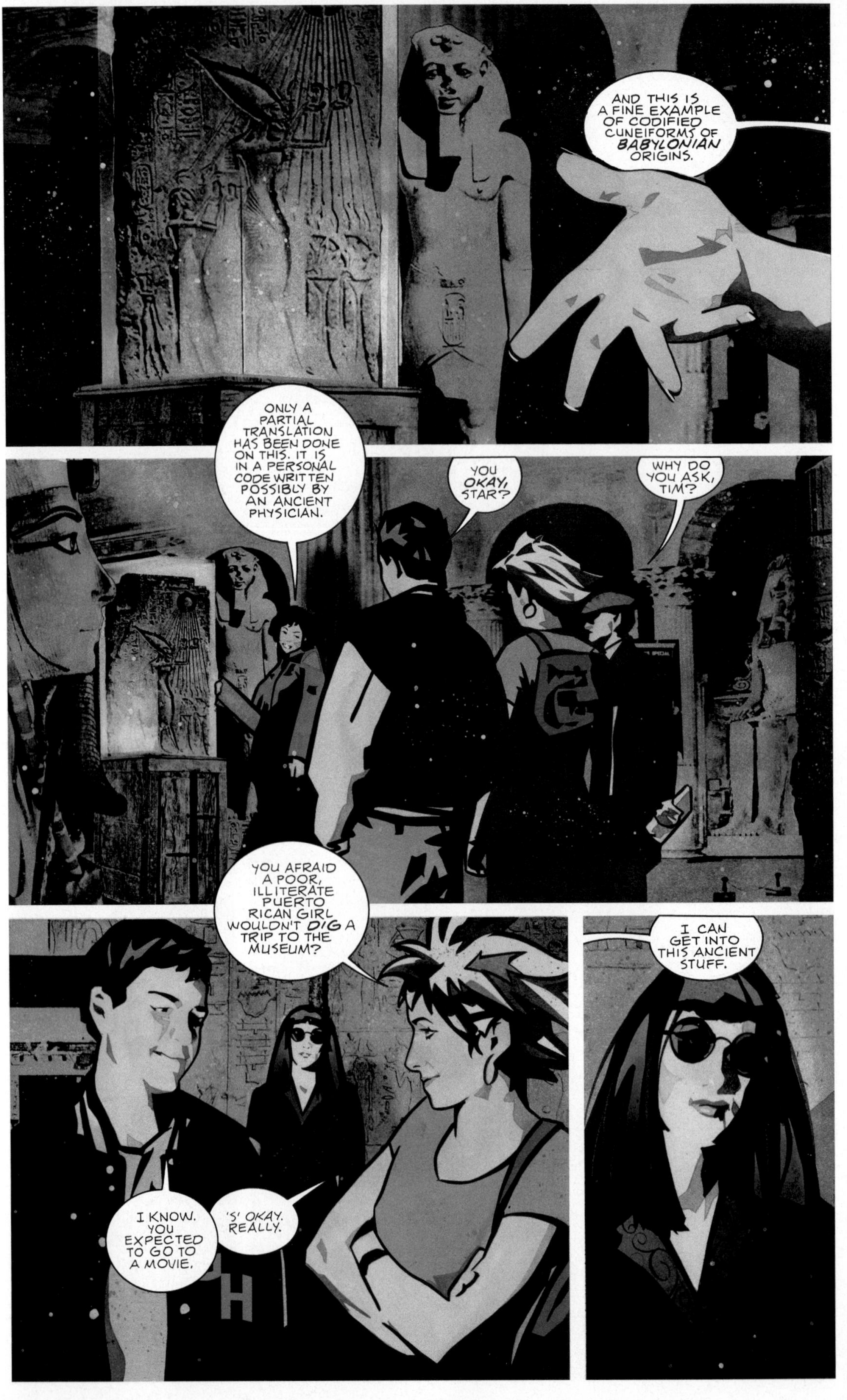
AND THIS IS A FINE EXAMPLE OF CODIFIED CUNEIFORMS OF BABYLONIAN ORIGINS.
ONLY A PARTIAL TRANSLATION HAS BEEN DONE ON THIS. IT IS IN A PERSONAL CODE WRITTEN POSSIBLY BY AN ANCIENT PHYSICIAN.
YOU OKAY, STAR?
WHY DO YOU ASK, TIM?
YOU AFRAID A POOR, ILLITERATE PUERTO RICAN GIRL WOULDN'T DIG A TRIP TO THE MUSEUM?
I KNOW. YOU EXPECTED TO GO TO A MOVIE.
'S' OKAY. REALLY.
I CAN GET INTO THIS ANCIENT STUFF.

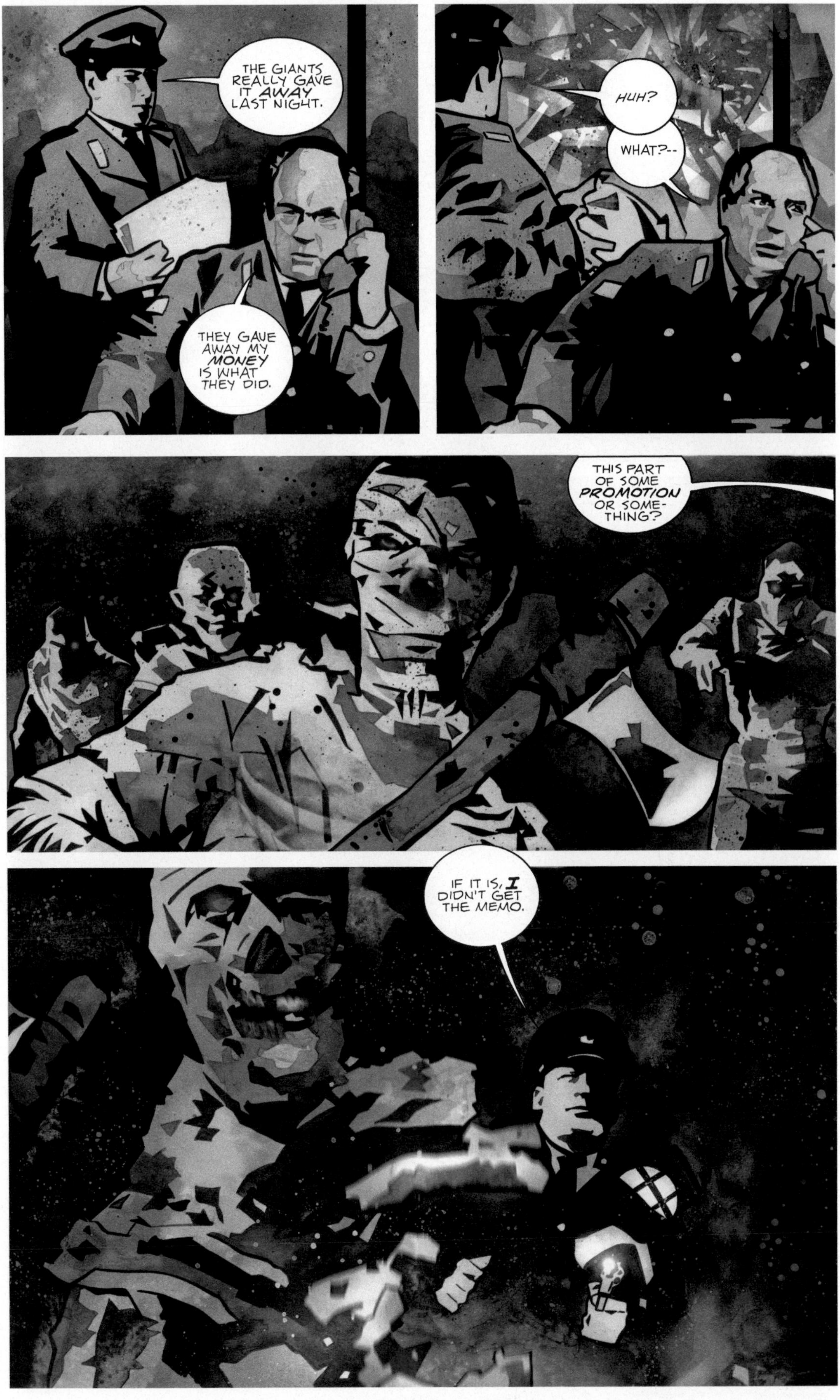
THE GIANTS REALLY GAVE IT AWAY LAST NIGHT.
THEY GAVE AWAY MY MONEY IS WHAT THEY DID.
HUH?
WHAT?--
THIS PART OF SOME PROMOTION OR SOME-THING?
IF IT IS, I DIDN'T GET THE MEMO.

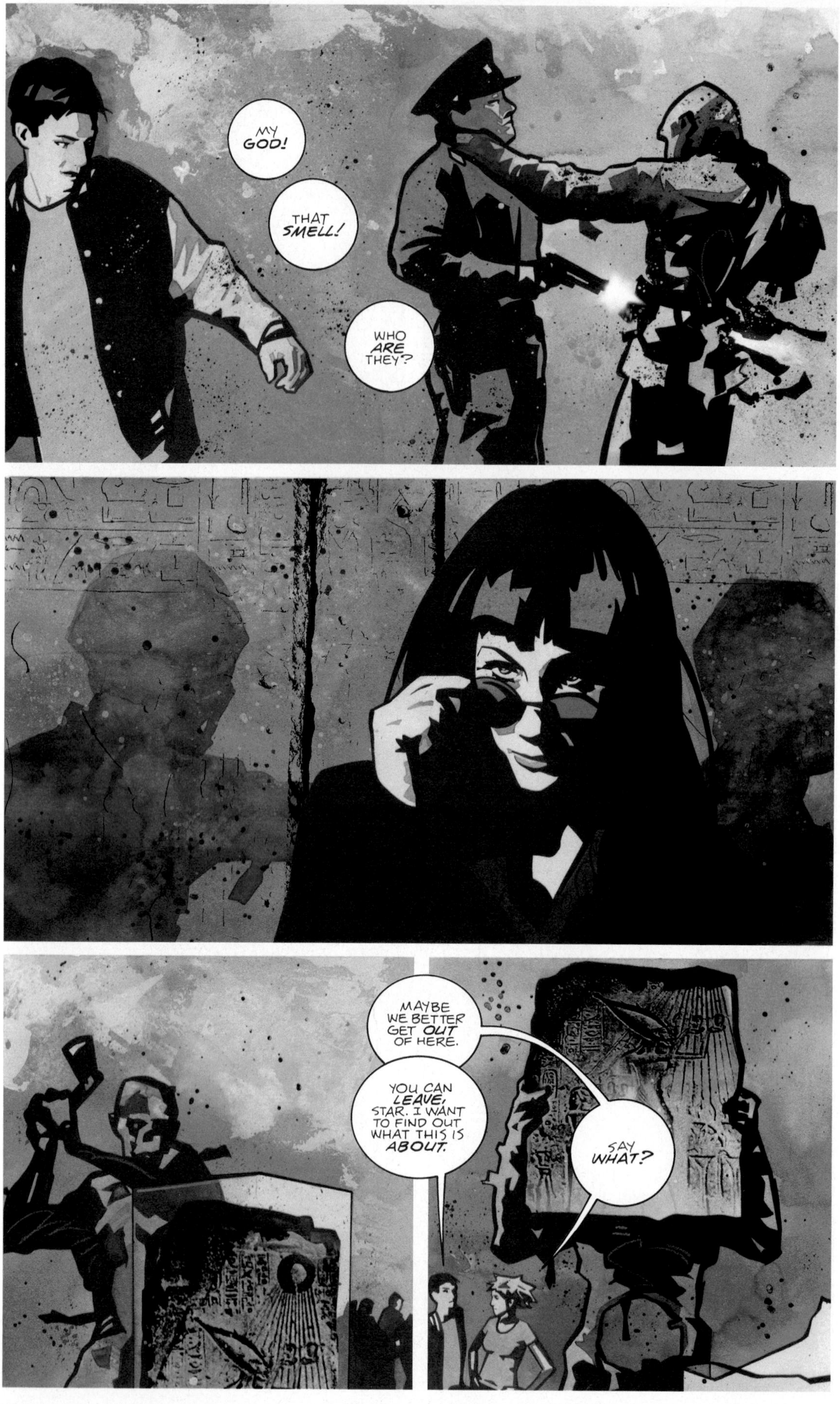
MY GOD!
THAT SMELL!
WHO ARE THEY?
MAYBE WE BETTER GET OUT OF HERE.
YOU CAN LEAVE, STAR. I WANT TO FIND OUT WHAT THIS IS ABOUT.
SAY WHAT?

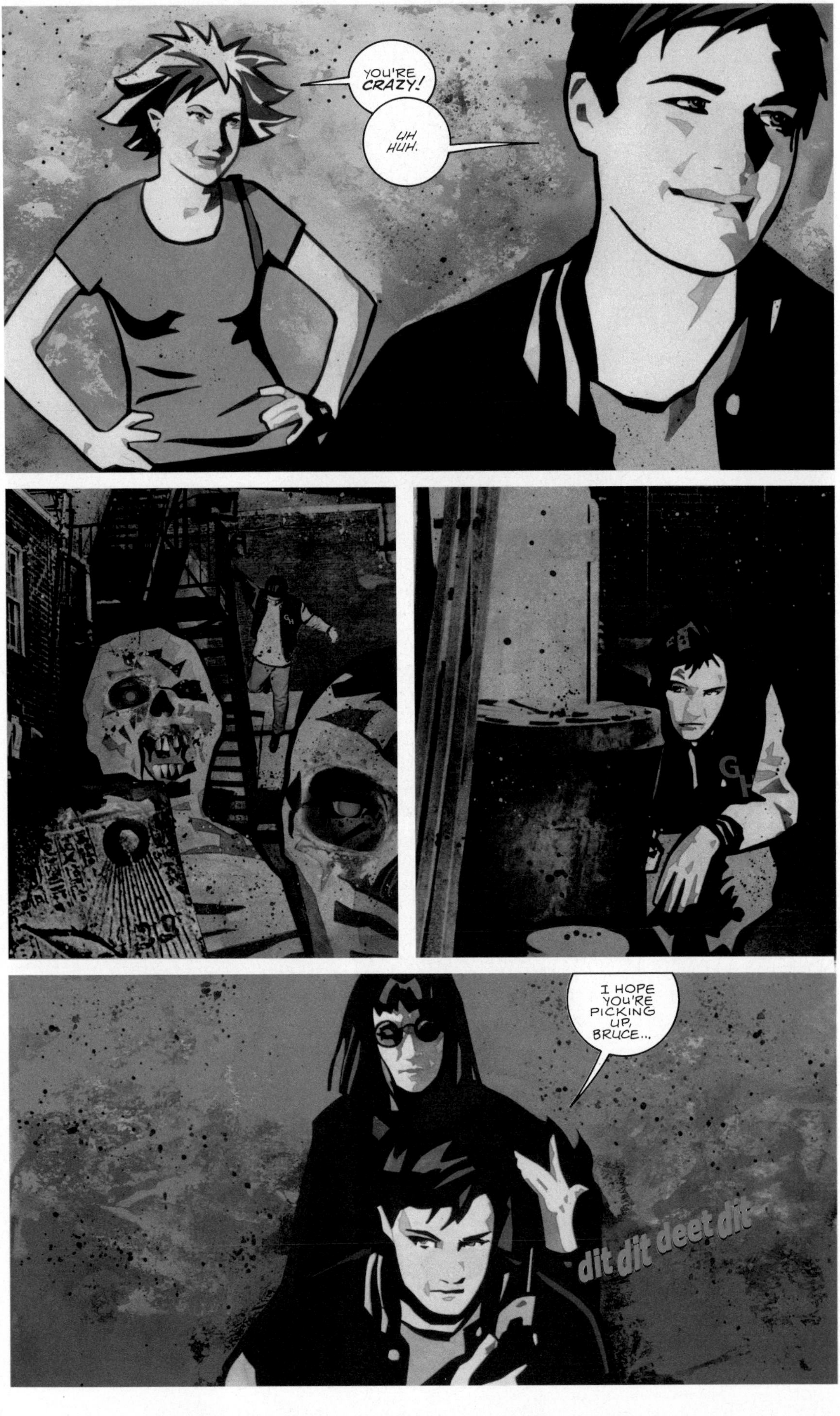
YOU'RE CRAZY!
UH HUH.
I HOPE YOU'RE PICKING UP, BRUCE...
dit dit deet dit

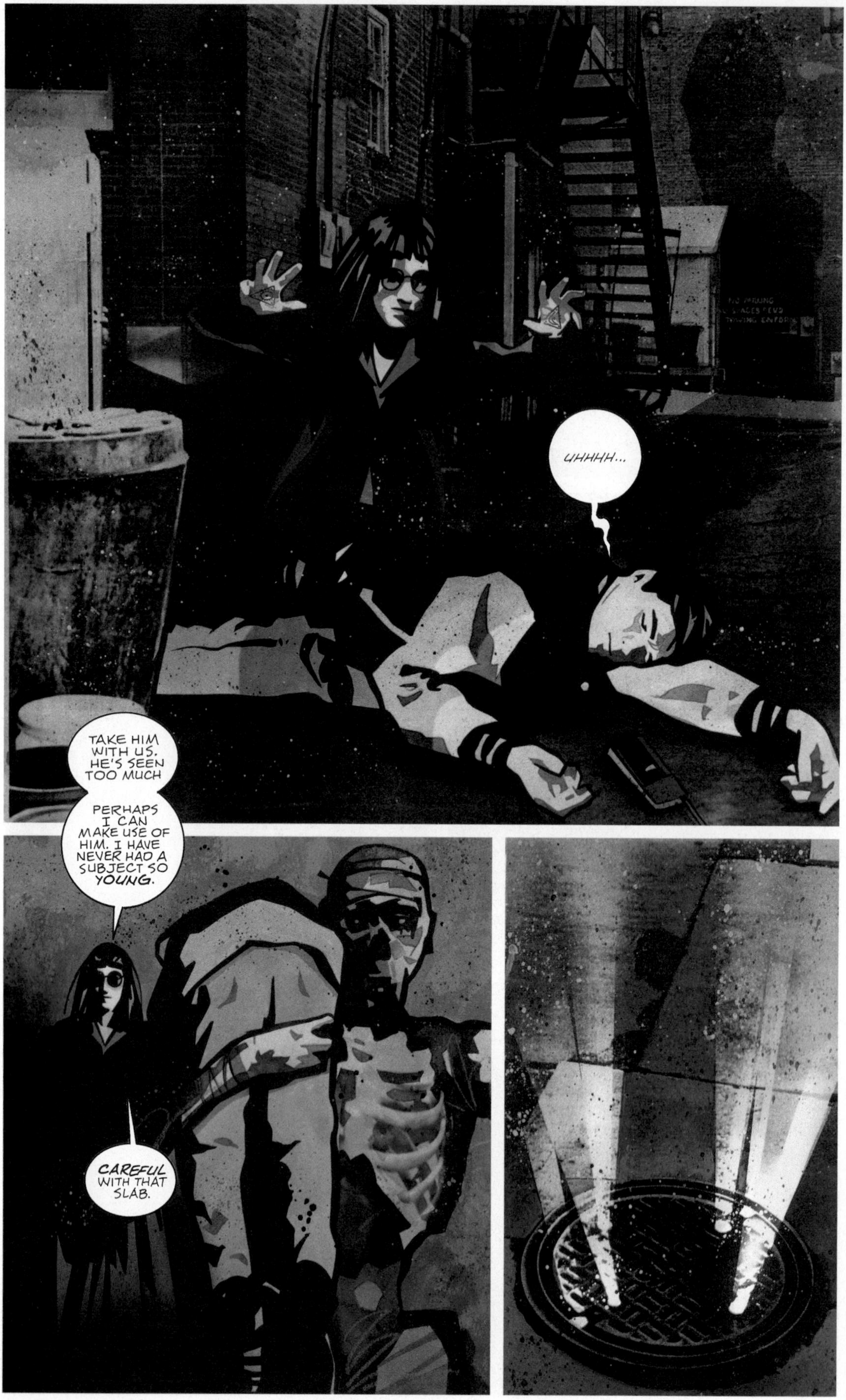
UHHHH...
TAKE HIM WITH US. HE'S SEEN TOO MUCH
PERHAPS I CAN MAKE USE OF HIM. I HAVE NEVER HAD A SUBJECT SO *YOUNG*.
CAREFUL WITH THAT SLAB.

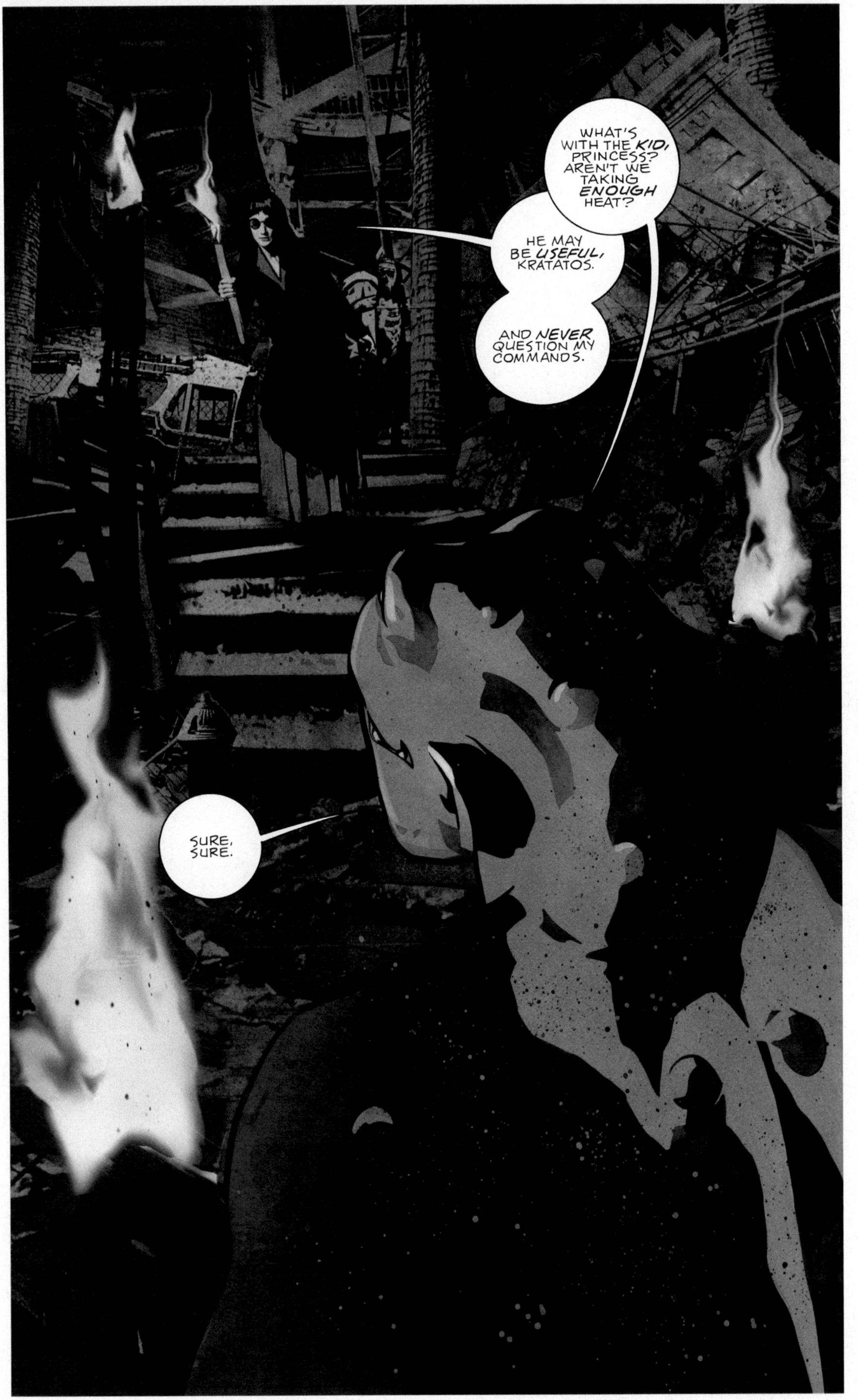
WHAT'S WITH THE KID, PRINCESS? AREN'T WE TAKING ENOUGH HEAT?
HE MAY BE USEFUL, KRATATOS.
AND NEVER QUESTION MY COMMANDS.
SURE, SURE.

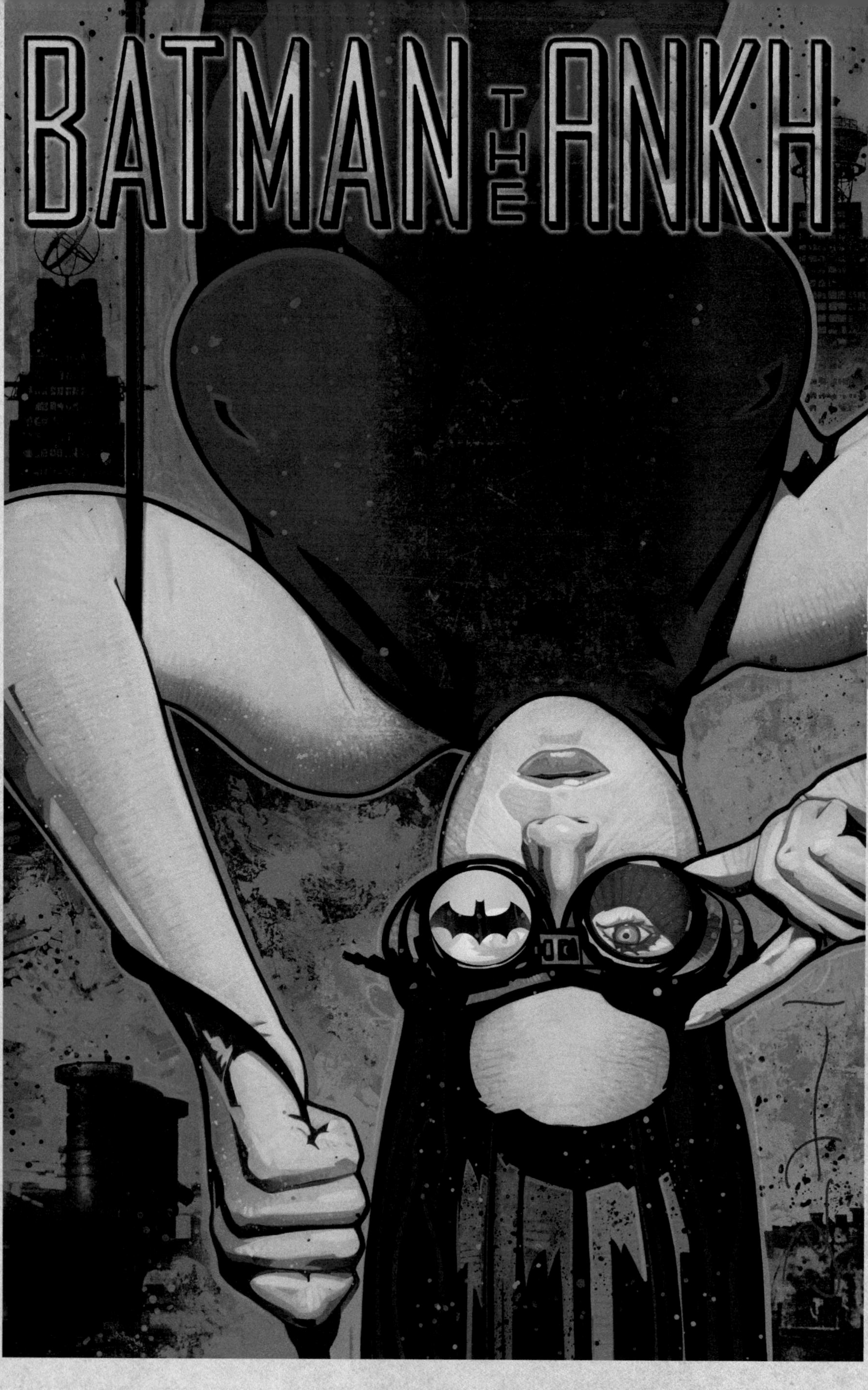
BATMAN THE ANKH

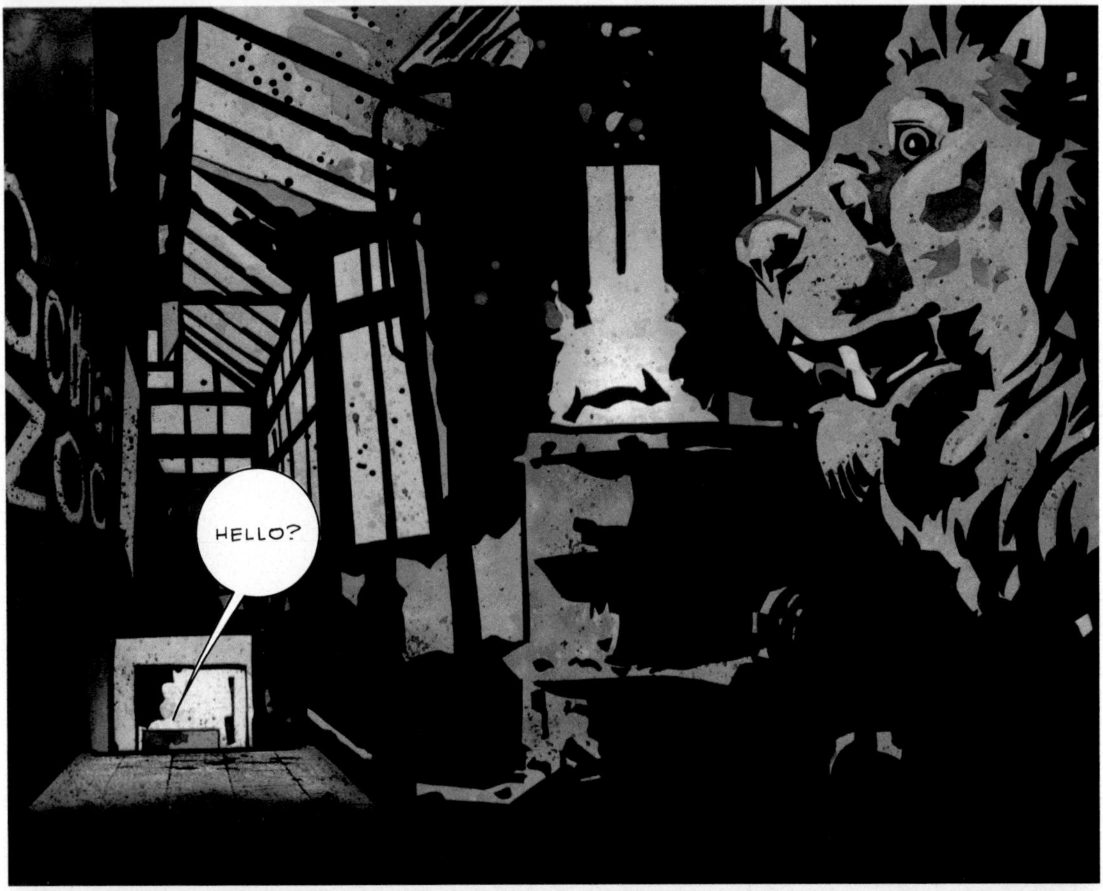
HELLO?

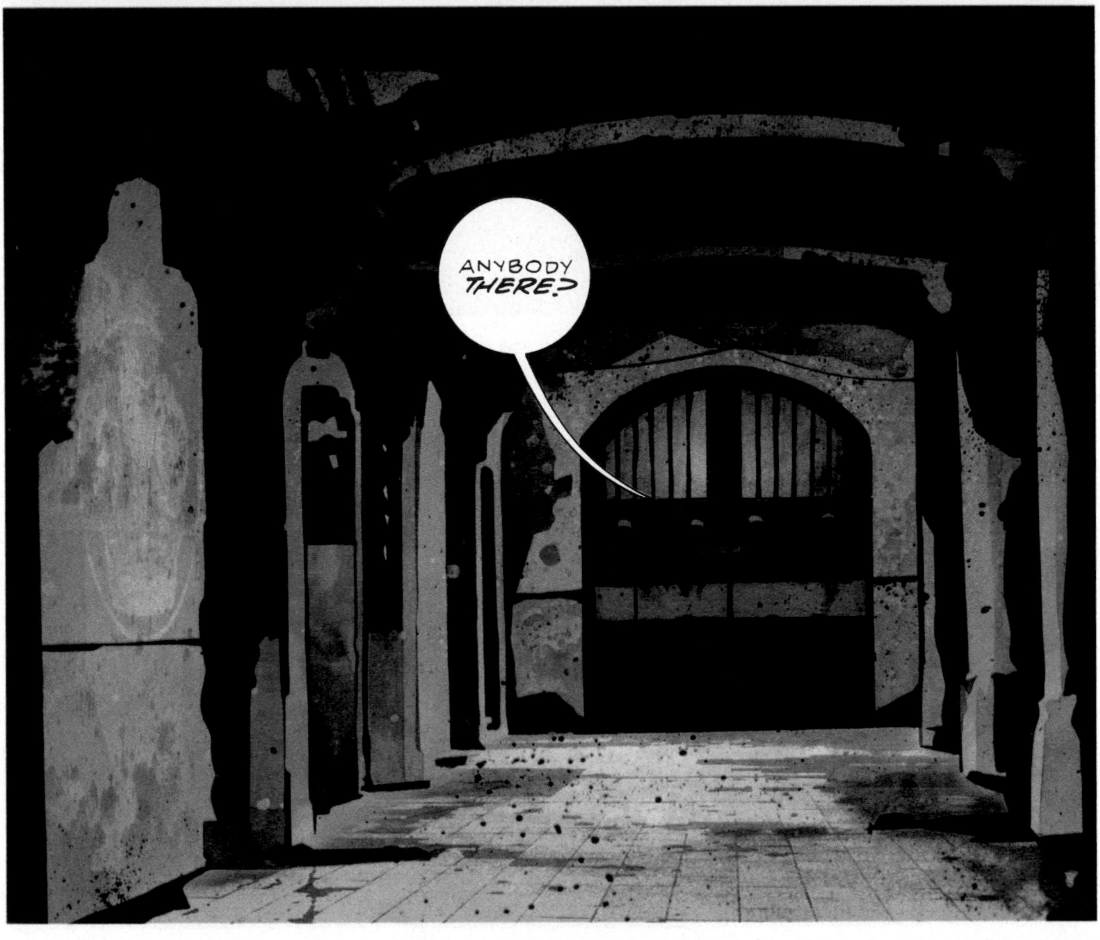
ANYBODY THERE?

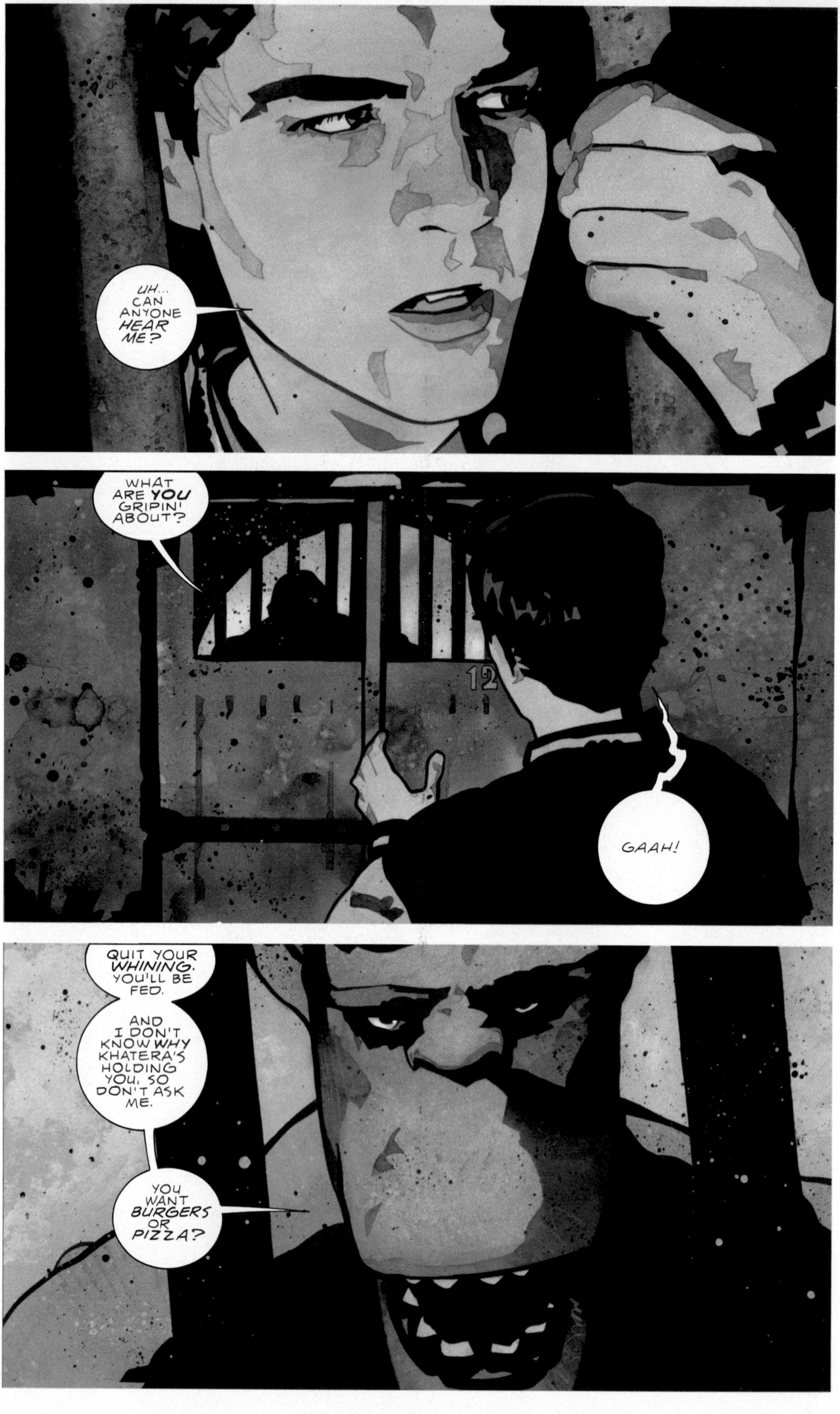
UH... CAN ANYONE HEAR ME?
WHAT ARE YOU GRIPIN' ABOUT?
GAAH!
QUIT YOUR WHINING. YOU'LL BE FED.
AND I DON'T KNOW WHY KHATERA'S HOLDING YOU, SO DON'T ASK ME.
YOU WANT BURGERS OR PIZZA?

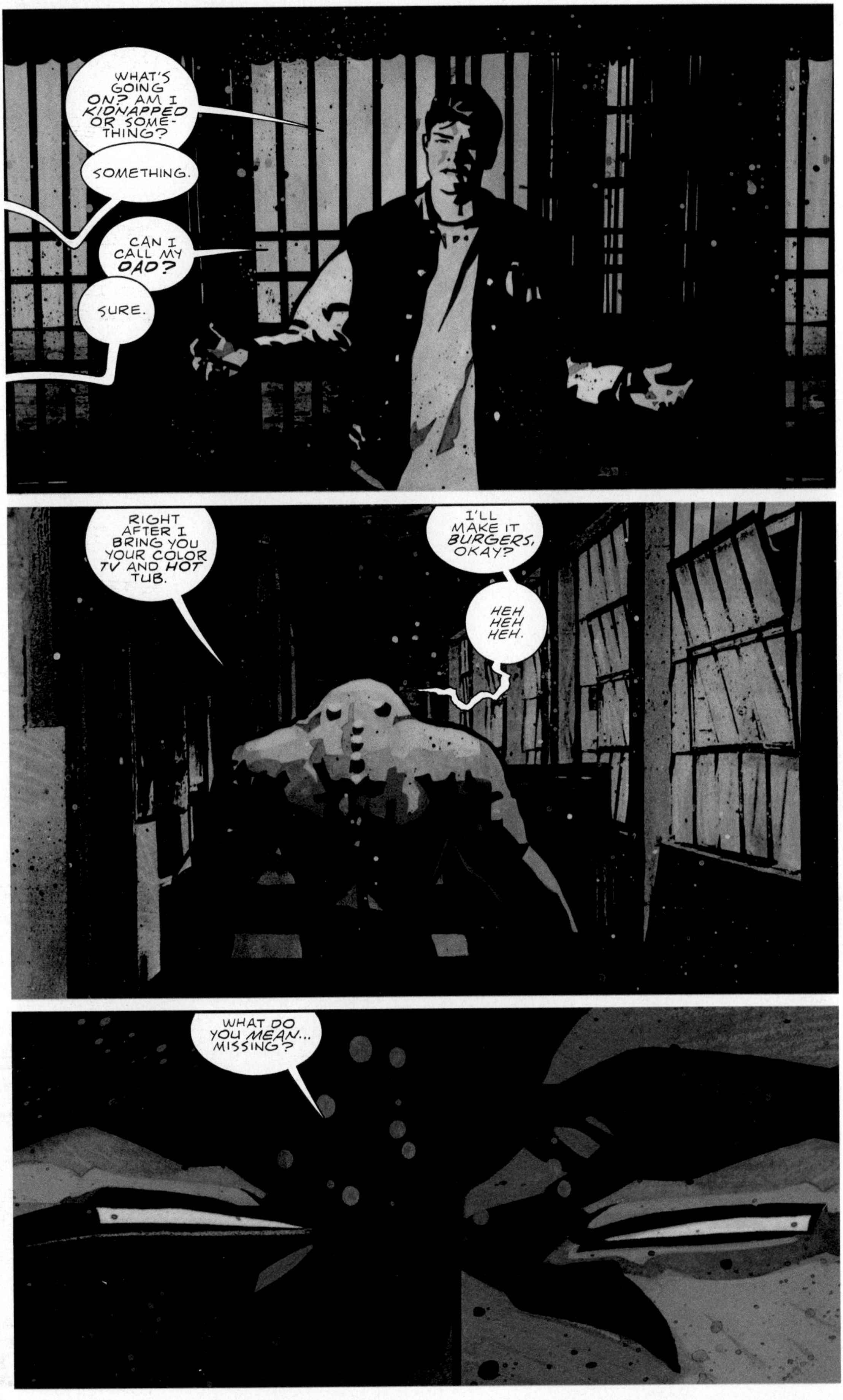
WHAT'S GOING ON? AM I KIDNAPPED OR SOME-THING?
SOMETHING.
CAN I CALL MY DAD?
SURE.
RIGHT AFTER I BRING YOU YOUR COLOR TV AND HOT TUB.
I'LL MAKE IT BURGERS, OKAY?
HEH HEH HEH.
WHAT DO YOU MEAN... MISSING?

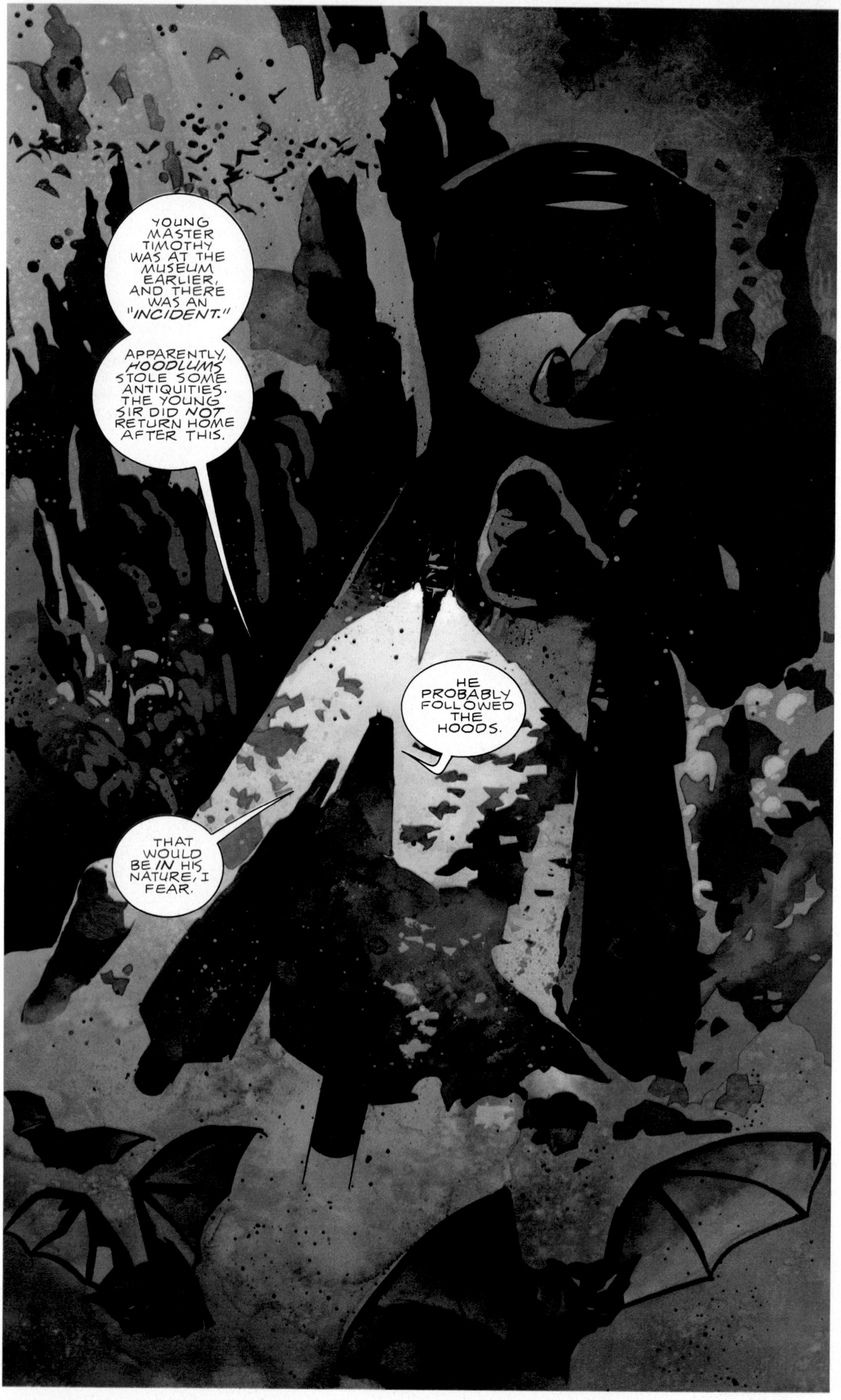
YOUNG MASTER TIMOTHY WAS AT THE MUSEUM EARLIER, AND THERE WAS AN "INCIDENT."
APPARENTLY, HOODLUMS STOLE SOME ANTIQUITIES. THE YOUNG SIR DID NOT RETURN HOME AFTER THIS.
HE PROBABLY FOLLOWED THE HOODS.
THAT WOULD BE IN HIS NATURE, I FEAR.

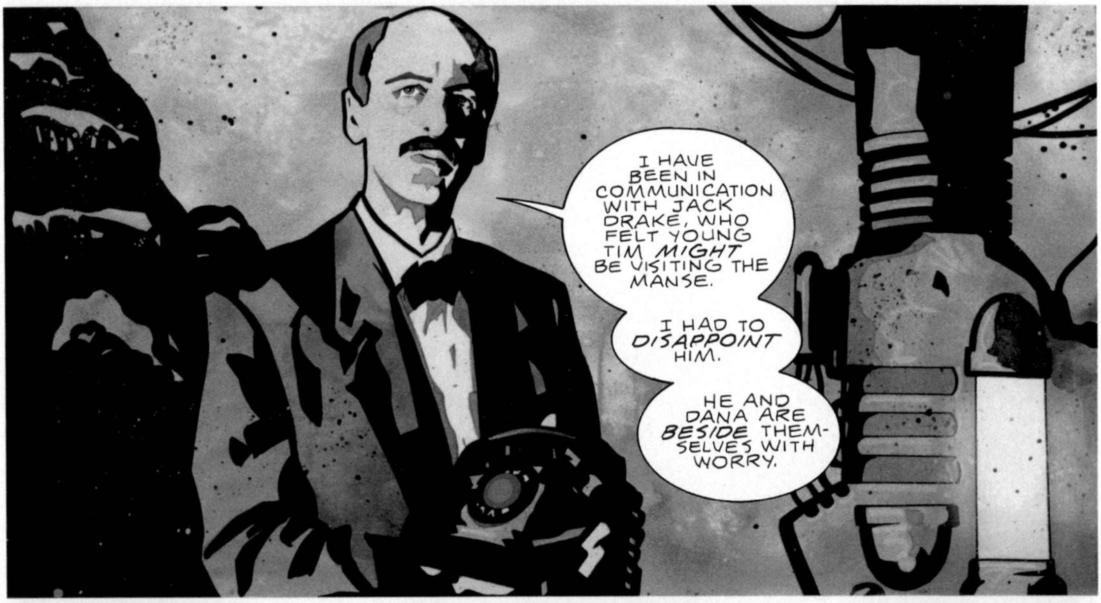
I HAVE BEEN IN COMMUNICATION WITH JACK DRAKE, WHO FELT YOUNG TIM *MIGHT* BE VISITING THE MANSE.
I HAD TO *DISAPPOINT* HIM.
HE AND DANA ARE *BESIDE* THEMSELVES WITH WORRY.

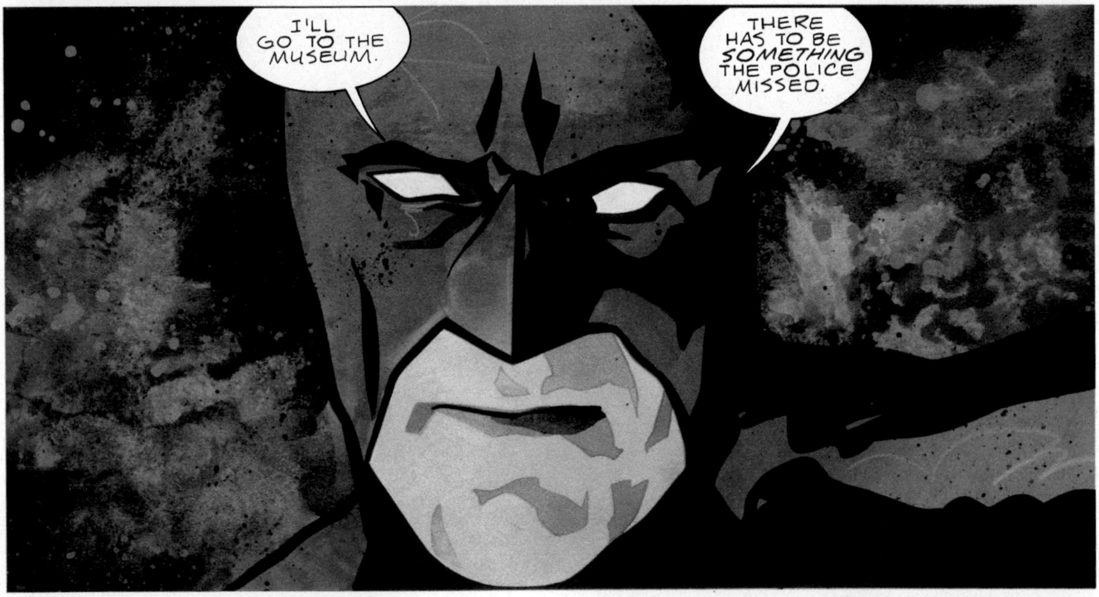
I'LL GO TO THE MUSEUM.
THERE HAS TO BE *SOMETHING* THE POLICE MISSED.

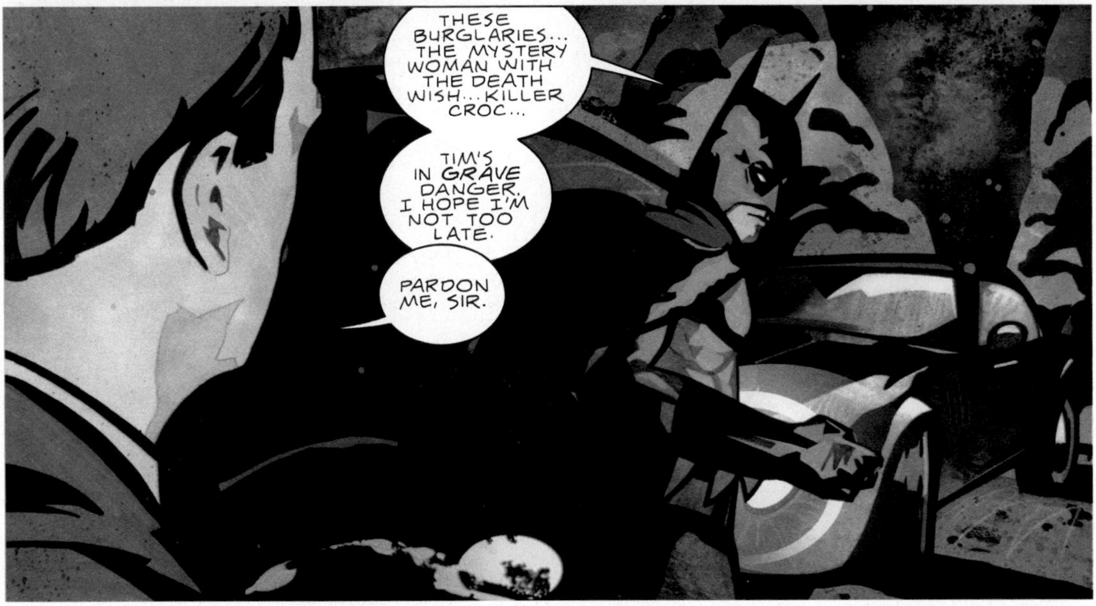
THESE BURGLARIES... THE MYSTERY WOMAN WITH THE DEATH WISH... KILLER CROC...
TIM'S IN *GRAVE* DANGER. I HOPE I'M NOT TOO LATE.
PARDON ME, SIR.

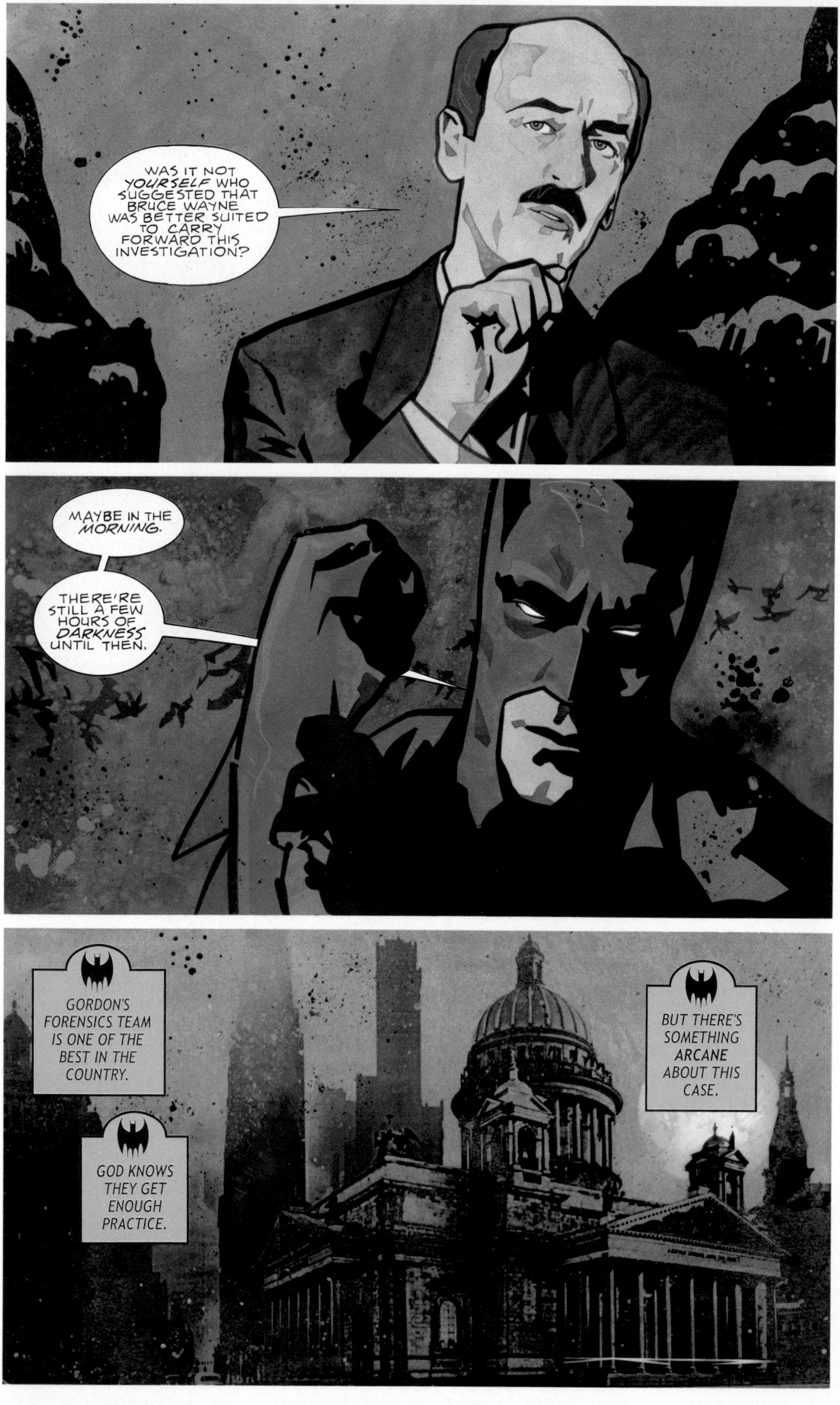
WAS IT NOT YOURSELF WHO SUGGESTED THAT BRUCE WAYNE WAS BETTER SUITED TO CARRY FORWARD THIS INVESTIGATION?
MAYBE IN THE MORNING.
THERE'RE STILL A FEW HOURS OF DARKNESS UNTIL THEN.
GORDON'S FORENSICS TEAM IS ONE OF THE BEST IN THE COUNTRY.
GOD KNOWS THEY GET ENOUGH PRACTICE.
BUT THERE'S SOMETHING ARCANE ABOUT THIS CASE.

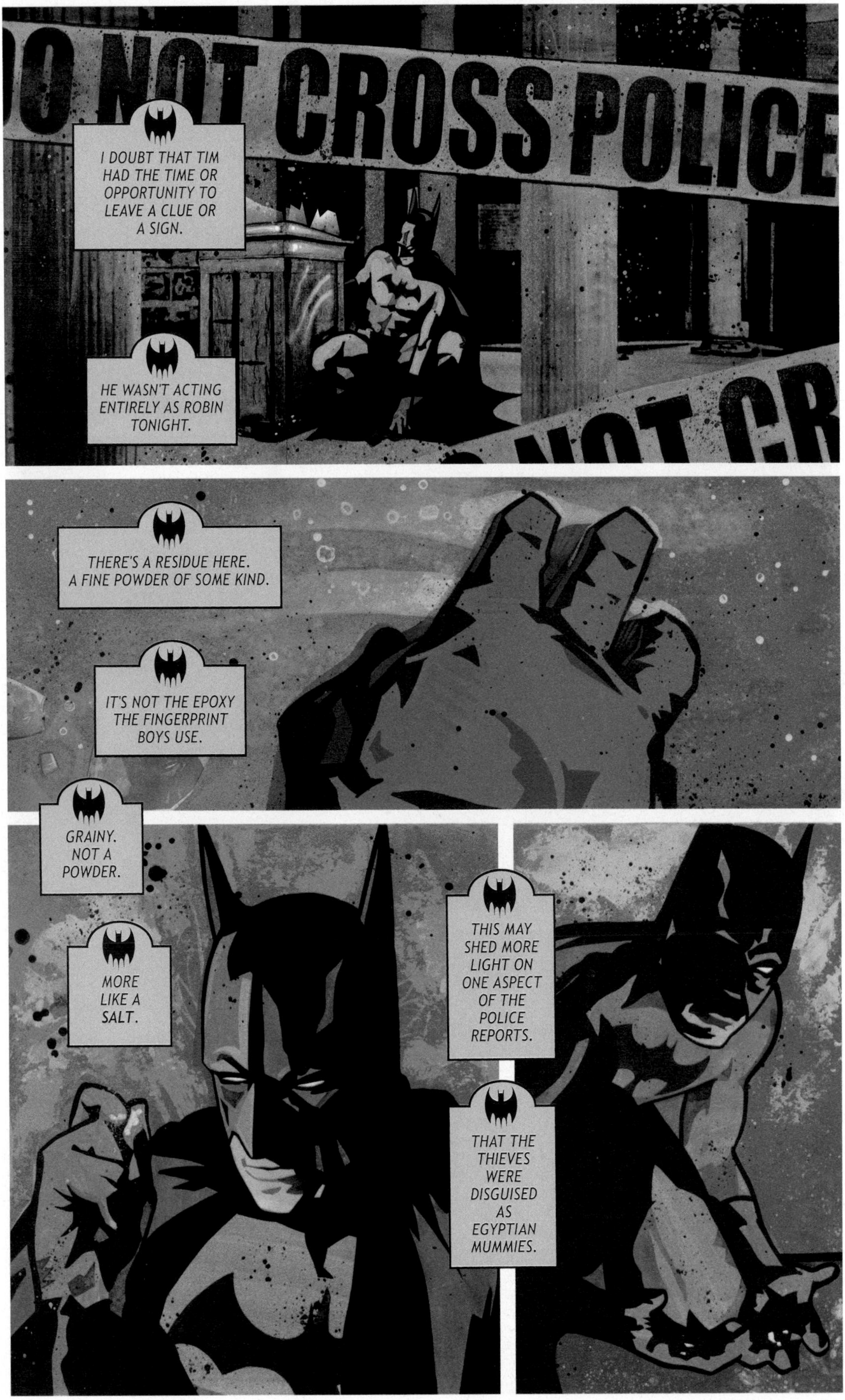
DO NOT CROSS POLICE
I DOUBT THAT TIM HAD THE TIME OR OPPORTUNITY TO LEAVE A CLUE OR A SIGN.
HE WASN'T ACTING ENTIRELY AS ROBIN TONIGHT.
THERE'S A RESIDUE HERE. A FINE POWDER OF SOME KIND.
IT'S NOT THE EPOXY THE FINGERPRINT BOYS USE.
GRAINY. NOT A POWDER.
MORE LIKE A SALT.
THIS MAY SHED MORE LIGHT ON ONE ASPECT OF THE POLICE REPORTS.
THAT THE THIEVES WERE DISGUISED AS EGYPTIAN MUMMIES.

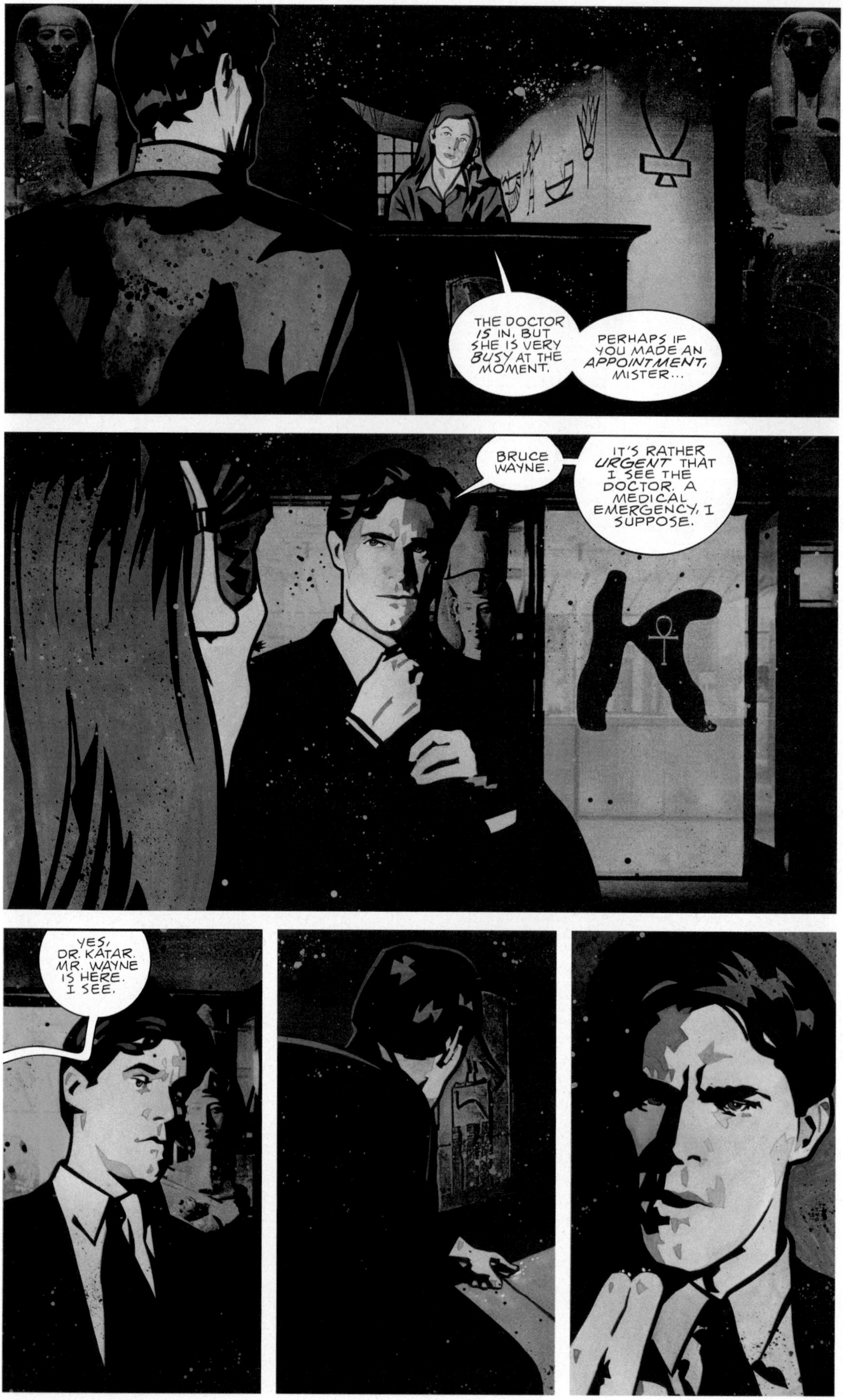
THE DOCTOR IS IN, BUT SHE IS VERY BUSY AT THE MOMENT.
PERHAPS IF YOU MADE AN APPOINTMENT, MISTER...
BRUCE WAYNE.
IT'S RATHER URGENT THAT I SEE THE DOCTOR. A MEDICAL EMERGENCY, I SUPPOSE.
YES, DR. KATAR. MR. WAYNE IS HERE. I SEE.

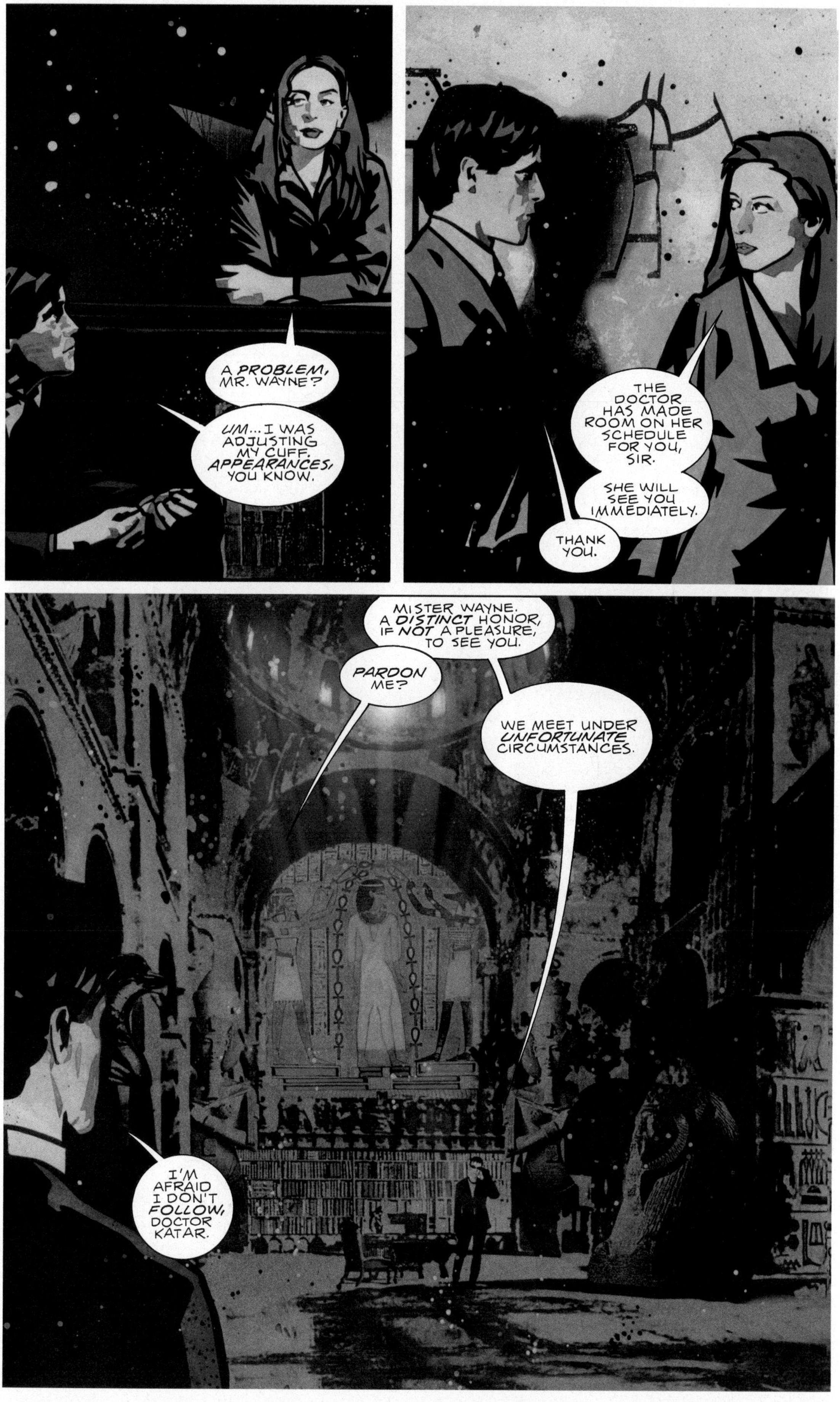
A PROBLEM, MR. WAYNE?
UM... I WAS ADJUSTING MY CUFF. APPEARANCES, YOU KNOW.
THE DOCTOR HAS MADE ROOM ON HER SCHEDULE FOR YOU, SIR.
SHE WILL SEE YOU IMMEDIATELY.
THANK YOU.
MISTER WAYNE. A DISTINCT HONOR, IF NOT A PLEASURE, TO SEE YOU.
PARDON ME?
WE MEET UNDER UNFORTUNATE CIRCUMSTANCES.
I'M AFRAID I DON'T FOLLOW, DOCTOR KATAR.

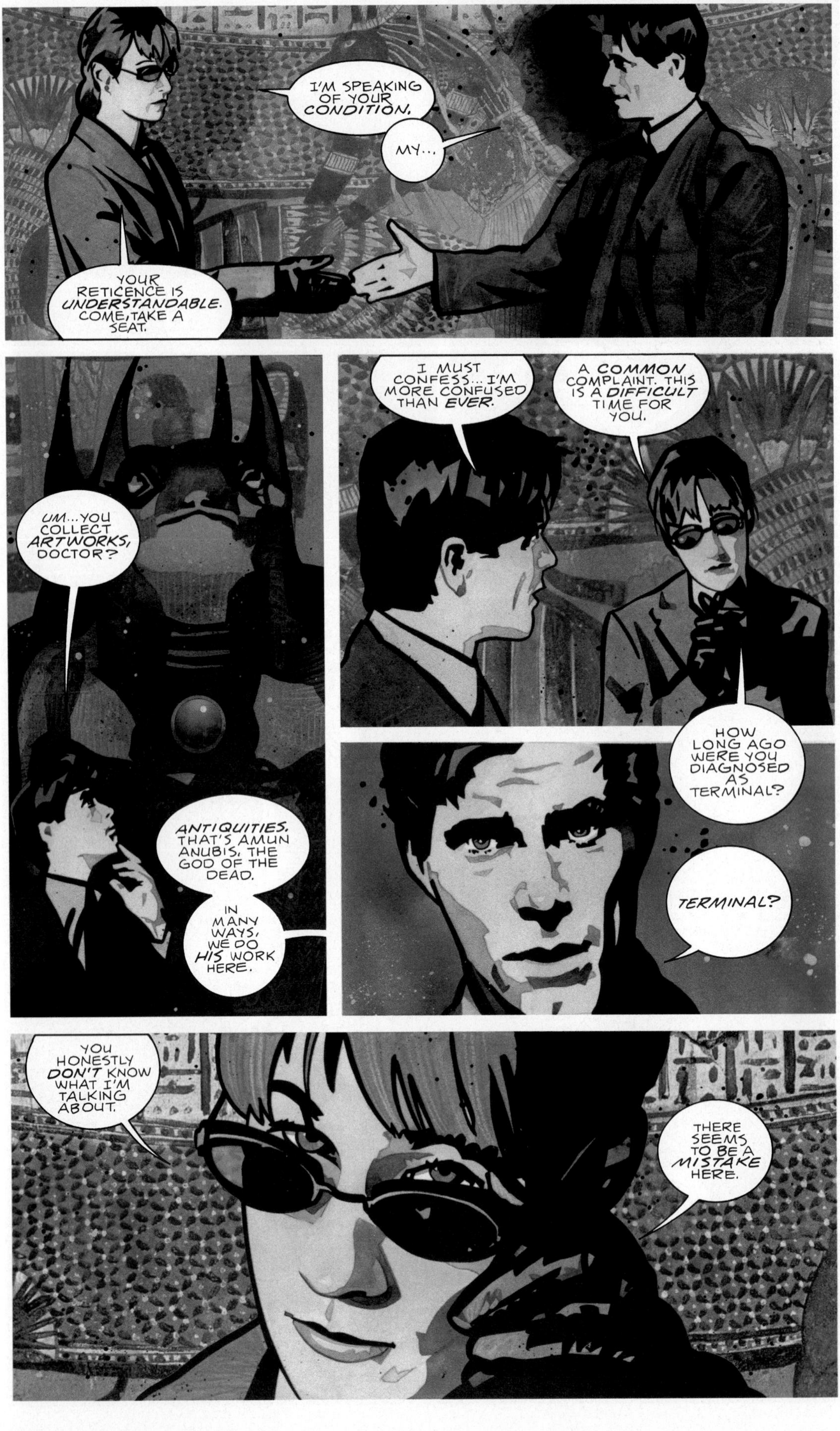
I'M SPEAKING OF YOUR CONDITION.
MY...
YOUR RETICENCE IS UNDERSTANDABLE. COME, TAKE A SEAT.
UM...YOU COLLECT ARTWORKS, DOCTOR?
ANTIQUITIES. THAT'S AMUN ANUBIS, THE GOD OF THE DEAD.
IN MANY WAYS, WE DO HIS WORK HERE.
I MUST CONFESS... I'M MORE CONFUSED THAN EVER.
A COMMON COMPLAINT. THIS IS A DIFFICULT TIME FOR YOU.
HOW LONG AGO WERE YOU DIAGNOSED AS TERMINAL?
TERMINAL?
YOU HONESTLY DON'T KNOW WHAT I'M TALKING ABOUT.
THERE SEEMS TO BE A MISTAKE HERE.

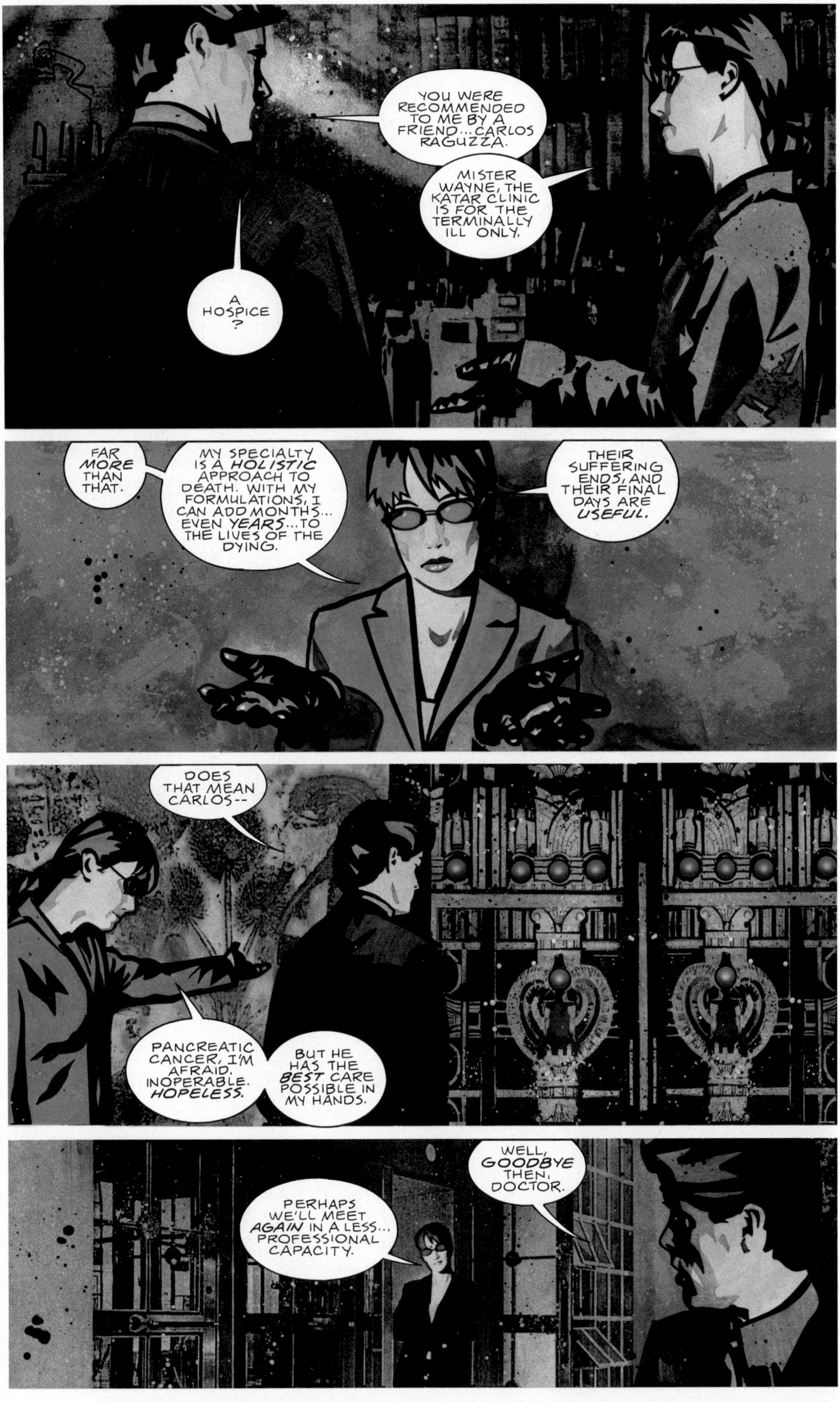
YOU WERE RECOMMENDED TO ME BY A FRIEND...CARLOS RAGUZZA.
MISTER WAYNE, THE KATAR CLINIC IS FOR THE TERMINALLY ILL ONLY.
A HOSPICE?
FAR MORE THAN THAT.
MY SPECIALTY IS A HOLISTIC APPROACH TO DEATH. WITH MY FORMULATIONS, I CAN ADD MONTHS... EVEN YEARS...TO THE LIVES OF THE DYING.
THEIR SUFFERING ENDS, AND THEIR FINAL DAYS ARE USEFUL.
DOES THAT MEAN CARLOS--
PANCREATIC CANCER, I'M AFRAID. INOPERABLE. HOPELESS.
BUT HE HAS THE BEST CARE POSSIBLE IN MY HANDS.
WELL, GOODBYE THEN, DOCTOR.
PERHAPS WE'LL MEET AGAIN IN A LESS... PROFESSIONAL CAPACITY.

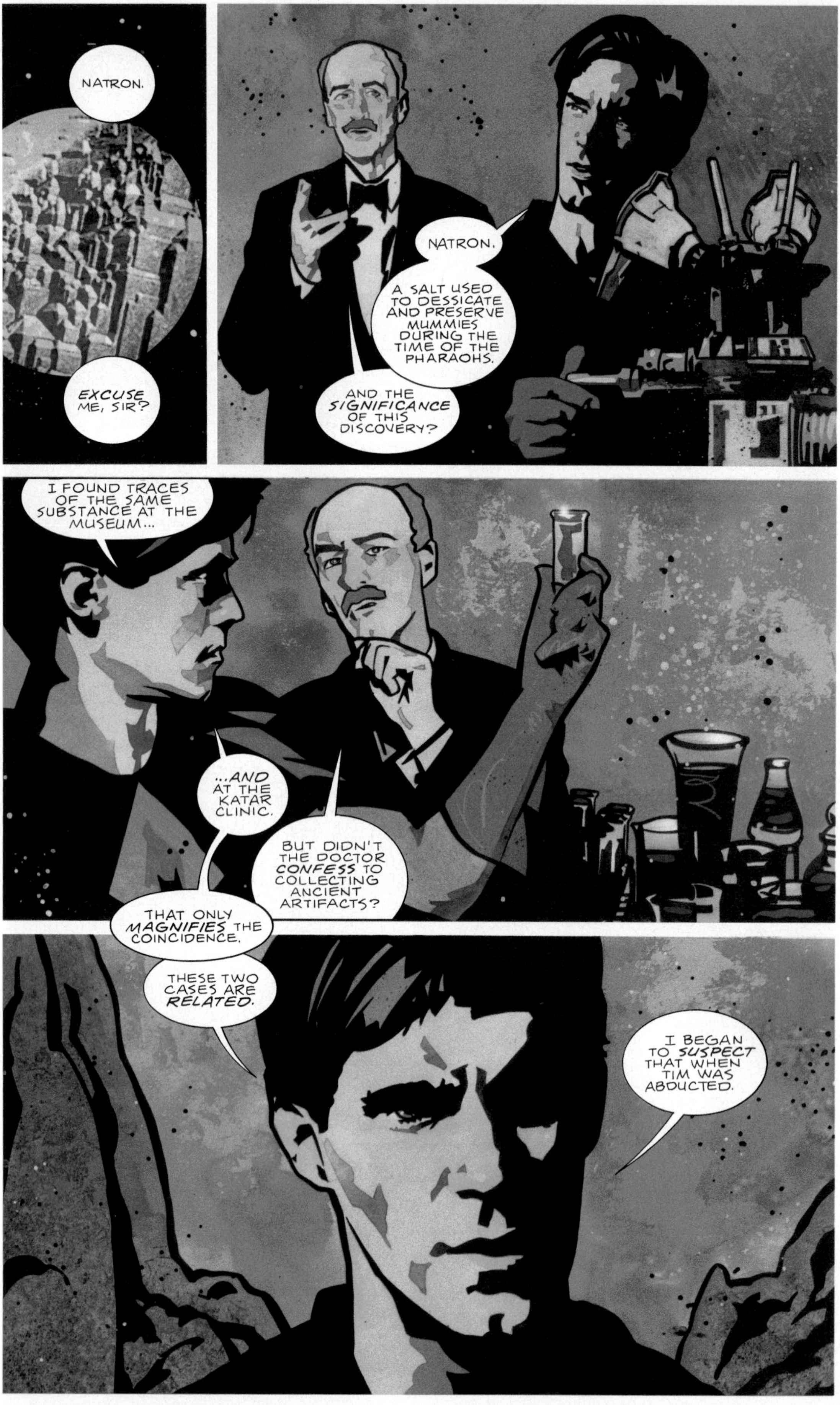
NATRON.
EXCUSE ME, SIR?
NATRON.
A SALT USED TO DESSICATE AND PRESERVE MUMMIES DURING THE TIME OF THE PHARAOHS.
AND THE SIGNIFICANCE OF THIS DISCOVERY?
I FOUND TRACES OF THE SAME SUBSTANCE AT THE MUSEUM...
...AND AT THE KATAR CLINIC.
BUT DIDN'T THE DOCTOR CONFESS TO COLLECTING ANCIENT ARTIFACTS?
THAT ONLY MAGNIFIES THE COINCIDENCE.
THESE TWO CASES ARE RELATED.
I BEGAN TO SUSPECT THAT WHEN TIM WAS ABDUCTED.

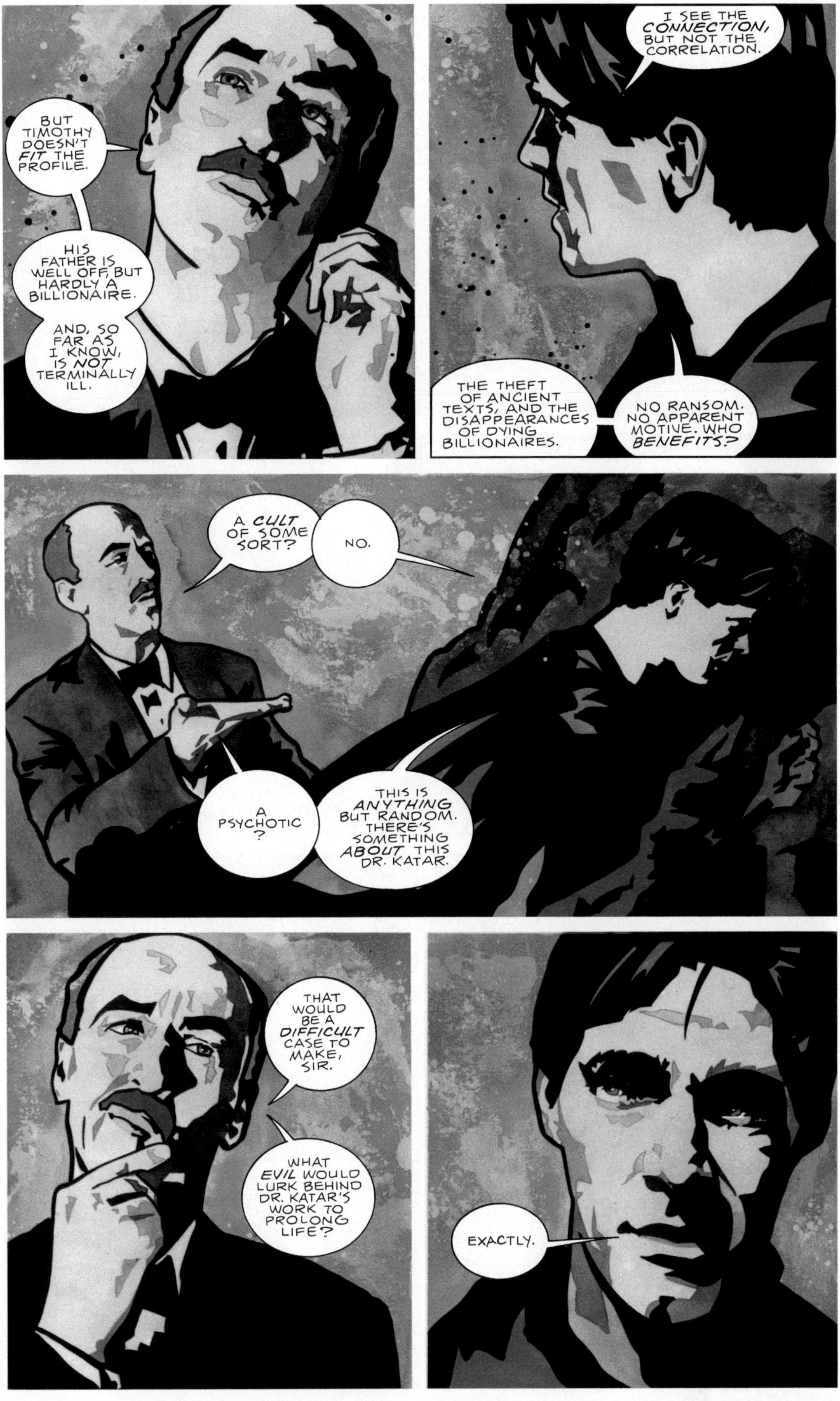
BUT TIMOTHY DOESN'T *FIT* THE PROFILE.
HIS FATHER IS WELL OFF, BUT HARDLY A BILLIONAIRE.
AND, SO FAR AS I KNOW, IS *NOT* TERMINALLY ILL.
I SEE THE *CONNECTION*, BUT NOT THE CORRELATION.
THE THEFT OF ANCIENT TEXTS, AND THE DISAPPEARANCES OF DYING BILLIONAIRES.
NO RANSOM. NO APPARENT MOTIVE. WHO *BENEFITS*?
A *CULT* OF SOME SORT?
NO.
A PSYCHOTIC?
THIS IS *ANYTHING* BUT RANDOM. THERE'S SOMETHING *ABOUT* THIS DR. KATAR.
THAT WOULD BE A *DIFFICULT* CASE TO MAKE, SIR.
WHAT *EVIL* WOULD LURK BEHIND DR. KATAR'S WORK TO PROLONG LIFE?
EXACTLY.

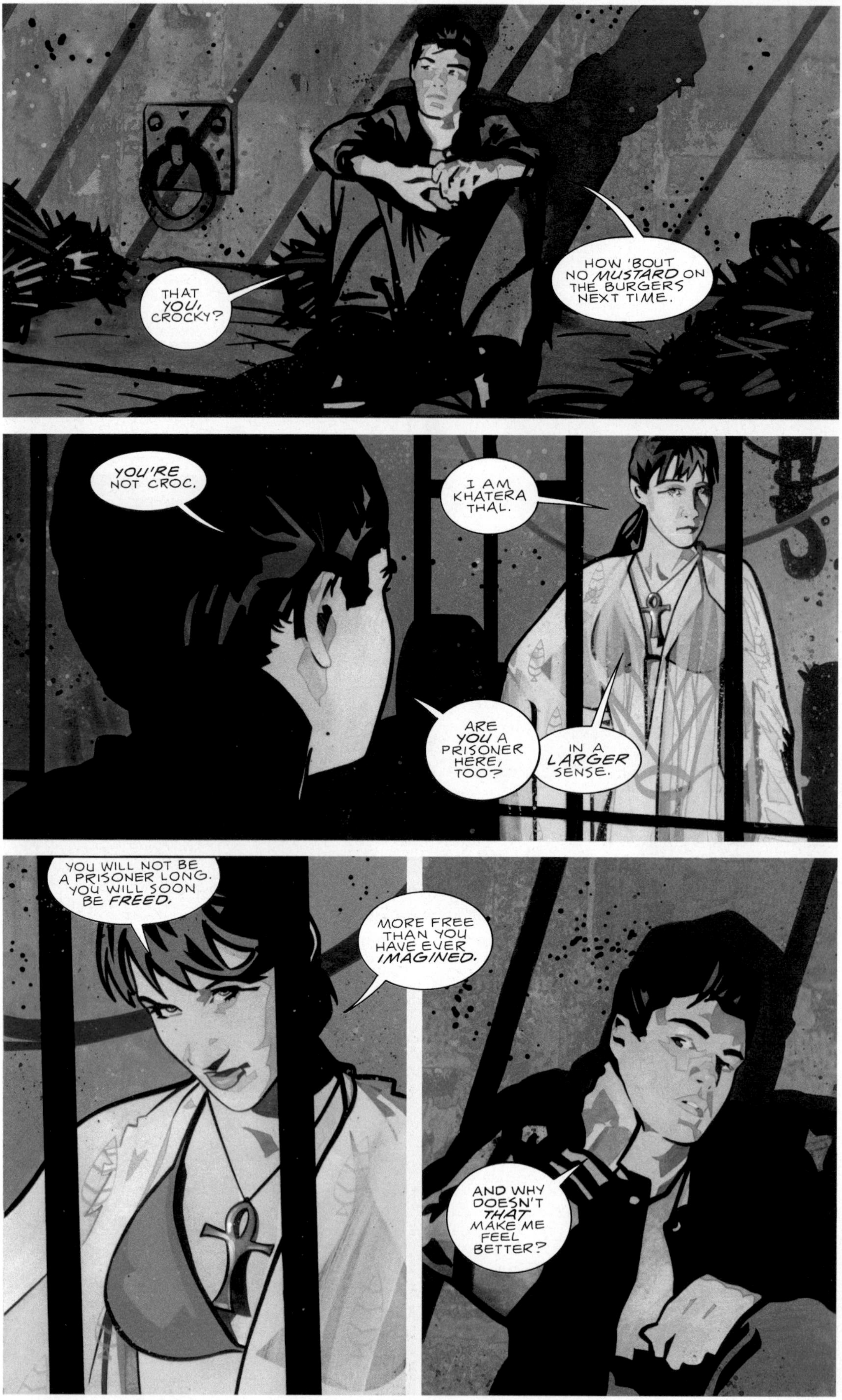

THAT YOU, CROCKY?
HOW 'BOUT NO MUSTARD ON THE BURGERS NEXT TIME.
YOU'RE NOT CROC.
I AM KHATERA THAL.
ARE YOU A PRISONER HERE, TOO?
IN A LARGER SENSE.
YOU WILL NOT BE A PRISONER LONG. YOU WILL SOON BE FREED.
MORE FREE THAN YOU HAVE EVER IMAGINED.
AND WHY DOESN'T THAT MAKE ME FEEL BETTER?

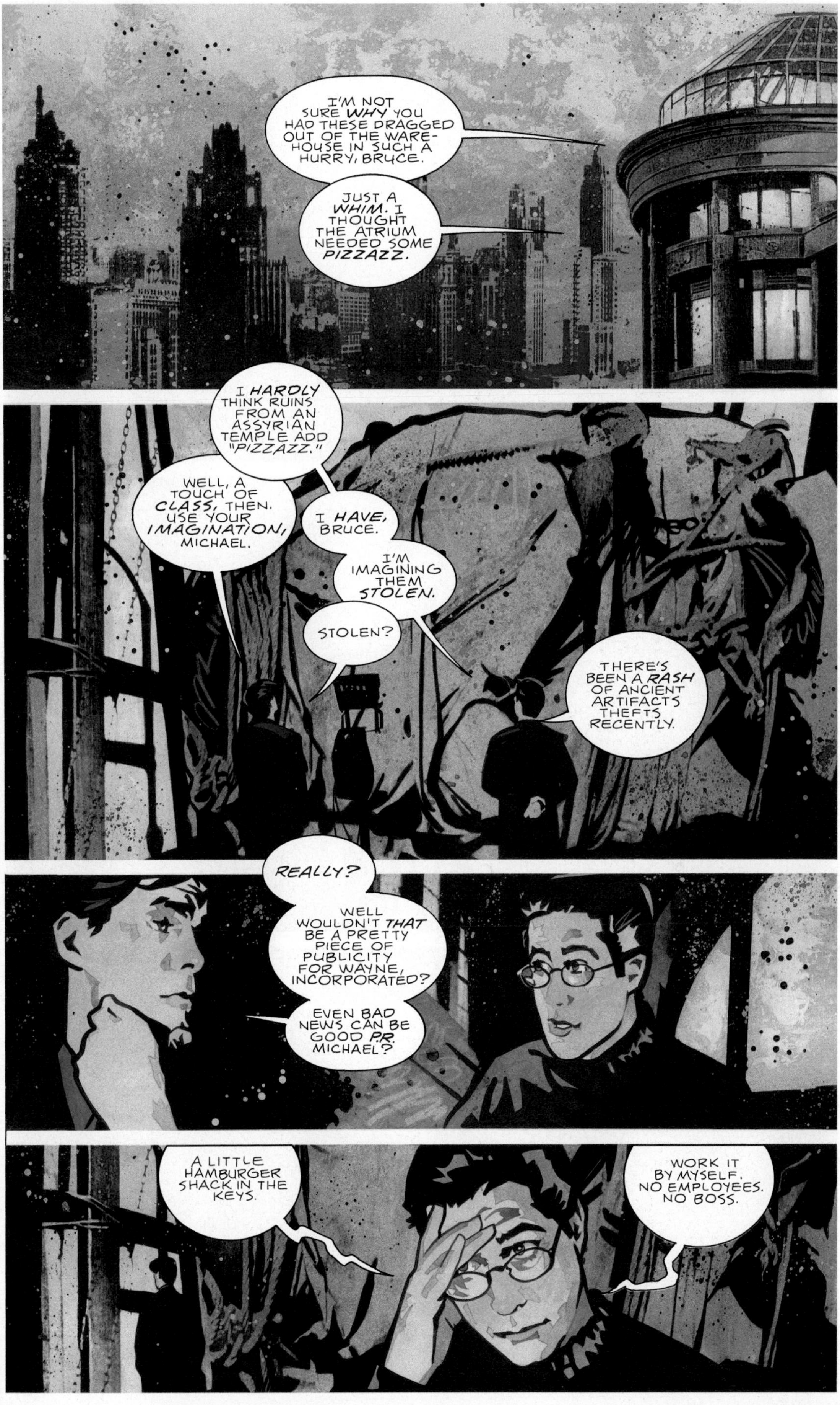
I'M NOT SURE WHY YOU HAD THESE DRAGGED OUT OF THE WAREHOUSE IN SUCH A HURRY, BRUCE.
JUST A WHIM. I THOUGHT THE ATRIUM NEEDED SOME PIZZAZZ.
I HARDLY THINK RUINS FROM AN ASSYRIAN TEMPLE ADD "PIZZAZZ."
WELL, A TOUCH OF CLASS, THEN. USE YOUR IMAGINATION, MICHAEL.
I HAVE, BRUCE.
I'M IMAGINING THEM STOLEN.
STOLEN?
THERE'S BEEN A RASH OF ANCIENT ARTIFACTS THEFTS RECENTLY.
REALLY?
WELL WOULDN'T THAT BE A PRETTY PIECE OF PUBLICITY FOR WAYNE, INCORPORATED?
EVEN BAD NEWS CAN BE GOOD P.R. MICHAEL?
A LITTLE HAMBURGER SHACK IN THE KEYS.
WORK IT BY MYSELF. NO EMPLOYEES. NO BOSS.

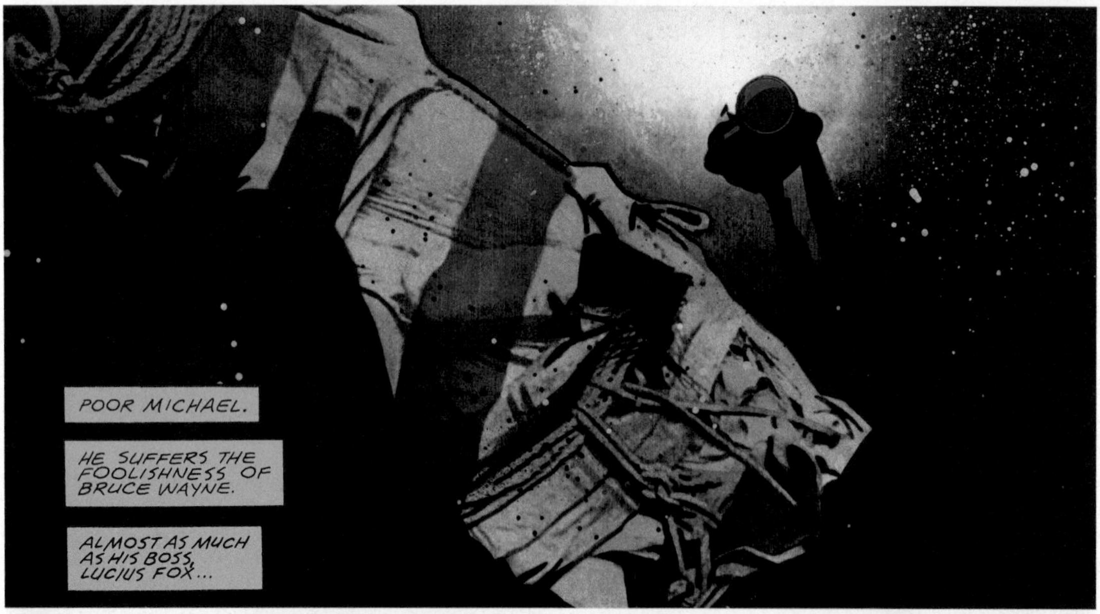
POOR MICHAEL.
HE SUFFERS THE FOOLISHNESS OF BRUCE WAYNE.
ALMOST AS MUCH AS HIS BOSS, LUCIUS FOX...
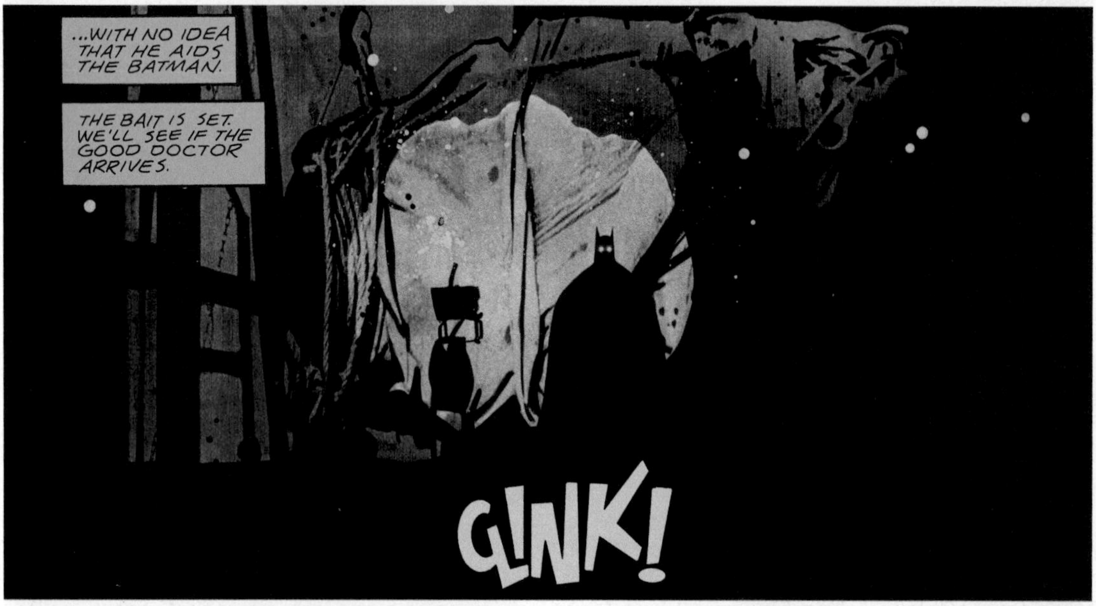
...WITH NO IDEA THAT HE AIDS THE BATMAN.
THE BAIT IS SET. WE'LL SEE IF THE GOOD DOCTOR ARRIVES.
GLINK!
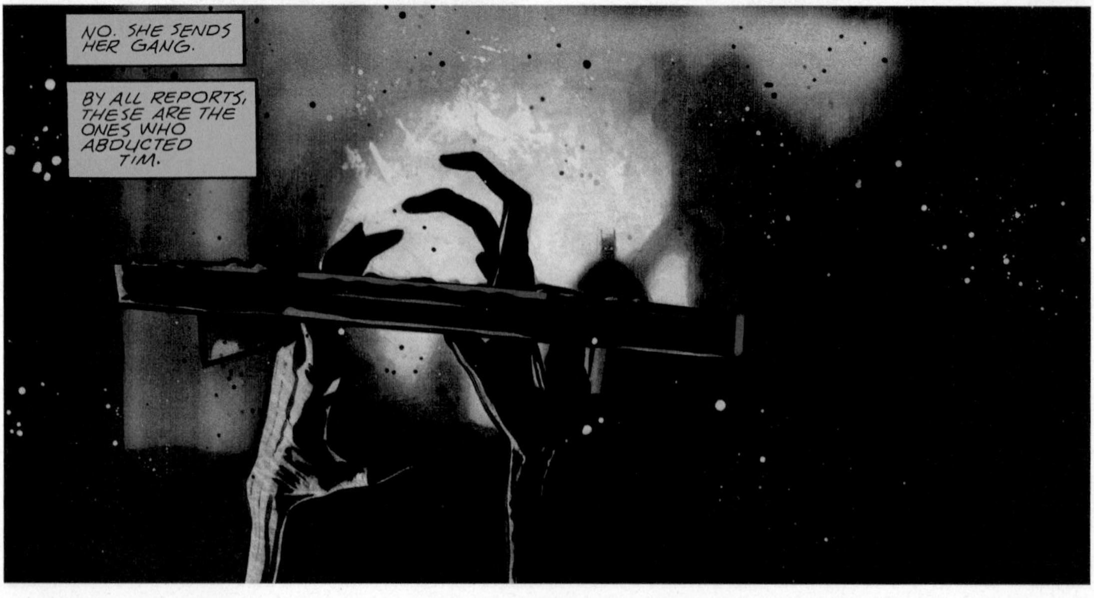
NO. SHE SENDS HER GANG.
BY ALL REPORTS, THESE ARE THE ONES WHO ABDUCTED TIM.

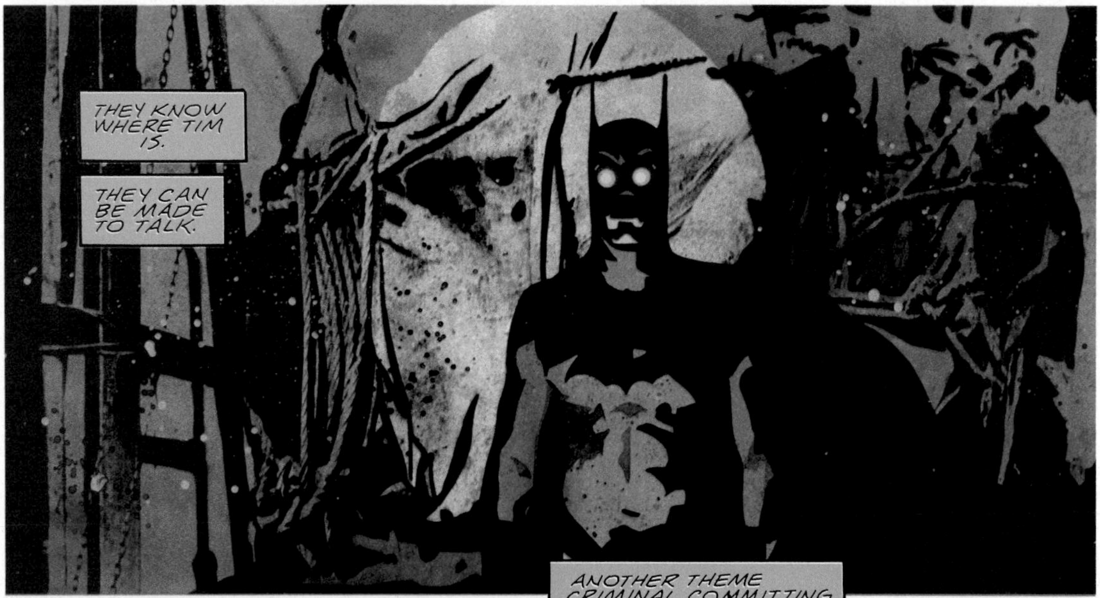
THEY KNOW WHERE TIM IS.
THEY CAN BE MADE TO TALK.

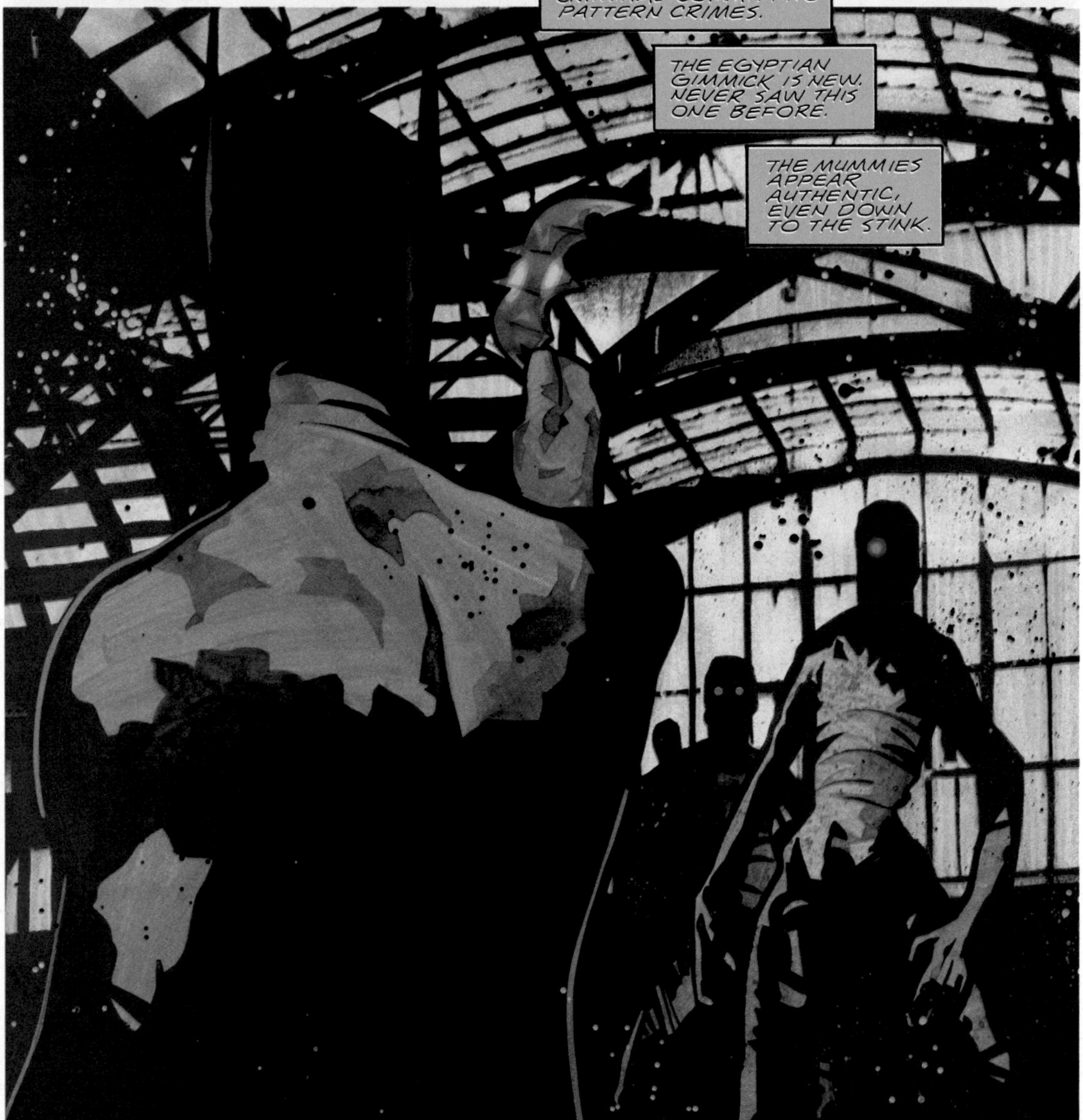
ANOTHER THEME CRIMINAL COMMITTING PATTERN CRIMES.
THE EGYPTIAN GIMMICK IS NEW. NEVER SAW THIS ONE BEFORE.
THE MUMMIES APPEAR AUTHENTIC, EVEN DOWN TO THE STINK.

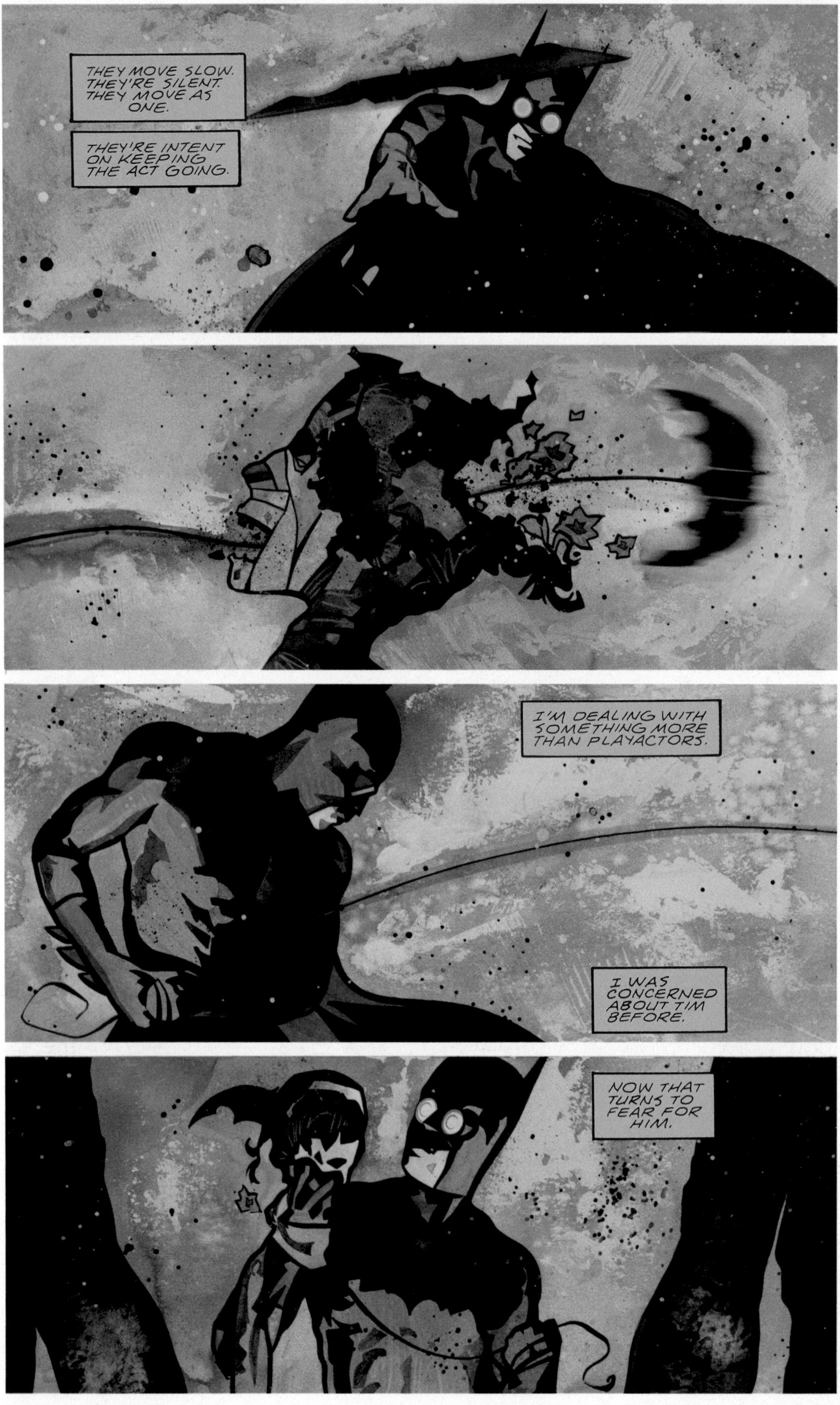
THEY MOVE SLOW. THEY'RE SILENT. THEY MOVE AS ONE.
THEY'RE INTENT ON KEEPING THE ACT GOING.
I'M DEALING WITH SOMETHING MORE THAN PLAYACTORS.
I WAS CONCERNED ABOUT TIM BEFORE.
NOW THAT TURNS TO FEAR FOR HIM.

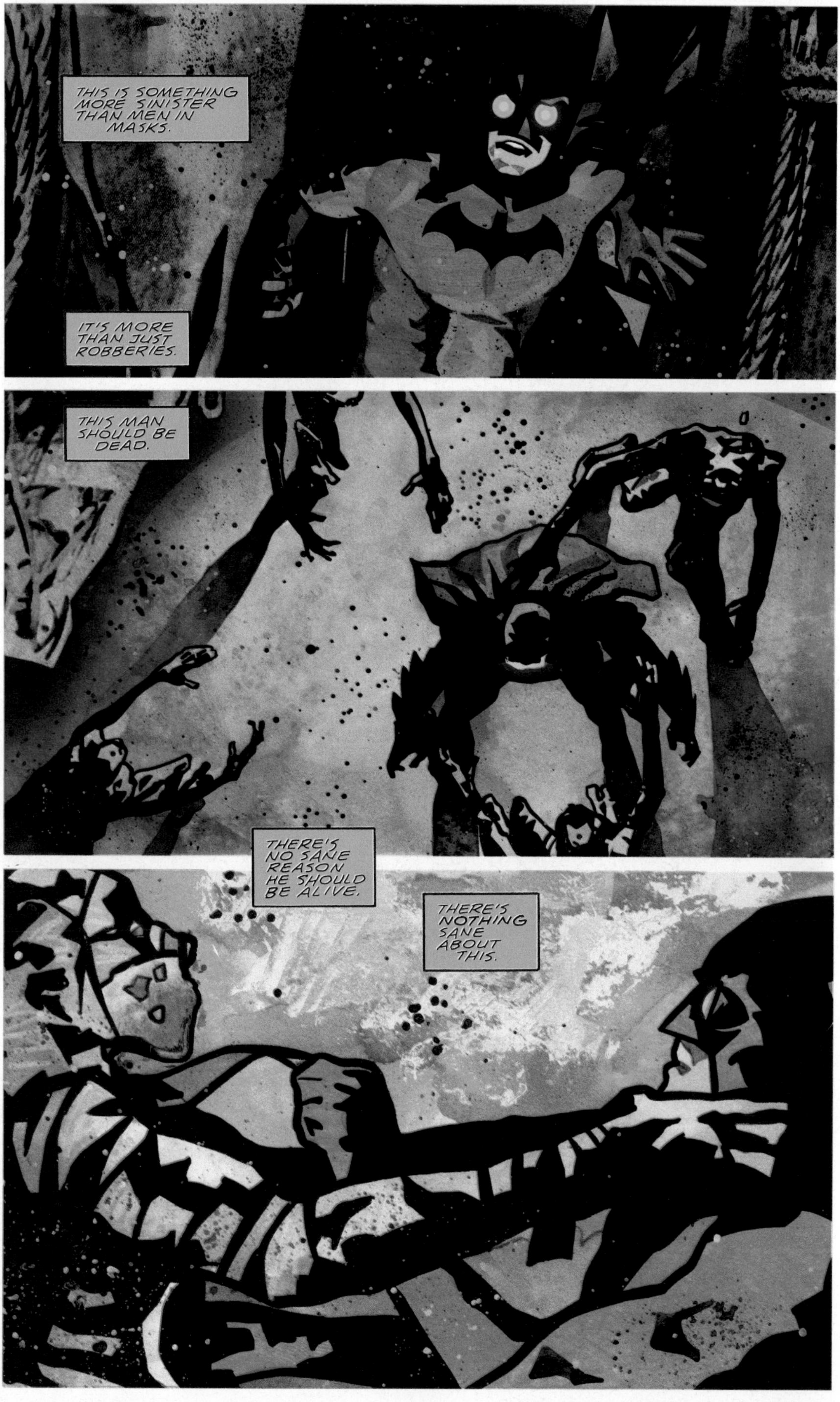
THIS IS SOMETHING MORE SINISTER THAN MEN IN MASKS.
IT'S MORE THAN JUST ROBBERIES.
THIS MAN SHOULD BE DEAD.
THERE'S NO SANE REASON HE SHOULD BE ALIVE.
THERE'S NOTHING SANE ABOUT THIS.

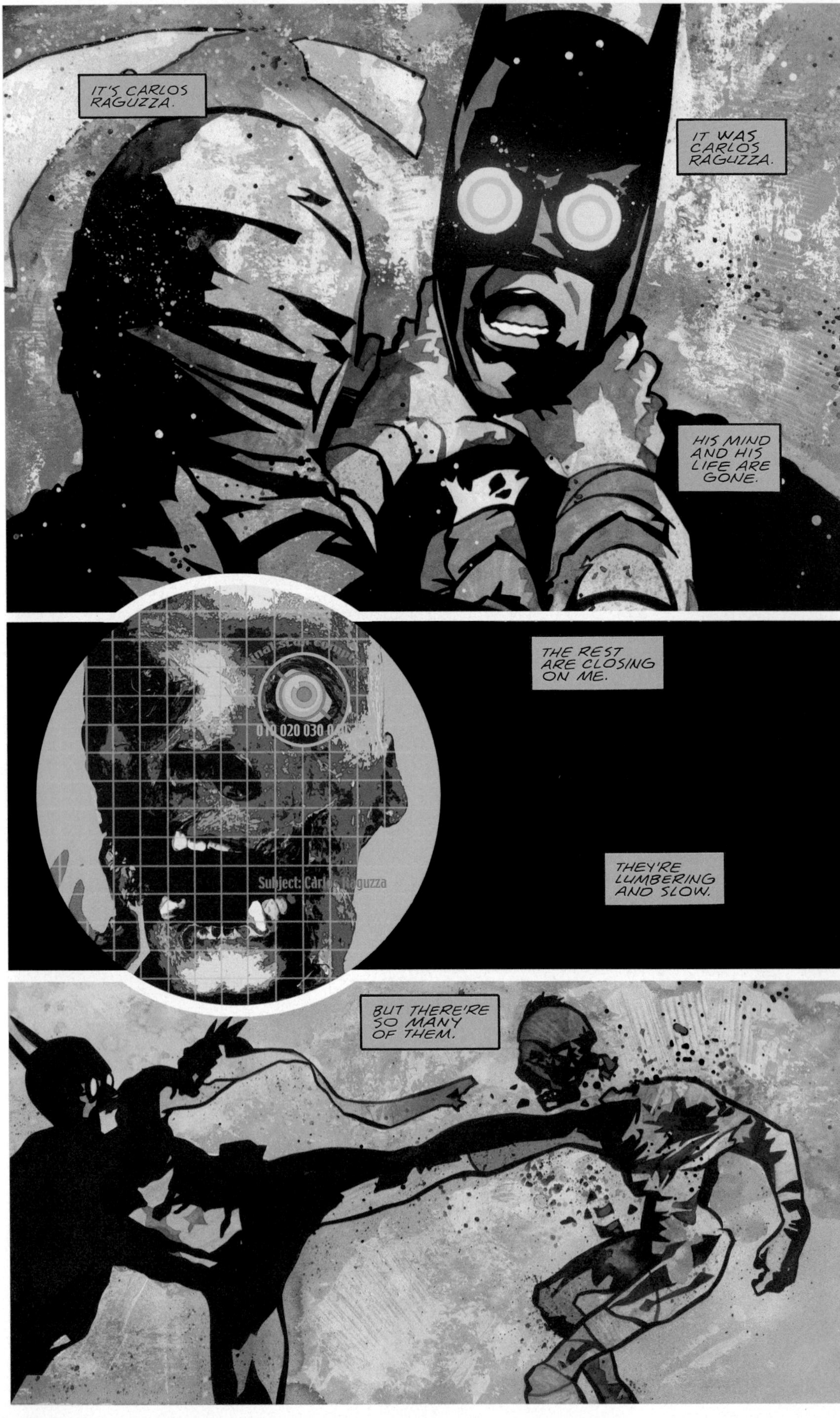

IT'S CARLOS RAGUZZA.
IT WAS CARLOS RAGUZZA.
HIS MIND AND HIS LIFE ARE GONE.
THE REST ARE CLOSING ON ME.
THEY'RE LUMBERING AND SLOW.
BUT THERE'RE SO MANY OF THEM.

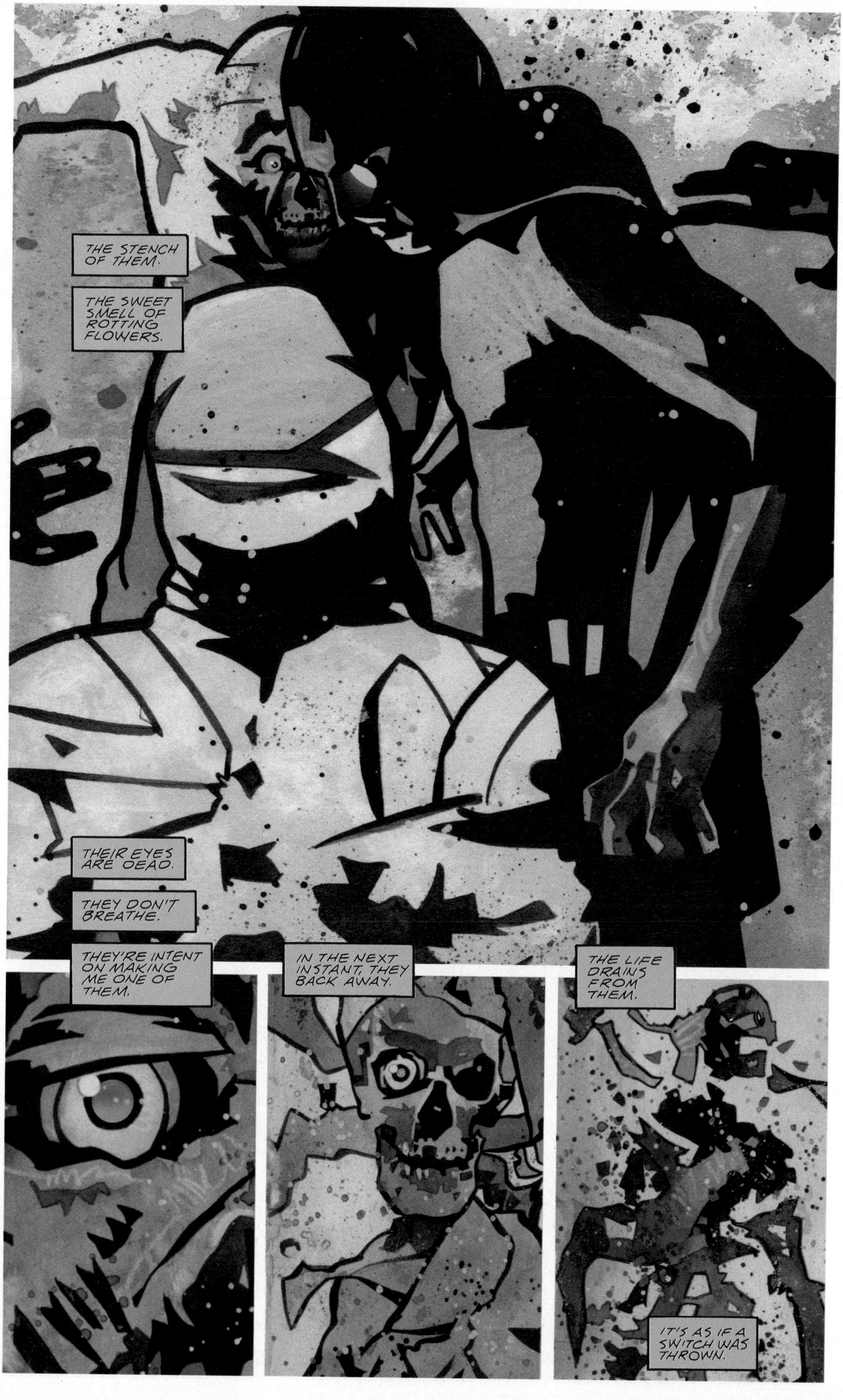
THE STENCH OF THEM.
THE SWEET SMELL OF ROTTING FLOWERS.
THEIR EYES ARE DEAD.
THEY DON'T BREATHE.
THEY'RE INTENT ON MAKING ME ONE OF THEM.
IN THE NEXT INSTANT, THEY BACK AWAY.
THE LIFE DRAINS FROM THEM.
IT'S AS IF A SWITCH WAS THROWN.

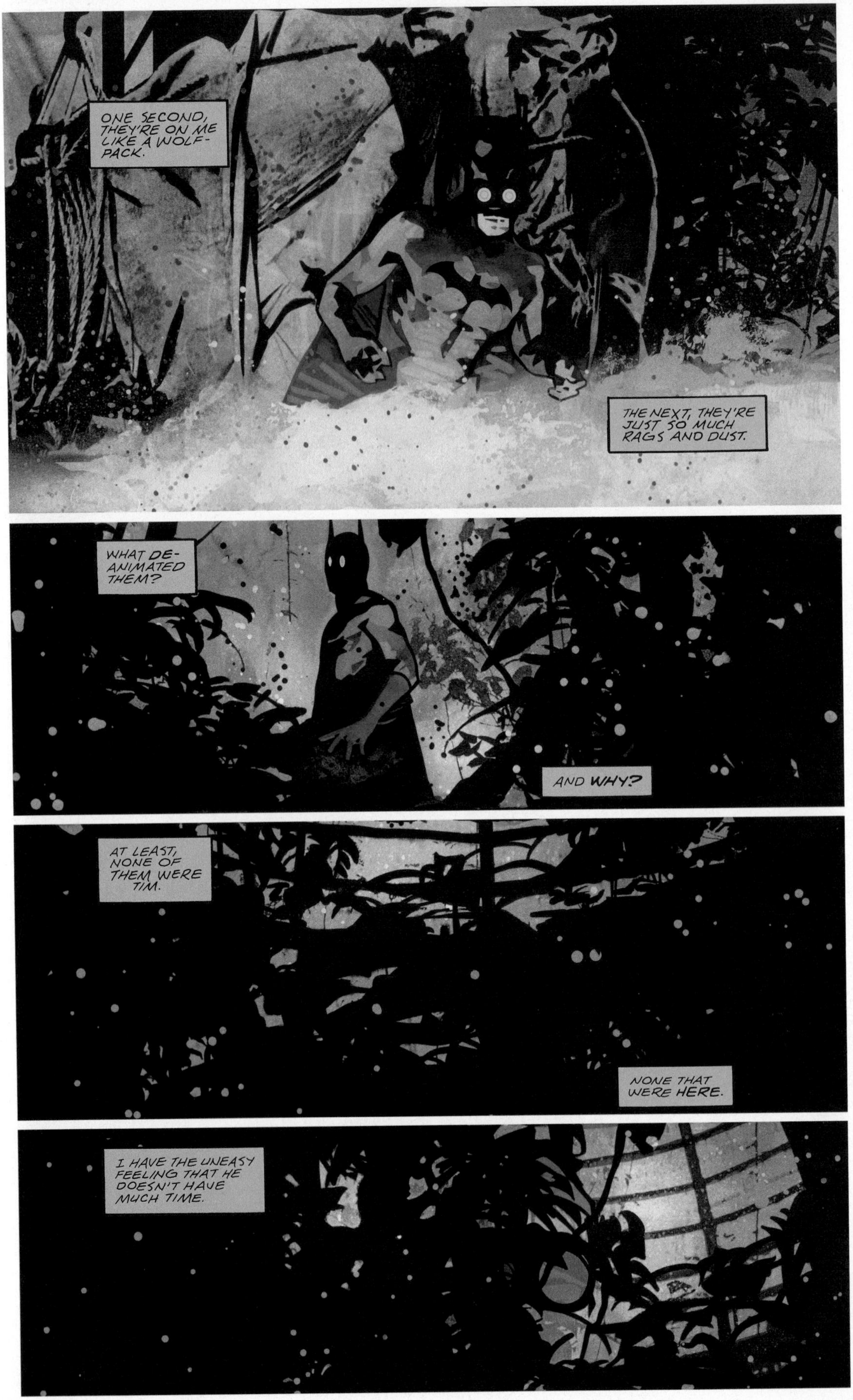
ONE SECOND, THEY'RE ON ME LIKE A WOLF-PACK.
THE NEXT, THEY'RE JUST SO MUCH RAGS AND DUST.
WHAT DE-ANIMATED THEM?
AND WHY?
AT LEAST, NONE OF THEM WERE TIM.
NONE THAT WERE HERE.
I HAVE THE UNEASY FEELING THAT HE DOESN'T HAVE MUCH TIME.

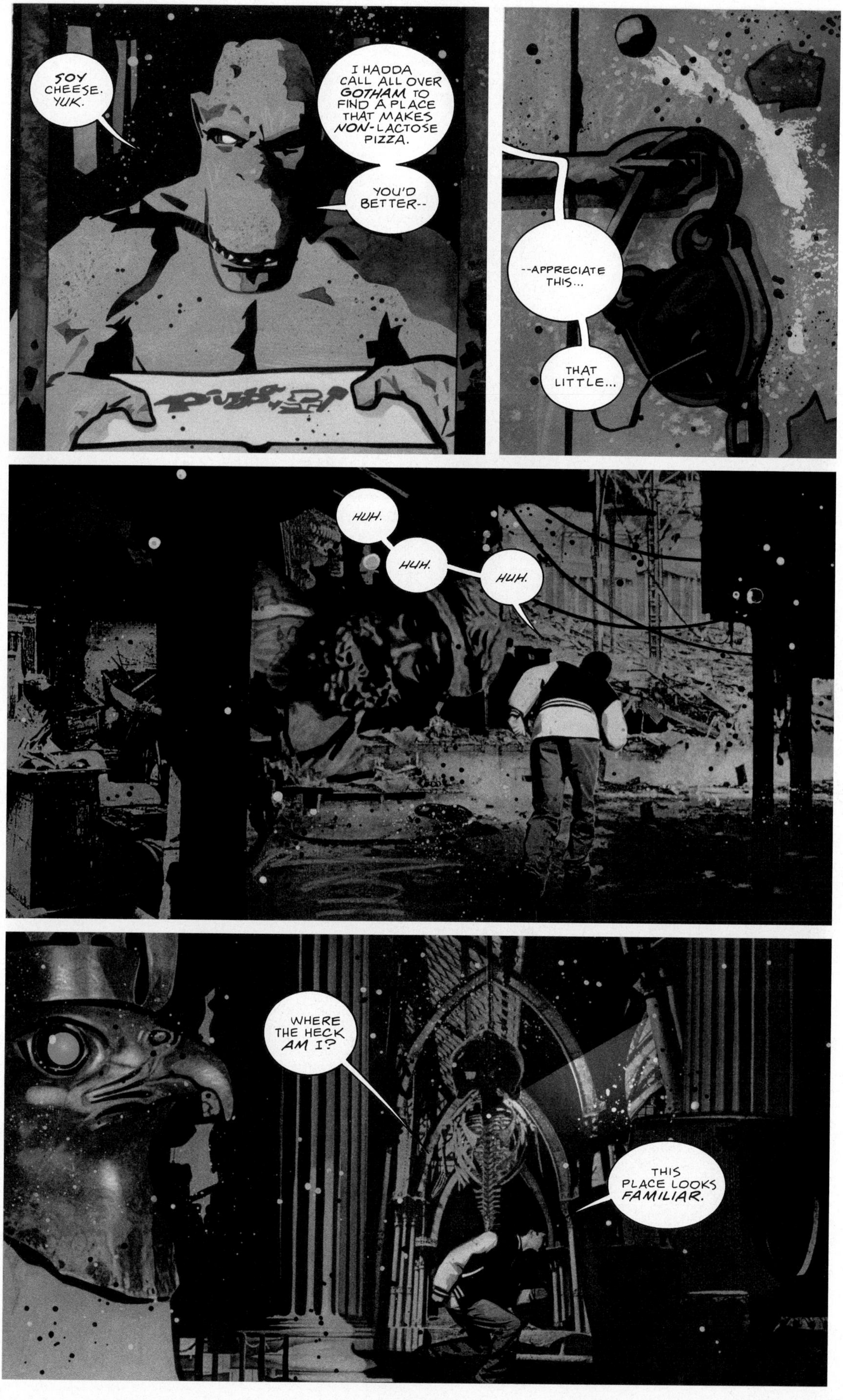
SOY CHEESE. YUK.
I HADDA CALL ALL OVER GOTHAM TO FIND A PLACE THAT MAKES NON-LACTOSE PIZZA.
YOU'D BETTER--
--APPRECIATE THIS...
THAT LITTLE...
HUH.
HUH.
HUH.
WHERE THE HECK AM I?
THIS PLACE LOOKS FAMILIAR.

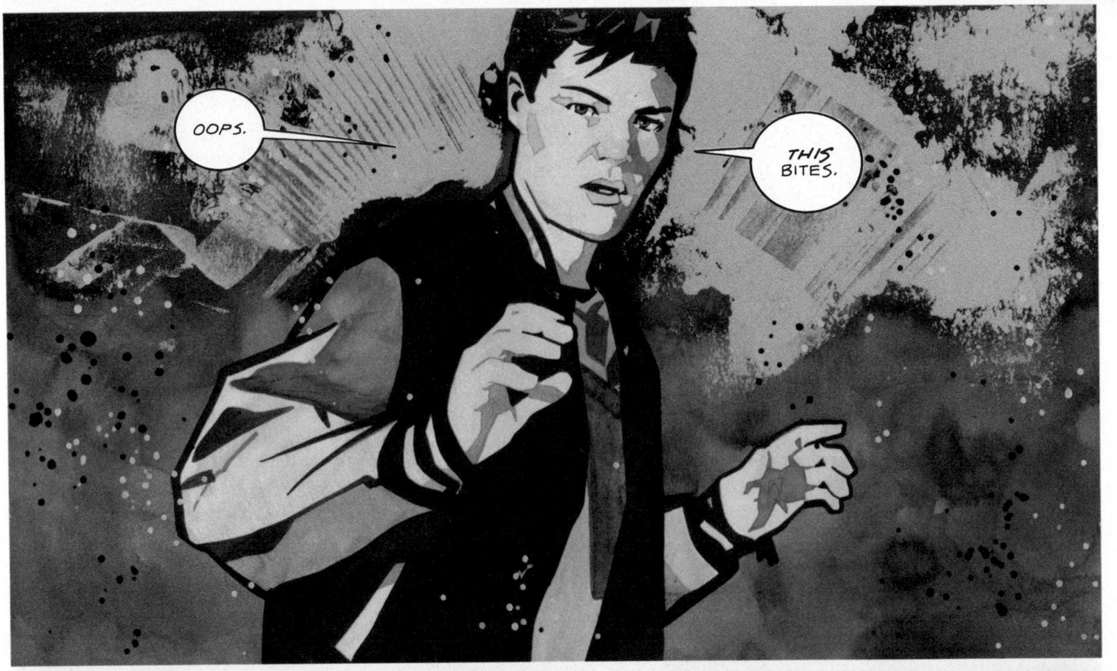
OOPS.
THIS BITES.

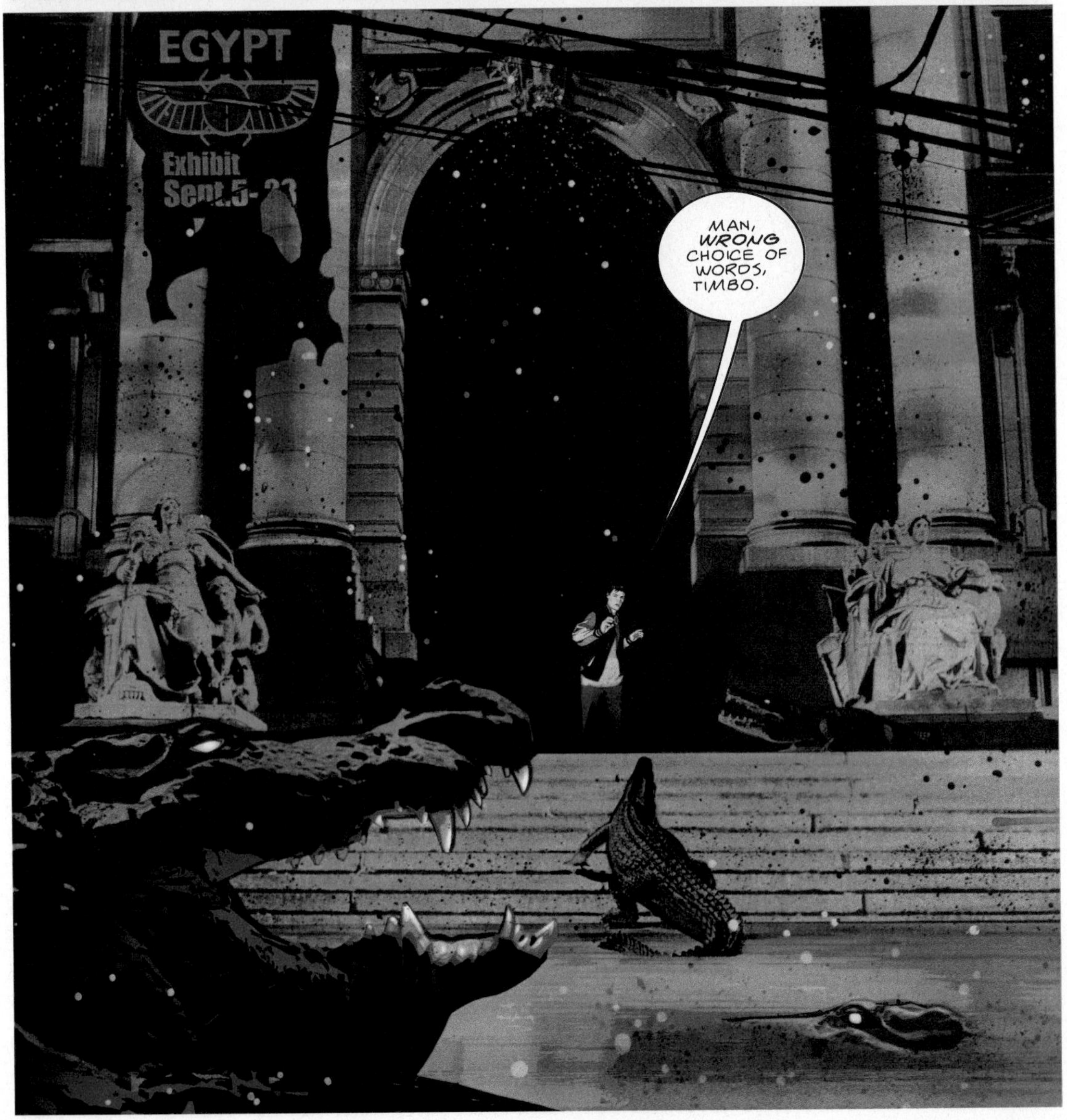
EGYPT
Exhibit
Sept.5-23
MAN, WRONG CHOICE OF WORDS, TIMBO.

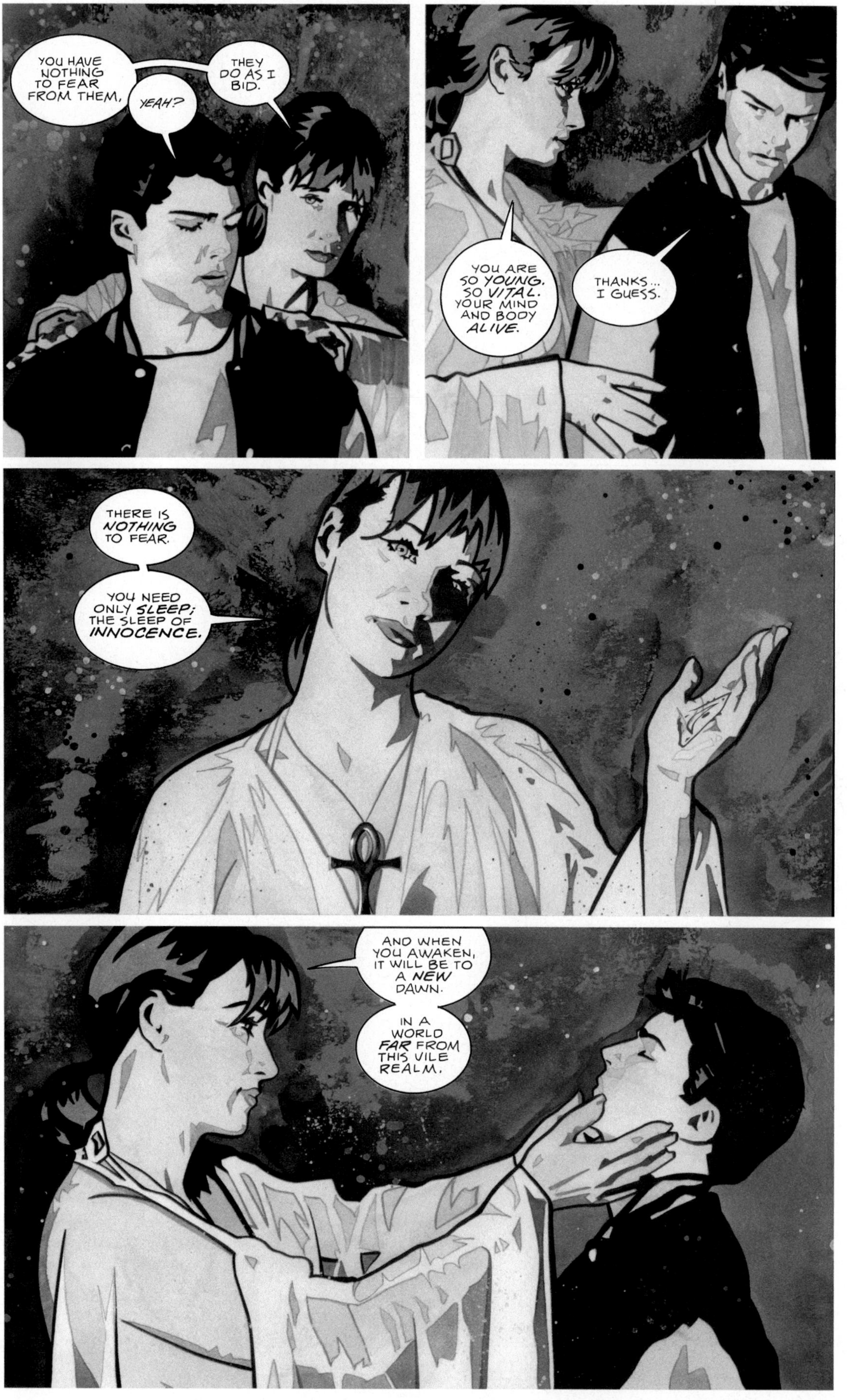

YOU HAVE NOTHING TO FEAR FROM THEM.
YEAH?
THEY DO AS I BID.
YOU ARE SO YOUNG. SO VITAL. YOUR MIND AND BODY ALIVE.
THANKS... I GUESS.
THERE IS NOTHING TO FEAR.
YOU NEED ONLY SLEEP; THE SLEEP OF INNOCENCE.
AND WHEN YOU AWAKEN, IT WILL BE TO A NEW DAWN.
IN A WORLD FAR FROM THIS VILE REALM.

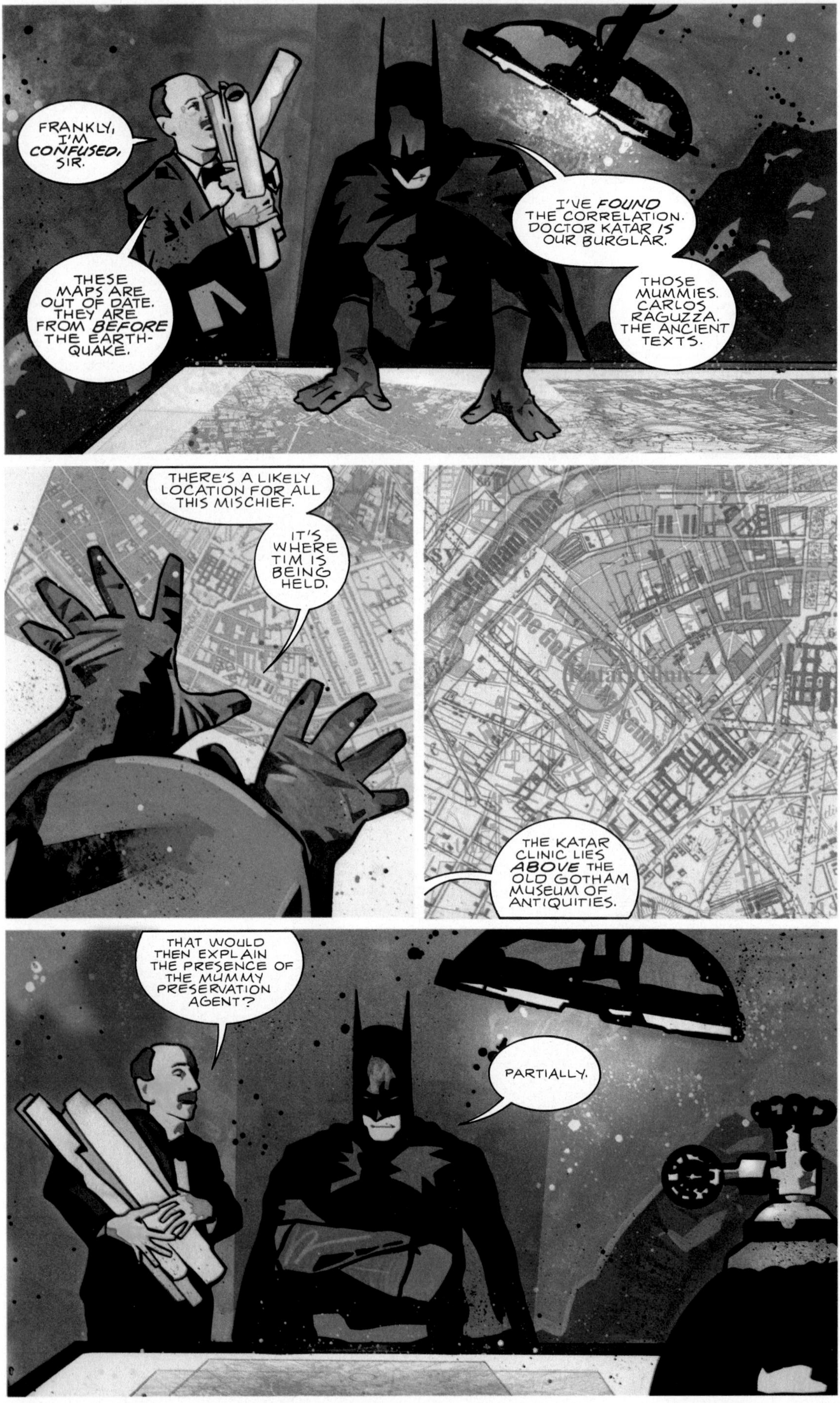
FRANKLY, I'M CONFUSED, SIR.
THESE MAPS ARE OUT OF DATE. THEY ARE FROM BEFORE THE EARTHQUAKE.
I'VE FOUND THE CORRELATION. DOCTOR KATAR IS OUR BURGLAR.
THOSE MUMMIES. CARLOS RAGUZZA. THE ANCIENT TEXTS.
THERE'S A LIKELY LOCATION FOR ALL THIS MISCHIEF.
IT'S WHERE TIM IS BEING HELD.
THE KATAR CLINIC LIES ABOVE THE OLD GOTHAM MUSEUM OF ANTIQUITIES.
THAT WOULD THEN EXPLAIN THE PRESENCE OF THE MUMMY PRESERVATION AGENT?
PARTIALLY.

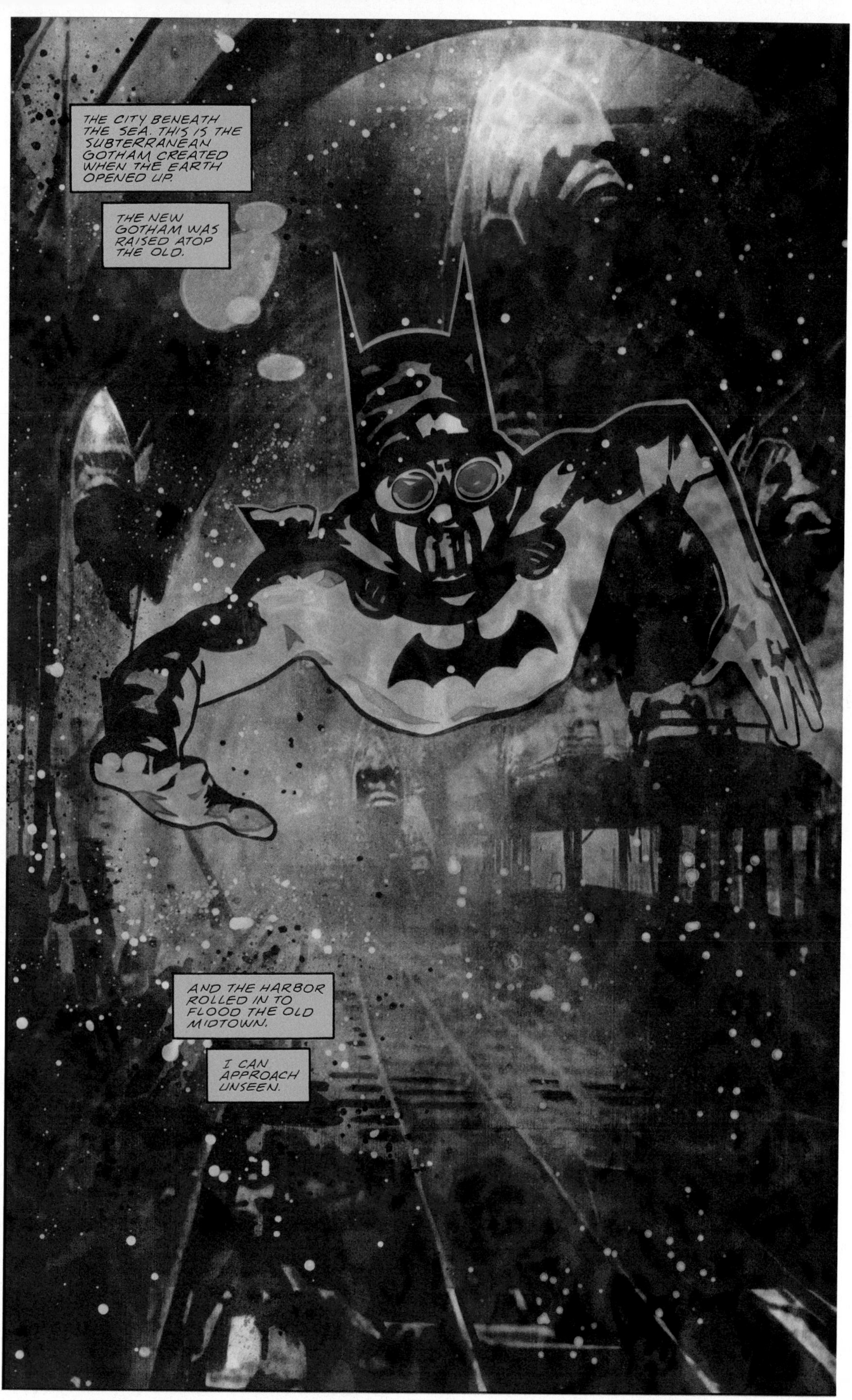
THE CITY BENEATH THE SEA. THIS IS THE SUBTERRANEAN GOTHAM CREATED WHEN THE EARTH OPENED UP.
THE NEW GOTHAM WAS RAISED ATOP THE OLD.
AND THE HARBOR ROLLED IN TO FLOOD THE OLD MIDTOWN.
I CAN APPROACH UNSEEN.

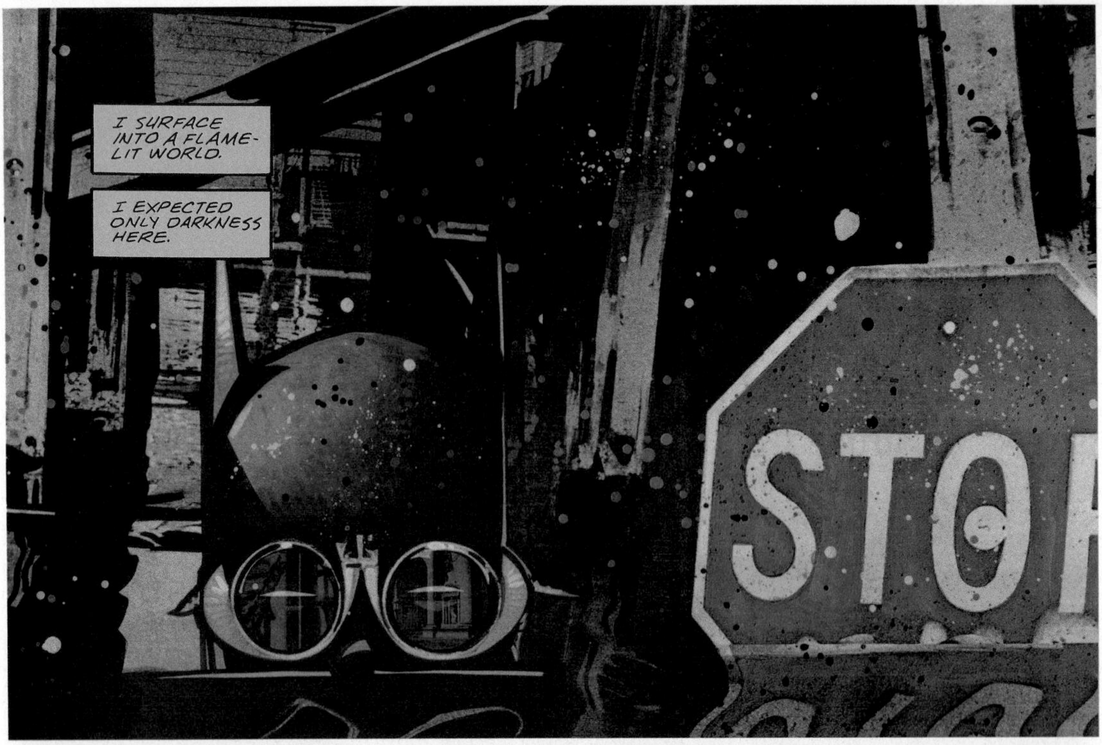
I SURFACE INTO A FLAME-LIT WORLD.
I EXPECTED ONLY DARKNESS HERE.
STOP

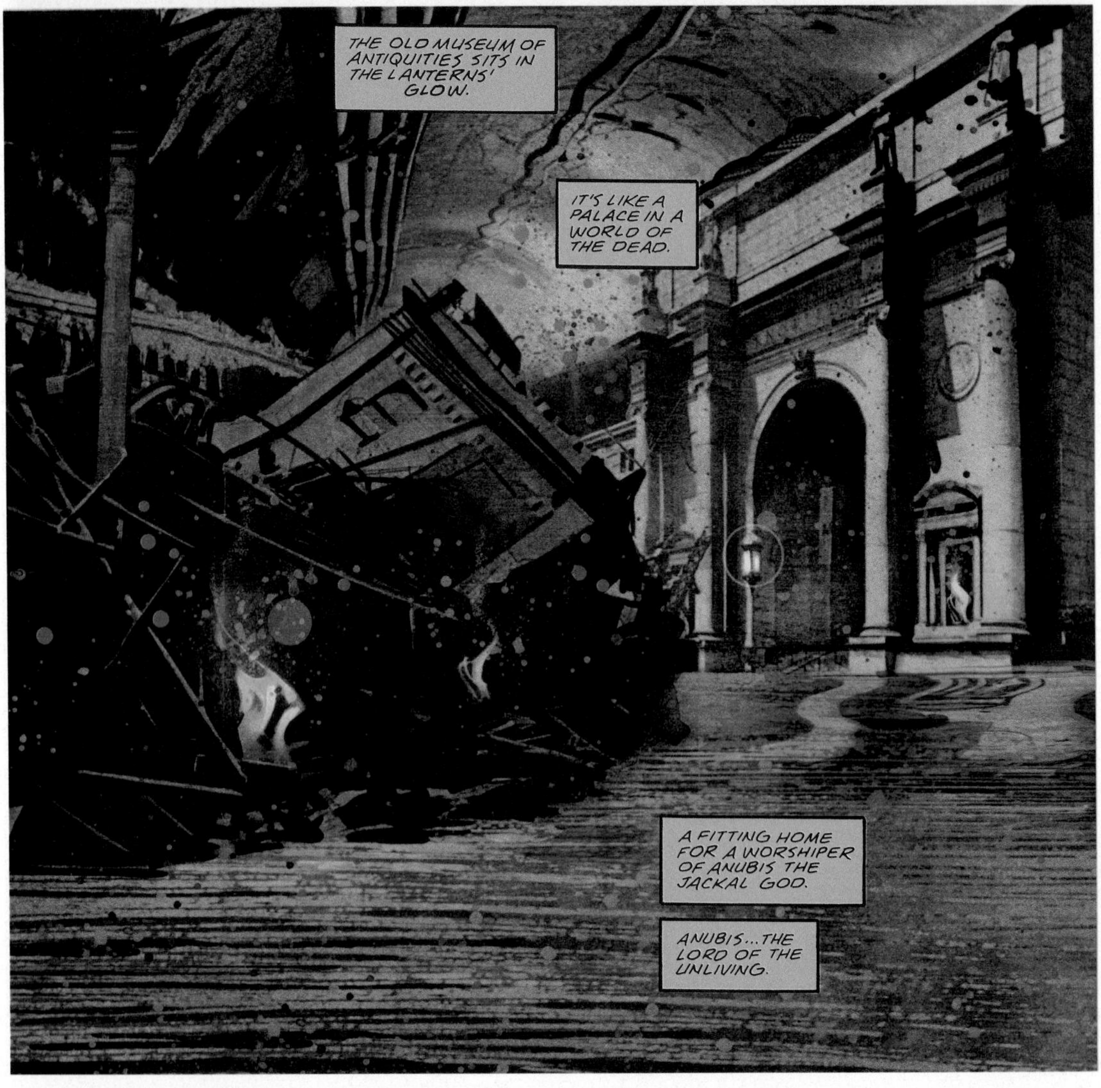
THE OLD MUSEUM OF ANTIQUITIES SITS IN THE LANTERNS' GLOW.
IT'S LIKE A PALACE IN A WORLD OF THE DEAD.
A FITTING HOME FOR A WORSHIPER OF ANUBIS THE JACKAL GOD.
ANUBIS...THE LORD OF THE UNLIVING.

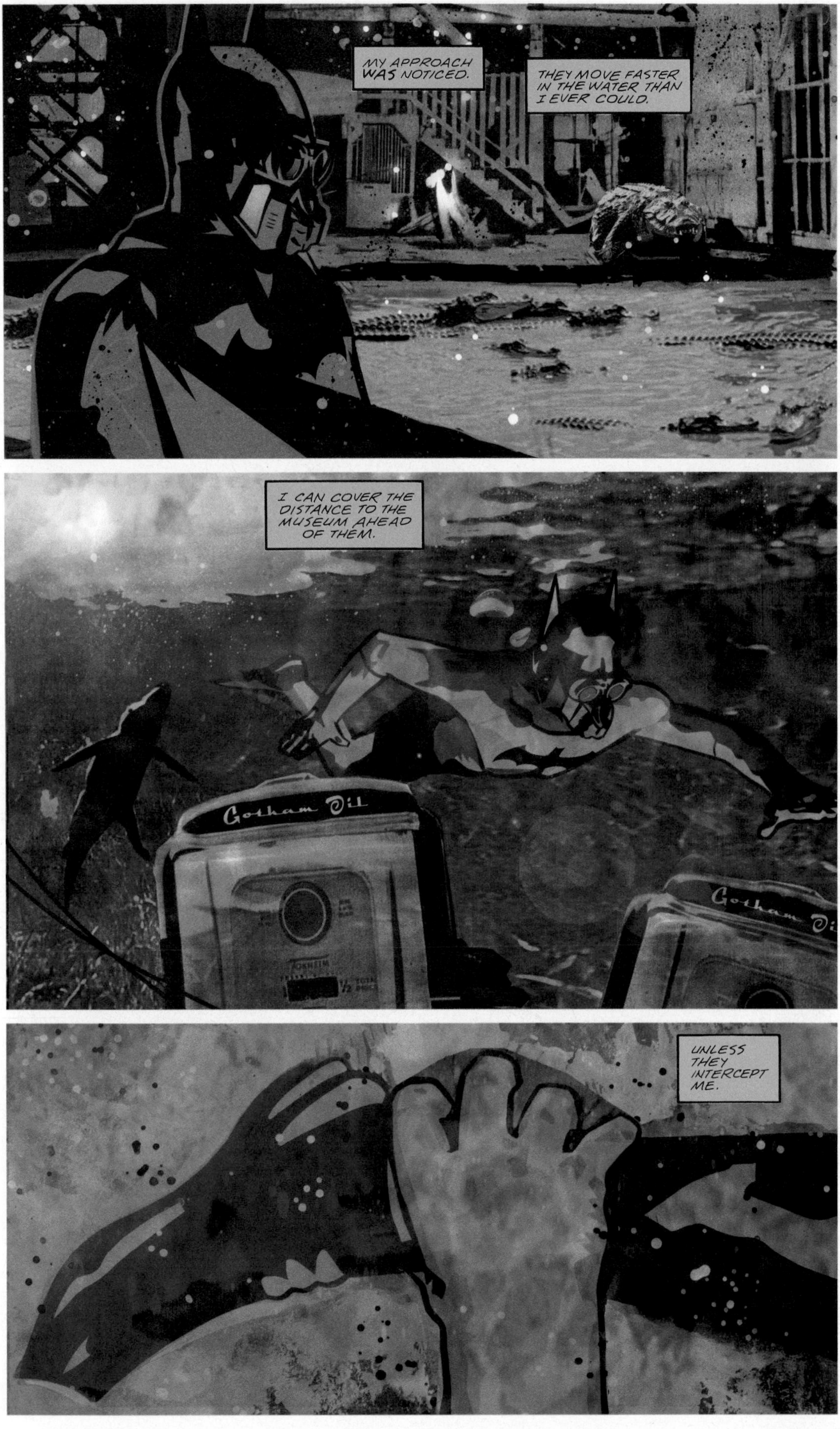
MY APPROACH WAS NOTICED.
THEY MOVE FASTER IN THE WATER THAN I EVER COULD.
I CAN COVER THE DISTANCE TO THE MUSEUM AHEAD OF THEM.
Gotham Oil
UNLESS THEY INTERCEPT ME.

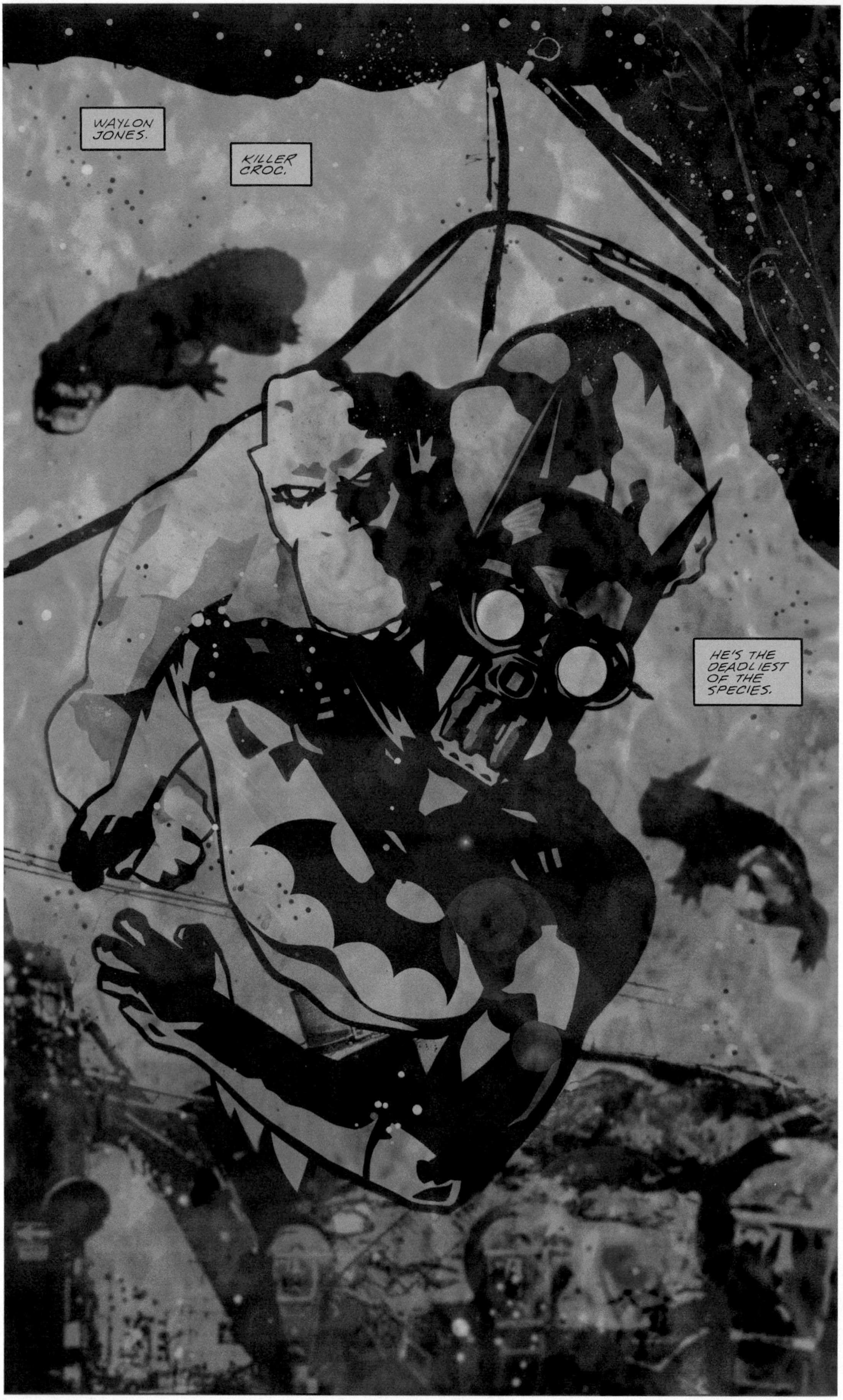
WAYLON JONES.
KILLER CROC.
HE'S THE DEADLIEST OF THE SPECIES.

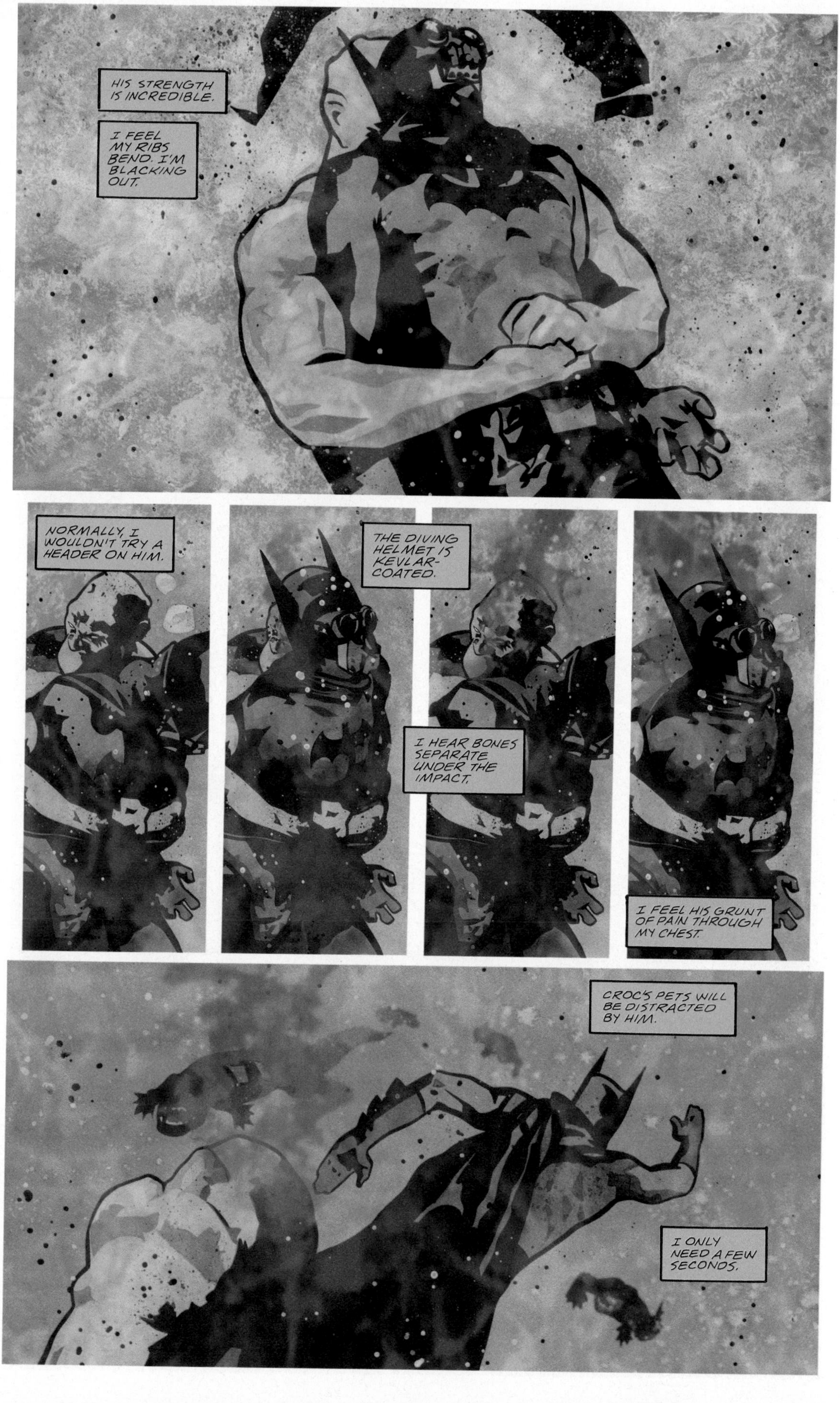
HIS STRENGTH IS INCREDIBLE.
I FEEL MY RIBS BEND. I'M BLACKING OUT.
NORMALLY, I WOULDN'T TRY A HEADER ON HIM.
THE DIVING HELMET IS KEVLAR-COATED.
I HEAR BONES SEPARATE UNDER THE IMPACT.
I FEEL HIS GRUNT OF PAIN THROUGH MY CHEST.
CROC'S PETS WILL BE DISTRACTED BY HIM.
I ONLY NEED A FEW SECONDS.

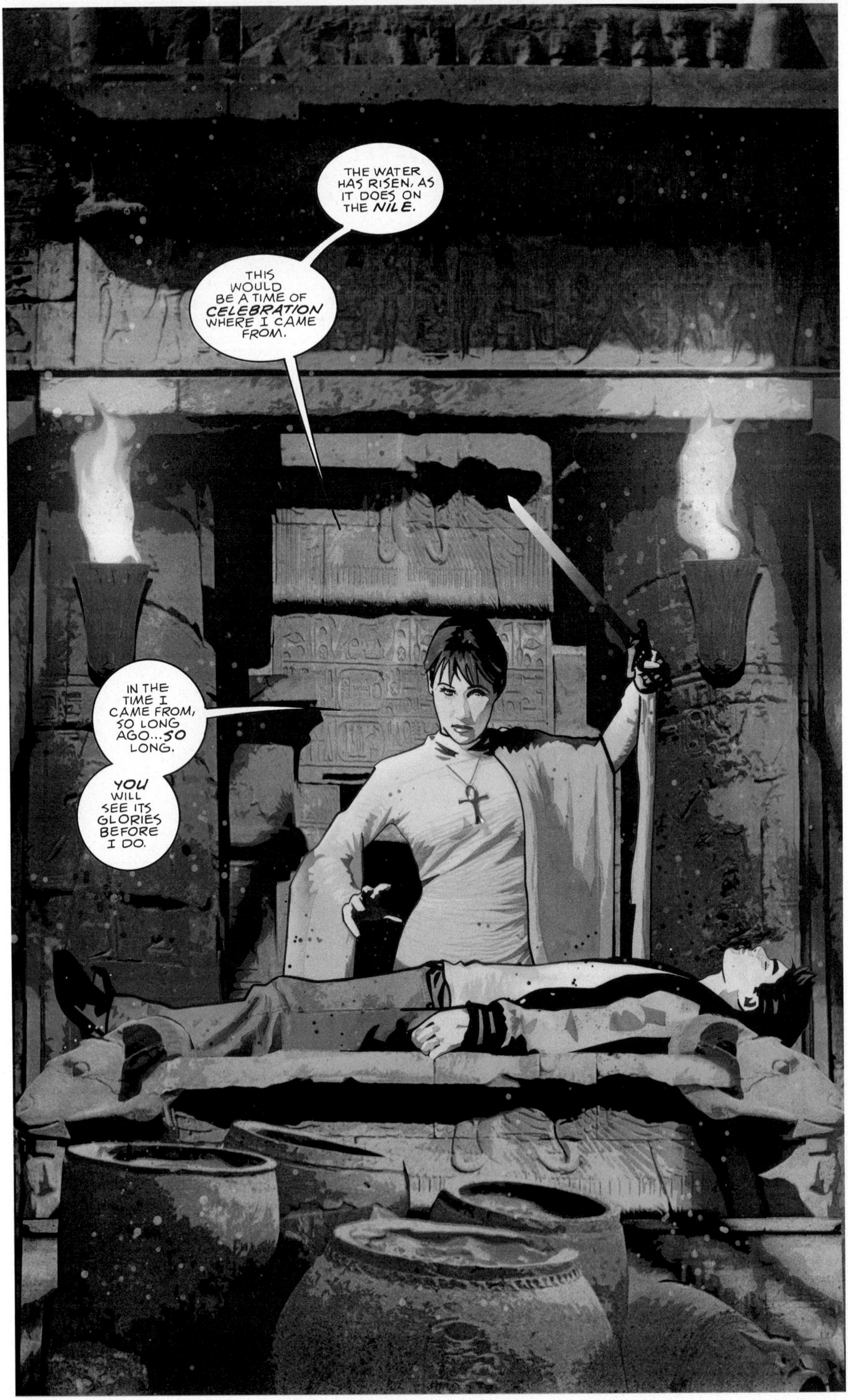

THE WATER HAS RISEN, AS IT DOES ON THE *NILE*.
THIS WOULD BE A TIME OF *CELEBRATION* WHERE I CAME FROM.
IN THE TIME I CAME FROM, SO LONG AGO...*SO* LONG.
YOU WILL SEE ITS GLORIES BEFORE I DO.

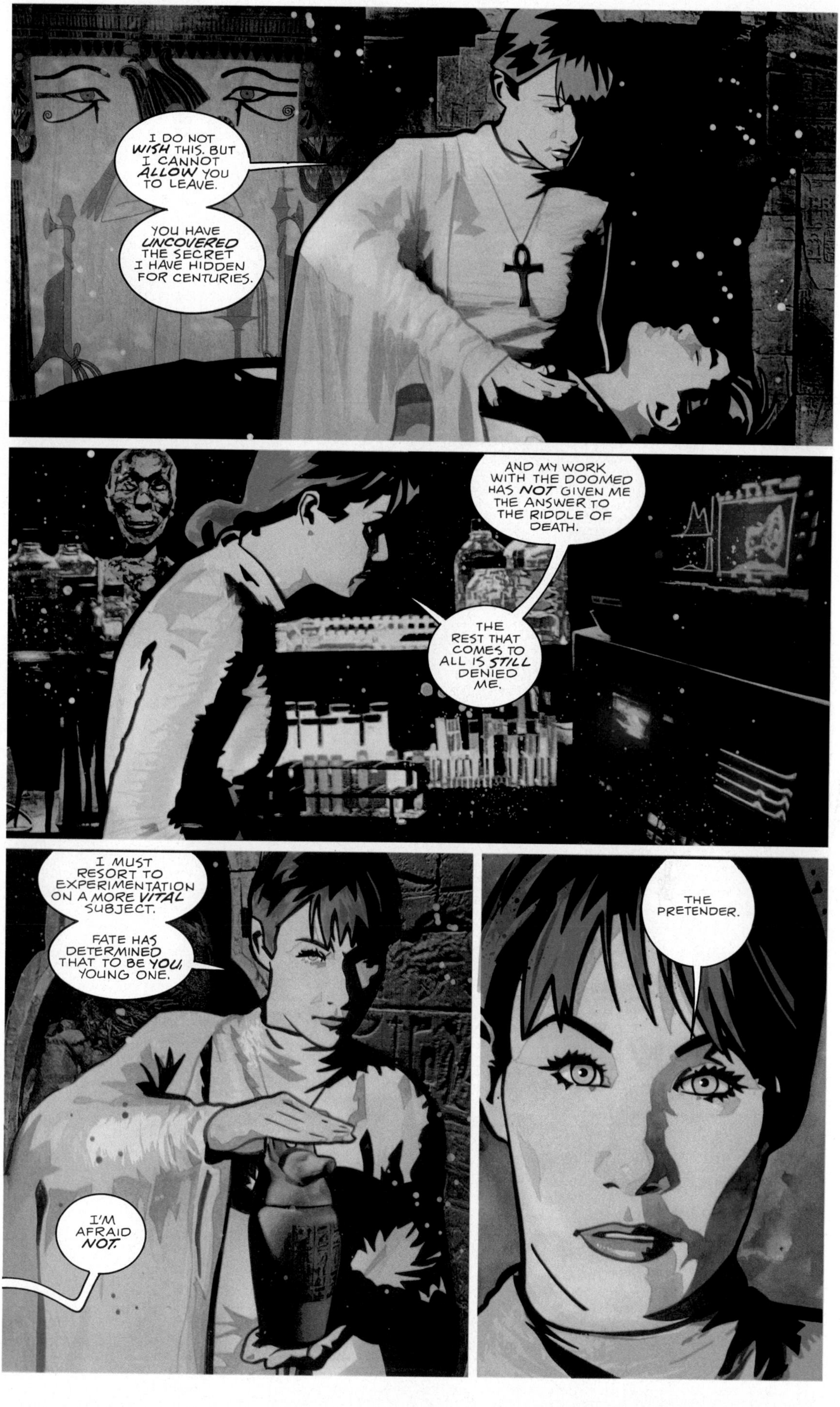
I DO NOT WISH THIS. BUT I CANNOT ALLOW YOU TO LEAVE.
YOU HAVE UNCOVERED THE SECRET I HAVE HIDDEN FOR CENTURIES.
AND MY WORK WITH THE DOOMED HAS NOT GIVEN ME THE ANSWER TO THE RIDDLE OF DEATH.
THE REST THAT COMES TO ALL IS STILL DENIED ME.
I MUST RESORT TO EXPERIMENTATION ON A MORE VITAL SUBJECT.
FATE HAS DETERMINED THAT TO BE YOU, YOUNG ONE.
I'M AFRAID NOT.
THE PRETENDER.

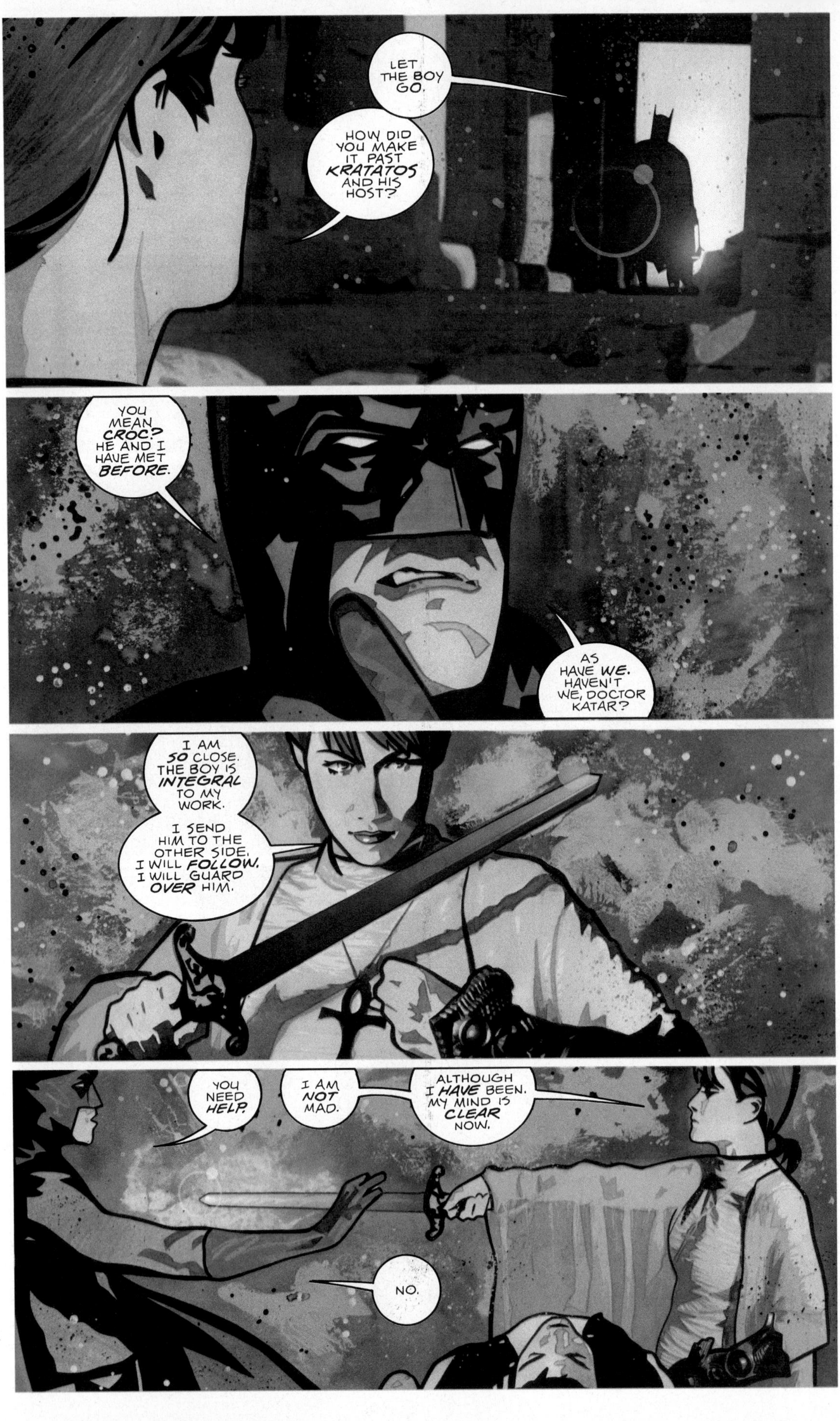
LET THE BOY GO.
HOW DID YOU MAKE IT PAST KRATATOS AND HIS HOST?
YOU MEAN CROC? HE AND I HAVE MET BEFORE.
AS HAVE WE. HAVEN'T WE, DOCTOR KATAR?
I AM SO CLOSE. THE BOY IS INTEGRAL TO MY WORK.
I SEND HIM TO THE OTHER SIDE. I WILL FOLLOW. I WILL GUARD OVER HIM.
YOU NEED HELP.
I AM NOT MAD.
ALTHOUGH I HAVE BEEN. MY MIND IS CLEAR NOW.
NO.

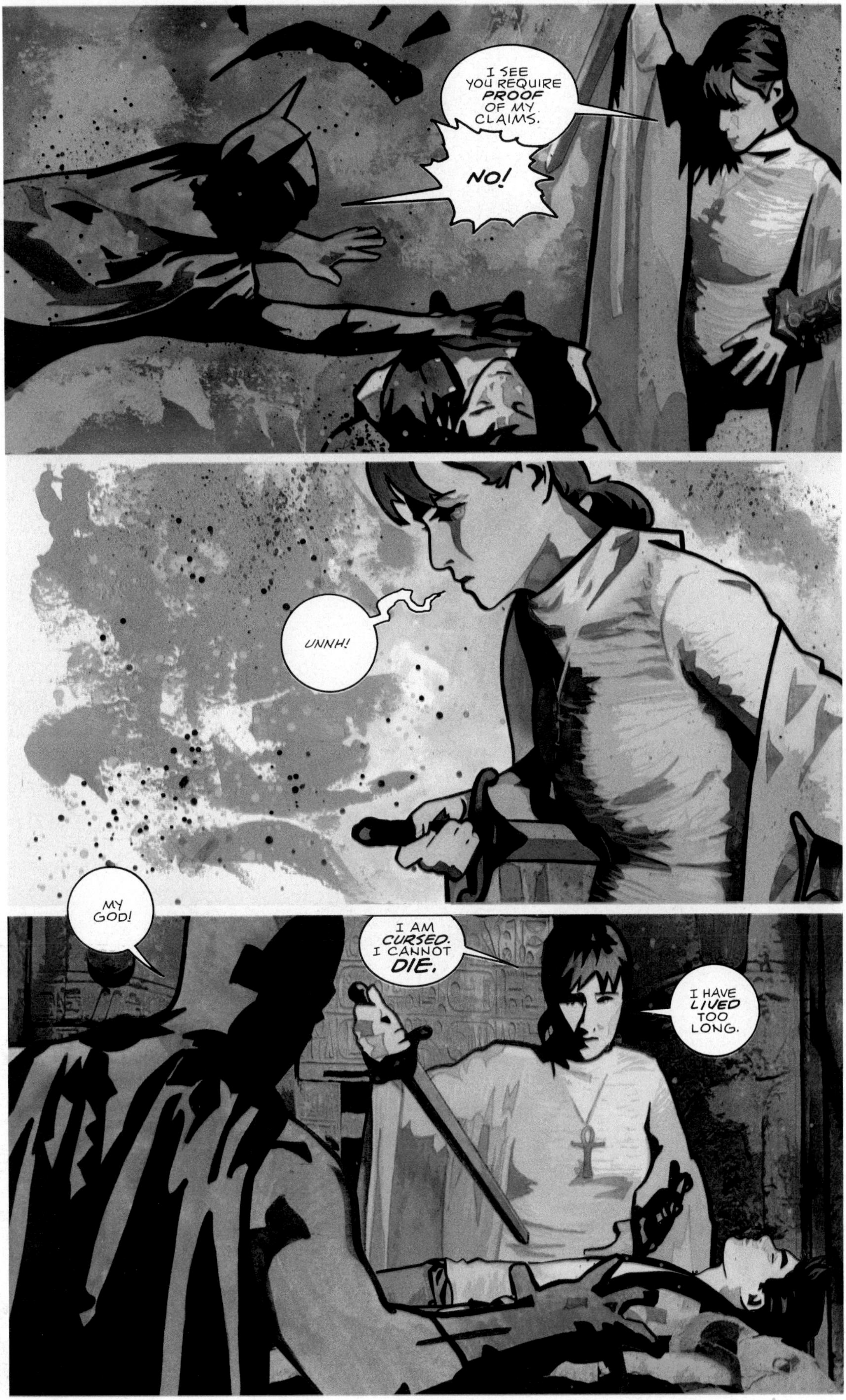
I SEE YOU REQUIRE PROOF OF MY CLAIMS.
NO!
UNNH!
MY GOD!
I AM CURSED. I CANNOT DIE.
I HAVE LIVED TOO LONG.

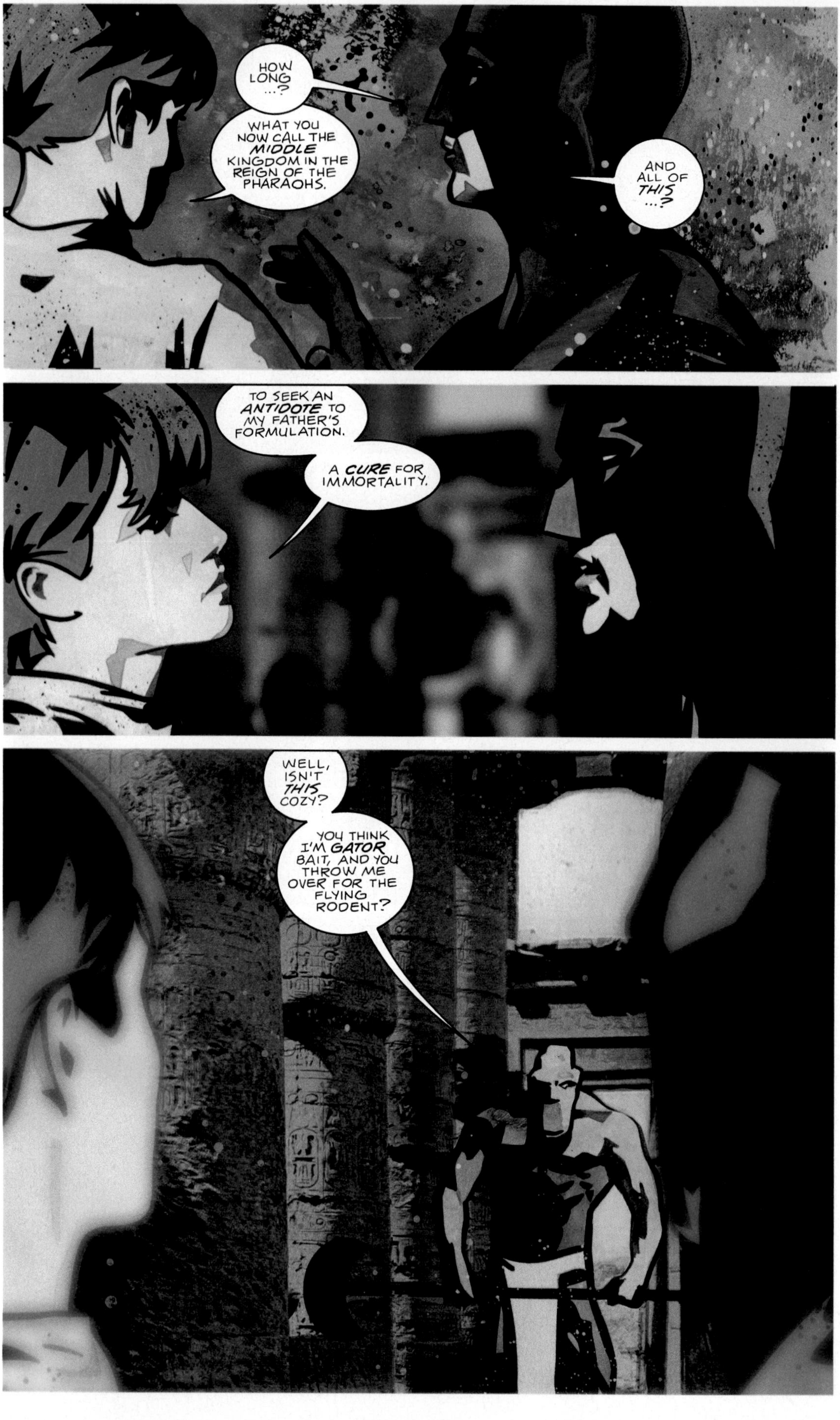
HOW LONG ...?
WHAT YOU NOW CALL THE MIDDLE KINGDOM IN THE REIGN OF THE PHARAOHS.
AND ALL OF THIS ...?
TO SEEK AN ANTIDOTE TO MY FATHER'S FORMULATION.
A CURE FOR IMMORTALITY.
WELL, ISN'T THIS COZY?
YOU THINK I'M GATOR BAIT, AND YOU THROW ME OVER FOR THE FLYING RODENT?

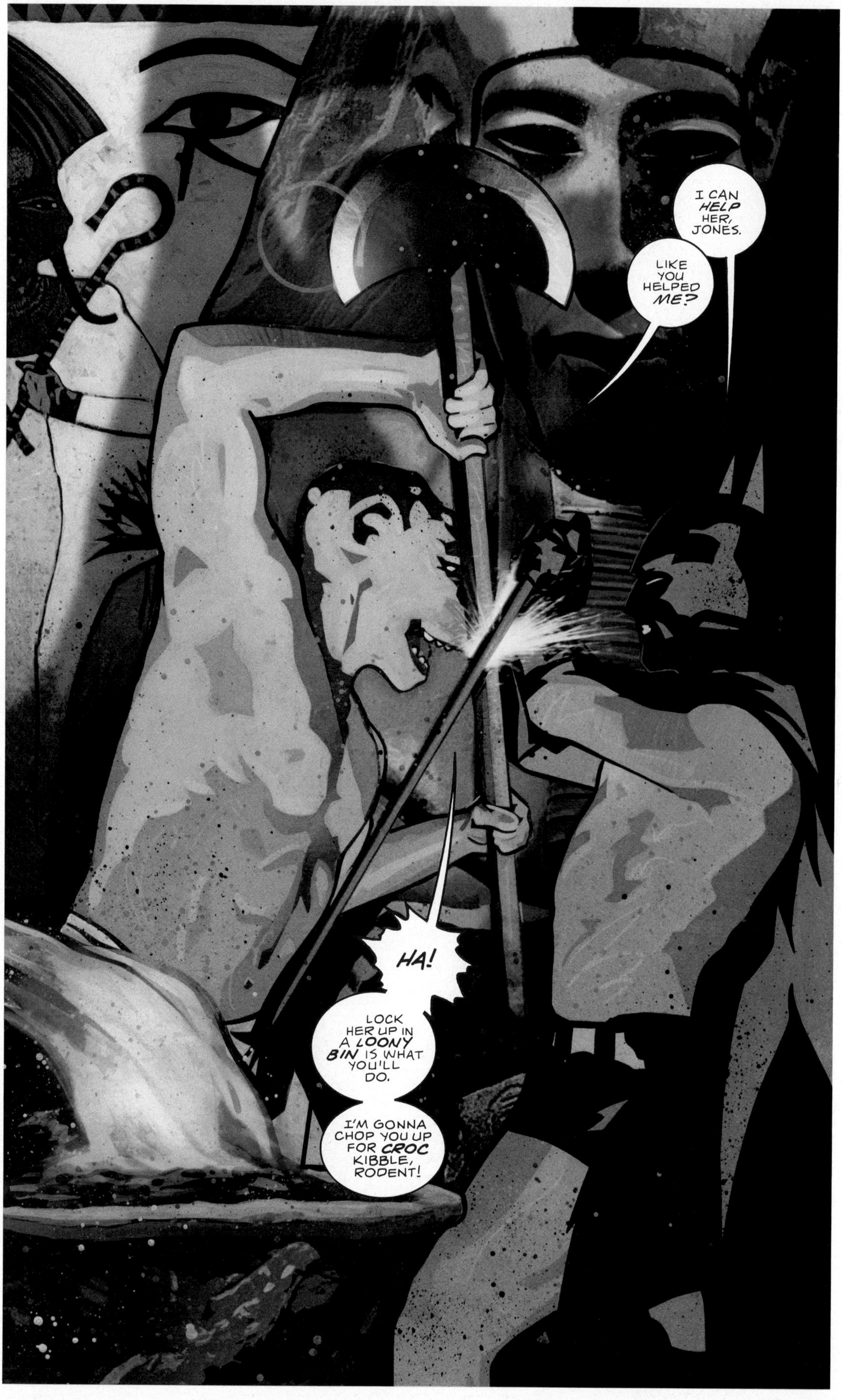
I CAN HELP HER, JONES.
LIKE YOU HELPED ME?
HA!
LOCK HER UP IN A LOONY BIN IS WHAT YOU'LL DO.
I'M GONNA CHOP YOU UP FOR CROC KIBBLE, RODENT!

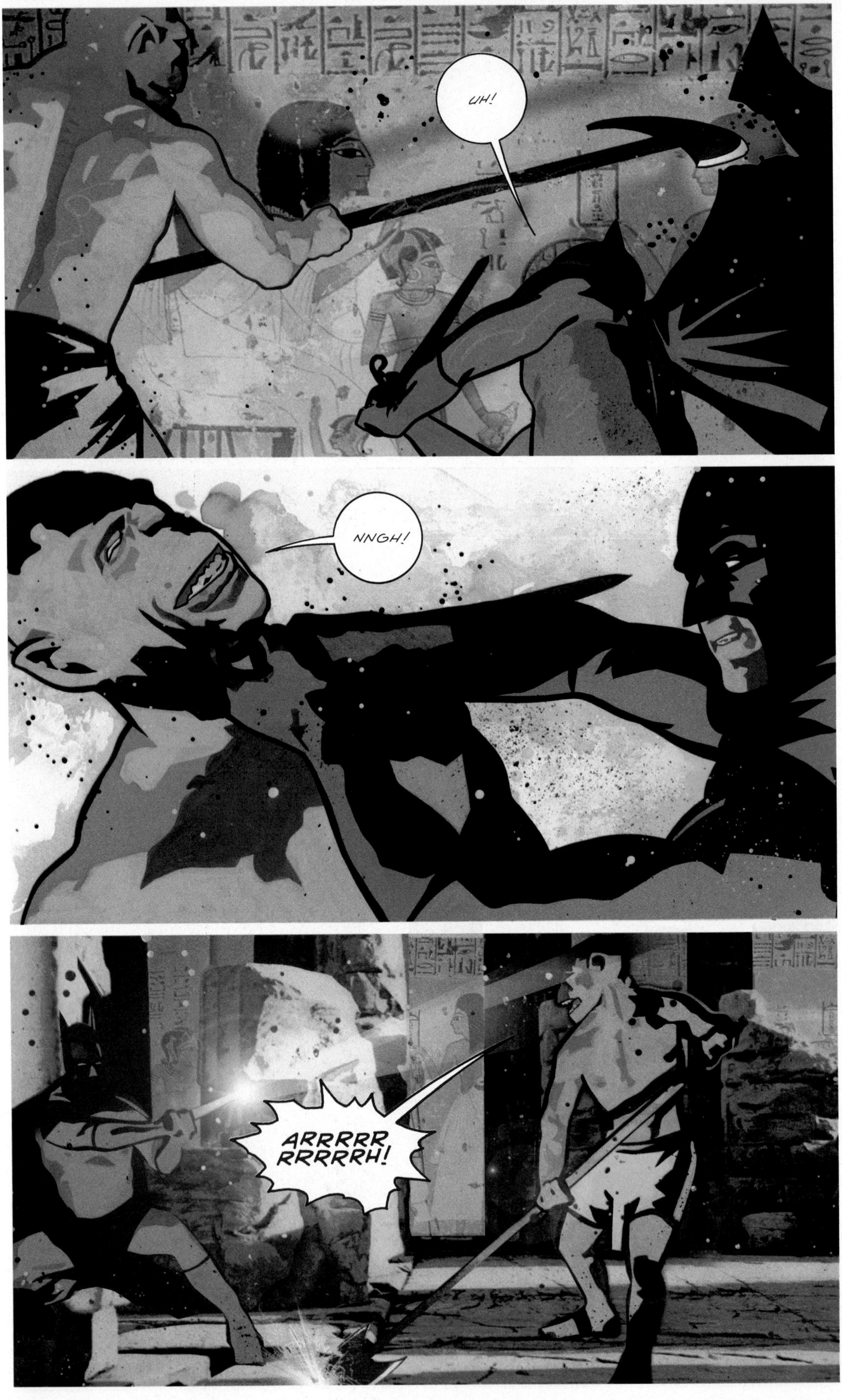
UH!
NNGH!
ARRRRR RRRRRH!

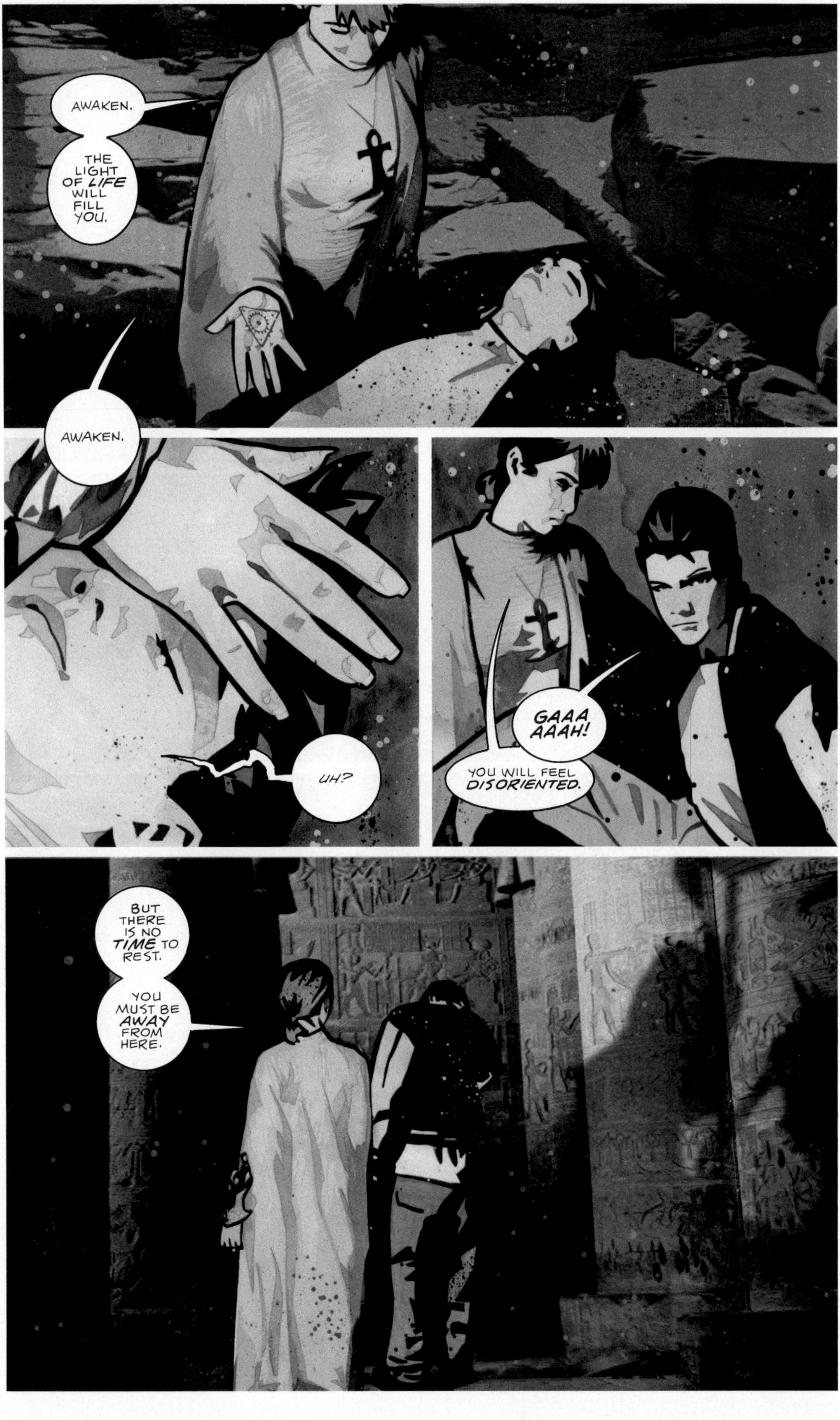
AWAKEN.
THE LIGHT OF *LIFE* WILL FILL YOU.
AWAKEN.
UH?
GAAA AAAH!
YOU WILL FEEL *DISORIENTED.*
BUT THERE IS NO *TIME* TO REST.
YOU MUST BE *AWAY* FROM HERE.

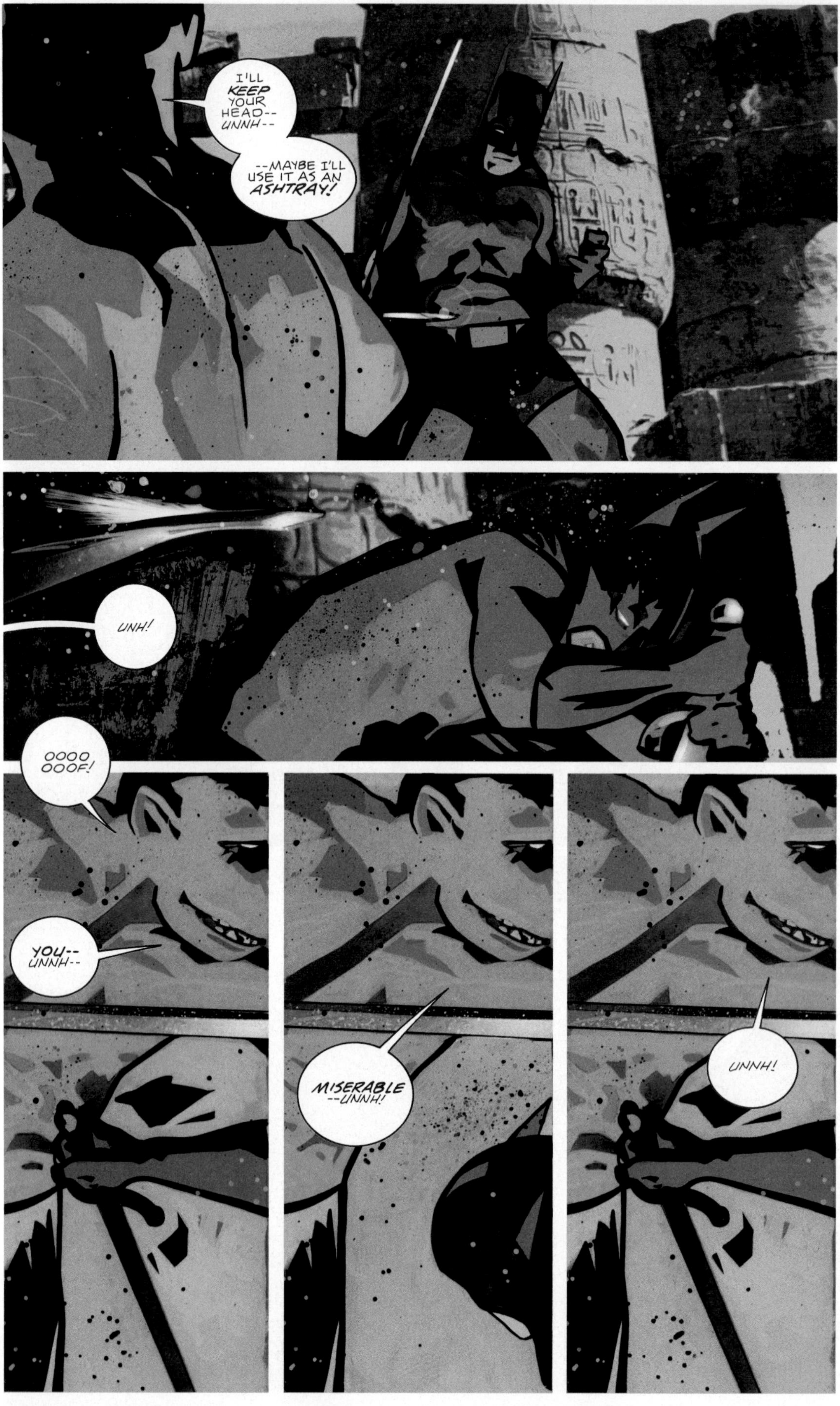
I'LL KEEP YOUR HEAD-- UNNH--
--MAYBE I'LL USE IT AS AN ASHTRAY!
UNH!
OOOO OOOF!
YOU-- UNNH--
MISERABLE --UNNH!
UNNH!

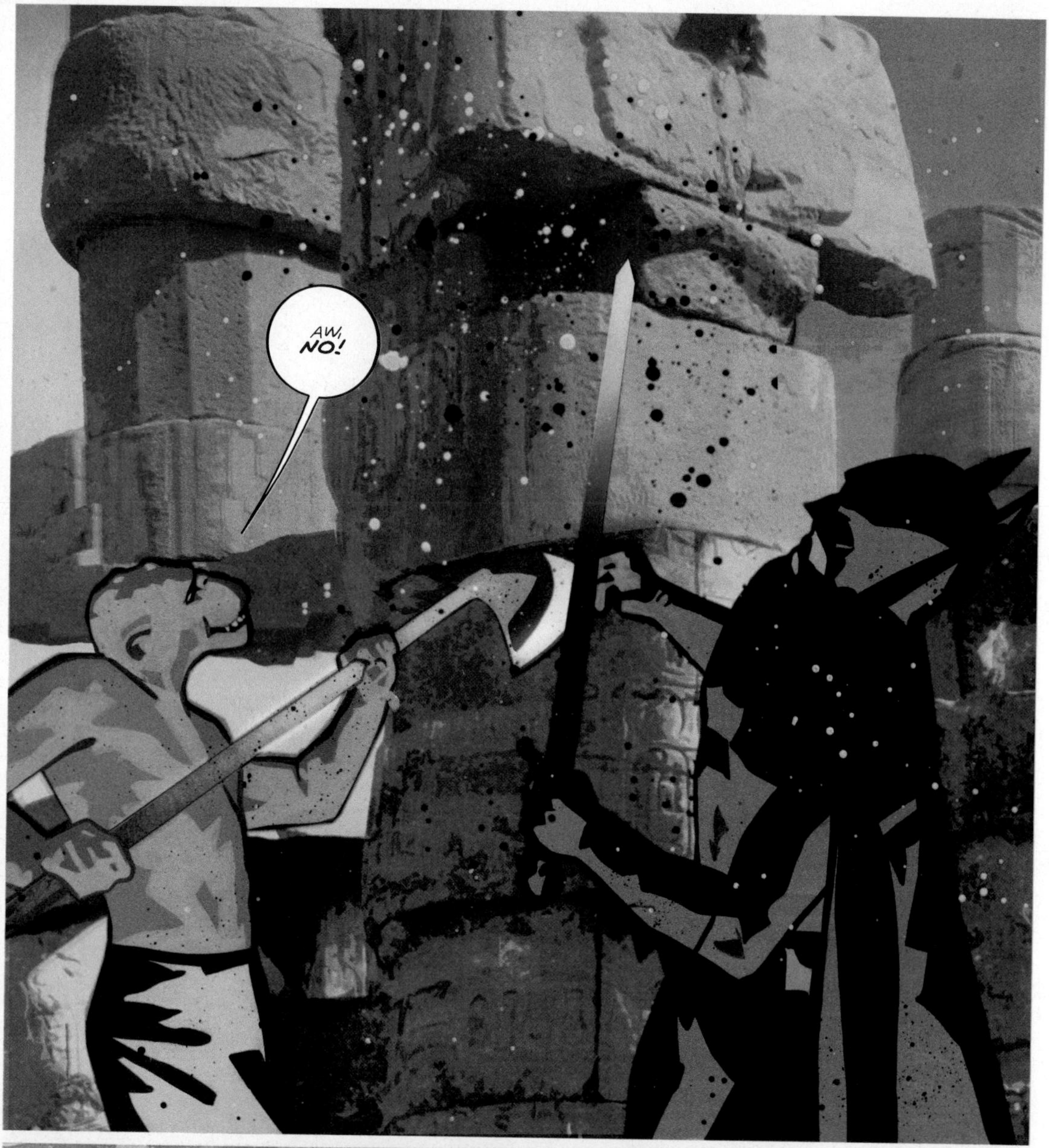
AW, NO!

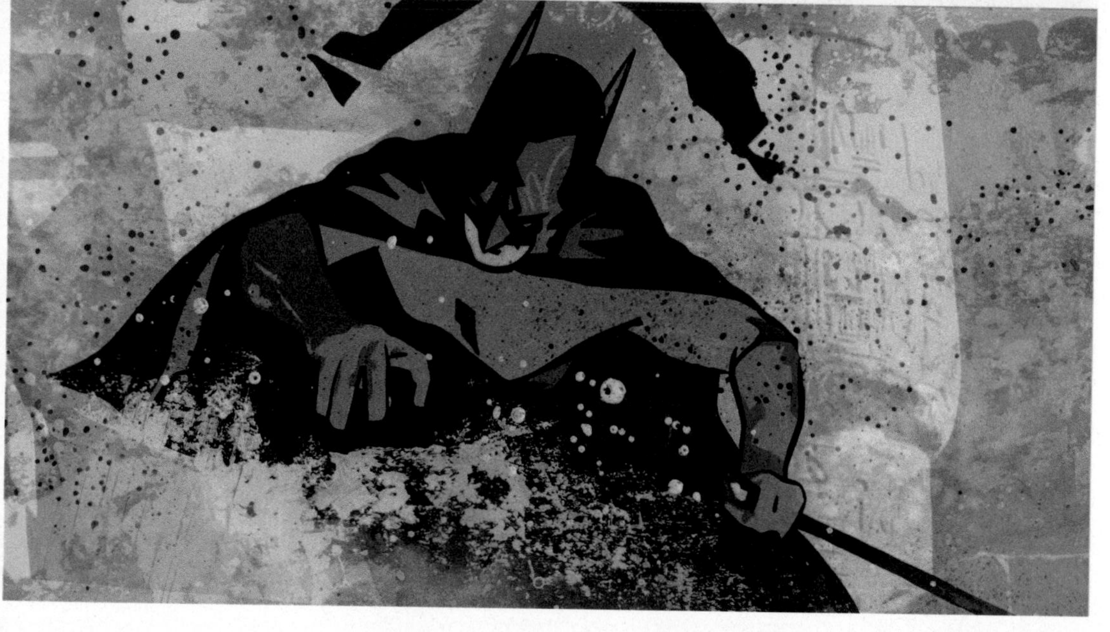

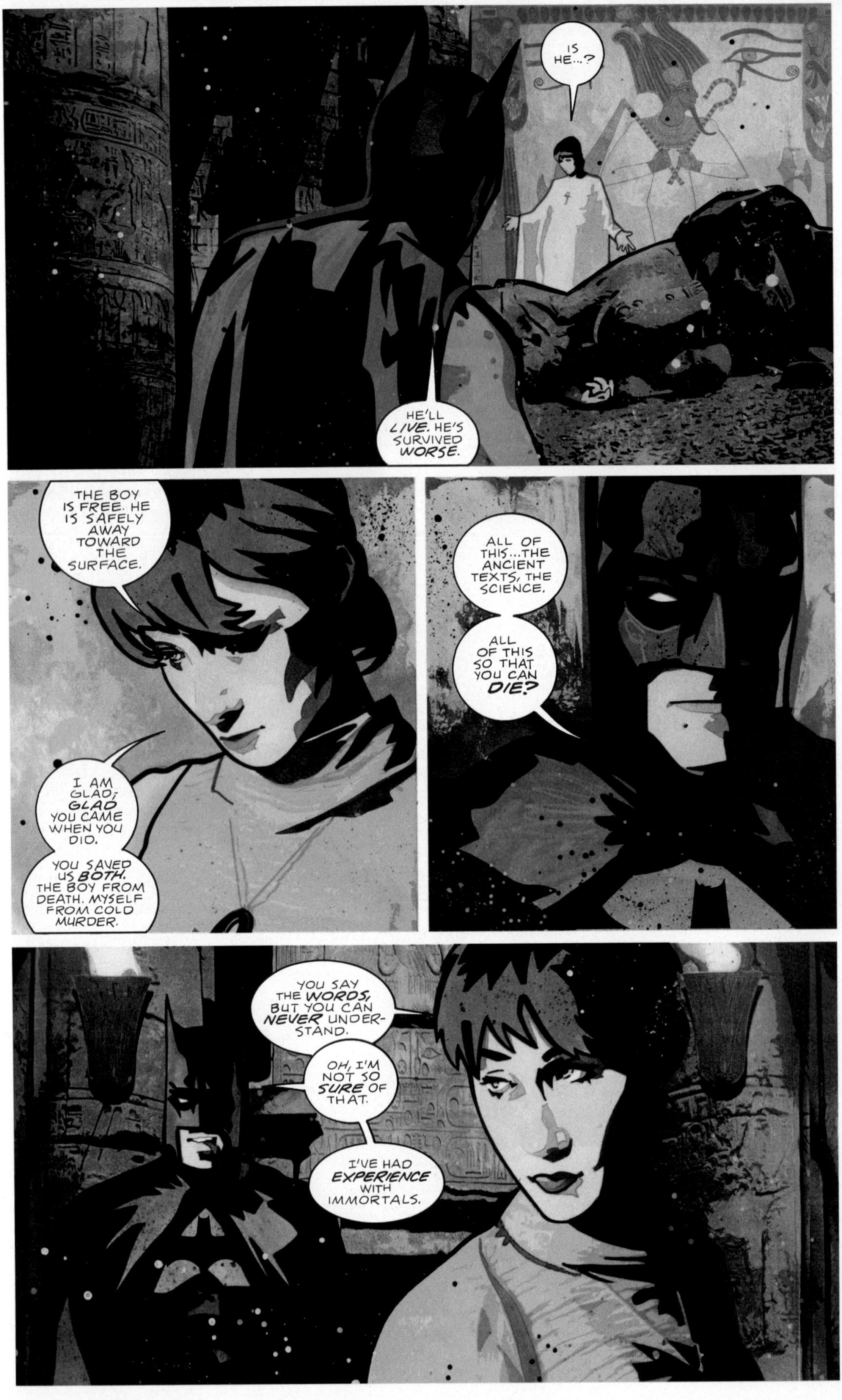
IS HE...?
HE'LL *LIVE.* HE'S SURVIVED *WORSE.*
THE BOY IS FREE. HE IS SAFELY AWAY TOWARD THE SURFACE.
I AM GLAD; *GLAD* YOU CAME WHEN YOU DID.
YOU SAVED US *BOTH.* THE BOY FROM DEATH. MYSELF FROM COLD MURDER.
ALL OF THIS...THE ANCIENT TEXTS, THE SCIENCE.
ALL OF THIS SO THAT YOU CAN *DIE?*
YOU SAY THE *WORDS,* BUT YOU CAN *NEVER* UNDER-STAND.
OH, I'M NOT SO *SURE* OF THAT.
I'VE HAD *EXPERIENCE* WITH IMMORTALS.

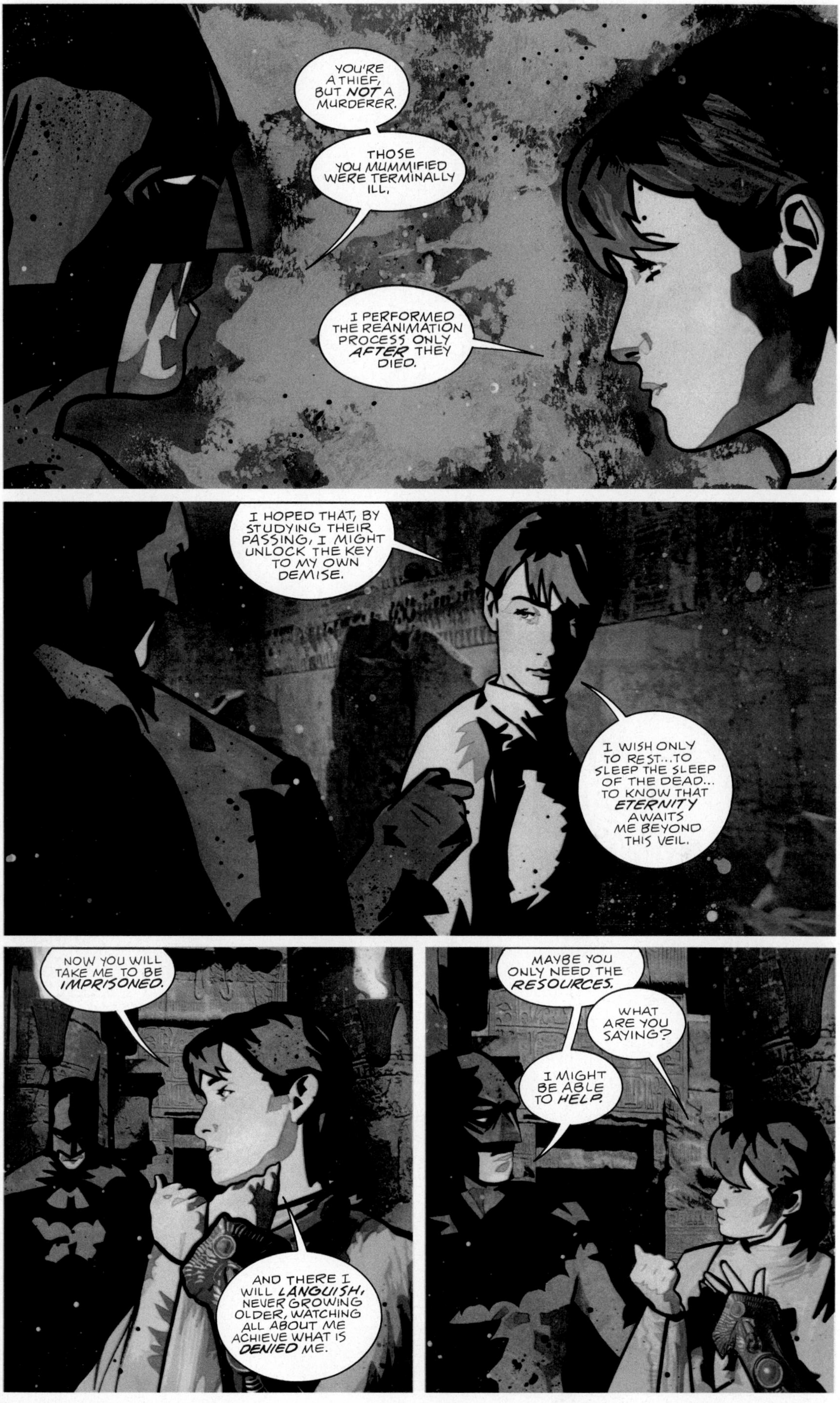
YOU'RE A THIEF, BUT NOT A MURDERER.
THOSE YOU MUMMIFIED WERE TERMINALLY ILL.
I PERFORMED THE REANIMATION PROCESS ONLY AFTER THEY DIED.
I HOPED THAT, BY STUDYING THEIR PASSING, I MIGHT UNLOCK THE KEY TO MY OWN DEMISE.
I WISH ONLY TO REST...TO SLEEP THE SLEEP OF THE DEAD...TO KNOW THAT ETERNITY AWAITS ME BEYOND THIS VEIL.
NOW YOU WILL TAKE ME TO BE IMPRISONED.
AND THERE I WILL LANGUISH, NEVER GROWING OLDER, WATCHING ALL ABOUT ME ACHIEVE WHAT IS DENIED ME.
MAYBE YOU ONLY NEED THE RESOURCES.
WHAT ARE YOU SAYING?
I MIGHT BE ABLE TO HELP.

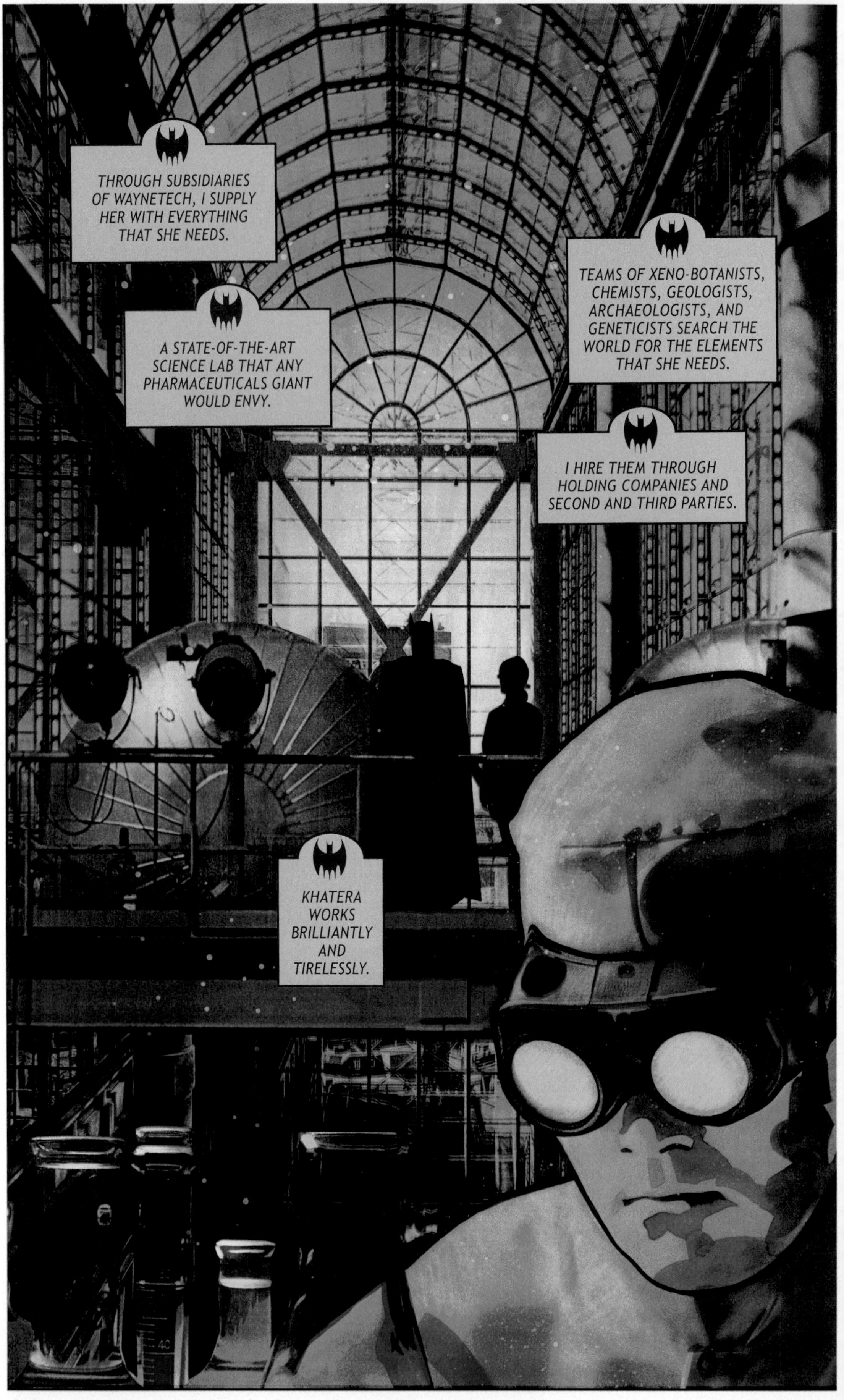
THROUGH SUBSIDIARIES OF WAYNETECH, I SUPPLY HER WITH EVERYTHING THAT SHE NEEDS.
A STATE-OF-THE-ART SCIENCE LAB THAT ANY PHARMACEUTICALS GIANT WOULD ENVY.
TEAMS OF XENO-BOTANISTS, CHEMISTS, GEOLOGISTS, ARCHAEOLOGISTS, AND GENETICISTS SEARCH THE WORLD FOR THE ELEMENTS THAT SHE NEEDS.
I HIRE THEM THROUGH HOLDING COMPANIES AND SECOND AND THIRD PARTIES.
KHATERA WORKS BRILLIANTLY AND TIRELESSLY.

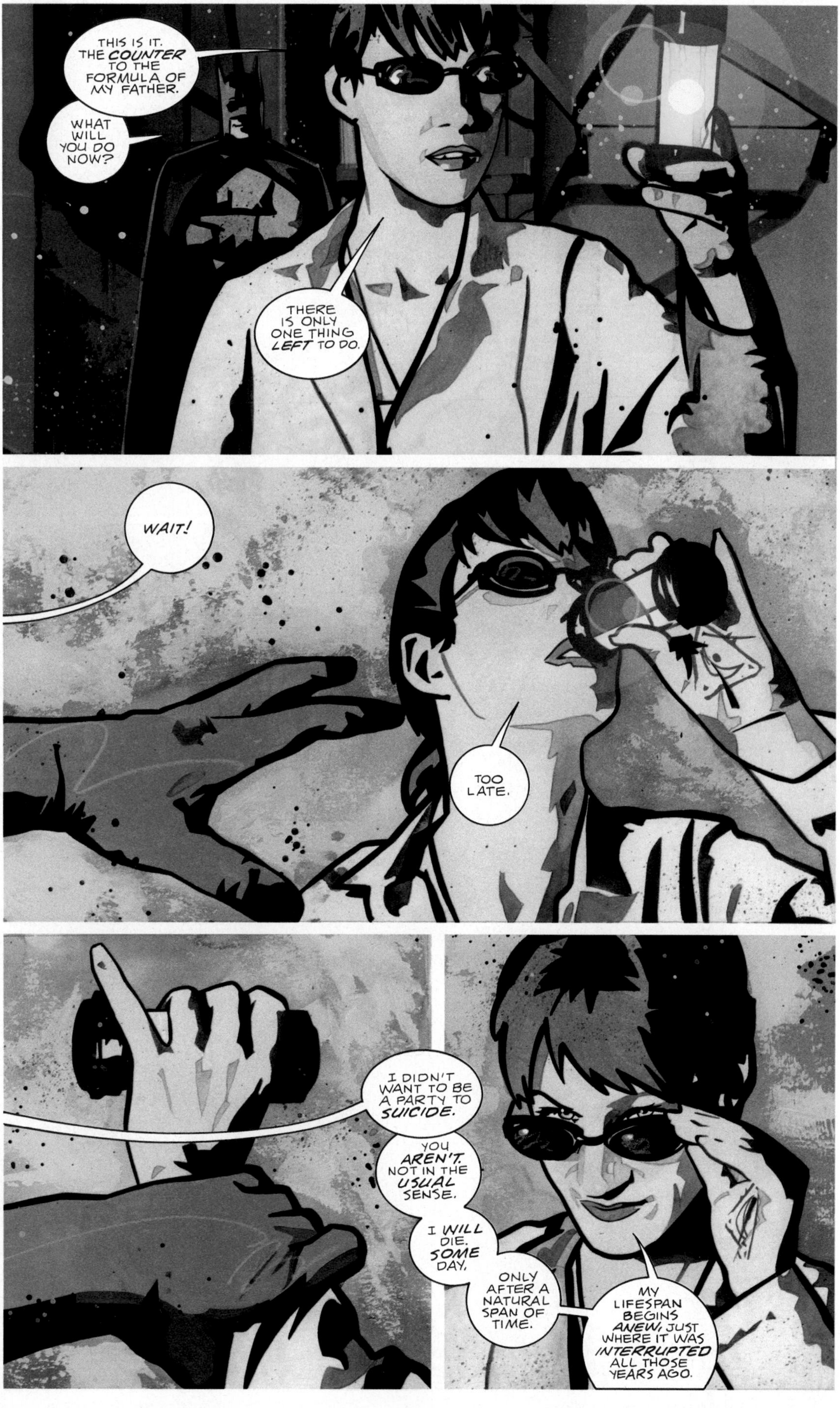
THIS IS IT. THE COUNTER TO THE FORMULA OF MY FATHER.
WHAT WILL YOU DO NOW?
THERE IS ONLY ONE THING LEFT TO DO.
WAIT!
TOO LATE.
I DIDN'T WANT TO BE A PARTY TO SUICIDE.
YOU AREN'T. NOT IN THE USUAL SENSE.
I WILL DIE. SOME DAY.
ONLY AFTER A NATURAL SPAN OF TIME.
MY LIFESPAN BEGINS ANEW, JUST WHERE IT WAS INTERRUPTED ALL THOSE YEARS AGO.

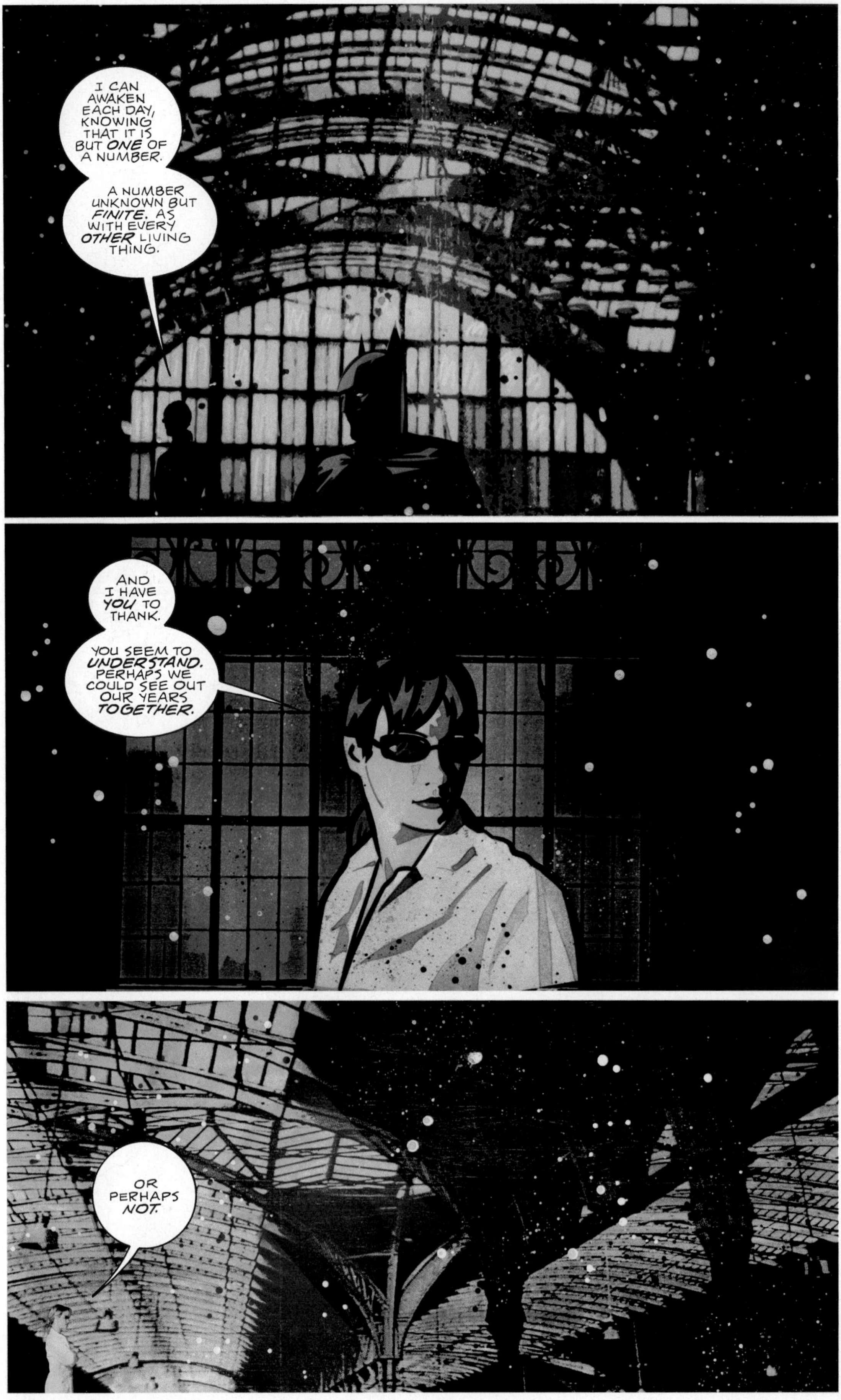
I CAN AWAKEN EACH DAY, KNOWING THAT IT IS BUT ONE OF A NUMBER.
A NUMBER UNKNOWN BUT FINITE. AS WITH EVERY OTHER LIVING THING.
AND I HAVE YOU TO THANK.
YOU SEEM TO UNDERSTAND. PERHAPS WE COULD SEE OUT OUR YEARS TOGETHER.
OR PERHAPS NOT.

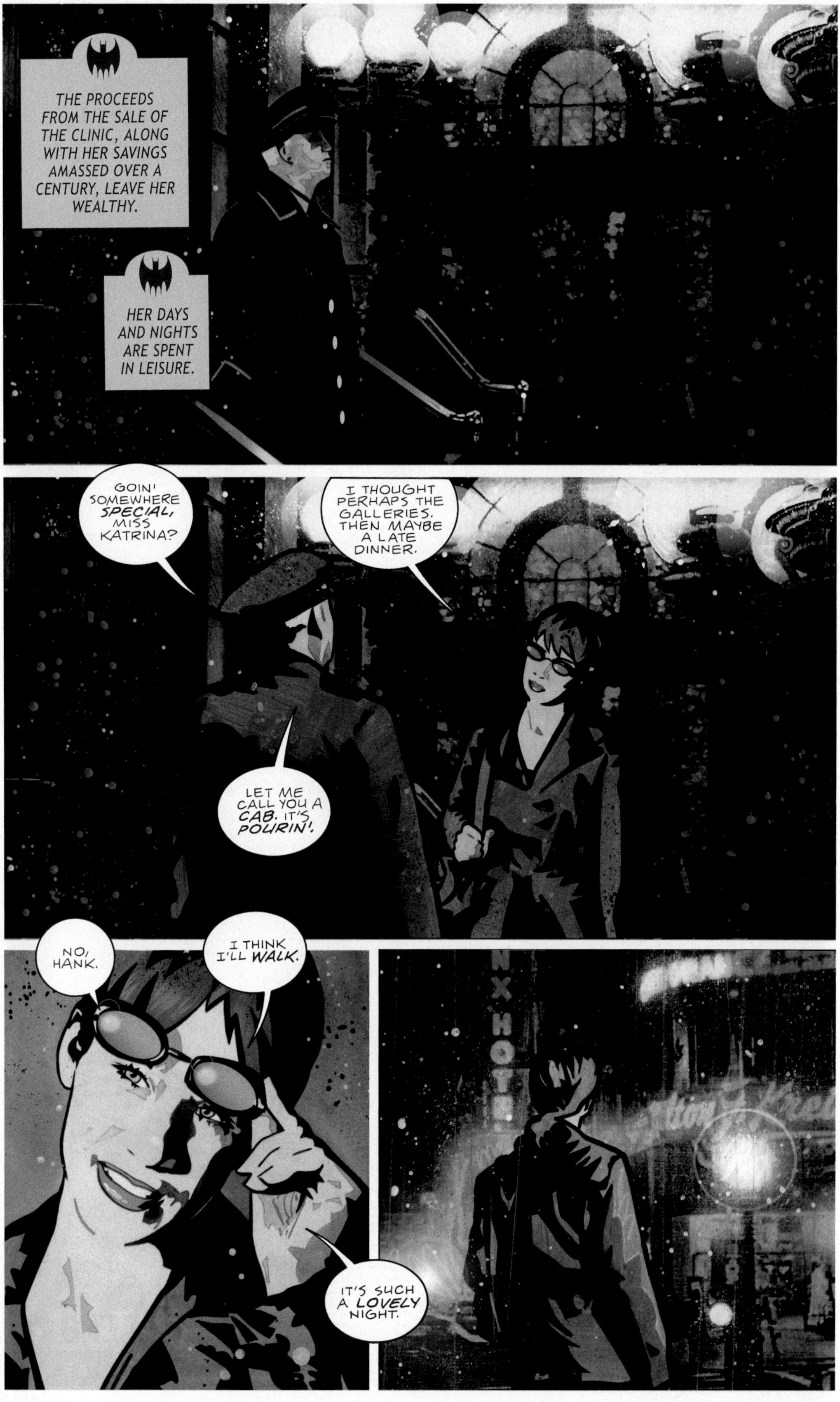
THE PROCEEDS FROM THE SALE OF THE CLINIC, ALONG WITH HER SAVINGS AMASSED OVER A CENTURY, LEAVE HER WEALTHY.
HER DAYS AND NIGHTS ARE SPENT IN LEISURE.
GOIN' SOMEWHERE SPECIAL, MISS KATRINA?
I THOUGHT PERHAPS THE GALLERIES. THEN MAYBE A LATE DINNER.
LET ME CALL YOU A CAB. IT'S POURIN'.
NO, HANK.
I THINK I'LL WALK.
IT'S SUCH A LOVELY NIGHT.

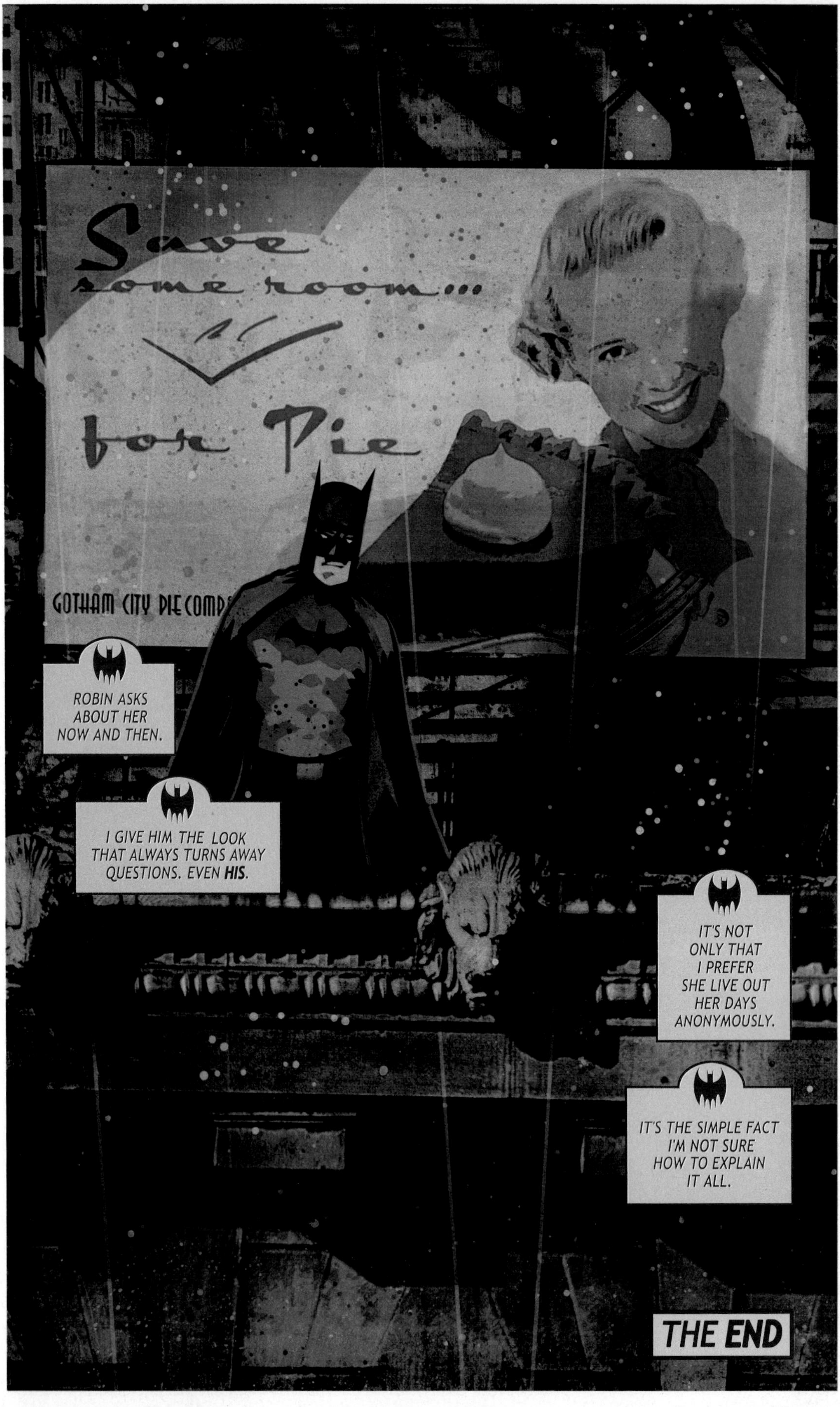

Save some room...
for Pie
GOTHAM CITY PIE COMP
ROBIN ASKS ABOUT HER NOW AND THEN.
I GIVE HIM THE LOOK THAT ALWAYS TURNS AWAY QUESTIONS. EVEN **HIS**.
IT'S NOT ONLY THAT I PREFER SHE LIVE OUT HER DAYS ANONYMOUSLY.
IT'S THE SIMPLE FACT I'M NOT SURE HOW TO EXPLAIN IT ALL.
THE END

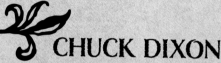

CHUCK DIXON

Chuck Dixon has over 30 years of experience in the graphic novel field as an editor, writer, and publisher. He has contributed well over 1,000 scripts to publishers like DC Comics, Marvel, Dark Horse, IDW, Hyperion, and others, featuring a range of characters from Batman to G.I. Joe to the Simpsons, and his comic book adaptation of J.R.R. Tolkien's *The Hobbit* continues to be an international bestseller. Considered to be one of the most prolific writers in his field, this award-winning storyteller has also scripted many creator-owned projects, including *Winterworld* and *Joe Frankenstein*, which reunited him with fellow Bane co-creator Graham Nolan.

In addition to his comics work, Dixon is currently writing two different series of action novels: *Bad Times* is a series about a team of former Army Rangers who travel back in time in search of treasure and adventure, and his Kindle-sensation Levon Cade books are dark tales of vigilante justice. Both are available now in paperback and digitally.

JOHN VAN FLEET

John Van Fleet was born into captivity and raised on Space Food Sticks and Bazooka gum. After graduating from Pratt Institute in Brooklyn, New York, he found instant success as a waiter. Unsatisfied with the food industry, John went on to make some art. His work can be found throughout the comic book industry in the form of graphic novels and as painted covers. Some of his comics titles include *Batman, Batman: The Chalice, Batman: The Ankh*, and *Cast Shadows* for DC Comics; *Typhoid* for Marvel; and *The X-Files* for Topps Comics. John's client list goes beyond comics to include book publishers, video game makers, film studios, and toy companies. When not working for the man, he creates 3D models. "It's just like when I was a kid working on Aurora monster models. Minus the effects of the glue." Examples of his work can be found at johnvanfleet.com.

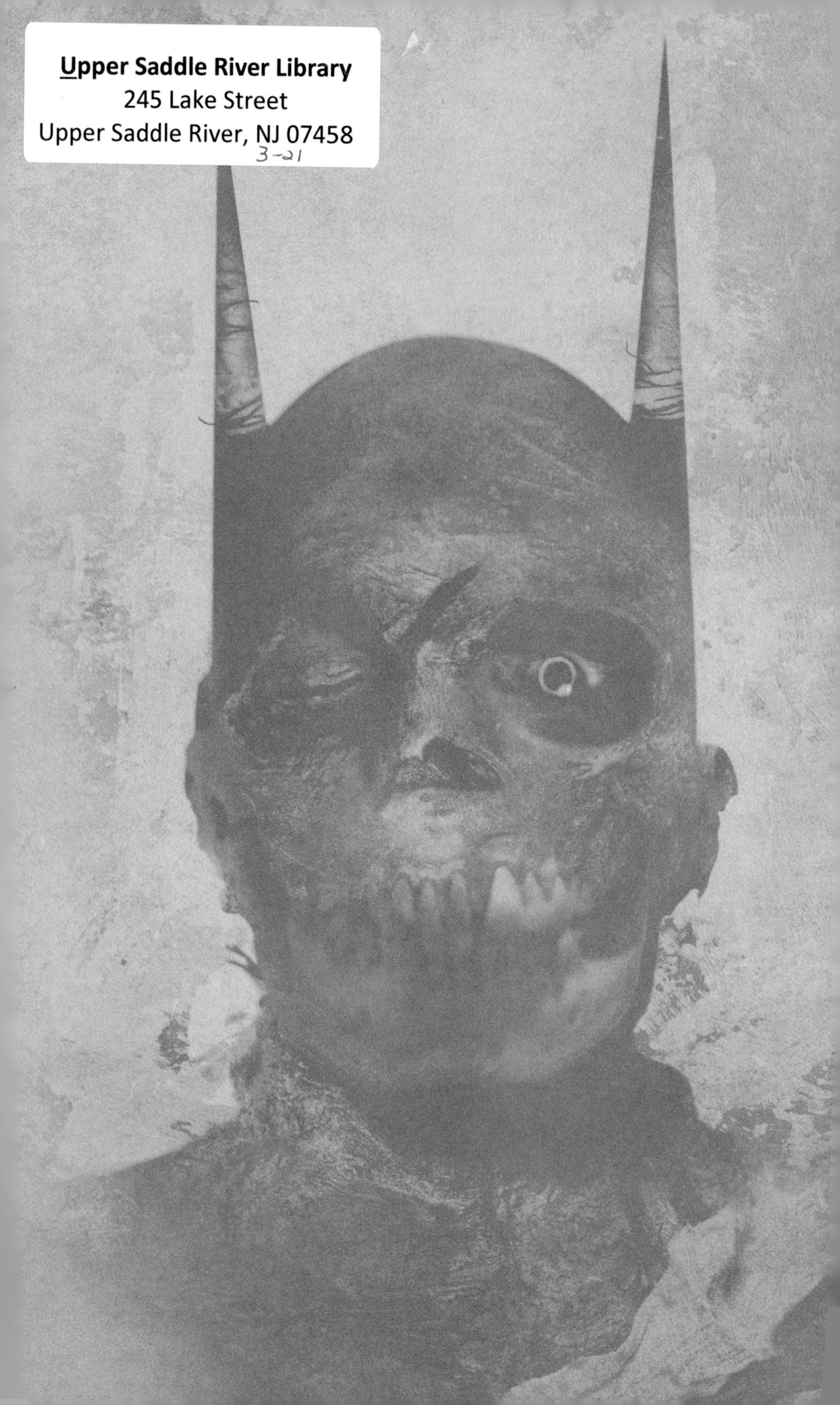